first year seminar: Perspective and Empowerment

Second Edition

CENGAGE
Learning™

Australia • Brazil • Japan • Korea • Mexico • Singapore • Spain • United Kingdom • United States

CENGAGE
Learning™

first year seminar: Perspective and Empowerment

Second Edition

Custom Editor: Kas Salazar, Cengage Learning

Front cover design:
Jennifer Mariko Chan, photo collage
Sacramento State Accelerated
College Entrance Student

Back cover design:
Alicia Guerra, sketch
Sacramento State General
Education Honors Student

Textbook cover layout:
Karen Booth,
Sacramento State University Public
Affairs

A significant number of articles from
this text are edited by:
Virginia N. Gordon, The Ohio State
University
Thomas L. Minnick, The Ohio State
University

Sacramento State Editors:
Executive Editors:
Lynn M. Tashiro, Director of First
Year Experience Programs
Rodolfo T. Santos, Coordinator of
First Year Programs

Chapter Editors:
Hui-Ju Huang
Lynne Fox
Julie Mumma
Denise Wessels
Valerie Becker
Roberta Ching
Ricky Gutierrez

Student Editor
John Kanemoto

For product information and technology assistance, contact us at
Cengage Learning Customer & Sales Support, 1-800-354-9706
For permission to use material from this text or product,
submit all requests online at **cengage.com/permissions**
Further permissions questions can be emailed to
permissionrequest@cengage.com

This book contains select works from existing Cengage Learning resources and was produced by Cengage Learning Custom Solutions for collegiate use. As such, those adopting and/or contributing to this work are responsible for editorial content accuracy, continuity and completeness.

Compilation © 2010 Cengage Learning.

ISBN-13: 978-1-111-40079-8

ISBN-10: 1-111-40079-2

Cengage Learning
5191 Natorp Boulevard
Mason, Ohio 45040
USA

Cengage Learning is a leading provider of customized learning solutions with office locations around the globe, including Singapore, the United Kingdom, Australia, Mexico, Brazil, and Japan. Locate your local office at:
international.cengage.com/region.

Cengage Learning products are represented in Canada by Nelson Education, Ltd.
For your lifelong learning solutions, visit **www.cengage.com/custom.**
Visit our corporate website at **www.cengage.com.**

Printed in the United States
of America

Brief Contents

———————————————————————————————■—

Contents

Chapter 3
What Does It Mean to Be an Educated Person? 101

Chapter 4
What Is the Value of a College Education? 141

Chapter 5
How Is Personal Development Related to Career and Community?   159

Chapter 6
What Is Diversity and Intercultural Competence?   183

Preface

—■—

What is this book?

The *First Year Seminar: Perspective and Empowerment* textbook is a collection of readings intended to connect first year college students to the intellectual culture of the university community. The chapters of this book correspond to the nine topics in the First Year Seminar course at Sacramento State. This anthology is a work in progress focused on the evolving needs of our student body and campus.

About the book cover:

The back cover portrays a student perspective of the first year of college. The simple sketch communicates the apprehension and hopes of first year students. The front cover illustrates the faculty and academic perspective of college. The photo collage represents the diversity of ideas, experiences, and interactions provided through a college education. The Sacramento State "flame of knowledge" is central and empowers students and faculty to explore new intellectual ideas. Between the front and back cover, these two perspectives, student and faculty, meet and interact through the selected articles to stimulate thinking, discussion, and action Learning is accomplished through the mutual interaction of faculty and students.

About the articles:

The articles in this book are a collection of viewpoints on college education. University administrators, faculty, staff, and students as well as historical figures, scholars, and journalists write these multiple perspectives. The contents of the articles address the learning goals of the First Year Seminar and have been selected to meet the developmental needs of first year students as well as the variety of faculty teaching the course. Select articles are followed by suggested assignments while other articles will have supporting curriculum available online.

For additional articles and curricular resources visit http://www.csus.edu/lc/fsfac/

An invitation to participate:

Both faculty and students are invited to contribute to the next edition, 2011/2012, of the First Year Seminar text. We look forward to the engaging intellectual discussions that are stimulated by this cross disciplinary project!

Lynn M. Tashiro, Ph.D.
Director, First Year Experience Programs
Professor of Physics, Academic Affairs

Acknowledgements

———■———

This collection of articles represents collaboration and contributions across many academic disciplines and departments including:

Reviewing and Editing by the First Year Experience Curriculum Committee:
Lynn Tashiro, First Year Experience Programs & Department of Physics, Academic
    Affairs
Hui-Ju Huang, Department of Teacher Education
Lynne Fox, Department of Philosophy
Julie Mumma, Department of Criminal Justice
Denise Wessels, Department of Child Development
Valerie Becker, Department of Teacher Education
Roberta Ching, Department of Learning Skills
Ricky Gutierrez, Department of Criminal Justice

Original manuscripts by:
Vanessa Arnaud, Department of Foreign Languages
Kim Bancroft, Department of Teacher Education
Melinda Wilson, Department of Theater and Dance
Al Levin, Department of Counselor Education
Julie Collier, David McVey, and Deb Marcus, Career Center

Special Contributions by:
Rodolfo T. Santos, First Year Experience Programs, Academic Advising Center -
    Student Affairs
Alexander Gonzalez, University President
Greg Wheeler, Department of Geology, Associate Dean Undergraduate Studies
Kathryn Palmieri, Associate Director, Academic Advising Center
Charlene Martinez, Director, Multi-Cultural Center
Renee Fabiano, Rene Fabiano Design
Karen Booth, Senior Designer, University Public Affairs
Sam Parsons, University Photographer, Academic Technology and Creative
    Services
Al Striplen, Counselor, Educational Opportunity Program
Rheena Munoz, First Year Experience Programs, Administrative Assistant Sup-
    port Coordinator
Jennifer Santos & Justin Gomez, Sacramento State Alumni

Student Contributions by:
John Kanemoto, Student Editor, Fall 2009–2010 Peer Mentor
Jennifer Mariko Chan, Accelerated College Entrance student
Alicia Guerra, General Education Honors Student
Lisa Franklin, Art History Major
Ashle Archangel, Fall 2008–2010 Peer Mentor
Diana Gonzalez, Fall 2008–2010 Peer Mentor
Mona Patel, Fall 2009 Peer Mentor
Kaely Mullins, Fall 2009 Peer Mentor
Kimmie Montgomery, General Education Honors Student, and Fall 2008 Peer
    Mentor

A Letter from the Student Editor

To the first year student,

As the 2010 FYE Student Editor, I spent the last few months reading every single page of this book before you. As a returning peer mentor and teacher-preparation mathematics major I believe every student has the potential to contribute to academic discourse and blossom while in college. Every moment of maturation will be inspired by personal willingness and awareness. Every moment in class, walking between classrooms, parking structures or residence halls, as well as studying has the possibility to teach you something about yourself, your community, and your future.

Many of you might wonder what the student editor's role is in the process of crafting this collection of articles, personal stories, and academic research. My job was to read each written piece submitted for this textbook and decided whether or not a first year student would find it beneficial. Now you may be thinking, this guy has no idea about what my passions, dislikes, and personal background truly are, how could he know what I need or find interesting? In response I offer the fact that I very recently sat at the same desk as you. On the first day of my first year seminar class I was nervous and a bit overwhelmed by the realization that I was truly in a college classroom. I've come a long way since that first day and have used the perspective gained during my journey to provide a student voice in this textbook.

I learned that the 2010 application and acceptance process for student admission to Sacramento State was the most competitive in decades. You not only graduated from the top third of your class, you successfully applied, and are now enrolled in a first year seminar with the excitement of a college career ahead of you. You made it here. I congratulate you with all my being.

The years you spend in college are quite short in the overall scheme of life however; these years can make a big impact on your thinking and your life. As a third year student, I found myself saying more often than not: "I can't believe I accomplished so much in such a short period of time." As a Sac State student, I started a student organization, became a student representative for social justice, participated in the Environmental Student Organization and the Future Math and Science Teacher Club. Did I mention that I attended athletic, cultural and social FYE events too! I do recognize my case is extreme, even insane, but from a student perspective there are only positive aspects to getting involved in campus life. Getting involved deepens your connection to the academic community to which you have now become a part of.

My request of you is that you utilize this reader as a tool and gateway for understanding the power of that degree you will grasp in your hand a few short years from now. Trust me, I remember receiving that syllabus the first day of class and wondering why in the world I would have to do so much reading, but after all I have accomplished by being in the FYE program, I am truly grateful to my orientation leader who suggested this opportunity.

Have an amazing semester and great time here at Sac State. I expect you to reach great heights as a proud Hornet!

Sincerely,

John Kanemoto

How to Keep a Journal

A fter most of the readings in this textbook, you will find "Suggestions for Your Journal." We strongly encourage you to get into the habit of keeping a written journal of your reactions to and reflections on your assigned readings. Such journaling will result in a record of your development as you think through both the essays and your experiences as a new student at your college or university. Because many new college students may not know what a journal at its best can be, or how to keep one, we offer the definition and suggestions that follow.

Why keep a journal? The type of journal we are suggesting that you write is a "response" journal in which you will record your ideas and feelings in response to the readings that you are assigned in each unit. Writing a journal can reveal how your thought processes work and how they develop or change, serve as a memory aid, and provide an informal way of keeping track of your ideas that may be less threatening than more formal writing assignments like essays and research papers. Writing in your journal means working to find the right words to express yourself, and so keeping a journal can help you make your ideas more specific, more concrete.

The purpose of a journal is usually to provide a record, often day by day, of the writer's own internal or spiritual growth. In this regard, both journals and the closely related form, diaries, are similar to a document once needed on every sailing ship, the captain's log. The log was a book in which the chief officer of the ship kept a daily record of the ship's travels. Entries were usually brief, providing the ship's location in longitude and latitude and perhaps a sentence or two about important events of the voyage: "Sighted a large group of whales to the west," for example, or "Finished the last fresh provisions today." The ship's log therefore became the skeleton of a history. For some writers, a diary can be very similar to a log. Depending on how much detail an author chooses to include, a diary can be as lean as a ship's log or substantially more informative. An important difference is that the ship's log was intended to be available to others, such as the ship's owners. A diary is almost always intended to be a private document. A journal, in the sense that we hope you will use the word, is similar to a log or diary in that the entries can be made daily and should be dated. Unlike a personal diary, the best journals are written with the expectation that sometime, someone besides the writer will probably read them. Yet they retain a sense of ease and intimacy as though the prospective readers were the author's good friends.

Keeping a journal can encourage you to think more critically by helping you to make connections between what an author has written and your agreements or disagreements with that author's point of view. For example, a typical journal entry may note:

Date: September 30, 2006 [Most journal entries should be dated!]
Essay: "College Major Doesn't Mean That Much" by William Raspberry

As I read Raspberry's advice to his daughter about not choosing a major right away, I wished that my parents had told me this. I felt really pressured to choose a major during orientation since everyone else seemed to know what they were doing. Now that I have been in college for a few weeks, I'm beginning to have second thoughts about majoring in engineering. The trouble is, I don't know what else to major in or even what I might be good at. I don't have to worry about a "career," as Raspberry puts it, if I stick with engineering. But I am not sure what an engineer does all day. Raspberry says to pick a major "on the pleasure principle" for what I enjoy studying. That sure isn't math and physics. And yet I was good in these subjects in high school, and so far in my college classes I have been doing at least average with everyone else in my classes. I think a good way to proceed is to stay in general with the engineering plan but add some other classes in areas—like Theater!—that I really enjoy. Maybe I can find a way to balance both options.

This entry starts with an idea from an assigned essay and develops it with the student's personal point of view, including her examples, generalizations, and relevant personal experiences. A journal entry is usually this length or longer: One perfect sentence might be adequate and expressive, but usually a reflective response will require some development. A paragraph is a common length for an entry, but some may be as long as several paragraphs—even amounting to an essay.

We recommend that you read every essay with an eye for what you personally can learn or take from that essay. Can you apply some comment or suggestion from that reading to your experience? How? Or why not? Our suggested topics are not meant to limit you but merely to serve as possible starting places. In addition, here are some practical tips for keeping a journal that many writers find helpful:

- In journal writing it is permissible to write as you would talk to a friend or trusted adviser. The content is more important than perfection of style, and you will often find the entries are more informative if you think about what you want to express without worrying too much about the style or form of expression you use.
- Write about the insights, feelings and emotions, or problems that you think about when reading the assigned essay. Don't worry if you may seem more negative than positive: It is entirely all right to disagree with an author.
- Sometimes as you are reading an assignment, it is handy to jot down notes with your reactions in a very brief form (just so you can understand them later!). Your journal entry can then be developed from these notes, as you think about them and put them into your own organization.
- Interact with and expand upon what the author is saying but do so in your own words, adding your own ideas.

■ Use any creative format that you think best expresses your responses. You may want to write in the form of a dialogue between you and the author or of a letter to a friend or to your parents.

Your course instructor will tell you how your journal entries will be used in class—that is, how they will fit into the course structure and count in your final grade. Some students find that they enjoy keeping a journal and continue the practice even after they are required to do so by a class. Many successful authors keep journals for decades and take from them their ideas for longer essays or books. And some journals have become important historical documents because, like the captain's log of an important voyage, they help others to navigate along one of the paths that eventually we all must find and follow.

A LETTER FROM THE PRESIDENT

Dear Students,

Welcome to Sac State.

I know from experience that arriving at a new campus can be intimidating.

I remember how I felt the first time I walked into a classroom as a freshman at Pomona College. The students there were very bright and well-prepared. They were familiar with challenging academic settings, many having gone to prestigious prep schools. In fact, many of them had already read the books we'd be reading that semester. I also soon discovered that many already had their careers planned out.

Alexander Gonzalez

My path was much different. In my family, making it through high school was amazing in itself. After high school I joined the Air Force and later worked at a job before beginning my studies at Pomona College. Those experiences were valuable, but I didn't feel as prepared or comfortable as my fellow students. I wondered how I would make it.

But I soon realized that to succeed, I would have to take my feelings of doubt and use them to my advantage. So even though I felt alone, I applied myself like never before.

I spent a lot of time in the library and made sure to be ready if a professor called on me. And I was successful.

After Pomona I attended Harvard Law School. When I left to pursue my passion for psychology in graduate school, I took with me the satisfaction that I had done very well – and had even worked over the summer at a prestigious law firm. Though my career still wasn't planned out, I knew that I could achieve anything I set my mind to.

I want you to know that at Sac State, you are not alone. You have the support of our entire campus community. We consider you to be part of our family.

That's one of the reasons we created the First Year Experience Program. It will give you opportunities to interact with your peers, make new friends and share methods for success.

Sac State is providing you with the same kinds of opportunities that I had. Whether you want to go on to graduate school, law school, begin your career – or if you're still exploring options – we are here to serve.

I hope you have a wonderful first year, and thank you for choosing Sac State.

Sincerely,

Alexander Gonzalez,
President

HOW DO PEOPLE LEARN
AS INDIVIDUALS AND AS A COMMUNITY?

Learning can be defined in many ways. It is not only the acquisition of knowledge and skills by instruction or study; it is also an accumulation through experience. Although students enter college after years of "learning," many find that college learning offers new and exciting challenges.

To First Year Students,

Growing up as a child I can clearly remember wanting to learn all the essentials of life and I wanted to learn them quickly. I remember hearing my grandmother state, "Learning takes time, persistence and effort. The race isn't given to the swift nor to the strong, but it is given to those who endure it."

Ashle Archangel,
Peer Mentor 08-10
Psychology Major

I've come to the conclusion that there is far more to learning than just being taught something. You actually must have experience behind the lessons taught and you have to be willing to make mistakes in order to correct the mishaps that may occur along the way. I believe that we simply learn by trial and error. We can never know what it feels like to get up, if we never make a mistake that causes us to fall down.

Learning is something that we have access to daily whether we choose to apply it to our lives or not. My first semester in college was a challenge because here at Sac State there is a unique sense of diversity. It was here that I was able to set aside some of my own life's lessons and begin to learn the life lessons of others. I now know what it means to "take a walk in someone else's shoes." Our experiences are part of our learning process. To learn isn't a hard task; however, it doesn't always happen flawlessly.

I'd like to leave you with a quote from Henry C. Link, "While one person hesitates because he feels inferior, the other is busy making mistakes and becoming superior."

Ashle Archangel

Understanding Who Is Smart

Jennifer James

Jennifer James is an urban cultural anthropologist and a highly regarded business speaker. A university professor for 14 years, she is the author of six books and has written a weekly newspaper column. In this essay James writes about a new vision of intelligence and how "system thinking" can help us understand change.

The debate over intelligence is a debate over higher standards. Over the past forty years, researchers of all kinds have uncovered the weaknesses of our tests and shown new respect for a broader-based definition of intelligence that reflects more than traditional fact retention and computation skills. Educators, in particular, are looking for a battery of tests that is more predictive of real-world success. The designers of a school testing program in California, for example, put a premium on the skills required for "reasonably deciding what to think and do." Among other things, students had to be able to determine the relevance of information, distinguish between fact and opinion, identify unstated assumptions, detect bias or propaganda, come up with reasonable alternatives or solutions, and predict possible consequences. Intelligence is the ability to make adaptive responses in new as well as old situations.

At Harvard, philosopher Nelson Goodman wanted to understand why some people were "creative" and others were not. In his work, Goodman expanded the concept of intelligence from "How smart is he or she?" to "How is he or she smart?" Motivation and interest in the task at hand—along with traits such as concentration, intention, purpose, drive and tenacity—emerged as important influences.

Howard Gardner, a psychologist who helped to conduct this research, thought of intelligence as the ability to solve problems or create products. He devised the following list of eight primary forms of intelligence (to which I have added one of my own):

1. **Verbal/linguistic intelligence.** This form of intelligence is revealed by a sensitivity to the meaning and order of words and the ability to make varied use of the language. Impromptu speaking, story-telling, humor, and joking are natural abilities associated with verbal/linguistic intelligence. So, too, is persuading someone to follow a course of action, or explaining, or teaching. Will Rogers had this form of intelligence. Good journalists also have it.

2. **Logical/mathematical intelligence.** This form of intelligence is easiest to standardize and measure. We usually refer to it as analytical or scientific thinking, and we see it in scientists, computer programmers, accountants, lawyers, bankers, and, of course, mathematicians, people who are problem solvers and *consummate* game players. They work with abstract symbols and are able to see connections

Reprinted with permission of Simon & Schuster from Jennifer James, *Thinking in the Future Tense*. © 1996 by Jennifer James.

between pieces of information that others might miss. Einstein is one of the best examples of someone with this form of intelligence.

3. **Visual/*spatial* intelligence.** Persons with this form of intelligence are especially deft at *conjuring* up mental images and creating graphic representations. They are able to think in three-dimensional terms, to re-create the visual world. Picasso, whose paintings challenged our view of reality, was especially gifted at visualizing objects from different perspectives and angles. Besides painters and sculptors, this form of intelligence is found in designers and architects.

4. **Body/kinesthetic intelligence.** This form of intelligence makes possible the connections between mind and body that are necessary to succeed in activities such as dance, mime, sports, martial arts, and drama. Martha Graham and Michael Jordan delighted audiences with their explosive and sensitive uses of the body. Because they know how we move, inventors with this form of intelligence understand how to turn function into form. They intuitively feel what is possible in labor-saving devices and processes.

5. **Musical/rhythmic intelligence.** A person with this form of intelligence hears musical patterns and rhythms naturally and can reproduce them. It is an especially desirable form of intelligence because music has the capacity to alter our consciousness, reduce stress, and enhance brain function. For example, students who had just listened to Mozart scored higher on standard IQ tests than those who had spent the same period of time in meditation or silence. Researchers believe that the patterns in musical themes somehow prime the same neural network that the brain employs for complex visual-*spatial* tasks.

6. **Interpersonal intelligence.** Managers, counselors, therapists, politicians, mediators, and human relations specialists display this form of intelligence. It is a must for workplace tasks such as negotiation and providing feedback or evaluation. Individuals with this form of intelligence have strong intuitive skills. They are especially able to read the moods, temperaments, motivations, and intentions of others. Abraham Lincoln, Mohandas Gandhi, and Martin Luther King, Jr., used interpersonal intelligence to change the world.

7. **Intrapersonal intelligence.** Sigmund Freud and Carl Jung demonstrated this form of intelligence, the ability to understand and articulate the inner workings of character and personality. The highest order of thinking and reasoning is present in a person who has intrapersonal intelligence. We often call it wisdom. He or she can see the larger picture and is open to the lure of the future. Within an organization, this ability is invaluable.

8. **Spiritual intelligence.** This form of intelligence is tentative; Gardner has yet to decide whether moral or spiritual intelligence qualifies for his list. It can be considered an *amalgam* of interpersonal and intrapersonal awareness with a "value" component added.

9. **Practical intelligence.** Gardner doesn't list this form of intelligence, but I do. It is the skill that enables some people to take a computer or clock apart and put it back together. I also think of practical intelligence as organizational intelligence or common sense, the ability to solve all sorts of daily problems without quite knowing how the solutions were reached. People with common sense may

or may not test well, but they have a clear understanding of cause and effect. They use intelligence in combination with that understanding.

QUALITIES OF MIND

Rate yourself on each of these forms of intelligence. What are your strengths and weaknesses? How are they reflected in the kind of work you do and your relationships with others?

	Low				Moderate				High	
	1	2	3	4	5	6	7	8	9	10

1. Verbal/linguistic

2. Logical/mathematical

3. Visual/spatial

4. Body/kinesthetic

5. Musical/rhythmic

6. Interpersonal

7. Intrapersonal

8. Spiritual

9. Practical

Don't let this list intimidate you. There is increasingly strong evidence that intelligence can be taught, despite ongoing arguments about genetic predetermination. Also, the levels of each of these forms of intelligence can vary from one person to the next. Albert Einstein had a high degree of logical and spatial intelligence, but his lack of personal skills was legendary. He left those details to others.

Regardless of the forms of our intelligence, we also need to know how we think. Researcher Gail Browning studies approaches to problem solving. She identifies four "styles" that people use to process information: analytical, conceptual, structural, and social. She concludes that most of us use more than one of them, depending on the problem before us. Her work helps us visualize thought processes, something that makes communication and negotiation easier. When forming a creative and productive team for problem solving or futuring consider combining different thinking styles.

Analytical thinkers are the most logical. They must have facts, figures, directions and reasons to approach problem solving. They want to design a system. They see themselves as straightforward, clear and purposeful. In a team meeting they ask, "Is this feasible?"

Conceptual thinkers accept information in almost any form. They enjoy a challenge and often plunge into the problem-solving process before considering what direction to take. They want to paint a picture. They don't mind mistakes. They usually suggest, "Let's look at this problem in a different way."

Structural thinkers draw comparisons and look for systematic links to determine the source of a problem. They prefer creating flow charts. They organize the components of the problem and the possible solutions and ask, "How does this apply to our situation?"

Social thinkers are the facilitators of group process. They talk to everyone; they weigh all the solutions equally; they may identify the best solution but not know how they reached it. In a team situation they ask, "What do you think of this idea?"

Review these four styles and combine them with the nine forms of intelligence outlined. Try to identify yourself and imagine how different problems or situations engage different aspects of your intelligence or thinking style. Create a perfect team for a problem you are currently trying to solve. What ideal set of minds would potentially be the most intelligent and the best at processing?

British researcher Edward De Bono, in a series of books on intelligence, believes he has the answer. He adds the term lateral thinking to this mix. He sees it as the most productive thinking process because it is easily taught and allows everyone in a group, regardless of their intelligence frame or thinking style, to operate with the same broad set of thinking tools.

Lateral thinking is similar to what others currently call critical or system thinking. It enables us to view a problem from all sides and understand all the alternatives before devising a solution. It requires us to abandon certainty and security, at least for the moment. De Bono's most useful exercise in lateral thinking is called PMI, an acronym for Plus, Minus, and Interesting. Participants are divided into small groups and are asked to evaluate what is good (plus), what is bad (minus), and what is interesting about an idea. In a session with a group of auto manufacturers, for example, De Bono posed the suggestion that all cars should be painted yellow. . . .

Table 1 on page 7 shows how the group reacted.

Exercises in lateral thinking work best if each category (good, bad, and interesting) is considered separately and in order when pondering an idea or a problem rather than brainstorming them in the random fashion preferred by conceptual thinkers. Such exercises can be particularly useful when you are floating some new idea or looking for a solution to some problem. They help people focus their perceptions and articulate their reactions and responses. *Common Ground*, a PBS series designed to bring opposing sides together on several controversial issues, used lateral thinking with powerful results. Participants were able to put aside rhetoric and emotion and find they had far more in common than they realized. . . .

We are all, to one degree or another, system thinkers. (I prefer the term system thinking to De Bono's lateral thinking because we are looking at the whole to understand the parts.) We must also combine disparate parts into coherent wholes to put together the puzzles and solve the problems of daily life. A system thinker believes in cooperation and knows that pooling or combining ideas, skills, and experience improves innovation, efficiency, and performance. I think of system thinking as broadscope intelligence and very much like synergy, a buzz-word in business in the 1990s. Companies that practiced synergy did so by buying or developing related businesses or by welding their existing units into a more coherent whole.

Social scientists used system thinking in the 1970s when they began working together to examine the "culture of poverty" as a whole. Edward Deming used it to fine-tune quality processes. The earliest ideas about man and environment as a whole organism represented system thinking. The interrelationship of mind and body in the healing process is another example. When we think about parts of a system, separate from the whole, we cut ourselves off from important information.

Table 1 Results of PMI Session: "All Cars Should be Painted Yellow."		
Good (Plus)	Bad (Minus)	Interesting
Easier to see on the roads.	Boring.	Interesting to see if shades of yellow arose.
Easier to see at night.	Difficult to recognize your own car.	Interesting to see if people appreciated the safety factor.
No problem in deciding which color you want.	Very difficult to find your car in a parking lot.	Interesting to see whether attitudes toward cars changed.
No waiting to get the color you want.	Easier to steal cars.	
Easier for the manufacturer.	The abundance of yellow might tire the eyes.	Interesting to see if trim acquired a different color.
The dealer would need less stock.	Car chases would be difficult for the police.	Interesting to see if this were enforceable.
It might take the "macho" element out of car ownership.	Accident witnesses would have a harder time.	Interesting to see who would support the suggestion.
Cars would tend to become transport items.	Restriction of your freedom to choose.	
In minor collisions the paint rubbed off onto your car would be the same color.		

System thinking can bridge the gap that sometimes exists between reality and our perception of reality. For example, unproductive workers, falling orders, and sagging profits are indicators of serious problems in any business. Our usual way of thinking may cause us to look at each in isolation. But system thinking helps us understand that all parts of a business or a process are connected, and that when one part is challenged, all the others are as well. We may look for productivity problems on the production line and create new incentives if salespeople are not doing well, but the real "cause" of our problems may be hidden in the system that underlies the entire enterprise. System thinking accepts the inter-relatedness of all things. System thinking is usually the best way to find out what is going on.

System thinking can help all of us understand the zigzags of change. It enables us to see the big picture. From that vantage point we can more easily perceive the changing realities of our work and lives and solve problems. Here are some of the basic characteristics of a system thinker:

- You are physically and intellectually alert.
- You are always wondering how things can be improved.
- You are able to resolve conflict by agreeing to disagree on some points and moving the discussion forward.
- You do not demand perfection from yourself or others.
- You are imaginative and creative.

- You are empathetic and compassionate.
- You are comfortable with chaos.
- You are a nonconformist in one way or another.
- You have a sense of humor.

The future challenges us to question our own minds and how we think, to reexamine our assumptions and see how they connect to the changing realities of our world. Thinking must become a more fluid process; I call it "water logic" because the future will require the development of a fluid, more adaptive level of reaction and response. As humanity evolves, creating ever more complex patterns, the ability to understand, synthesize, and adapt to those patterns will become basic intelligence.

 ## Vocabulary

As you think about this essay, these definitions may be helpful to you:

1. **consummate**   extremely skilled and accomplished
2. **spatial**   relating to three-dimensional space
3. **conjuring**   imagining
4. **amalgam**   combination of different elements
5. **synergy**   combined action or operation

 ## Discussion Questions

1. In her first paragraph, Jennifer James provides her own definition of intelligence. What is it?
2. What traits seem to be important in Nelson Goodman's expanded concept of intelligence?
3. Why are Howard Gardner's eight basic forms of intelligence important in broadening our concept of intelligence? Is the form that James adds to Gardner's list different from the others? How?
4. Do you agree with the author's addition of "practical intelligence"? Why?
5. What is "lateral thinking"? How can it be used in problem solving?
6. What are the characteristics of "system thinking," according to the author? How can system thinking be used to analyze problem areas?

Suggestions for Your Journal

What does being intelligent mean to you? On which of the eight forms of intelligence do you rate yourself highest? Lowest? Which do you think are most important for being successful in college? In the real world? Are you intelligent in some ways that Gardner or James have not described?

How Do You Perceive and Process Information?

Constance Staley

Style—we all have it, right? What's yours? Baggy jeans and a T-shirt? Sandals, even in the middle of winter? A stocking cap that translates into I-just-rolled-out-of-bed-before-class? When it comes to appearance, you have your own style.

Think about how your mind works. For example, how do you decide what to wear in the morning? Do you turn on the radio or TV for the weather forecast? Jump on the Internet? Stick your head out the front door? Throw on whatever happens to be clean? We all have different styles, don't we?

So what's a learning style? A learning style is defined as your "characteristic and preferred way of gathering, interpreting, organizing, and thinking about information."[1] The way you perceive information and the way you process it—your perceiving/processing preferences—are based in part on your senses. Which sensory modalities do you prefer to use to take in information—your eyes (visual-graphic or visual-words), your ears (aural), or all your senses using your whole body (kinesthetic)? Which type of information sinks in best? Do you prefer teachers who lecture? Teachers who use visuals such as charts, web role-plays, and create simulations?

To further understand your preferred sensory channel, let's take this example. You decide to buy a new car and you must first answer many questions: What kind of car do you want to buy—an SUV, a sedan, a sports car, a van, or a truck? What are the differences between various makes and models? How do prices, comfort, gas mileage, and safety compare? Who provides the best warranty? Which car do consumers rate highest? How would you go about learning the answers to all these questions?

- **Visual:** Some of us would **look**. We'd study charts, graphs, and photographs comparing cars, mileage, fuel tank capacity, maintenance costs, and customer satisfaction. We learn from pre-organized, visual representations.
- **Aural:** Some of us would **listen**. We'd ask all our friends what kind of cars they drive and what they've heard about cars from other people. We'd pay attention as showroom salespeople describe the features of various cars. We learn through sounds by listening.
- **Read/Write:** Some of us would **read** or **write**. We'd buy a copy of *Consumer Reports* annual edition on automobiles, or copies of magazines like *Car and Driver,* and write lists of each car's pros and cons. We learn through words by reading and writing.
- **Kinesthetic:** Some of us would want to **do it**. We'd go to the showroom and test drive a few cars to physically try them out. We learn through experience when all our sensory modalities are activated.

---

[1]Davis, B. (1993). *Tools for teaching.* San Francisco: Jossey-Bass, p. 185.

What would you do? Eventually, as you're deciding which vehicle to buy, you might do all these things, and do them more than once. But learning style theory says we all have preferences in terms of how we perceive and process information.

After reading the car-buying description, you probably have a gut feeling about your own style. However, take a few minutes to answer the questions about yourself in the exercise—for confirmation or revelation—to verify your hunches or to learn something new about yourself.

VARK Learning Styles Assessment

1. You are helping someone who wants to go downtown, find your airport or locate the bus station. You would:
   a) draw or give her a map.
   b) tell her the directions.
   c) write down the directions (without a map).
   d) go with her.

2. You are not sure whether a word should be spelled "dependent" or "dependant." You would:
   a) see the word in your mind and choose by the way different versions look.
   b) think about how each word sounds and choose one.
   c) find it in a dictionary.
   d) write both words on paper and choose one.

3. You are planning a group vacation. You want some feedback from your friends about your plans. You would:
   a) use a map or website to show them the places.
   b) phone, text or email them.
   c) give them a copy of the printed itinerary.
   d) describe some of the highlights.

4. You are going to cook something as a special treat for your family. You would:
   a) look through the cookbook for ideas from the pictures.
   b) ask friends for suggestions.
   c) use a cookbook where you know there is a good recipe.
   d) cook something you know without the need for instructions.

5. A group of tourists want to learn about the parks or wildlife reserves in your area. You would:
   a) show them internet pictures, photographs or picture books.
   b) talk about, or arrange a talk for them, on parks or wildlife reserves.

   c) give them a book or pamphlets about the parks or wildlife reserves.
   d) take them to a park or wildlife reserve and walk with them.

6. You are about to purchase a digital camera or cell phone. Other than price, what would most influence your decision?
   a) Its attractive design that looks good.
   b) The salesperson telling me about its features.
   c) Reading the details about its features.
   d) Trying or testing it.

7. Remember a time when you learned how to do something new. Try to avoid choosing a physical skill, like riding a bike. You learned best by:
   a) diagrams and charts—visual clues.
   b) listening to somebody explaining it and asking questions.
   c) written instructions—e.g. a manual or textbook.
   d) watching a demonstration.

8. You have a problem with your knee. You would prefer that the doctor:
   a) show you a diagram of what was wrong.
   b) describe what was wrong.
   c) give you a pamphlet to read about it.
   d) use a plastic model of a knee to show what was wrong.

9. You want to learn a new software program, skill or game on a computer. You would:
   a) follow the diagrams in the book that came with it.
   b) talk with people who know about the program.
   c) read the written instructions that came with the program.
   d) use the controls or keyboard and try things out.

10. I like websites that have:
    a) interesting design and visual features.
    b) audio channels where I can hear music, radio programs or interviews.
    c) interesting written descriptions, lists and explanations.
    d) things I can click on or try out.

11. Other than price, what would most influence your decision to buy a new non-fiction book?
    a) The cover looks appealing.
    b) A friend talks about it and recommends it.
    c) You'd quickly read parts of it.
    d) It contains real-life stories, experiences and examples.

12. You are using a book, CD or website to learn how to take photos with your new digital camera. You would like to have:
    a) diagrams showing the camera and what each part does.
    b) a chance to ask questions and talk about the camera and its features.
    c) clear written instructions with lists and bullet points about what to do.
    d) many examples of good and poor photos and how to improve them.

13. Do you prefer a teacher or a presenter who uses:
    a) diagrams, charts or graphs?
    b) question and answer, talk, group discussion or guest speakers?
    c) handouts, books or readings?
    d) demonstrations, models, field trips, role plays or practical exercises?

14. You have finished a competition or test and would like some feedback. You would like to have feedback:
    a) using graphs showing what you had achieved.
    b) from somebody who talks it through with you.
    c) in a written format, describing your results.
    d) using examples from what you have done.

15. You are going to choose food at a restaurant or cafe. You would:
    a) look at what others are eating or look at pictures of each dish.
    b) ask the server or friends to recommend choices.
    c) choose from the written descriptions in the menu.
    d) choose something that you have had there before.

16. You have to give an important speech at a conference or special occasion. You would:
    a) make diagrams or create graphs to help explain things.
    b) write a few key words and practice your speech over and over.
    c) write out your speech and learn from reading it over several times.
    d) gather many examples and stories to make the talk real and practical.

Source: N. Fleming. (2001–2007). *VARK, a Guide to Learning Styles.* Version 7.0. Available at http://www.vark-learn.com/english/page.asp?p=questionnaire. Adapted and used with permission from Neil Fleming.

Scoring the VARK

Let's tabulate your results.

Count your choices in each of the four VARK categories.

(a)	(b)	(c)	(d)
————	————	————	————
Visual	Aural	Read/Write	Kinesthetic

Now that you've calculated your scores, do they match your perceptions of yourself as a learner? Could you have predicted them? The VARK's creators believe that *you* are best qualified to verify and interpret your own results.[2]

---

[2]Fleming, N. D. (1995). I'm different; not dumb: Modes of presentation (VARK) in the tertiary classroom. In A. Zeimer (Ed.), *Research and Development in Higher Education, Proceedings of the 1995 Annual Conference of the Higher Education and Research Development Society of Austral-asia*

	Everyday Study Strategies	Exam Preparation Strategies
VISUAL	• Convert your lecture notes to a visual format. • Study the placement of items, colors, and shapes in your textbook. • Put complex concepts into flowcharts or graphs. • Redraw ideas you create from memory.	• Practice turning your visuals back into words. • Practice writing out exam answers. • Recall the pictures you made of the pages you studied. • Use diagrams to answer exam questions, if your instructor will allow it.
AURAL	• Read your notes aloud. • Explain your notes to another auditory learner. • Ask others to "hear" you understanding of the material. • Record your notes or listen to your instructors' podcasts. • Realize that your lecture notes may be incomplete. You may have become so involved in listening that you stopped writing. Fill your notes in later by talking with other students or getting material from the textbook.	• Practice by speaking your answers aloud. • Listen to your own voice as you answer questions. • Opt for an oral exam if allowed. • Imagine you are talking with the teacher as you answer questions.
READ/WRITE	• Write out your lecture notes again and again. • Read your notes (silently) again and again. • Put ideas and principles into different words. • Translate diagrams, graphs, etc., into text. • Rearrange words and "play"with wording. • Turn diagrams and charts into words.	• Write out potential exam answers. • Practice creating and taking exams. • Type out your answers to potential test questions. • Organize your notes into lists or bullets. • Write practice paragraphs, particularly beginnings and endings.
KINESTHETIC	• Recall experiments, field trips, etc. Remember the real things that happened. • Talk over your notes with another "K" person. • Use photos and pictures that make ideas come to life. • Go back to the lab, your manual, or your notes that include real examples. • Remember that your lecture notes will have gaps if topics weren't concrete or relevant for you. • Use case studies to help you learn abstract principles.	• Role-play the exam situation in your room (or the actual classroom). • Put plenty of examples into your answers. • Write practice answers and sample paragraphs. • Give yourself practice tests.

Figure 1

You can take the VARK online at http://www.vark-learn .com/english/page. asp?p=questionnaire and your results will be tabulated for you.

Using Your VARK Preferences

Knowing your preferences can help you in your academic coursework. If your highest score (by 4 or 5 points) is in one of the four VARK modalities, that particular learning modality is your preferred one.[3] If your scores are more or less even between several or all four modalities, these scores mean that you don't have a strong preference for any single modality. It's estimated that 60 percent of the population is multimodal, which gives most of us flexibility in the way we learn.[4] A lower score in a preference simply means that you are more comfortable using

---

(HERDSA), HERDSA, 18, 308–313; Fleming, N. D., & Mills, C. (1992). Not another inventory, rather a catalyst for reflection. *To Improve the Academy,* 11, 137–149. Available at http://www. ntlf.com/html/lib/suppmat/74fleming.htm.
[3]Fleming, I'm different; not dumb.
[4]Neil Fleming, personal communication, November 14, 2006.

other styles. If your VARK results contain a zero in a particular learning modality, you may realize that you do indeed dislike this mode or find it unhelpful. "Why would anyone want to use *that* mode?" you may have asked yourself in the past. It may be helpful to reflect on why you omit this learning modality. To learn more about your results and suggestions for applying them, see Figure 1 for your preferred modality.

Your highest score represents your preferred learning style; your lowest score, your least preferred. Most college classes emphasize reading and writing; however, if your lowest score is in the read/write modality, don't assume you're academically doomed. VARK can help you discover alternative, more productive ways to learn the same course material. As Fleming writes, knowing your VARK scores doesn't naturally help you become a better learner any more than jumping on a scale helps you slim down. You must take the next step and do something about it![5]

Learning style descriptions aren't meant to put you into a cubbyhole or stereotype you. And they certainly aren't meant to give you an excuse when you don't like a particular assignment. You may learn to adapt naturally to a particular instructor or discipline's preferences, using a visual modality in your economics class to interpret graphs and a kinesthetic modality in your chemistry lab to conduct experiments.

Of course, you'll be required to use all four modalities in college. You'll have to read your literature assignments and write your English papers, even if read/write isn't your preferred style. Different disciplines require different kinds of information access. As one skeptic of learning styles writes, "At some point, no amount of dancing will help you learn more algebra." Actually, some teachers do use dance to help students learn math, and there are plenty of other kinesthetic techniques that work well, like solving actual problems, rather than simply re-reading a chapter in your math book.[6]

Visual, Aural, Read/Write, and Kinesthetic Learning Strategies

Regardless, you may also find that you need to deliberately and strategically re-route your learning methods in some of your classes, and knowing your VARK preferences can help you do that. Learning to capitalize on your preferences and translate challenging course material into your preferred modality may serve you well. Remember these suggestions about the VARK, and try them out to see if they improve your academic results.

1. VARK preferences are not necessarily strengths. However VARK is an excellent vehicle to help you reflect on how you learn and begin to reinforce the

---

[5]Fleming, N., & Baume, D. (2006, November). Learning Styles Again: VARKing up the right tree!, *Educational Developments*, 7.4, 4–7.

[6]Chabris, C. F. (2009, April 27). How to wake up slumbering minds. *Wall Street Journal*. Available at http://online.wsj.com/ article/SB124079001063757515.html. (2008, May 10). Do the math dance: Mathematicians and choreographers use dance to teach mathematics. *Science Daily*. Available at http://www.sciencedaily.com/videos/2008/0503-do_the_math_dance.htm.

productive strategies you're already using or select ones that might work better.

2. If you have a strong preference for a particular modality, practice multiple suggestions listed in Figure 1 for that particular modality. Reinforce your learning through redundancy.

3. Remember that an estimated 60 percent of people are multimodal. In a typical classroom of 30 students (based on VARK data): 17 students would be multimodal, 1 student would be visual, 1 student would be aural, 5 students would be read/write, 6 students would be kinesthetic, and the teacher would most likely have a strong read/write preference![7]

---

[7]Fleming, N. D. (2005). *Teaching and learning styles: VARK strategies.* Christchurch, NZ: Microfilm Limited.

Freshmen Can Be Taught to Think Creatively, Not Just Amass Information

David C. Finster

Dr. David C. Finster is professor of chemistry and chair of the chemistry department at Wittenberg University of Springfield, Ohio. He has been a recipient of the Wittenberg Distinguished Teaching Award.

Finster describes how he applies Perry's theory of cognitive development to his teaching methods and how he uses student-based teaching in his classes. He challenges his students to think about *how* they solve a chemistry problem in addition to finding the solution.

Not long after I embarked on my teaching career, I realized that to be an effective teacher one must first know something about learning. To try to convey knowledge with no understanding of the process of receiving it is to forget the principles of communication. My questions about learning led me to the work of the educational psychologist Jean Piaget on *cognition* in children. His insights, which beautifully explain how children learn to think about problems and to make sense of the world around them, were critical for me. Indeed, understanding how to foster a child's natural growth from simplistic to more complex and abstract thinking processes seems to me vital for any teacher.

But what about college freshmen? Are they just "big children"? In the sense that they are still wrestling with the turmoils of adolescence, now compounded by the independence and responsibility of college life, perhaps so. But in the sense that they are making the transition to what Piaget calls formal *operational* thought, they are not.

A clearer view of cognition in college students came to me from the work of William Perry. He studied the college experience through lengthy interviews with students over several years and then formulated a "developmental scheme" based on his findings. His charting of the intellectual and ethical growth of college students reveals much about the processes of learning and teaching.

Perry's scheme describes progressive stages of development in young people of the ability to comprehend the difference between information and knowledge, to understand the roles of teacher and student, and to make considered decisions in resolving life's simple and complex dilemmas. At the first stage, they are "dualists," with a right-or-wrong view of the world. They see knowledge as a collection of facts to be memorized and authority figures as having all the answers. At the middle stage, they develop a more complex worldview, recognizing that there can be a variety of opinions and viewpoints on an issue. Later they become capable of evaluating those different perspectives through reasoning and judgment, and, finally, they are able to make decisions and commitments based on their own value system. This latter stage is crucial in the formulation of individual identity.

Perry notes nine distinct developmental "positions" along the way to maturity, which must be gone through sequentially—that is, one cannot advance from the second to the fifth position without going through the third and fourth. Most students come to college in "late *dualism*," or at the third position, believing that the purpose of education is to accumulate information and that people in authority have the right answers. Their ability at that stage to see multiple perspectives on an issue is very limited. The way to promote their progress along Perry's scheme is to challenge them to think of the stage just beyond their current level while providing the necessary support to help them do so.

A good teacher seeks not only to build students' knowledge of the content of a discipline but also to teach them to think critically as they learn. The second aim may explain the difficulty some students have in learning at the college level. Critical thinking—that is, the ability to evaluate different perspectives and challenge assumptions—comes at a stage in the Perry model that is beyond students in the "dualist" position. Teachers naturally prefer teaching their disciplines at that level, however, and many expect their students to welcome this broadening aspect of their education. Dualists, on the other hand, see education differently.

A problem arises when the gap between where students are in their intellectual development and where their teachers teach is too large. Most teachers are aware of the gap, but find that time-honored teaching methods do not readily bridge it. Some choose to ignore it, because they are loath to "water down" their courses. Others eliminate it by reducing their goals to a more elementary level and teaching information rather than thinking skills.

The latter tactic is encouraged in our educational system, because content is readily measured by testing, and so "mastery" of a subject can be easily demonstrated. Unfortunately, teachers who resort to it *entrench* their students in the early stages of development by reinforcing a simplistic view of education.

An alternative solution to the problem would be to adopt a developmental instructional method. Using that approach, a teacher begins by recognizing where students are in their ability to understand the purpose of education, to see a difference between information and knowledge, and to think for themselves in the classroom. The aim is then to foster their intellectual growth from that point on.

A favorite saying of mine is that the purpose of college is to calm the disturbed and disturb the calm. Part of good teaching is challenging the way students think, while at the same time providing them with mental and emotional tools to resolve the dilemmas they face. In this manner, we help them grow *incrementally* and become mature adults.

Developmental-instruction theory holds that success in fostering intellectual growth depends in large part on the degree of personal interaction in the educational environment. Small classes are therefore important, because in addition to avoiding the impersonal atmosphere of large lectures, they allow a two-way exchange between teacher and student. Such exchanges play a vital part in active participatory learning and in the development of critical-thinking skills.

Another tenet of development theory is that the first year of college is crucial in tapping students' potential to grow intellectually. So, while large sections of introductory courses are efficient in terms of allocating teaching resources, the freshman year is the worst time for "mass education" because it reinforces the early stage idea that the purpose of education is to amass information.

As a chemistry professor, I have adopted developmental theory in teaching science courses. I begin by challenging the notion that science is Truth—a classic dualistic belief woven into our culture from the time of Galileo and Newton. There are multiple perspectives possible in many aspects of science, and, while I point out that in some cases only one answer to a scientific question is the right one, I present alternative perspectives as often as I can in class. Discussing applications of science that both create and solve special dilemmas provides ample opportunity for examining different perspectives.

In teaching my chemistry classes, I focus on process as much as on content. *How* one solves a problem in chemistry is as important as the solution, particularly when one is learning. I therefore avoid multiple-choice tests in favor of examinations that force my students both to solve the problem and to explain how they approached it. I try to lecture in an interactive way also, by engaging students in the process of thinking through an argument rather than just presenting them with the facts and theories. They begin to become educated scientists by discussing historical and current scientific issues in class, in assignments, and on tests.

Writing is a well-recognized method of exposing students' thought processes to themselves, and I assign my students term papers that require them to investigate a contemporary, controversial issue in science and then present their conclusions clearly. In fact, I "think developmentally," even when I am prescribing the format for writing up their lab reports.

The changes in the way I approach my classes that have resulted from my study of developmental theory may seem insignificant individually, but in combination they have added, for me, a new and exciting dimension to my teaching. As I listen to students talk about learning and life, I hear Perry's positions and stages review themselves. His model has given me a framework for understanding my students' assumptions about education—particularly as they conflict with mine. It helps me guide their progress with a sense of direction. Student-based teaching has worked for me, and I am convinced that the Perry model can be applied profitably to any discipline.

 Vocabulary

As you think about this essay, these definitions may be helpful to you:

1. **cognition**   the process of knowing, including awareness and judgment
2. **operational**   ready to undertake a destined function
3. **dualism** a theory that considers reality to consist of two irreducible elements or modes
4. **entrench**   to establish solidly
5. **incrementally**   changing by small amounts or degrees

Discussion Questions

1. How has the work of Piaget, a French psychologist and philosopher, influenced Finster's understanding of cognition, or how individuals learn in the broadest sense?
2. Describe the "dualists'" way of thinking according to Perry.
3. How can students be encouraged to progress beyond their current level of thinking, according to Perry?
4. How does Finster describe a "good teacher"?
5. What specific steps does Finster take to apply Perry's ideas in his teaching chemistry?

 ## How Can These Ideas Apply to You?

1. Are you a "late dualistic" thinker according to Finster's definition? Explain.
2. Do you agree with Finster's description of a "good teacher"?
3. Have you ever experienced a teacher who is teaching "above your head"? What did you do?
4. Why does Finster think the first year is the worst time for "mass education"?
5. Do you think Finster's methods of teaching are effective? Why? Would you enjoy chemistry if taught by Finster's methods?

Standing Up for Yourself—Without Stepping on Others

Ruthann Fox-Hines
Counseling Psychologist
Counseling and Human Development Center
University of South Carolina

In high school, when I had to talk in front of a class the paper shook louder than my voice. I have so many "if onlys" when I think back to how I could have handled my college experience differently—how much I missed academically and socially because I wasn't assertive. I didn't talk to professors. I let folks take advantage of me. I allowed friendships to disintegrate because I wouldn't bring up things that bothered me until they had reached crisis level. I was a beautiful example of the passive person. In graduate school, I switched to the opposite extreme—aggressiveness; nobody was going to push me around. I was going to be tough. That didn't win me many points, either.

It wasn't until after graduate school that I learned about assertiveness and studied and acquired the skill involved. Now I have a Ph.D. degree and am a licensed counseling psychologist in my fifteenth year with a university counseling center. I'm a director and vice president of Resource Associates, Inc., a consulting firm. I'm the mother of a young man with (not "at") whom I can talk. I can get up in front of 300 people and hold their attention. I can get the service I desire in most stores, and I can deal with issues involving friends and colleagues. Assertive behavior has made such a difference in both my professional and personal life that I want to share it with you.

In this article, I'll describe the skills of positive communication, often called "assertive behavior." Assertive behavior is always based on mutual respect and on personal responsibility. I hope this article motivates you to examine your forms of interacting and to seek further training.

The Importance of Communication Skills

In college and beyond, the skills of standing up for yourself effectively, of communicating your wants, needs, feeling, and ideas in a positive manner are extremely important. Concerned parents or teachers who look out for you may not be around when you need them, and mind-readers are extremely rare. It's up to you to communicate your needs specifically, clearly, and with respect for yourself and the other person.

Stop and think a moment of the many occasions when you wished you had such skills! Perhaps you needed to talk to an advisor about getting into a course, or had to ask an instructor to explain an obscure point in a lecture. Maybe you and your roommates have never agreed upon living arrangements and responsibilities. Resisting pressures from overly concerned parents, equitably sharing responsibilities on a committee, having your input heard and valued in classes, handling job interviews successfully, negotiating work requirements such as salary and hours—all these situations call for the skills of positive communication.

Some people find it easy to stand up for themselves, but many find themselves on the receiving end of negative results and reactions. If standing up for your rights is very difficult for you, you may go through life hoping someone else will figure out what you want and do your standing up for you. The sad truth is, someone else rarely will.

Varieties of Communication

Most of us picked up our communication skills in a rather disorganized fashion. We probably began by imitating parents, other family members, and our peers. You might compare this to learning grammar exclusively from everyday conversations, without once consulting a grammar book.

Not standing up for yourself, or standing up in a poor way, tends to cause frustration and poor relationships with others. Generally, if we do our learning in the pick-it-up-as-you-go-along school, our communication of feelings, and needs, will tend to fall into one of three categories, or some combination of all three.

1. *Passive*: not speaking up, hinting, whining, poor-me routines.
2. *Aggressive*: speaking up in a put-down way, demanding, pressuring.
3. *Passive-aggressive*: speaking up in a confused way saying one thing and doing another ("Sure, I'll be there on time," and showing up late).

None of these attempts at communication is particularly well received by other people. The poor communicator is frequently disappointed, rejected, or even avoided.

Assertive Behavior

The most effective and positive ways of standing up for yourself and of communicating your needs and feelings properly are referred to as assertive behaviors. *Assertiveness* is clear, direct, respectful, responsible communication—verbal and nonverbal. It can be so much more effective than passive or passive-aggressive forms of communication because your chances of being heard and understood are greater, and the chances of the receiver of your communication drawing away, closing his or her ears to what you have to say, or coming back at you fighting are less. If others hear and understand you, and don't feel the need to protect themselves from you, your chances of getting an acceptable response are much greater.

One definition of assertiveness labels it as behavior that permits a person to stand up for his or her rights without denying others their rights. This definition is extremely important. If we simply stand up for our rights, we'll probably come across as aggressive. If we focus exclusively on the rights of the other person, we become passive. Attention to our own *and* others' rights is important in learning to be assertive.

And what are those rights? They include personal rights, such as the right to your own feelings, and interpersonal rights, such as the right to ask others for what you want or need. To avoid denying others their rights, you need to be aware of, and consciously acknowledge, the rights of others. For example, although you have the right to ask a favor, other people have the right to tell you they refuse to grant it.

Mutual Respect and Personal Responsibility

To stand up assertively for your rights, two conditions completely or partially missing from other forms of communication must be present: mutual respect and personal responsibility.

Basically, these conditions can be expressed in the following manner: I respect myself and my right to my ideas, feelings, needs, wants, and values, and I respect you and your rights to the same. I take responsibility for myself. I don't require you to be responsible for me and for figuring out what I am; I'll figure it out for myself.

Passive, passive-aggressive, and aggressive behaviors tend to lack respect for the self and/or the other person, and all three tend to be irresponsible forms of behavior.

Examples of Inappropriate Behaviors

An example may help you distinguish the various behaviors. You are serving on a class committee, and one of the other students isn't doing her share of the work. You're becoming extremely frustrated and worried about the grade you may receive on the project if this other person doesn't come through. The *passive* approach might be to hint about the deadline, and leave it up to the other person to figure out that you're concerned. Using this approach, you show that you're not respecting your own feelings and needs enough to make them known and that you're putting the major responsibility for figuring out what you mean on the other person.

The *passive-aggressive* approach might be to complain to another committee member. This shows a lack of respect for the person you should be addressing. Haven't you often said, "I wish he would respect me enough to come to me instead of talking to others about me." This behavior is irresponsible because you probably hope that the person you complain to will take the responsibility of saying something to the individual at fault.

The *aggressive* approach might be to confront the individual in this manner: "You're messing it up for the rest of us. How can you be so inconsiderate? If you don't have your part ready by tomorrow, I'm telling the professor!" This attack ignores the other person's feelings entirely and possibly overlooks mitigating circumstances of which you may be unaware. Thus, it is disrespectful.

If these three forms of address are incorrect and inappropriate, what is the assertive, or proper, approach?

The Assertive Approach

The *assertive* approach respects the other person and does not attack her, yet still deals with the issues and is responsible enough to express feelings and wishes clearly (in specific words, not by implication or tone of voice).

Such a communication might sound like this: "Mary, I have a problem. Our project is due next week, and I'm worried we won't have it ready on time. I had my part ready yesterday, the day we agreed on. I figure you probably have a heavy load and may have forgotten we agreed on that date. Still, I'm frustrated and worried that we won't have a good project. Would you please make this a priority, and do your part so we can meet either tomorrow afternoon or noon the next day at the latest? I'd very much appreciate it."

The other person may feel embarrassed, but there's a good chance she won't feel as if you attacked her, and therefore won't be forced to take a defensive position. When people are attacked, they defend themselves either by "flight" or "fight." Using flight, they passively comply to another's wishes, but resentment builds inside them. Using fight, they openly throw back accusations or fight subversively (passive-aggressive) by getting the work done, but in a rather slipshod fashion.

On the other hand, when you approach people in a respectful and open manner, chances are they'll hear you more clearly and respond in a more positive manner.

Formula for Assertiveness

To make assertive communication your method for standing up for yourself, you may find the following formula helpful: RÆ, R¨, S.

Respect the Other Person

RÆ reminds you to communicate respect for the other person. Incidentally, respect does not necessarily mean liking, admiring, or agreeing with that person. It simply acknowledges that the other person *is* a person with the same basic rights as you. In other words, you can dislike someone's behavior or disagree with her or him and still offer basic human respect.

We communicate respect both in speech and in actions, in the words we choose to use, and in the nonverbal expressions that accompany the words. The verbal expression may be as simple as saying, "Excuse me," as you move through a crowd getting off an elevator, instead of pushing your way through silently. Your words may acknowledge that the other person has his or her own set of values and needs: "I realize you have established certain criteria for grades in this class . . . " is a good opener when you're about to discuss a possible grade change with a professor.

The verbal communication may even express empathy: "I realize you have a heavy load." It may offer the benefit of the doubt: "I'm sure it probably just slipped your mind." Respect for other people means giving them what we want to receive: courtesy, acknowledgement, and empathy.

Nonverbal communications of respect for others may be expressed in gestures, facial expression, and tone of voice. Such communications may be more significant than words. Said in the wrong tone of voice, "I realize you have a heavy load" could have an opposite and sarcastic meaning. Attention to your nonverbal communications becomes essential to learning effective and positive methods of standing up for yourself.

Nonverbal expressions that communicate respect for others include a clear, relatively gentle, and unhurried manner of speaking, eye contact when another person is talking, uncrossed arms to signal openness, and giving others appropriate physical space so they don't feel crowded or intimidated. Cultural differences exist in nonverbal as well as verbal communication. Because of this, you should not take certain nonverbals as signs of disrespect when the individual expressing them is of a different cultural background. For example, Mediterranean, Latin American, and Middle Eastern people need much less space between themselves and others (as little as twelve inches) than their Northern European or North American counterparts (who require as much as three feet). Unless we're aware of differences like these, we could interpret such behavior as intimidating and disrespectful.

Respect Yourself

R" reminds you to respect yourself and to accept personal responsibility for your feeling, wants, and actions. A major way to accomplish this verbally is to use the first-person singular pronoun: I, me, my—especially the "I." Say "I feel . . . ," not "You make me feel . . ."; "I need more time," not "That's not a lot of time" (indirect, almost a hint) or "Give me more time" (a demand). Say "I don't want to . . . ," not "Well, maybe . . . ," or "No! How could you ask me that?"

Nonverbal communication of self-respect also includes such things as eye contact and open body movements. Both imply that you believe what you say and have nothing to hide. Holding your head up instead of lowering it tends to communicate assurance rather than fear. Ending a spoken sentence with a softened, slightly lowered voice instead of an "up in the air" question mark shows that you have confidence in what you're saying.

Be Specific

S stands for specificity, or being specific, which develops from personal responsibility and respect for the other person. Specificity means being responsible enough to figure out your views, feelings, and wants and being able to communicate them as clearly as possible. It means avoiding labels or generalities about other people and their behavior. Instead of saying, "How can you be so inconsiderate?" when a smoker allows smoke to blow in your direction, you might try this: "I'm having a problem with smoke from you cigarette. Would you please blow it in the other direction?"

Avoid labels such as "inconsiderate," "lazy," and "poor attitude." Don't you feel attacked when others use these labels on you? Talk about the behaviors that lead you to think about those labels. Avoid generalities such as "love,""attention," and "respect." Instead, determine the specific behaviors you include in your definitions of those vague terms, and talk about those behaviors. For instance, if you don't like someone to keep looking at a magazine when you're talking to her, don't say, "You don't respect me." Instead, you might try saying, "I'm uncomfortable when I talk to someone and don't get eye contact. When we talk, I'd appreciate it if you'd put your magazine down. It would help a lot."

Choosing the Proper Response: An Example

To see the formula at work, let's go through an example. Mark is a relatively conscientious student. His roommate John seems to be majoring in partying. John cuts classes and regularly borrows Mark's notes from the two classes they share. Although Mark has been rescuing John by giving him his notes whenever John asks (being the "good guy"), he is beginning to feel used. One important lesson from this example is that "rescuers become victims." If you do for others what they can and should do for themselves, they tend to demand more and more and value what they get less and less.

Mark's first mistake was not to make his position clear at the start. A suggestion I can't stress too strongly is: the more you take responsibility for yourself—know what you feel and what your priorities and wants are, and make them clearly known to others—the fewer problems you'll have down the road.

The first time John asked to borrow the notes, Mark could have said, "I know you missed class and need the material (*acknowledging John's plight: RÆ*). But I don't usually lend my notes. I'll let you use them this time, but in the future, please don't ask. Find someone else or talk to the instructor" ("I" *statements of a clear policy and Mark's wishes*: R¨ *and* S).

If John pressures him, Mark may need to protect himself by tightening his communication and using what is sometimes referred to as a "broken record": No matter what John says, Mark responds by repeating the major message: "I don't lend my notes." Here is an example:

JOHN: Ah, come on. I thought we'd be able to take care of each other in classes (*a guilt trip*).

MARK: (*resisting the guilt and focusing on the major issue*) I don't lend my notes out. This time I said okay, but from now on, no.

JOHN: Hey, what kind of buddy are you? I thought we could count on each other.

MARK: John (*using the other person's name may make him more attentive*), I don't lend my notes. I hope you'll respect that and not use it to judge whether or not I'm a good buddy.

At this point, John may start to head out of the room in a huff.

MARK: Hey, John, I'm sorry you've taken my not lending out notes that way. I hope later you'll accept my position.

Since Mark didn't take care of this issue at the outset, he's reaching a frustrating point and probably establishing a negative pattern of interaction with John. He could slip into a passive approach easily, avoiding his room as much as possible so he can avoid John. Or he could become passive-aggressive and let his frustration show in his voice, make sarcastic remarks, or even give John the wrong notes. Finally, he could explode in an aggressive outburst: "Don't you ever take your own crummy notes? I'm sick and tired of doing all your work for you. Find someone else to mooch off. And, by the way, I'm also sick and tired of. . . ." Here, all Mark's other little frustrations with John may come pouring out.

Any of these alternatives will result in added frustration on Mark's part, distancing between the two, or even fight or flight on John's part: a loud argument, sneak attacks, or stony silences. There's a good chance that both will be seeking new roommates at a time when reshuffling may be difficult.

The Assertive Approach

The assertive approach, while not guaranteeing that Mark will get what he wants from John, at least opens the door for such a possibility. First, Mark needs to separate the issues he has with John—notes, noise, privacy, or whatever—and decide which issues he wants to deal with first. Dealing with individual issues is better than dumping a whole load of complaints on a person all at once. Mark should also find a time when he can talk to John alone. Complaints made in front of others tend to be disrespectful and cause the other person to be more defensive. Then he might say, "John, I know I've been lending you my notes for X and Y classes. (*By acknowledging his own part, Mark is showing respect for John:* RÆ.) But I'm beginning to feel used. I don't mind lending my notes if someone is sick, but I really don't like doing it on a regular basis ("I"*statements and clarity of feeling and wishes:* R¨ *and* S). I know I should have said something earlier (*again,* R¨, *accepting responsibility that isn't John's*). I want to break that pattern. From now on, I'm not lending my notes, and I'm asking you not to ask me for them. Find someone else or talk with the instructor" (*more "I" statement and a clear statement of what he doesn't want and what he wants from John:* R¨ *and* S). If John pushes, Mark can resort to the "broken record" described earlier.

Learning Effective Communication Skills

Since assertiveness, which encompasses standing up for yourself effectively and communicating in a positive manner, is a behavior pattern, we can learn these methods of interacting as skills. Learning communications skills is similar to learning to drive a car. First, you practice in "safe" places such as the driveway or empty parking lots. Later, as you feel more comfortable with your skills, you try driving on the streets and, eventually, in five o'clock traffic. When you first learn to drive, such skills as braking smoothly feel unnatural and awkward. Later, after practicing, you reach a point where you don't even have to think about it.

The same is true with communication skills. First, you try simple skills in such places as a training group. When you first try this new communication, they may feel funny (uncrossing your arms, for example, if you're in the habit of keeping them crossed). Later, with practice, you find you can use these behaviors in the "real world." Still later, you'll find you don't have to think much about them. At that point, they've become natural.

The best way to learn assertive behavior skills is through special training seminars. Most colleges and universities, through their counseling centers or continuing education programs, and many community organizations such as the YWCA and YMCA offer workshops, short courses, or seminars in assertiveness. Books listed at the end of this article may also be useful to you. Remember, though, that reading and learning aren't enough. Practice is the essential ingredient.

Suggested Activities

1. Explain to a friend outside of class that assertiveness is not the same as aggressiveness.

2. Indicate the type of communication in each of the following examples: assertive (AS), passive (P.), passive-aggressive (PA), aggressive (AG).

   _____ a. A mother indicates she would like her daughter, a college student, to come home each weekend. The student replies: "Mom, I know you love me and want what's best for me. Right now, with studies and the friendships I'm trying to establish, what's best for me is to have most of my weekends ends here. I won't be coming home except at breaks, but I promise I'll write or call at least once a week. Thanks for understanding."

   _____ b. You're asked to do a favor. Your reply: "Are you kidding? Hell, no!"

   _____ c. You're a student and need to borrow a classmate's notes. You say to her: "I don't know what I'm going to do. I missed Carter's class last Friday and that test of his is next week. Oh, Lord, I know I'm going to do awful. I'll probably flunk."

   _____ d. Someone pays you a compliment. You reply: "Thank you. I appreciate your noticing."

   _____ e. You're upset with a friend who usually walks in late for meetings. He does it again. You say: "Oh, look. Sam's on time for a change!"

   _____ f. You'd like to ask your roommate to play the stereo more softly. You say: "Mark, I don't have any problems with the fact that you enjoy the stereo loud. What I have a problem with is that, when I'm here and trying to study, the loud stereo breaks my concentration. When I'm out, do as you like. But, please, when I'm here, keep it lower. I'd appreciate it a lot."

Answers: a. AS   b. AG   c. P   d. AS   e. PA   f. AS

3. This classroom exercise can help both in the practice of assertive nonverbal behavior and in the personal coaching and cheering needed to remember we have certain rights. This exercise will take from thirty to sixty minutes of class time; parts a and b can be done ahead of time outside of class.

    a. Mark the rights listed below that are especially important to you and which you have some difficulty affirming:

        _____ 1. To lead my own life, make my own decisions, make choices, and take the consequences.

        _____ 2. To have my own values and to act on those values in a responsible manner.

        _____ 3. To control my own body, time, money, or property.

        _____ 4. To have all my feelings, positive and negative, and to express these feelings in a responsible way.

        _____ 5. To have my own opinions, ideas, and perceptions and to express them in a responsible, nondogmatic way.

        _____ 6. To have needs and act to meet them.

        _____ 7. To express my needs, make requests, ask for information, ask for special consideration.

        _____ 8. To refuse requests and invitations.

        _____ 9. To *not* feel what others would like me to feel. To not share values and perceptions that others would like me to share.

        _____ 10. To be imperfect, make mistakes, and act to correct them.

        _____ 11. To change feelings, values, opinions, ideas, and behaviors.

        _____ 12. To stop and think when confronted, invited, or asked to do a favor.

    All these rights depend on your willingness to allow them to others; for example, you have the right to say no if you permit that right to others

    b. Pick out one right that is the most important to you—that is, if you worked on remembering you had that right and began behaving in terms of possessing it, your life might be improved. Write it out in the space provided. (You may think "I want all those rights"; if so, for now, for the purposes of the exercise, focus on one. As that one becomes yours through affirmation, go on to the others.)

    _____

    _____

    c.   (approximately 10 minutes) In class, pair up and practice assertively reading and saying the following sentence plus the right you chose to work on. To practice assertively:

        1.   sit up straight; feet flat on the floor (well-balanced); head up, not lowered.

        2.   make eye contact with your partner (hold the paper or book up so you don't have to keep looking down at the desk or lap).

        3.   keep facial expression serious and don't laugh either during or after.

        4.   make sure your voice is strong and goes down at the end of the affirmed right.

        5.   go slowly enough to be meaningful; don't rush.

I _____ (your name), as a worthy human being, who respects the rights of others, have the *perfect* right to: (read the right you have written out in part b).

As you practice with a partner, give each other specific feedback such as "Your eye contact was good" or "It would be better if you slowed down a bit." Practice several times until you accomplish an assertive affirmation.

    a.   (approximately 10 minutes) Pairs join other pairs (form groups of four or six) and go around the group, each doing an assertive affirmation.

    b.   Practice assertive affirmations at home, making eye contact with yourself in a mirror. (During the next class, each person could then do an assertive affirmation after home practice.)

    c.   The instructor may want to lead a discussion about how things would be different if all students allowed themselves to have the right they have not let themselves have until now.

4.   In this class exercise for role-playing practice, divide the class into teams of three (one or two teams of four, if necessary).

    a.   Each team should write up one or two situations that call for assertive behavior: roommate or dating issues, interactions with professors, resisting pressures, and interactions with parents, for example. Students could do this individually ahead of time, and teams could choose from among the situations brought in. Put the situations in a pile and have each team draw a situation.

    b.   (approximately 15 minutes) Teams plan a role-playing demonstration of assertive handling of the situation they draw. One member might play the roommate, friend, or professor; another plays the person who assertively handles the situation; the third (and fourth) member would serve as a helper to the one being assertive, reminding the assertive member of the rights involved and suggesting RÆ, R", S phrasing and nonverbal behavior.

    c.   (approximately 5 minutes per role play) Each team presents its role play to the class.

    d.   Class can then follow each role-playing demonstration with some discussion of how it was handled and suggestions for improvement (approximately 5 minutes per role play). For further practice, teams could later switch situations and redo them or come up with new ones to practice.

A word about role playing: Have fun. This kind of practice is necessary. Skills are not learned through mere reading. Trying them out is necessary. Since the skills are new, it is natural to feel a bit awkward. Feeling "natural" only comes with practice.

5.   Contact your college or university counseling center or continuing education department for information regarding workshops or seminars on assertive behavior.

6.   Get together with friends or fellow students who are interested in developing these skills. Use the workbook *Assert Yourself* by Galassi and Galassi (see Suggested Readings) as a guide, or your instructor or college may be able to acquire the game, Assert with Love, High Consciousness Games, Inc., PO Box 3206, Kansas City, Kans. 66103

Suggested Readings

Butler, Pam. *Self Assertion for Woman*. San Francisco: Canfield Press, 1981.

Emmons, M. L., and R. E. Alberti. *Your Perfect Right*. San Luis Obispo, Calif.: Impact Publishers, 1974.

Galassi, J., and M. Galassi. *Assert Yourself*. (workbook) New York: Human Sciences Press, 1977.

Jacubowski, R. and A. J. Lang. *The Assertive Option*. Champaign, Ill.: Research Press, 1978.

Tips on Becoming Personally Effective

Susan Jones Sears

Well known for her work in counselor education, Susan Jones Sears is a professor emerita in the College of Education at the Ohio State University. In this essay, she offers some practical tips for becoming a competent and successful student.

Whether you are a new college student or a more experienced one, you are probably impressed with the number of talented and highly skilled individuals in your classes—individuals who seem to know more than you do and who are motivated, bright, and dedicated. With increasing competition in the classroom and the workplace, individuals have begun searching for a psychological edge, an advantage to help them excel and be recognized as competent students and workers. Think about the concept of personal effectiveness—personal behaviors and skills that result in enhanced performance in college, at work, and in life. As you begin your college career and prepare for the work world, you can benefit from reflecting upon what it takes to excel.

What are the ingredients of success? During the last three decades, hundreds of books have been written with the intent of helping people improve themselves and increase their chances for success. Techniques for improving your personality, learning to communicate more effectively, and managing stress are all familiar topics to readers who avail themselves of the self-help books in their local bookstores or on the Internet. In the early 1980s, those interested in improving their performance read *Peak Performers* by Charles Garfield; in the latter 1980s and early 1990s, they read *The Seven Habits of Highly Effective People* by Stephen Covey. In the 2000s, Philip C. McGraw is the latest self-help guru.

Today, many books on coaching are generating a lot of attention and discussion. Professional athletes and actors have used the services of coaches for decades, and now ordinary individuals are hiring coaches to give them advice and offer strategies on how to improve their personal and professional lives.

If you study high achievers or personally effective individuals, you begin to see that they function at higher levels not because of a single talent but, rather, because certain factors, taken together, result in greater accomplishment. Individuals who know what they want to do in life, who have a vision, a game plan, or a purpose or goal, are more successful than those who do not. If you have a sense of purpose, you will naturally attract those who are going in the same direction. What is your purpose or goal in life? What are you trying to achieve? Maybe you want to find a major or a career that you will enjoy and [that will] bring you

From Susan Jones Sears and Virginia N. Gordon, *Building Your Career—A Guide to Your Future,* 3rd edition (Upper Saddle River, NJ: Prentice Hall, 2002). Reprinted with permission of Pearson Education Inc., Upper Saddle River, NJ.

fulfillment, or maybe you want to travel to learn about other cultures. Take a few minutes to think about your goal or purpose for the year.

Replacing Distractions with Energy Boosters

Petty annoyances are often small irritants, but they tend to become real hassles when they are not dealt with. They drain your energy and distract you from your quest for success. Perhaps something around the house or apartment is broken, but you can't seem to get around to repairing it. Or your roommate is a "night owl" and you are not.

Maybe one of your own bad habits is annoying you! Your notes are disorganized and scattered, and when it is time to study for a test, you procrastinate. Or maybe a friend has a habit of making fun of you or putting you down when you make even a small mistake. You have tolerated it but find yourself getting angrier each time it happens. Many of us tolerate petty annoyances and really don't realize how much they are irritating us, wearing us down, and draining our energy. Write down a list of the things you are putting up with or tolerating that are draining your energy. Now set aside a day within the next week to tackle some of these petty annoyances. Try to eliminate everything on your list that you can.

Some annoyances take time to eliminate. If you are having difficulty in a relationship and want to rebuild or repair it, you probably can't do it in a day. But at least you can begin. When you succeed in working through the annoyances that bother you the most, you should reward yourself by indulging in some favorite activity.

Simplifying Your Life

One way to attract something new in your life is to make space—get rid of the clutter, toss out old notes, clothes, and memos, and sell those old books and CDs. Ask yourself: "Have I used this in the past six months?" If your answer is no and it isn't a seasonal item, toss it. If you don't know where to start, take one part of a room at a time. Give your usable items to a local charity. Someone will appreciate what has been cluttering up your space. Getting rid of things you do not need can invigorate you and create the sensation of starting anew.

Once you have rid yourself of the clutter in your life, look at your schedule. If your schedule is packed with stuff to do, people to meet, and places to go, it may be time to simplify. People who are too busy can miss opportunities because they don't notice what is going on around them and don't have time to think. Consolidate your credit cards so you don't spend so much time paying and keeping track of bills. Turn your cell phone off. Before you say yes to a social event, make certain it is really something you want to do.

Managing Your Time Effectively

Do you attend classes, study as hard as you can, and then run to your part-time or full-time job? Do you find yourself complaining that there aren't enough hours in the day? If you feel pressured for time, perhaps you should take a week and track your time in one-hour increments. Keep a notepad in your pocket or bookbag and write down what you are doing each hour from the time you rise until you go to bed. Writing just a few words will allow you to keep track of how you are spending your time. At the end of the week, quickly calculate how much time you spend on major life activities such as attending classes, studying, talking on the phone, sleeping, watching television, listening to music, hanging out with your friends, e-mailing, texting or instant messaging. Are you surprised by how you spend your time? In what areas do you think you are wasting your time? How can you reschedule your time so you will use it more effectively?

Learning to Say No

Are you overcommitted with work and social obligations? Do you find yourself participating in activities that don't really interest you? Perhaps you need to learn to say no. Women in particular are brought up in our society to please and to be liked. As a result of this kind of socialization, they find it harder to say no when asked to do favors or take on extra work. Some fear that saying no will turn off their friends, but in reality it doesn't. Often your friends and colleagues respect you more when they learn they cannot take advantage of you. Learning to say no is one way of getting control of your time and your life.

Managing Your Money Well

During the last 20 years, it has become acceptable to have debts. Your parents probably saved money before they purchased a cherished item, whereas you may find it easy to simply charge the cost to your credit card. The costs of immediate gratification (charge it now) can be high. First, the interest rate on debt is high. Second, too much debt can lead to stress that can drain your energy, making it difficult for you to be your best and attract the people and opportunities you want. Instead, if you pay off the balance on your credit cards each month, you will feel lighter, more free, and in control of your life.

Building a Strong Network of Friends

Part of your success in life and work is having some close friends with whom you can laugh, love, and celebrate your and their successes. Be aware of the people around you, and get to know those who are particularly interesting. With our increased mobility, we sometimes have to create our own communities, a circle of friends with whom we feel comfortable and supported. Some create this circle of friends at college or at work, and others find opportunities to create friendships at church or in clubs. Be proactive and create your own network of friends.

Making Time for Yourself

Life can become boring if we do not have something to look forward to. Taking a walk, talking to friends, taking a hot bubble bath, or listening to your favorite music are just a few examples of activities that might be pleasurable and inspiring to you. Taking time for yourself is an important way to keep balanced in today's hectic world. Think about the activities that you really look forward to doing, and then how can you change your schedule to include them in your daily life.

Identifying and Managing Stress

If you are to become truly effective, you must begin to identify the sources of stress in your life and learn to manage stress at work, school, and home. Stress can be either a positive or a negative force. It is negative when it interferes with your ability to function at your optimal level. It is positive when it enhances your performance or your effectiveness. That is the key to stress management.

What does the term *stress* really mean? According to psychologist Donald Meichenbaum, you experience stress when you appraise an event (a demand on you, a constraint, an opportunity, or a challenge) as having the potential to exceed the resources you have available. You may think it's too hard, too frightening, or too challenging. Stressors or events that can create anxiety vary greatly from individual to individual. Three classifications are:

■ *external* physical stimuli, such as heat, cold, crowding, loud noises
■ *interpersonal* difficulties with others
■ *internal* stimuli, such as our own thoughts or feelings

Although stressors are specific to individuals to some extent, universal categories of stressors are environmental stressors, life stress events, and daily hassles.

Environmental stressors include things such as noise, crowding, commuting time, worry about crime, traffic and pollution, economic difficulties, isolation, restricted leisure opportunities, and job insecurity. These often are a function of where you live and sometimes your socioeconomic class.

Life stress events are major occurrences that create stress and require people to change and adapt. Holmes and Rahe identified 43 life events that cause significant stress and assigned each event a weight, using what they called "life change events." Events that call for a greater amount of change and adaptation are assigned a higher number of life change units. For example, the death of a spouse is assigned a very high weight. Holmes and Rahe used their instrument, the Social Readjustment Rating Scale, to measure the amount of life stress a person was experiencing. They found that too many life stress events forced the body to adapt and change so much that those stresses weakened the immune system.

In fact, researchers have made connections between life stress events and both physical and mental illness. Evidence has shown that life stress events contribute to emotional disorders, heart disease, accidents, and other conditions. Whether individuals who experience stressful life events subsequently become ill, however, also depends on their personal vulnerability, as well as the amount of social and emotional support available to them.

Daily hassles (for instance, physical appearance, concerns about weight, too many things to do, and losing or misplacing things) are also stressors. Until the early 1980s, little research had been done on the effect of minor but more common daily hassles. Since then, researchers have paid considerable attention to studying effects of hassles on health. Hassles seem to vary depending on age and, to some extent, the circumstances in which people find themselves. Some common daily hassles for students are:

■ Taking tests or exams
■ Worrying about not meeting academic deadlines
■ Not knowing how to study effectively
■ Taking difficult and demanding classes

Strategies for Managing Stress

Preventive approaches such as relaxation training are important to any stress management program. The term *relaxation training* refers to any technique whose purpose is to decrease the negative symptoms the human body experiences under stress. If individuals can be taught to relax, they should be able to produce voluntarily an alternative physiological response to offset the negative stress symptoms. For example, if a stress reaction results in increases in muscle tension, blood pressure, or heart rate, the voluntarily induced state of relaxation can reverse these increases.

Engaging in a healthy lifestyle goes a long way in managing stress. Individuals who experience the physiological effects of stress are endangering their health. If they also are practicing unhealthy habits that weaken the body's ability to resist stress, their level of stress may increase. Clearly, if you are stressed, you should practice good eating habits, use alcohol only moderately if at all, not smoke, and get regular exercise.

Accepting and Adapting to Change

Change is anything that causes us to shift from old and familiar ways or situations to ones that are new, different, and often challenging. More than a decade ago, Alvin Toffler talked about "waves of change" that are accelerating at a faster and faster pace. The rate of change in today's world is greater than any other time in our history. Global competition, almost unbelievable advances in technology, particularly communication technologies, and a knowledge and information explosion all contribute to this fast-paced change. Learning how to adapt and adjust to change is a critical skill that can be learned.

In times of rapid change, you must be able to adapt quickly. Below are several suggestions on how to adapt to change rather than ignore or resist it:

■ Withhold judgment and tolerate ambiguity or uncertainty until you see the results of whatever changes you are experiencing.
■ Be flexible and try new approaches.
■ Stay current about changes and trends in your field and try to understand their potential impact.
■ Anticipate the new skills needed in your field and acquire them.
■ View change as part of a natural process of growth.
■ Look to the future; don't glorify the past beyond its worth.

■   Scan your environment and reassess your goals regularly.

Think about the changes that have occurred in your life in the last 18 months. How did you respond? For example, did you try to avoid change at all costs, complain about the change, reluctantly change, or see change as an opportunity and develop ways to deal with it? At times, change can create situations in which you feel you have little or no control over events going on around you. When that happens, we usually experience anxiety or stress. Although we cannot always control what is happening in life, we can control our reaction it. We can decide how to react to change so it does not overwhelm us.

The personal characteristics and skills outlined above can give you the psychological edge in school, work, and life in general. As you establish your educational and career goals, developing these habits, attitudes and skills can enhance your success in all areas of life.

Works Cited

Covey, Stephen. *The Seven Habits of Highly Effective People*. New York: Simon and Schuster, 1989.

Garfield, Charles. *Peak Performers*. New York: Avon, 1986.

Holmes, T. H., and Rahe, R. H. "The Social Readjustment Rating Scale." *Journal of Psychosomatic Research*, 11(2), 213–218, 1967.

Meichenbaum, Donald. *Stress Inoculation Training*. New York: Pergamon Press, 1985.

Toffler, Alvin. *The Third Wave*. New York: William Morrow, 1980.

 ## Discussion Questions

1. What does becoming a "personally effective student" mean to you? Does being a competent college student differ from being a competent high school student? If so, how?
2. Which of the author's suggestions for improving your daily life would be the most difficult for you to accomplish? (For example, do you have trouble saying no when friends ask for a favor?)
3. What are some stressors in your life, and what can you do to alleviate them?

 ## Suggestions for Your Journal

Reflect on your ability to accept and adapt to change. Since you began college, what changes (for example, in your daily routine, in the classroom, in your relationship with your parents) have been the most difficult to deal with? The easiest?

What has surprised you the most about how being a college student has changed your life?

The Harvard Guide to Happiness
Kate Zernike

Lost in the current obsession to get into "The Best U" is something most adults readily admit, at least in hindsight:

It doesn't matter so much where you go to college, but what you make of the experience.

So how to make the most of it?

In 1986, Derek Bok, then the president of Harvard, summoned a professor at the Graduate School of Education and asked him to evaluate how well the university educated its students and ways it might improve. Why, Dr. Bok wanted to know, did some students have a great experience while others did not?

The professor, Richard I. Light, a statistician by training, gathered colleagues and deans from twenty-four other institutions to examine the question and come up with a scientific method to find the answer.

Over ten years researchers interviewed sixteen hundred Harvard students, asking a range of questions about everything from what they did in their spare time to the quality of teaching and advising. They looked for patterns—say, what made certain courses effective. They also correlated students' academic and personal choices with their grades and how happy and intellectually engaged they said they were. The goal was to determine which factors were more likely to improve learning and overall happiness. A factor always linked to success would be rated 1, one with a significant relationship to success would be 0.50, and one with no effect would be 0. (Not every factor got a rating because of inconsistencies in how questions were asked.)

Fifteen years later, Harvard has made policy changes based on the study, like assigning students homework to do in groups and scheduling some classes'later in the day so discussions can continue over dinner.

"It turns out there are a whole range of concrete ways students can improve their experience," said

Professor Light, who teaches at the John F. Kennedy School of Government as well as at the education school. Professor Light has gathered the best ideas in a book, *Making the Most of College* (Harvard University Press, 2001) The suggestions are often simple. "Still," he said, "It's amazing how little thought people give to these decisions."

1. *Meet the faculty.* Professor Light now tells each of the students he advises the same thing at the beginning of each term: "Your job is to get to know one faculty member reasonably well and get that faculty member to know you reasonably well. If you do nothing else, do that." On the most opportunistic level, this means that at the end of four years—two semesters each—the student has eight professors to write recommendations for jobs or for graduate school.

But more important, the relationship makes a student feel more connected to the institution.

The most satisfied students in the Harvard interviews sought detailed feedback and asked specific questions of professors and advisers— not "Why didn't I get a better grade?" but "Point out the paragraphs in this essay where my argument faltered."

And don't try to hide academic problems. The researchers working for Professor Light interviewed a sample of forty students who stumbled academically in their first year. The twenty who asked for help improved their grades, the twenty who did not spiraled downward—isolated, failing and unhappy.

2. *Take a mix of courses.* Nearly without exception, the students in the study who were struggling were taking nothing but large introductory courses that were needed to complete their degree. Why? To get them out of the way. Advice from well-meaning parents often goes something like this: first year, take required courses. Second year, choose a major. Third year, take advanced classes required for your major. Save fun electives, like dessert, for last.

The trouble is, introductory courses range across so much material they often fail to offer students anything to sink their teeth into. So when it comes time to choose a major, students don't know what really interests them. By senior year, when taking courses that stimulate them, they are wondering why they didn't take more courses in Japanese/medieval social history/statistics earlier. Those who treat the early years like a shopping excursion, taking not only required classes but also ones that pique their interest, feel more engaged and happier with their major.

"The less-satisfied students were the ones who said, 'My tack was to get all the requirements out of the way,'" Professor Light said. "The successful students do the exact opposite."

The corollary to this recommendation: Take small classes, which encourages faculty interaction and a feeling of connectedness. Taking classes with fifteen or fewer students had a 0.52 correlation with overall engagement and a 0.24 correlation with good grades— both considered significant.

3. *Study in groups.* Doing homework is important, but what really matters is doing it in a way that helps you understand the material. Students who studied on their own and then discussed the work in groups of four to six, even just once a week, understood material better and felt more engaged with their classes. This was especially true with science, which requires so much solitary work and has complicated concepts.

4. *Write, write, write.* Choose courses with many short papers instead of one or two long ones. This means additional work—more than twelve hours a week versus fewer then nine, or about forty percent more time—but it also improves grades. In a class that requires only one twenty-page paper at the end of the term, there is no chance of recovering from a poor showing. Courses with four five-page papers offer chances for a midcourse correction.

And the more writing, the better. In all of Professor Light's research, no factor was more important to engagement and good grades than the amount of writing a student did. Students in the study recommended taking courses with a lot of writing in the last two years, when you have adjusted to the challenges of being in college and are preparing to write a long senior thesis.

5. *Speak another language.* Foreign language courses are the best-kept secret on campus. Many students arrive with enough skills to test out of a college's language requirement. But language was the most commonly mentioned among "favorite classes." Sixty percent of students put them in the category of "hard work but pure pleasure"; fifty-seven percent of those interviewed again after leaving college recommended not testing out. Why? Classes are small, instructors insist on participation, students work in groups, and assignments include lots of written work and frequent quizzes, allowing for repeated midcourse corrections. In short, foreign language courses combine all the elements that lead to more learning and more engagement.

6. *Consider time.* In the Harvard interviews, there was one striking difference between those who did well in their courses and those who did not: Those who did well mentioned the word "time"; those who did not never used the word. Students reported that they did not succeed when they studied the way they had in high school, squeezing in twenty-five minutes in a study hall, thirty-five minutes after sports practice and forty-five minutes after dinner. Grades and understanding improved when they set aside an uninterrupted stretch of a few hours. Professor Light even suggests keeping a time log for a few weeks and showing it to an adviser, who can help figure out the best way to allocate time.

7. *Hold the drum.* Students often flounder in college because they do not have the same social or family support network they had at home. Those who get involved in outside activities, even ones not aimed at padding a resume or a graduate school application, are happiest. Professor Light tells the story of one young woman arriving unhappy in her adviser's office. When the adviser encouraged her to do something beyond her studies, she demurred. She had no talent; she could not play on a team or sing in the choir. "How about band?" her adviser prodded. She replied that she did not play an instrument. "That's OK," he said. "Ask them if you can hold the drum." Years later, when asked to describe why her college experience had been so positive, she repeatedly referred to the band, which got her involved at pep rallies and football games and introduced her to a diverse range of students.

Students who have worked hard to get into college, Professor Light said, tend to arrive and say, "Academic work is my priority, and doing other things will hurt that." In fact, the Harvard research found otherwise.

"What goes on in situations outside of class is just as important, and in some situations, it turns out to be a bigger deal than what happens in class," he said. "Very often an experience outside of class can have a profound effect on the courses students choose and even what they want to do with their lives."

The study found that students who worked long hours at a job had the same grades as those who worked a few hours or not at all. Students who volunteered actually had higher grades and reported being happier. The only students whose outside activities hurt their grades were intercollegiate athletes. Still, Professor Light said, they are the happiest students on campus.

Active Learning

James Twining

James E. Twining is on the faculty at the Community College of Rhode Island. This essay is from his book *Strategies for Active Learning*. In this essay he presents an overview of learning that has a very practical application.

How people learn is an intriguing subject. Ask a group of students what they do when given a reading assignment, and most will respond, quite logically, "I read it." If you then ask, "How do you know when you've completed the assignment?" the answer is typically, "I've completed it when I'm finished reading." Neither response says much about how learning takes place.

Knowing when an assignment is complete is at the heart of the learning process. It suggests that the purpose of the assignment is clearly understood and that the activities necessary to complete the work are also known. More important, this knowledge suggests that each of us is responsible for our own learning, for taking charge of the learning process. Think about what that means.

Studies done by psychologists and others show that active learners— those who take charge of their learning—are successful learners. One result their research demonstrates is that students who use appropriate study methods, such as underlining key ideas and taking notes, remember more from a study period than those who do not. Furthermore, the research shows that those students who search for ways to improve their methods of study and who further develop their skills are much more likely to become successful learners. But most of all, these studies show that active and successful learners are aware of how to think about a learning situation, such as studying a textbook chapter in preparing for an exam, and how to regulate the learning process, such as making specific plans to pass a test successfully. . . .

As people grow, they learn many things that are quite difficult to grasp at first but eventually become so familiar that they are done automatically. Learning to ride a bicycle is one of these tasks. Think of how many rules riding a bike requires us to know: Keep the wheel straight, keep pedaling, hold your balance, watch where you're going, and so on. Yet once bike riding is learned, you do it automatically. You don't think about holding your balance; you just do it, naturally.

Learning how to learn is a bit like learning how to ride a bike. It is not always easy, it is sometimes confusing, and it doesn't guarantee success, particularly in the beginning. But knowing how to learn, how to use specific strategies, and to make good study habits a routine practice improves the likelihood of success.

Learning is also like problem solving. Each course assignment is essentially a problem to be solved. Your job is to get from point X, an assignment to learn a subject about which you have little or no knowledge, to point Y, a thorough understanding of the material and the increased potential for success on an examination. But to get from point X to point Y, to solve the problem, means moving in steps—doing things first, second, and so forth until completion. And because of the many steps to learning, it is useful to think about grouping them in three major stages: planning, monitoring, and evaluating.

Active learners plan how they will accomplish a task. They monitor their work carefully to make sure things are working as they had planned. And they evaluate their results to be sure they have accomplished the task, to be sure that they are now successful learners. That's why you need to look closely at how this learning process works. . . .

Planning is the first step in successful learning. Planning is, in fact, an integral part of everyday life. People make plans to go out. They make plans to see friends. They make plans for the weekend. It seems quite reasonable, therefore, that people also make plans for learning.

One approach to planning . . . considers four types of information: the characteristics of the learner, the critical tasks or specific assignments, the nature of the materials, and the learning strategies necessary to complete the task.

Good planning requires first that you know yourself, know your characteristics as a learner. . . . The more aware you are of how you learn, of your strengths and weaknesses, and of how you can build your strengths, the more successful you are likely to be in learning how to learn. . . .

Do you take good notes, or should you learn how to take better notes? Are you able to retain much that you study, or should you learn more efficient memory techniques? These are the issues of self-awareness. To accomplish any task, you must be aware of how best to guide your learning.

You must also plan with purpose. What is the critical task, the specific assignment to be completed? How will you be evaluated? What method of testing will the instructor use? How will you know before the exam whether your efforts are succeeding?

Imagine, for instance, that your assignment is to read a chapter in your sociology text on socialization (how people become a part of their community) and to prepare for a quiz on the difference between socialization in highly developed urban communities and in more traditional rural communities. The assignment is the critical task; it creates the purpose for your study: (1) what you need to do— read the chapter on socialization; (2) what you need to know— the differences between the two communities; and (3) how to judge when you are done—to test your knowledge of the differences. You fulfill your purpose, and you are done when you know those differences. . . .

Next, consider the nature of the study material. What type of material is it? Is it typical of a textbook chapter or a magazine article? How is it organized? Differences, for example, are frequently presented with comparison and contrast patterns. Is there a plan of action most appropriate to this type of material? These questions suggest a couple of important points.

On the one hand, you need to be aware of how different reading materials are organized. Recognize, for instance, the difference between the organization of textbook chapters, which are very explicit (new ideas are both explained and illustrated) and the organization of short stories, which are less explicit (new ideas are introduced via the interaction of character, plot, and setting). These differences influence your choice of method to study the material.

On the other hand, different types of study material present different organizational clues. Textbook authors frequently signal important parts of the text with phrases like "the key point here" and "to summarize." The clues in the short story are more general. Understand the characters—how they are presented, how they behave, what the consequences of their thoughts and actions are— and you will understand the story. Reading materials differ in their purpose and structure, and these differences determine how best to study them. . . .

Next, good planning requires that you determine which learning strategies are most useful for the task, the material, and your strengths as a learner. What strategies will make you an efficient and effective learner? . . . But for the moment, look again at the hypothetical sociology assignment.

The task is to know the differences in socialization for urban and rural communities. Because the material follows standard textbook organizations, the information should be fairly explicit. As you think about your reading habits, you realize that you sometimes lose your concentration while reading textbooks and that careful underlining helps you stay alert and keep track of important facts. Imagine then that the strategy you choose may look something like this:

- My purpose is to know the differences in socialization between urban and rural societies.
- I will read the text to answer this question: "What is the difference between rural and urban patterns of socialization?"
- I will underline important ideas as I read to keep track of the information.
- Once I have completed my reading, I will review my underlined points to be sure I understand them and that they help answer the question.
- I will also reread sections I find confusing.
- To evaluate my understanding, I will give myself a written self-test to see if I know the differences and can explain them.
- Reviews and additional self-tests will depend on my previous successes. My success on my self-test will determine when I'm done.

This, of course, is just one example, but it does suggest how planning works. To be successful, you should consider (1) your characteristics as a learner, (2) the critical tasks of learning, (3) the nature of the materials to be learned, and (4) the variety of learning strategies available.

As soon as you put your plan into play, begin monitoring. Start by observing your activities to see if your plan and your strategies are working successfully. Try to decide if the material you are studying makes sense, if your approach is appropriate to the assigned task, and if your progress is proceeding efficiently. Remember that learning always carries time limits.

Self-Questioning

You might think of the monitoring process, at least initially, as a self-questioning procedure. You can examine your progress by asking a series of questions about your purpose, your task, and your response. You might consider checking your work with these questions:

_____ Is my purpose clear?
_____ Am I able to identify important ideas?
_____ Does my underlining and note-taking aid my comprehension?
_____ Are the questions I ask about the subject being answered by the text?
_____ Can I summarize the main points in the material I've studied?
_____ Am I using effective memory techniques to help me retain the information? . . .

Also consider the importance of monitoring your reading comprehension, because reading is such an integral part of all study. Reading is a continuous process of interpreting what is happening in the text and predicting what will happen next. To the extent you understand—comprehend—the material, you will succeed in learning it. To the extent you don't, your comprehension will break down. . . .

Three basic strategies are generally suggested to help you monitor your comprehension in the reading for study: note-taking, questioning, and summarizing.

Note-Taking

Note-taking has long been considered an effective strategy for learning because it requires the learner to pay close attention to the text and to construct, through notes, a meaningful interpretation of the text. *Paraphrasing*—rewriting in your own words—the important information from the text also helps clarify its meaning. Note-taking creates the opportunity for you to think about the material you are reading, thereby increasing your ability to understand and remember its most important points.

Questioning

Questioning strategies work much like note-taking strategies in that questioning also requires the learner to pay close attention to the text. Specifically, questioning helps you to identify important ideas in the text, to use those ideas to ask further questions, and to think of possible answers to those questions.

For example, thinking about the note-taking paragraph above, you might ask, "How can note-taking increase my comprehension?" Then your recall of the details of the paragraph—"Notes help me think about what I'm reading"— answers the question and checks your understanding. Furthermore, self-generated questions increase your awareness of the learning process and your potential for success because they make you a more active learner. . . .

Summarizing

Summarizing is another useful technique for monitoring comprehension. Summarizing helps organize large quantities of information into a condensed, more easily remembered version and tests your understanding. Effective summarizing aids learning by making you identify key elements of a text once again and restate, or reorganize, that information in a meaningful fashion.

Good summaries focus on the main point of a reading selection, identify major supporting points, and eliminate all unnecessary information. Imagine yourself writing a summary of a short article about the negative influence of television on children's reading habits. An effective summary requires that you:

- Ignore unnecessary material. For example, exclude issues other than reading habits.
- Delete *redundant*, or repeated, points. For example, eliminate repeated examples or additional statements making similar points about the negative influence of television.
- Use general statements to consolidate details. For example, summarize the conclusions from different examples of television watching.
- Select important topic sentences. For example, find statements in the text that explain the negative influence of television.
- Invent topic sentences where necessary to focus on key information. For example, create a sentence that links heavy viewing and low reading scores.

Summarizing helps you to monitor your comprehension by keeping you alert to important points and it helps you to comprehend by requiring you to organize information in a meaningful way. . . .

Evaluating your success in learning means judging whether or not you have achieved your purpose and are able to retain what you have learned. In practice, it is a continuous cycle of self-testing and review. Regular self-testing promotes successful academic performance.

Self-Testing

Self-testing is a natural part of learning in everyday life as in academic life. Imagine that you are having some friends over for dinner and you want to prepare something very special. You decide first to look for a fancy seafood dish in your favorite cookbook. But once you find a recipe, study it carefully, and imagine how tasty it is, you realize you have no experience with such a dish. What if the recipe is a flop with your guests?

The answer for many people is to cook the new dish ahead of time to gain practice before it's time to cook for friends. That first cooking is not simply practice; it is also a self-test. It is one way to judge your ability to handle the job ahead of the actual test. The same is true of self-tests in academic life (the cooking example is somewhat similar to the way laboratory classes promote understanding in science courses). The test provides you with an opportunity to judge your understanding of a subject prior to a formal examination. Self-testing prepares you for the actual experience. . . .

Review and Memory

Evaluation also contains a review component. All students recognize the hazardous effects of forgetting. In fact, it is not uncommon for students to find themselves staring blankly at a test question, searching for an answer they know they studied but have completely forgotten.

Why does memory fail? There are many reasons. You may, for instance, not understand the material and, therefore, not remember it. Understanding is probably the most important element of good memory. You may very well understand the material while you are reading, but the information may seem so obvious that it is merely included in your short-term memory and quickly lost as you continue reading. . . .

To your benefit, a few basic study strategies will increase your memory and support your continuous review. The strategies are spaced study, active rehearsal or recitation, *overlearning*, and relearning. . . .

Spaced study means simply: Don't try to learn everything at once. Fatigue undermines learning and remembering primarily because of a loss in concentration. To study for three or four 45-minute periods with a 5- or 10-minute break between is much better for learning than to study for three or four hours straight. Smaller units of time with clear purpose, good concentration, and effective strategies will aid learning and memory, especially if supported by follow-up reviews. A good sequence, for instance, might be to study for three 45-minute periods and then to review that material in the fourth period. . . .

Active rehearsal or recitation of material studied is an excellent technique for storing information in your long-term memory. Practicing your knowledge by thinking aloud is also a good method for regular review. You can "rehearse" material—talk it over with yourself—at any time, and then use self-tests to judge your accuracy. The point is to give yourself repeated practice through verbal rehearsal. . . .

Another useful technique is "overlearning." Common sense may suggest that once you learn something, the job is complete. It is learned. Overlearning seems a waste of time. But the fact of the matter is that once you learn something, it can still be rather quickly forgotten. Therefore, it is frequently worth your time to overlearn important information. Overlearning gives you more practice, and learners who give themselves more practice remember more of what they learn. When you think you're done with analyzing or memorizing some material, practice it a few more times; you'll do much better in the long run. . . .

A final aid to memory is relearning—sometimes referred to as the savings technique. Simply stated, it is easier to learn—or relearn—information previously studied than it is to learn new information. That idea is probably obvious to you. It's a bit like riding a bicycle. Even if you haven't been on a bike in years, riding quickly comes back to you if you once learn how. The benefit of ease in relearning lends further support to the review process. Once something is learned, it is much easier to relearn or retain if it is reviewed from time to time. And once you have thoroughly reviewed, you can evaluate the accuracy of your knowledge through self-testing. . . .

Planning, monitoring, and evaluating each are critical stages in the learning process (see Figure 1). They are not always easy to apply and they don't guarantee success. They do give the learner a sense of direction and allow active learners to take charge of their learning. Each stage offers you the opportunity to think about your learning and to direct and control it. The goal is for you to establish habits for learning, to develop automatic approaches to thinking about learning, approaches that allow you to decide for yourself how to get from point X to point Y most effectively, most efficiently, and most successfully.

Figure 1

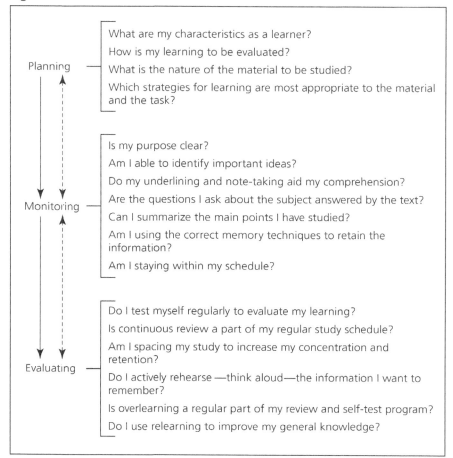

Planning
- What are my characteristics as a learner?
- How is my learning to be evaluated?
- What is the nature of the material to be studied?
- Which strategies for learning are most appropriate to the material and the task?

Monitoring
- Is my purpose clear?
- Am I able to identify important ideas?
- Do my underlining and note-taking aid my comprehension?
- Are the questions I ask about the subject answered by the text?
- Can I summarize the main points I have studied?
- Am I using the correct memory techniques to retain the information?
- Am I staying within my schedule?

Evaluating
- Do I test myself regularly to evaluate my learning?
- Is continuous review a part of my regular study schedule?
- Am I spacing my study to increase my concentration and retention?
- Do I actively rehearse —think aloud—the information I want to remember?
- Is overlearning a regular part of my review and self-test program?
- Do I use relearning to improve my general knowledge?

Vocabulary

James Twining tries to help readers by defining complex words within his text. How does he define each of the following?

1. paraphrasing
2. redundant
3. overlearning

 ## Discussion Questions

1. What do some research studies indicate about successful learners, as cited by the author?
2. What does Twining mean by "learning to learn"?
3. What are the four types of information you must have to formulate a plan for learning, according to the author?
4. What three basic strategies does Twining suggest for monitoring your comprehension in reading?
5. How can you evaluate whether your learning is successful?

 ## How Can These Ideas Apply to You?

1. How do you approach a learning task? How are your techniques the same as, or different from, those suggested by the author?
2. What approaches do you use when learning different subjects (e.g., foreign language, English, math)?
3. How do you know when you have successfully learned something—even before you get your grade on a test?

Student Expectations Seen as Causing Grade Disputes

Max Roosevelt

Prof. Marshall Grossman has come to expect complaints whenever he returns graded papers in his English classes at the University of Maryland.

"Many students come in with the conviction that they've worked hard and deserve a higher mark," Professor Grossman said. "Some assert that they have never gotten a grade as low as this before."

He attributes those complaints to his students' sense of entitlement.

"I tell my classes that if they just do what they are supposed to do and meet the standard requirements, that they will earn a C," he said. "That is the default grade. They see the default grade as an A."

A recent study by researchers at the University of California, Irvine, found that a third of students surveyed said that they expected B's just for attending lectures, and 40 percent said they deserved a B for completing the required reading.

"I noticed an increased sense of entitlement in my students and wanted to discover what was causing it" said Ellen Greenberger, the lead author of the study, called "Self-Entitled College Students: Contributions of Personality, Parenting, and Motivational Factors," which appeared last year in The Journal of Youth and Adolescence.

Professor Greenberger said that the sense of entitlement could be related to increased parental pressure, competition among peers and family members and a heightened sense of achievement anxiety.

Aaron M. Brower, the vice provost for teaching and learning at the University of Wisconsin-Madison, offered another theory.

"I think that it stems from their K-12 experiences," Professor Brower said. "They have become ultra-efficient in test preparation. And this hyper-efficiency has led them to look for a magic formula to get high scores."

James Hogge, associate dean of the Peabody School of Education at Vanderbilt University, said: "Students often confuse the level of effort with the quality of work. There is a mentality in students that 'if I work hard, I deserve a high grade.' "

In line with Dean Hogge's observation are Professor Greenberger's test results. Nearly two-thirds of the students surveyed said that if they explained to a professor that they were trying hard, that should be taken into account in their grade.

Jason Greenwood, a senior kinesiology major at the University of Maryland echoed that view.

"I think putting in a lot of effort should merit a high grade," Mr. Greenwood said. "What else is there really than the effort that you put in?"

"If you put in all the effort you have and get a C, what is the point?" he added. "If someone goes to every class and reads every chapter in the book and does everything the teacher asks of them and more, then they should be getting an A like their effort deserves. If your maximum effort can only be average in a teacher's mind, then something is wrong."

Sarah Kinn, a junior English major at the University of Vermont, agreed, saying, "I feel that if I do all of the readings and attend class regularly that I should be able to achieve a grade of at least a B."

At Vanderbilt, there is an emphasis on what Dean Hogge calls "the locus of control." The goal is to put the academic burden on the student.

"Instead of getting an A, they make an A," he said. "Similarly, if they make a lesser grade, it is not the teacher's fault. Attributing the outcome of a failure to someone else is a common problem."

Additionally, Dean Hogge said, "professors often try to outline the 'rules of the game' in their syllabi," in an effort to curb haggling over grades.

Professor Brower said professors at Wisconsin emphasized that students must "read for knowledge and write with the goal of exploring ideas."

This informal mission statement, along with special seminars for freshmen, is intended to help "re-teach students about what education is."

The seminars are integrated into introductory courses. Examples include the conventional, like a global-warming seminar, and the more obscure, like physics in religion.

The seminars "are meant to help students think differently about their classes and connect them to real life," Professor Brower said.

He said that if students developed a genuine interest in their field, grades would take a back seat, and holistic and intrinsically motivated learning could take place.

"College students want to be part of a different and better world, but they don't know how," he said. "Unless teachers are very intentional with our goals, we play into the system in place."

 Discussion Questions:

1. Do you think that you deserve a high grade if you work hard? Explain.

2. Do you merit at least a "B" if you attend class and do the readings? Why or why not?

3. Do you agree or disagree with the following statement: "if students developed a genuine interest in their field, grades would take a back seat, and holistic and intrinsically motivated learning could take place." Have you ever experienced your grades "taking a back seat" and developing a genuine interest in a subject? Explain.

How Can these Ideas Apply to You?

1. How do you know when you have successfully learned something – even before you get your grade back?
2. What do instructors need to do in order to clarify their grading system? What do you need to do in order to understand how your instructors grade?

Submitted by Vanessa Arnaud

Avoiding Plagiarism

Sharon Williams

Definition of plagiarism: To present the ideas or writings of another person as your own.

Writers sometimes plagiarize ideas from outside sources without realizing that they are doing so. Put simply, you plagiarize if you present other writers' words and ideas as your own. You do not plagiarize if you "provide citations for all direct quotations and paraphrases, for borrowed ideas, and for facts that do not belong to general knowledge" (Crews and VanSant, 407).

General Advice for Using Sources

The best way to avoid plagiarism is to keep control of your argument. You should include ideas from other sources only when those ideas add weight to your argument. Keep the following suggestions in mind when you are using material from other sources:

- Select carefully. Quotations should give weight to your argument. In general, do not select quotations which only repeat points you have already made.
- Be sure to integrate all ideas from other sources into your own discussion.
- Introduce direct quotations with your own words. After quoting, explain the significance of quotations.
- Avoid quoting more than is needed. Most of the time, brief quotations suffice.
- Use direct quotations only when the author's wording is necessary or particularly effective. Some disciplines discourage direct quotations. Check with your professor.
- If you are using material cited by an author and you do not have the original source, introduce the quotation with a phrase such as "as is quoted in...."
- End citation alone is not sufficient for direct quotations; place all direct quotations within quotation marks. Be sure to copy quotations exactly as they appear.
- To avoid any unintentional failure to cite sources, include all citation information on notecards and in your first draft.

At all times, stay in control of your argument and let your own voice speak for you.

A Common Pitfall: The Notetaking Stage

Plagiarism often starts with the notetaking stage of the research process. If possible, have a clear question in mind before heading off to the library so you will not waste time taking extraneous notes. When taking notes, be sure to distinguish between paraphrases and direct quotations. When you are copying a direct quotation, be extremely precise. Note all the information you will need for the citation and copy the quotation exactly as it appears. Some writers use only direct quotations when notetaking so there can be no confusion as to whether a note is a paraphrase or a direct quotation. Other writers color-code notes: one color for paraphrases, another for quotations. To ensure that you are not copying wording or sentence structure when paraphrasing, you might find it helpful to put the source material aside. In summary, be consistent and conscious of whatever notetaking method you decide to use.

Examples

Sometimes writers do not recognize when their use of other writers' ideas constitutes plagiarism. Versions of the following source can help you see the difference between acceptable paraphrasing and plagiarism (taken from *The Bedford Handbook for Writers*, 508).

Original Source #1

If the existence of a signing ape was unsettling for linguists, it was also startling news for animal behaviorists (Davis, 26).

Version A

The existence of a signing ape unsettled linguists and startled animal behaviorists (Davis, 26).

Comment: Plagiarism. Even though the writer has cited the source, the writer has not used quotation marks around the direct quotation "the existence of a signing ape." In addition, the phrase "unsettled linguists and startled animal behaviorists" closely resembles the wording of the source.

Version B

If the presence of a sign-language-using chimp was disturbing for scientists studying language, it was also surprising to scientists studying animal behavior (Davis, 26).

Comment: Still plagiarism. Even though the writer has substituted synonyms and cited the source, the writer is plagiarizing because the source's sentence structure is unchanged.

Version C

According to Flora Davis, linguists and animal behaviorists were unprepared for the news that a chimp could communicate with its trainers through sign language (Davis, 26).

Comment: No plagiarism. This is an appropriate paraphrase of the original sentence.

Original Source #2

The joker in the European pack was Italy. For a time, hopes were entertained of her as a force against Germany, but these disappeared under Mussolini. In 1935 Italy made a belated attempt to participate in the scramble for Africa by invading Ethiopia. It was clearly a breach of the covenant of the League of Nations for one of its members to attack another. France and Great Britain, the Mediterranean powers, and the African powers were bound to take the lead against Italy at the league. But they did so feebly and half-heartedly because they did not want to alienate a possible ally against Germany. The result was the worst possible: the league failed to check aggression, Ethiopia lost her independence, and Italy was alienated after all (J. M. Roberts, *History of the World.* New York: Knopf, 1976, p. 845).

Version A

Italy, one might say, was the joker in the European deck. When she invaded Ethiopia, it was clearly a breach of the covenant of the League of Nations, yet the efforts of England and France to take the lead against her were feeble and half-hearted. It appears that those great powers had no wish to alienate a possible ally against Hitler's rearmed Germany.

Comment: Plagiarism. The writer has taken entire phrases from the source, and there is no citation. The writer's interweaving of his or her own language does not mean that the writer is innocent of plagiarism.

Version B

Italy was the joker in the European deck. Under Mussolini in 1935, she made a belated attempt to participate in the scramble for Africa by invading Ethiopia. As J.M. Roberts points out, this violated the covenant of the League of Nations (Roberts, 845). But France and Britain, not wanting to alienate a possible ally against Germany, put up only feeble and half-hearted opposition to the Ethiopian adventure. The outcome, as Roberts observes, was "the worst possible: the league failed to check aggression, Ethiopia lost her independence, and Italy was alienated after all" (Roberts, 845).

Comment: No plagiarism. The writer properly acknowledges the one use of Roberts's ideas. (Note that the writer has chosen to use only one idea from the source and has integrated that idea into his or her own argument.)

A Final Note

Learning how to use the ideas of others to add weight to your ideas involves effort and a commitment to academic honesty. It is not always clear exactly when or how to use sources, and sometimes you will need advice. Since your professors are most familiar with the expectations of their disciplines, they are the best people to ask.

Works Cited

Crews, Frederick and Ann Jessie VanSant. *The Random House Handbook,* 4th edition. New York: Random House, 1984.

Fowler, H. Ramsey and Jane Aaron. *The Little, Brown Handbook.* Glenview, Ill.: Scott, Foresman and Co., 1989.

Hacker, Diana. *The Bedford Handbook for Writers.* Boston: St. Martin's Press, 1991.

Williams, Sharon (2001). "Avoiding Plagiarism." Retrieved Jan. 20, 2005 from www.tarleton.edu/"mkerr/Avoid_Plagiarism.htm.

Technology Skills: Wireless, Windowed, Webbed, and Wikied

Constance Staley

Ah, technology . . . Does it make our lives simpler or more complicated? Have you ever stayed up until the wee, small hours playing an online game? Do you live to text? Do you run, not walk, to any nearby computer to check your Facebook account? Or, on the other hand, do you hate the thought of facing dozens of e-mails after you've been away on a trip?

Many of us have a love-hate relationship with technology: We love the convenience but hate the dependence. But in college, information literacy and technology skills will be other keys to your academic success. You'll need to know things like how to use Microsoft Word with agility to produce a polished essay, how to design an information-rich and visually compelling PowerPoint presentation, and how to use one or more of the many course management systems available like Blackboard. You don't have to be a technology guru, but you will need to call upon your technology skills to conduct research for your college classes. Many college students are tech savvy, but their skills are more about entertainment than education. In fact, a recent study suggests that many students actually overestimate their technology skills when it comes to using software that is often related to class assignments.[1]

Use Technology to Your Academic Advantage

When you first arrive on campus or even before, you'll see evidence of technology everywhere. Your school may send out regular updates about campus events on Twitter. You may be asked to respond to an on-screen quiz in class by using your cell phone. You'll get an e-mail account and be sent official college documents, like your tuition bill and weather alerts. You will take entire courses or parts of courses online so that you can learn on your own time at your own pace. Many of your instructors will use course management systems, streaming video, and websites in the classroom to increase your learning. And the good news is that 60.9 percent of college students say it helps.[2] Furthermore, not only is technology helping students learn now, but exciting new developments are on the horizon. Soon (and to some extent, already) new "killer apps" will combine into one smartphone or laptop, it's projected. WiMAX will be the new state of the

[1]Grant, D. M., Malloy, A. D., & Murphy, M C. (2009). A comparison of student perceptions of their computer skills to their actual abilities. *Journal of Information Technology Education*, 8. Available at http://jite.org/documents/Vol8/JITEv8p141-160 Grant428.pdf.
[2]Guess, A. (2007, September 17). Students' "evolving" use of technology. *Inside Higher Ed*. Available at http://www.inside highered.com/news/2007/09/17/it; Caruso, J. B., & Salaway, G. (2007, September). Key findings: The ECAR study of undergraduate students and information technology, 2007. *Educause*. Available at http://net.educause.edu/ir/library/pdf/ ERS0706/EKF0706.pdf.

art (Worldwide Interoperability for Microwave Access) with increased broadband to let you do more. And "fixed mobile convergence" will allow you to do several things simultaneously: read a text message from one person and talk on the phone to someone else.[3] Technology will become an even more highly integrated part of learning in the future. What academic benefits does technology provide?[4] Let's look at some examples of the advantages technology will offer you in college. Technology will help you:

■ **Manage your courses.** Many of your college classes will be conducted partially or wholly online, using technology shells, like Blackboard, eCollege, Moodle, Desire2Learn, or eCompanion. Course management systems help you:

- Track grades, assignments, and tests
- Take sample tests and quizzes (or real ones)
- Get the course syllabus
- Turn in assignments online
- Access readings and other course materials
- Post to an online discussion[5]

■ **Interact with course content, classmates, and your instructor.**
You may have heard the term "Web 2.0." It's not a new version of the Internet. It refers to creative uses of it, like Facebook, Wikis, and blogs, where instead of just reading passively, users help create the content.

For example, your instructor may post a question or comment and ask you to post your responses online and to respond to those of your classmates. Everyone can get to know you by your online personality, and some students say they become better writers by reading other students' responses to their blogs (Web logs). You may watch a YouTube clip in class, insert one into a presentation you create as a class assignment, or post one yourself related to your life as a student. Or you may be asked to contribute to a Wiki, today's online, editable encyclopedia. Anyone can add information or change content (currently there are more than 13 million articles in more than two hundred and fifty languages on the most extensive of these sites[6]). In addition to these Web 2.0 possibilities, you will undoubtedly use e-mail, Facebook your classmates, and listen to podcasts, if your professor posts an audio version of her lecture. Typically, aural learners enjoy podcasts and kinesthetic learners enjoy the interactivity of Web 2.0.

■ **Complete assignments.** Your college classes will ask you to use at least three types of software in your academic work:

- Microsoft Word allows you to type, edit, alphabetize, index, footnote, and do many other things to prepare papers for your classes.

---

[3]Shinn, S. (2009, January–February). Dial M for mobile. *BizEd*, pp. 32–39.
[4]Caruso, J. B., & Salaway, G. (2007, September). Key fi ndings: The ECAR study of undergraduate students and information technology, 2007. *Educause*. Available at http://net.educause .edu/ir/library/pdf/ERS0706/EKF0706.pdf.
[5]Ibid.
[6]See http://en.wikipedia.org/wiki/Wikipedia.

- Microsoft PowerPoint, used as an electronic visual aid for oral presentations, allows you to create an on-screen guide for your listeners (and you, if you glance periodically and subtly for clues).

- Microsoft Excel spreadsheets are good for tabulating, record keeping, and organizing.

How Tech Savvy Are You?

Many college students spend hours on the Internet downloading their favorite tunes and uploading their favorite photos. They think they know technology. But do they? Here's an important question: What kinds of computer skills will help you excel in college and what kind of skills are employers looking for? Look at the lists below. Which of the following tasks can you perform *right now* (without clicking on "help" or Googling)? These software applications are considered to be the "industry standard" used in most organizations.

	Basic	Moderate	Advanced
MS Word	open a document bold text cut and paste undo and redo change the page orientation	count words highlight text insert page numbers justify a paragraph add bullets	alphabetize lists create footnotes use Autocorrect record/run macros merge documents
MS PowerPoint	create slides delete slides insert clip art choose a design template add new slides	animate slides change background colors add transitions between slides create and run a slide show print slides, handouts, and outlines	merge slides from another slideshow insert hyperlinks edit hyperlinks change animation timing change animation order
MS Excel	create spreadsheets move data around make calculations create a chart copy/merge cells	use the SUM function to create formulas use the fill handle to copy a cell use a VBA macro freeze panes format cells, rows, and columns	create formulas using the IF function use absolute references use Excel as a database use VLOOKUP use PivotTables

In one recent study, college students overestimated their software skill levels, particularly on Word and Excel. Although they perceived their skills as average or high, when tested, their performance didn't measure up. Computer literacy is a critical job requirement. If you're surprised by how few checkmarks you were able to make above, now is the right time to gear up! Take an online tutorial, sign up for a workshop on campus, or enroll in a computer literacy class. Not only will you be able to apply your skills to all your classes, but you'll be ramping up for the job waiting for you in the world of work.[a]

[a]Hendry, E. (2009, July 20). Students may not be as softwaresavvy as they think, study says. *The Wired Campus: The Chronicle of Higher Education.* Available at http://chronicle .com/blogPost/Students-May-Not-Be-as/7276; Grant, D. M., Malloy, A. D., & Murphy, M C. (2009). A comparison of student perceptions of their computer skills to their actual abilities. *Journal of Information Technology Education, 8.* Available at http://jite.org/documents/Vol8/JITEv8p141-160Grant428.pdf.

The industry standard for these applications is generally the Microsoft products listed here, although other possibilities exist. If you need help learning any of these applications, your campus techies, instructors, or online tutorials (which can easily be found by Googling) can help. If you're a techie yourself, you can venture into other software applications like Flash, Camtasia, iMovie, or Adobe Acrobat to make your academic work look even more professional.

■ **Increase your learning.** You may also find yourself using textbook websites, like the one you're using for *FOCUS on College Success.* Often these websites are tied closely to they textbook you're using in class, and they contain information and activities to enrich your learning experience, like videos, quizzes, and iAudio chapter summaries. Use these resources to help you master course material.

The Internet: The Good, the Bad, and the Ugly

The Good

For many of us, the Internet is how we get our news, our research, our entertainment, and our communication. When it comes to all the potential benefits of the Internet, think about advantages like these:

■ **Currency.** While some of the information posted on the Internet is outdated, much of it is up-to-the-minute. Reports, articles, and studies that might take months to publish in books or articles are available on the Web as soon as they're written.

■ **Availability.** The Internet never sleeps. If you can't sleep at 2:00 a.m., the Internet can keep you company. Unlike your real instructor who teaches other classes besides yours and attends marathon meetings, Professor Google is always in. For the most part, you can check your e-mail or log onto the Internet from anywhere, any time.

■ **Scope.** You can find out virtually anything you want to know on the Internet from the recipe for the world's best chocolate chip cookie to medical advice on everything from Athlete's Foot to Zits. (Of course, real human beings are usually a better option for serious questions.)

■ **Interactivity.** Unlike other media, the Internet lets you talk back—instantly and constantly. You can add to your Facebook page daily or edit a Wikipedia entry whenever you like.

■ **Affordability.** As of June 2009, there were 1,668,870,408 online Internet users worldwide; more than 227 million Americans are online today.[7] For most, when it comes to the Internet, the price is right. After you buy a computer, and pay a monthly access fee, you get a great deal for your money.

---

[7]Internet World Stats. Available at http://www.internetworldstats .com/stats.htm.

The Bad

Too much of a good thing can be bad. When anything becomes that central to our lives, it carries risks like the following:

- **Inaccuracy.** Often we take information presented to us at face value, without questioning it. But on many Internet sites, the responsibility for checking the accuracy of the information presented there is yours. Bob's Statistics Home Page and the U.S. Census Bureau's website are not equally valid. Not everything published online is true or right.

- **Laziness.** It's easy to allow the convenience of the Internet to make us lazy. Why go through the hassle of cooking dinner when you can just stop for a burger on the way home? The same thing applies to the Internet. The ultimate use some students think is downloading someone else's paper.[8] Why bother doing hours of library research on the topic for your paper when others have already been there, done that, and published it on the Internet? And today's global online "paper mills" make it easy to plug in your credit card number and buy your paper online, perhaps one even authored by someone on the other side of the globe![9] For one thing, if you don't give the rightful author credit, that's plagiarism, which can give you a zero on an assignment, or even cause you to fail a course. But another thing worth considering is that the how of learning is as important as the what. If all you ever did was cut, paste, and download, you wouldn't learn how to do research yourself. You may never have to give your boss a five-page paper on the poetry of Wordsworth— but you may need to write a five-page report on your customers' buying trends over the last six months. No one's researched that particular topic before. Your job now is to develop your skills so that you can do it then.

- **Overdependence.** A related problem with anything that's easy and convenient is that we can start depending on it too much. National studies report that many of us lack basic knowledge. We can't name the Chief Justices of the Supreme Court or the President of Pakistan. Are we so dependent on the Internet that we're relying on it for information we should learn or know?[10] Using the Internet as your sole source of information can lure you into surface, rather than deep learning. When information is reduced to screen shots, soundbites, and video clips, it's easy to become an information "nibbler," someone who takes nothing but quick "bytes." Many questions don't have quick answers, and many problems don't have simple solutions.[11]

---

[8]Simon, H. A. (1996). *Observations on the sciences of science learning.* Paper prepared for the Committee on Developments in the Science of Learning for the Sciences of Science Learning: An Interdisciplinary Discussion. Department of Psychology, Carnegie Mellon University.
[9]Bartlett, T. (2009, March 20). Cheating goes global as essay mills multiply. *Chronicle of Higher Education*, 55(28), p. A-1.
[10]Billout, G. (2008, July/August). Is Google making us stupid? *The Atlantic.com*. Available at http://theatlantic.com/doc/print/ 2000807/google.
[11]Wood, G. (2004, 9 April). Academic original sin: Plagiarism, the Internet, and librarians. *The Journal of Academic Librarianship*, 30(3), 237–242. Carr, N. (2008, July/August). Is Google making us stupid? *The Atlantic*. Available at http://www.the atlantic.com/doc/200807/google; Nelson, F. (2009, April 29). Podcast: Is Twitter making us stupider? *Full Nelson: Information Week*. Available at http://www.informationweek.com/ blog/main/archives/2009/04/podcast_is_twit. html;jsessionid= UMBB25NKOCXS1QE1GHPSKHWATMY32JVN.

Netiquette: Online Manners Matter

Professionalism is important in college, and it doesn't just apply to how you act in class, like getting to class on time or turning in your assignments when they're due. Online communication like e-mail has netiquette (or network etiquette) rules like these:

1. Don't send a message you don't want to risk being forwarded to someone else. Once you send a message, you can't take it back, and it may reappear in a very awkward place!

2. Don't hit the "send" key until you've given your-self time to cool off, if you're upset. You may want to edit what you've written into a more humane, more polite version of the same message.

3. Don't forward chain e-mails. At the very least, they're a nuisance, and sometimes, they're illegal.

4. Don't do business over your school e-mail account. Sending all 500 new students in your residence hall an invitation to your family's restaurant grand opening is off-limits. Besides, sending messages to lots of people at once is called "spam," and it can really gum up the works.

5. Don't spread hoaxes about viruses or false threats. You can get into big trouble for that.

6. Don't type in all CAPS. That's called SHOUTING, and it makes you look angry.

7. Don't be too casual. Use good grammar and correct spelling. Your instructors consider e-mails to be academic writing, and they'll expect professionalism from you.

8. Don't forget important details. Include everything the reader needs to know. For example, if you're writing to an instructor, give your full name and the name of the course you're writing about. Professors teach more than one class and have many students.

9. Don't hit the "Reply to All" key, when you mean to hit the "Reply" key. Many e-mail message writers have been horrified upon learning that hundreds or thousands of people have read something personal or cranky that was meant for just one reader.

10. Don't forget to fill in the subject line. That gives readers a chance to preview your message and decide how soon they need to get to it.

How Not to Win Friends and Influence People Online

All four of these e-mail messages from students violate the rules of netiquette. See if you can identify the rule number from the Netiquette box that's been violated in each case.

From Matt	Rule: _____

Professor X, I just looked at the online syllabus for Academic Success 101. Why didn't you tell us that our first paper is due on Monday? I will be very busy moving into a new apartment this weekend. Writing an essay for your class is the last thing I want to have to think about.

From Tiffany	Rule: _____

Prof X, i didn't know u were makin us write a paper over the weekend. i won't be able to do it. i hop you don't mind.

From Xavier	Rule: _____

PROFESSOR X, I CAN'T GET MY PAPER DONE BY MONDAY. LET ME KNOW WHAT I SHOULD DO.

From Dameon	Rule: _____

Hey, Section 3 Can you believe our instructor? She assigns a big writing assignment after only one day of class! Who in their right mind would be remotely interested in sitting in their crummy little room writing a bunch of meaningless junk, when we haven't even learned anything yet? What kind of teacher are we stuck with here? Somebody out there respond to me, OK? I'm totally hacked off!

As a class, discuss your responses and see if you all agree on which rules were broken in the four examples provided.

The Ugly

The Internet can be used in foul ways. Take a look at one student's social networking page shown below and see if you can guess where things are headed.

Like the hypothetical Victoria Tymmyns (or her online name, VicTym) featured in this figure, some students publish inappropriate, confidential, and potentially dangerous information on their Facebook and MySpace accounts. Victoria has posted her address, phone numbers, and moment-by-moment location. You can see that she's now being stalked. And other kinds of danger can result from bad judgment, too. What some students post just for fun can later cost them a

ISpy.com   RMSU

Basic Info [edit]

Name: Victoria Tymmyns
Looking For: A Good Time
Residence: 456 Pine Valley
Birthday: June 12, 1990

Contact Info [edit]

Email: VicTym@rmsu.edu
AIM Screenname   VicTym
Mobile: 719.111.1112
Current Address: 123 Fake St.
                     Great Bluffs, CO 80900

Personal Info [edit]

Activities: Drinkin' at "Annie Oakley's" every Fri. night.
                     Karaoke at "All That Jazz" every Sat. night.

Favorite Music: Black Flag, NIN, DK, the Clash
Favorite Movies: Shrek, Dracula

Work Info [edit]

Company: Common Grounds Coffee Shop
Schedule: Work M – F 7AM –2PM

View More Photos of Me

Status   edit

Doin' shots at Annie Oakley's!

RMSU Friends

425 friends at RMSU   See All

Seymore Bonz   N.O. Body

Friends in Other Networks

Cal (51)
UF (40)
CMU (63)
KSCC (7)
RMSU (425)

The Wall [edit]

N.O. Body wrote: at 11:00am August 1, 2010
Saw u dancing at Annie Oakley's!! Whatta hottie! We should meet.

N.O. Body wrote: at 1:00pm August 1, 2010
Aw come on! U know u want to meet me!

N.O. Body wrote: at 3:02pm August 1, 2010
Still no response? What 's up? Do u wanna play or not?

Seymore Bonz wrote: at 4:27pm August 1, 2010
R we still hookin up w/the gang at Annie Oakley's tonight?
Meet you guys at the front door at 10.

N.O. Body wrote: at 5:20pm August 1, 2010
Sounds fun. Maybe i'll see u there.

Bay-Bee Face wrote: at 10:17pm August 2, 2010
Can you believe how we much we rocked last night? What was the deal with that guy who kept staring at us? He gave me the creeps!! You switched shifts w/Mary right? Working at 4?

N.O. Body wrote: at 12:39pm August 2, 2010
Gee, BTW u were dressed, I just assumed u liked being stared at... U looked really cute at work.

N.O. Body wrote: at 2:21pm August 3, 2010
What's the matter sweetheart? U looked unhappy to see me at work today. Why didn't u talk to me? BTW, nice house u got. Who knew you lived in such a nice neighborhood.

N.O. Body wrote: at 12:57pm August 5, 2010
Nice dog u have. Ur parents must be outta town—no one's been home all night.

N.O. Body wrote: at 7:26pm August 5, 2010
U never showed up for ur shift today. I waited all day for u. Saw your friends. They said somebody poisoned your dog. That's a shame—such a yappy little thing. I hate stuck-up women. Guess I'll just have to find u in person...

job opportunity. If your webpage has provocative photos of you or descriptions of rowdy weekend activities that you wouldn't want your grandmother to see, remove them! If you call in sick on the job, but it's described as a hangover on your Facebook page, you may be looking at some serious consequences. (Employers regularly check these sources for insider information on current employees as well as new applicants.)

What does all of this have to do with you? Everything! It's important to remember that the Internet itself is neutral. It can be used constructively or destructively, based on the choices you make. It can be an exciting, invigorating, essential part of your college experience. Use it wisely!

COLLEGES:
HOW AND WHY WERE THEY CREATED?
HOW ARE THEY DIFFERENT
FROM HIGH SCHOOL?

Knowing the history and mission of higher education, including Sacramento State, will provide a perspective to understand the value and purpose of a university education. This understanding will enable you to navigate the university system and build relationships with your professors and classmates. Intellectual roles, responsibilities, and expectations are different in college than they are in high school. Sacramento State student Diane Gonzalez shares some insight on this topic in the following letter.

Diana Gonzalez,
Peer Mentor 08-10
Counseling Graduate
Student

To First Year Students:

In the beginning, colleges were created to educate wealthy young white men who wanted to become part of the clergy. Originally, state colleges were only accessible to people who wanted to pursue a teaching career. Today, a college education is accessible to nearly everyone. Colleges now have the goal of educating people on diverse topics and the ability to create social change and give freedom to those who would otherwise be oppressed. Colleges now exist for each individual to become a critical thinker and gain a voice.

College is very different from high school. In high school, teachers tell students what is expected of them. Teachers want students to be able to regurgitate material instead of inputting their own opinion. It is almost as if students are passive learners who merely go to class and accept what the teacher is saying. High school teachers still hold authority over their students and are seen as disciplinarians in the classroom environment. However, in college, professors appreciate students' opinions, thoughts and concerns. College professors place a high value on voicing one's opinions, and sometimes they even like it when you disagree with that they have to say. In college students have a choice of what they want to learn and they are expected to take charge of their education. In high school, you are also concerned with fitting in and hanging out with the right people. In college, it is different. College is a time to explore and find out who you truly are. It is a time to make your own choices. It is a time when teachers or parents will only be able to provide guidance. Ultimately, college is about making your own decisions. Just because someone says something, does not mean we don't have every right to ask for an explanation so we can make educated decisions. College. . .it will be an amazing experience that will stay with you for the rest of your life!

Diana Gonzalez

American Higher Education: A Brief History

William H. Halverson

William H. Halverson is associate dean emeritus of University College at The Ohio State University, Columbus, Ohio. A philosopher by training, Dr. Halverson is now widely known for his recent translations from Norwegian.

This essay presents a brief history of higher education in the United States. Although modeled initially after the great English universities, the American university has developed into a unique institution.

The modern American university is the product of a number of historical developments occurring over a period of several centuries. The story of higher education in America begins with the establishment of a small number of colonial colleges in the seventeenth and eighteenth centuries. Harvard College, founded in 1636, was first, followed by the College of William and Mary (1693), Yale (1701), the College of New Jersey, now Princeton (1746), King's College, now Columbia (1754), the College of Philadelphia, now University of Pennsylvania (1755), the College of Rhode Island, now Brown (1765), Queen's College, now Rutgers (1766), and Dartmouth (1769). These nine institutions, all of which are still in existence, constitute a complete roster of the colleges established in colonial America.

The colonial colleges were deliberately modeled after the great English universities, Oxford and Cambridge. Harvard's first degree formula makes it very explicit: the degree is being bestowed "according to the manner of Universities in England." Degree requirements, curriculum, administrative regulations, procedures for handling matters involving student discipline—all were initially copied from the English universities. The familiar names for the four college classes—freshman, sophomore, junior, and senior— come from the same source.

The colonial colleges were established in order to ensure that the colonies would be supplied with literate and humane intellectual leaders, especially clergymen. A college had to be established in the middle colonies, says an early Princeton historian, because "the bench, the bar, and seats of legislation, required such accomplishments, as are seldom the spontaneous growth of nature, unimproved by education" (Samuel Blair, *An Account of the College of New Jersey*, 1764). Yale was established in order that there might be a school "wherein youth may be instructed in the arts and sciences, who through the blessing of Almighty God may be fitted for public employment, both in church and civil state" (Franklin B. Dexter, *Documentary History of Yale University*, 1916). The *perpetuation* of humane learning in the New World and, as an integral part of this, the training of a literate clergy—these were the aims in the service of which the colonial colleges were established.

Reprinted by permission of the author.

Given the same Old World models and similar aims, the colonial colleges quite naturally developed similar educational programs. These programs had the following characteristics:

1. They were intended for men only, indeed, for men who aspired to the Christian ministry or to some other position among the "learned elite."
2. All students in a given institution took exactly the same course of study.
3. The prescribed course of study consisted of those things that every "educated gentleman" was expected to know. A student was required to have mastered both Latin and Greek before being admitted to college. Once admitted he spent by far the greatest amount of his time studying the classics: Livy, Xenophon, Herodotus, Thucydides, Horace, Demosthenes, Plato and Aristotle, Cicero, Euclid, Homer and Tacitus. In addition to the classics the curriculum included such subjects as Hebrew (once required of all students at Yale), ethics, politics, mathematics, botany, and theology.

Change occurred very slowly in the curriculums of the colonial colleges. No one seriously questioned the assumption that classical studies should form the bulk of a gentleman's education. As the impact of the Enlightenment began to be felt in the New World, however, pressures began to mount to broaden the curriculum to include more mathematics and natural science, some exposure to English language and literature, and some study of modern foreign languages (especially French). Philadelphia College under Provost William Smith, and the College of William and Mary under the influence of Thomas Jefferson (who was a member of the Board of Visitors), led the way in establishing these curricular changes. In varying degrees the other colleges moved, though more slowly, in the same direction. In the main, however, the colonial colleges continued throughout the colonial period to educate their young men according to the model brought to the New World by the English settlers.

The Post-Revolutionary Era

The decades immediately following the close of the Revolutionary War, from about 1780 to 1860, saw a number of developments that were to have a permanent effect on the shape of higher education in this country. In terms of sheer size, the enterprise of higher education increased from just nine permanent colleges at the end of the colonial era to 179 by the year 1860. Nearly all the permanent institutions established during this period—152 of the 173—were private colleges founded and controlled by various religious denominations. The remaining 21 were public institutions with either state or city support and control.

Curriculums also underwent some important changes during this period. As colleges were established in the new territories opened up by the Louisiana Purchase of 1803, it became apparent to many that a strict "classical education" was ill suited to meet the highly *utilitarian* needs of a new nation. Vast new territories needed to be brought under cultivation, cities needed to be established, railroads needed to be built, minerals lay waiting to be discovered and mined. For these purposes, what was clearly needed was not familiarity with Virgil and Homer but increasing mastery of science and technology. The age of higher education for "gentlemen only" was past: the system needed to be changed to "furnish the agriculturalist, the manufacturer, the mechanic, or the merchant with the education that will prepare him for the profession to which his life is to be devoted" (Francis Wayland, *Report to the Corporation of Brown University*, 1850).

Mounting pressures for an educational program specifically designed to serve such needs led in 1824 to the establishment of Rensselaer Polytechnic Institute "for the education of Architects, Civil, Mining, and Topographical Engineers." The older colleges, which heretofore had responded to similar pressures by adding such things as chemistry, geology, economics, law, medicine, and other profession-oriented studies to their curriculums, now began to establish separate departments or schools of engineering on their campuses. Within a period of eight years (1847 to 1855) technical schools or departments were established at Harvard, Yale, Dartmouth, Brown, and the University of Pennsylvania. Scientific and technical training had quite evidently become a permanent and important part of higher education in America.

With the broadening of curriculums and the establishment of professional courses of study, the old practice of requiring all students to take the same courses was no longer tenable. Students were still required to take certain courses that were presumed to be essential to any educated person, but beyond this each student elected those courses that he and his adviser judged best in terms of his particular goals. This system continues to be used in most American colleges and universities today.

This period also saw the beginning of the training of teachers as a specific and identifiable educational task. The "*normal school* movement" began, actually, in two small private schools established during the 1820s in Vermont and Massachusetts. The first public normal school was established at Lexington, Massachusetts, in 1839, and by 1860 similar institutions had been established in nine of the then thirty-four states. The first permanent university professorship in education was established at the State University of Iowa in 1855.

Higher education for women also made its first appearance in this country during the first half of the nineteenth century. An early product of the feminist movement, colleges for women were first established in the South— Wesleyan Female College in Georgia (1836), Judson College in Alabama (1838), and Mary Sharp College for Women in Tennessee (1852). Despite a widespread belief that women were intellectually inferior to men and, moreover, too delicate to endure prolonged intellectual effort, the practice spread to Illinois (Rockford College), to New York (Elmira College), and finally even to that citadel of masculine education, venerable old New England. Vassar, Wellesley, and Smith were among the first to institute a curriculum based on the traditional pattern in men's colleges.

Meanwhile, a number of colleges were taking the daring step of admitting *both* men and women. Oberlin, founded in 1833, was the first coeducational college in North America, admitting women as well as men as early as 1837. The University of Utah opened its doors in 1850 to both male and female students, and thus became the first *public* institution of higher education to "go coeducational." By 1860 there were about a dozen coeducational colleges, and by the end of the century coeducation was the standard pattern in most American colleges and universities.

The period from 1780 to 1860 may be characterized, then, as one of great "horizontal" growth in American higher education. Existing curriculums were broadened, new curriculums were added, new institutions were established, the opportunity for higher education was made available to greatly increased numbers of students. Yet, as recently as 1860, the university as we know it today did not exist. Some very important ingredients had yet to be added.

The Late Nineteenth Century

Although a number of attempts were made prior to 1860 to establish "public" universities, the principles of public support and public control of institutions of higher education did not catch on easily. When Americans thought of institutions of higher learning, the models that immediately occurred to them were the privately controlled older colleges and the denominationally controlled colleges established by various religious groups as the settlers moved westward. Even when public funds were appropriated for the support of a "state university," the board of control of the institution was commonly self-perpetuating and looked upon any attempt at public control as unwarranted interference in its affairs.

The great breakthrough for public education occurred in 1862 with the passage of the Morrill Act. This act, which was the subject of much controversy for several years prior to its adoption under President Lincoln, authorized grants of land to each state "for the endowment, support, and maintenance of at least one college where the leading object shall be, without excluding other scientific and classical studies, and including military tactics, to teach such branches of learning as are related to agriculture and the mechanic arts, in such manner as the legislatures of the states may respectively prescribe, in order to promote the liberal and practical education of the industrial classes in the several pursuits and professions of life." Within nine years (despite the intervening Civil War), thirty-six states had taken formal action to take advantage of the new law. Today every state in the union has at least one land-grant school.

The impact of the land-grant concept on American higher education cannot be overestimated. The principle of public support for higher education was established once and for all. Moreover, the Act makes it clear that higher education is not only for the wealthy or for those entering the learned professions: these institutions are to "promote the liberal and practical education of the industrial classes in the several pursuits and professions of life." Henceforth colleges would teach whatever was necessary in order to prepare young men and women for the infinite variety of roles required in a dynamic and growing society.

Notwithstanding the Morrill Act, very few African-American students received the benefits of public higher education during the nineteenth century, and several institutions devoted to the education of these neglected students were established to fill the void. Morehouse College (Georgia), Howard University (Washington, D.C.), and Fisk University (Tennessee) were all founded in 1867.

A second major influence on American higher education at this time was the example of the great German universities, especially the University of Berlin. The German university in the nineteenth century was not primarily a place of instruction: it was a place of bold and original research. The proper business of a professor, according to the German model, was not to instruct the young but to push forward the frontiers of human knowledge, to discover truths that had not been known before. He would, indeed, share the results of his efforts with mature young scholars—graduate students—who might wish to study with him, but routine instruction in the simple rudiments of his subject was no part of his task.

Some few universities were established in this country for the explicit purpose of emulating the German model—Johns Hopkins in 1876, Clark University in 1889, and the University of Chicago in 1892. In the main, however, American educators responded to the German example by superimposing a graduate school upon the undergraduate structure that was already there. With the completion of this two-story structure, the modern university came into being.

Imagine, then, an institution that combines on one campus all of the developments catalogued in the preceding pages: it is a picture of the modern American university. The colonial college, suitably modified, lives on in the college of arts and sciences. The learned professions have their respective homes in the colleges of law and medicine. Engineering, agriculture, business, education—all are integral parts of virtually every large public university today. And overarching all of these, serving as a place of advanced study and research for thousands of scholars from all over the world, is the graduate school.

Three Major Tasks

Hundreds, perhaps thousands, of different activities are carried on in the various colleges and schools of a modern university. How does all of this activity "fit together" to constitute some kind of definable mission? What does society now expect its universities to accomplish? One of the major tasks of a university, obviously, is *instruction*, both undergraduate and graduate. Our society, being highly complex, requires many more highly trained people than were required when the colonial colleges were established. It is to the universities, and increasingly to the public universities, that society looks for its needed supply of doctors, lawyers, engineers, teachers, business executives, etc., without which our kind of civilization could not exist.

A second major task of a modern university is *research*. A modern university without a significant effort in research is as unthinkable as a university without students: it is implicit in the very concept of a university. Most of the major advances in human knowledge in the past hundred years have been made by researchers whose work has been carried out under the auspices of a major university. Since World War II much of this research effort has been supported by federal funds provided under research contracts between the federal government and the participating universities.

A third major task of a modern university is *public service*. This task, too, is implicit in the concept of a land-grant university. County agents, whose task it is to assist farmers to benefit from the findings of agricultural research—to promote "scientific farming"—are typically affiliated with the College of Agriculture of a land-grant university. Many universities maintain testing and research centers where local industries can, on a contract basis, refine and improve their products.

University professors are often called upon to serve as expert consultants to business firms, school systems, federal and state agencies, and other organizations who have need of their particular expertise.

Virtually everything that a university does is related to one or more of these three major tasks. Together they constitute what may be called the overall "mission" of the university.

These three major tasks are interrelated in a wide variety of ways. The graduate students who assist a professor in pursuing a research project are, in the process, acquiring the up-to-date knowledge that they will need in order to serve as effective instructors of undergraduate students. The research professor who develops a new process for, say, increasing the durability of rubber becomes thereby a uniquely valuable consultant to the tire industry. The historian whose research turns up new evidence regarding the administration of Abraham Lincoln may, as a result, produce changes in the content of an undergraduate course in American history. Instruction, research, and public service may, at times, vie with one another for the university's human and material resources, but ideally they are complementary and in fact are mutually reinforcing in numerous ways.

 ## Vocabulary

As you think about this essay, these definitions may be helpful to you:

1. **perpetuation**   causing to last indefinitely
2. **utilitarian**   useful or designed for use rather than beauty
3. **normal school**   a two-year school for training teachers

 ## Discussion Questions

1. Where did American higher education have its origins?
2. Why were the colonial colleges established?
3. What were the first curricula like?
4. What significant changes were made in the post-Revolutionary period?
5. What significant event happened in the late nineteenth century? What impact did it have on higher education even to today?
6. A second Morrill Act passed in 1890. It stipulated that no federal money would go to a state that denied admission to its land grant college on the basis of race—unless "separate but equal" facilities were available to students who would be denied for the reason of race. In your view, was this second Morrill Act, which established the so-called "1890 schools," a good or bad piece of federal legislation? Why?

How Can These Ideas Apply to You?

1. How would you be different as a student in an early colonial college as compared with what you experience today?

2. What changes in the post-Revolutionary era would have affected you the most as a student of that period (e.g., as a pre-engineering student, as a teacher-in-training, as a woman, as an African American)?

3. How would your education as a community college student differ from your education as a four-year college student?

Loneliness

Barbara M. Newman and Philip R. Newman

Barbara and Philip Newman are the authors of many books on human development. They are especially well known for *Development Through Life: A Psychological Approach,* now in its eighth edition. Barbara Newman is professor and chair of the Human Development and Studies Department at the University of Rhode Island. Philip Newman is a lecturer in the same department.

Some students may experience feelings of loneliness as they enter a new and foreign college environment. The authors describe loneliness as a common college experience and suggest that friendships can play a key role in overcoming it.

College brings new opportunities for friendship, but it also brings new experiences of isolation and loneliness. Many college students leave the comfort and familiarity of their support system at home for a new environment. Others break ties with old friends who have gone to work or entered the military right after high school. The early weeks and months of college are likely to bring deep feelings of isolation and loneliness. These feelings are intensified because students usually approach the transition to college with such positive anticipation. They often do not even consider that this change will bring any sense of *uprootedness* or loss.

Loneliness is a common experience of college life. An estimated 25 percent of the college population feel extremely lonely at some time during any given month. These feelings are likely to be most noticeable during the freshman year because of the sharp contrast between the structure of high school life and the independence expected of students in college. However, loneliness can be a theme throughout the college years. The process of becoming an individual brings with it a new appreciation for one's separateness from others. As young people discover their own uniqueness, from time to time they are bound to feel that no one else really understands them.

Your parents may also experience periods of loneliness. They miss the physical presence of a person they love. They miss the daily interactions. Now and again, they may yearn for things to be more like they were and wish to be less separate.

Loneliness can be classified into three categories: *transient,* situational, and chronic.[1] *Transient loneliness* lasts a short time and passes. College students may feel this kind of loneliness when their friends are out on dates and they are alone in the dorm. This type of loneliness may occur when a student is the only one

---

[1]These categories are adapted from J. Meer, "Loneliness," *Psychology Today,* July 1985, pp. 28–33.

to take a certain position in a discussion; the only black student in a class; or the only one working out in a large, empty gym.

Situational loneliness accompanies a sudden loss or a move to a new city. Students commonly experience this kind of loneliness when they first come to college, especially if they are away from home. Most of us are *disoriented* when we move to a new town. Going to college is no different. Despite the many new and wonderful facets of college life, most young people experience situational loneliness due to the loss of the supportive, familiar environment of their homes and communities.

Your parents may undergo situational loneliness because of the loss of your presence. Even though they have planned and saved for this opportunity, they may experience intense loneliness following your departure. Rather than trying to create a myth that no one is feeling lonely, parents and college students can help each other through this time by admitting their loneliness and doing their best to reduce it. Frequent telephone calls, letters, and visits home in the first few months can ease the feelings of loss.

Chronic loneliness lasts a long time and cannot be linked to a specific event or situation. Chronically lonely people may have an average number of social contacts, but these contacts are not meaningful in helping the person achieve the desired level of intimacy. Chronically lonely people often seem reluctant to make contact with others. There appears to be a strong relationship between social skills and chronic loneliness. People who have higher levels of social skill, including friendliness, communication skills, appropriate *nonverbal* behavior, and appropriate response to others, have more adequate social support and experience lower levels of loneliness.

You may not recognize that you suffer from chronic loneliness until you are away at college. While children are living at home, parents are usually able to provide the amount of social support their children need. At college, children may find it extremely difficult to replace the level of trust and closeness that were provided by family members and high school friends.

Inadequate friendship relationships may actually interfere with your academic performance as well as your physical and mental health. Substantial research evidence supports the relationship between inadequate social support and *vulnerability* to illness. People who are part of a strong social support system are more likely to resist disease and to recover quickly from illnesses when they occur. Their general outlook on life is more optimistic.

A college student's circle of friends plays a key role in keeping the young person integrated into the social environment. Friends look in on you when you are sick; they make sure you have an assignment if you miss class; they invite you to join them if they are going to a party, a special lecture, or a campus concert. Friends worry about you and remind you to take care of yourself. Friends monitor your moods and prevent you from becoming too preoccupied or too discouraged. Friends value you and support your emerging identity. They understand the importance of the questions you are raising, and they encourage you to say what's on your mind. Building and maintaining satisfying friendships are key ingredients to feeling at home and succeeding in college.

Vocabulary

As you think about this essay, these definitions may be helpful to you:

1. **uprootedness**   in psychology, a sense of being displaced
2. **transient**   passing through with only a brief stay or sojourn
3. **disoriented**   having lost a sense of time, place, or identity
4. **nonverbal**   involving minimal or no use of language
5. **vulnerability**   openness to attack or damage

 ## Discussion Questions

1. What factors may trigger loneliness in a college student?
2. What are the three categories of loneliness described by the authors?
3. How does transient loneliness differ from chronic loneliness?
4. Why are students with little or no social support more vulnerable to illness?
5. What is the hardest part of maintaining a friendship?

 ## Suggestions for Your Journal

Did you experience situational loneliness when you started college? How did it feel? Do you know students who are lonely? How can building and maintaining friendships be helpful in overcoming loneliness? How can you as a friend help another student through lonely times?

On Academic Freedom
William H. Halverson and James R. Carter

William H. Halverson is associate dean emeritus of University College at The Ohio State University. After completing academic studies focused on philosophy, Halverson authored well-known textbooks for college philosophy classes. More recently, he has translated several books from Norwegian into English. James R. Carter, also a philosopher by education, is assistant dean of the College of Arts and Sciences at the University of Louisville, where he directs the Advising Center. In the following essay, Halverson and Carter define the notion of academic freedom, which is at the heart of a university as established and perpetuated in Western cultures.

People create institutions to serve a variety of purposes that they regard as important. They establish hospitals in order to care for the sick, retail stores to sell goods to consumers, banks to manage transactions involving the exchange of money, radio and TV stations to provide various sorts of program materials to the public, and so on. An institution is a means to an end, a way of doing something that society has decided needs to be done.

The Purpose of a University

What, then, is the purpose for which society has created universities? Why do people spend millions of dollars to build buildings—libraries, laboratories, classrooms, and the like—and additional millions to enable people like us (students, teachers) to occupy those buildings? What is a university for? What is its mission?

Try this: the unique mission of a university is the discovery, preservation, and dissemination of truth.

The discovery of truth: that is the heart and soul of the university. You must not think of professors and students as, respectively, those who already know the truth and those who do not. Professors have an edge on students by virtue of having been at the business of learning a bit longer than most students—but they would be the first to tell you, if they are candid, that even after many years of diligent study, their knowledge of the truth is limited, fragmentary, and mixed with error.

Our Common Ignorance

The professor's problem is the problem of human beings generally: we can rarely be certain that what we have learned, what we believe, is the *truth*. For many thousands of years, scholars believed that the earth was flat, and that it was stationary in the center of the universe, and that the sun, the planets, and the stars revolved around it. These beliefs, we now know with a high degree of certainty, were in error. We may be inclined to laugh at those silly people of yesterday who held such childish views. But let us not laugh too loudly, for it is highly likely

Reprinted by permission of the authors.

that among the beliefs you and I hold today are some that will appear as foolish to future generations as the flat-earth theory does to us. Truth and error do not wear labels that enable us easily to distinguish between them. Our situation, then, may be described as follows. We (that is, all people) hold many opinions, some of which are probably true and some of which are probably false. In addition, there are many matters about which we are totally ignorant, and about which we therefore have no opinions at all. Our task, if we wish to know the truth, is to rid ourselves so far as possible of both ignorance (no opinions) and error (false opinions), to exchange ignorance and error for the truth.

Seeking the Truth

How does one go about this? How does one attempt to determine the truth or falsity of any assertion? Clearly, one must look to the evidence that appears to be relevant to the truth or falsity of that assertion. *Paradoxically, the surest way to establish the truth of an assertion is to try to disprove it.* If there is some evidence in support of an assertion, and if nobody can find any evidence against it after making a reasonable effort to do so, then there is at least some reason to believe that the assertion may be true. Until, of course, some contrary evidence turns up, in which case one has to start all over again.

Thus we arrive at the following *axiom:* one who desires to know the truth concerning any matter must be persuaded by the evidence, and by the evidence alone. Anything or anybody who attempts to compel a conclusion based on anything other than the evidence is to that extent an enemy of truth.

Academic Freedom

Academic freedom is the opportunity to hold opinions based on the best evidence one has and to speak those opinions without fear of reprisal. Academic freedom means free and open discussion, a liberty to read what you want, to debate any issue, to defend new views and reinterpret or criticize old ones in an open forum.

Academic freedom can exist only when two conditions are met. First, it can exist only in a community of open and intelligent individuals who recognize that in principle every legitimate question deserves an answer, and that the legitimacy of question and answer cannot merely be assumed but must be shown capable of withstanding criticism. Second, academic freedom requires that this community make truth its common purpose, and free and open discussion the means to it. Unless both conditions are met, any freedom that there is will be purely accidental, and not very secure.

It is therefore an essential part of this idea to promote and provide for the intellectual development of every member of the academic community. In this community, it is not only those who have already cultivated a high degree of intellectual understanding who have a place. There must also be room for those who are just beginning their intellectual development. Students in each new generation must be allowed their skepticism; they must have time to examine and criticize even the most fundamental, most widely held views. But they in turn must be open to criticism and direction from their teachers and peers.

How does this notion of academic freedom affect your life? The university's need to maintain academic freedom means that *your* freedom to inquire is essential. You cannot be free if there is prejudice in the academic community. The idea of academic freedom requires that the individuals in the university actively help one another through the basic intellectual tactic of challenge and response. In his essay *On Liberty,* John Stuart Mill reminds us of this, and of the unique mission of an academic community, when he writes, "Complete liberty of contradicting and disproving our opinion, is the very condition which justifies us in assuming its truth. . . ."

Enemies of Academic Freedom

Anyone or anything that tends to inhibit free inquiry and discussion concerning any matter, or that attempts to compel a conclusion based on anything other than the relevant evidence, is by definition an enemy of academic freedom. And there are, unfortunately, many such enemies.

Some of these enemies are purely internal, within the individual. They can be rooted out only by great effort on the part of that individual.

One of these is *fear.* The most comfortable opinions to hold are those that we have held the longest, and so we fear the discomfort of abandoning long-held opinions. The most comfortable opinions to hold are those that are widely held by those whose esteem we crave, and so we fear to adopt opinions that we know will be unpopular. A sage once said, "I never learned anything of importance without feeling a sense of loss because of the old and familiar but mistaken view that had to be abandoned." But we are human, and we fear such loss—even though it be for the sake of truth.

Sheer laziness is an enemy of academic freedom. It is easier, it takes less effort, simply to adopt a view that one has heard expressed by someone else than to study the evidence and draw one's own conclusion. But the easy way, unfortunately, is not the best way, for it gives us no basis for distinguishing between opinions that are true and those that are false.

Undue respect for tradition is yet another internal enemy of academic freedom. Indeed, the opinions of one's forebears deserve considerable respect, for they represent the accumulated wisdom of many generations. Still we must not be bound by them, and we must be willing to abandon them if the weight of the available evidence suggests that they are mistaken. For we, too, will pass on a fund of accumulated wisdom to the next generation, and those who receive it have a right to expect of us that it will contain relatively more truth and less error than that with which we began.

Perhaps the more obvious enemies of academic freedom are the external enemies. Every one of us is capable of being such an enemy and probably has in fact acted as one at one time or another. If in the course of a discussion one shouts down a would-be participant instead of allowing him or her to speak, one is playing the enemy. The same is true if one heckles, and so prevents from being heard, a speaker who holds views with which one disagrees. An instructor who uses the threat of a bad grade to compel agreement (or the *appearance* of agreement) with his or her own views is violating the academic freedom of students.

The administrator who denies promotion or *tenure* or a salary increase to an instructor because the instructor advocates views with which the administrator disagrees is violating the academic freedom of that instructor. A citizen who demands the ouster of a faculty member on the grounds that he or she holds views that are "dangerous" or "unorthodox" is asking (usually without realizing it) that academic freedom be abolished.

We repeat: anyone or anything that tends to inhibit free inquiry and discussion concerning any matter, or attempts to compel a conclusion based on anything other than the relevant evidence, is by definition an enemy of academic freedom. That academic freedom has so many enemies, both internal and external, underscores the important fact that the pathway to truth is not an easy one to find or to follow.

Academic freedom, then, is by no means a cloak for nonsense. It does not confer approval upon ideas that are *demonstrably* false, unsupported by evidence, or just downright silly. To the contrary: academic freedom makes it more likely that in due course such ideas will be shown up for what they are, and that views that are supported by the evidence—that is, truth—will prevail. In an institution whose business is the discovery, preservation, and *dissemination* of truth, academic freedom is the *sine qua non*—the "without which nothing," the essential condition in the absence of which it would cease to be a university.

Vocabulary

As you think about this essay, these definitions may be helpful to you:

1. **paradoxically** in a manner seemingly contradictory to common sense and yet perhaps true.

2. **axiom** a fundamental notion or idea that is assumed to be true

3. **tenure** used within universities, this term denotes an earned privilege of assured continued employment following a long period—usually seven years—of probation during which a faculty member is evaluated on teaching ability, research productivity, and community service

4. **demonstrably** capable of being proved, either logically or by reference to the real world

5. **dissemination** dispersal; thus, universities are said here to exist for spreading the truth (by teaching and publishing, for example), not hiding it

Discussion Questions

1. Identify and explain the paradox in the statement, "the surest way to establish the truth of an assertion is to try to disprove it."

2. What, according to Halverson and Carter, are the two necessary conditions without which academic freedom cannot exist?

3. Halverson and Carter argue that "one who desires to know the truth concerning any matter must be persuaded by the evidence, and by the evidence alone." What else are people persuaded by?

4. What, according to Halverson and Carter, are the enemies of academic freedom?

5. How, according to Halverson and Carter, should we regard the opinions we have received from people we respect?

 ## Suggestions for Your Journal

Fear, laziness, and undue respect for tradition—have you ever struggled with these internal enemies of academic freedom? Write a journal entry in which you select one of these and advise a younger friend how to deal with them successfully.

Academic freedom seems to be in conflict with the idea of majority rule. Do you agree? Why or why not?

How does the university differ from other institutions that seem to be, or ought to be, concerned about the truth—churches, for example, or the federal government?

The Difference Between High School and College

Jack W. Meiland

Jack Meiland is a former director of the Honors Program at the University of Michigan at Ann Arbor. This essay is from his book *College Thinking: How to Get the Best Out of College.*

Most high school students believe that college work will be similar to the content of their high school courses, which involved factual information. This essay describes how the expectation of college courses is different and what new types of intellectual work are required.

Since you know what high school work is like, we can approach the nature of college work by comparing college with high school. College freshmen believe that there must be a difference between high school and college, but their ideas about what the difference is are often radically mistaken. Students often see the function of high school as the teaching of facts and basic skills. They see high school as a continuation of elementary and junior high school in this respect. In senior high school, one learns physics and chemistry, trigonometry, American and world history—all subjects in which the "facts" to be learned are harder, but in which the method is much the same as in elementary and junior high school. The method of study most commonly used is memorization, although students are also called upon to apply memorized formulas in working problems and to make deductions in mathematical proofs. There are some exceptional high school classes, and some exceptional high schools, in which this is not so. But by and large, the perceived emphasis in secondary education is on learning facts through memorization. The secondary schoolteacher holds a position of authority because he or she has mastered factual information. Tests demand recitation of facts; papers require compilation of facts.

It is only natural, then, that the typical student sees college along these same lines. Reinforced by the relation between elementary school, junior high, and high school, the students usually believe that the relation between high school and college is the same as that between junior high school and high school. They believe that the difference between high school and college is that college courses are simply more difficult and that they are more difficult because they present more difficult factual information; they examine more difficult factual information; they examine more difficult topics; they go over topics covered in high school but in a more detailed and painstaking way.

College is taken to be different from high school only in being more difficult. Unfortunately this belief is reinforced by the actual content and method of presentation of typical freshman courses and programs. For example, in the first semester, a freshman might take a course in English composition, a beginning physics course, a course in a foreign language, and perhaps a lower-level survey course in social science or history. These courses are often indistinguishable from high school courses.

New Types of Intellectual Work

At the same time, college freshmen sometimes suspect or expect that college is or should be different *in kind* (not just in difficulty) from high school—that somehow intellectual activity in college is or should be of a distinctly different and higher level. And this expectation is fulfilled when the student gets beyond the introductory survey courses. There the instructors do seem to expect something different *in kind* from the student, though without telling the student explicitly and in detail what this is.

The good college teacher presents some information, in the sense of "what is currently believed." But such a teacher also spends much time talking about *the basis* on which this information is currently believed. *A large part of college work consists of discussing and examining the basis of current beliefs.*

The difference between high school and college is not that there is intellectual activity in one and not in the other. The difference is that college work requires that students engage in a *different kind* of intellectual activity, in addition to the activity of understanding the material that is presented. The first type of intellectual activity in both high school and college is understanding the material. Even here, though, college requires a different and higher type of understanding. Once the material is understood, the college student must perform another sort of intellectual work on the material, namely critical examination and evaluation. A main difference, then, between high school and college is that *new types of intellectual work* are required at the college level.

Material is presented in college not as something to be believed on the basis of authority but as something to be believed because such belief is rationally justified and can be rationally defended. Thus, much work in college—and, I would say, the work that is characteristic of college—deals with the rational justification of belief. College teachers are concerned not merely with imparting information but also, and mainly, presenting and examining the basis on which this information is or should be believed. They do this because they want this material to be believed on the basis of reason rather than on the basis of authority. It is a basic *presupposition* of the modern mind that rationally based belief is better than belief based on authority, on faith, or on some other nonrational process. Thus, much time in college is spent investigating the *rationality* of this or that belief.

It is important to notice that once we make this shift from authority to rational evaluation, the mode of presentation of the material—and the way in which we regard the material—also changes. Material that is presented on the basis of authority is presented as factual and given an air of being absolutely and unchangeably true. Material that is presented on the basis of rational justification is presented as belief, as theory, as *hypothesis,* sometimes as *conjecture*—as material supported to a greater and lesser degree by argument and evidence. And this difference in mode of presentation makes an enormous difference in how the material is regarded. What is treated in high school as eternal and unchangeable fact that human beings have discovered in their continual and relentless progress toward total knowledge will be treated in college as belief that may perhaps be well supported at the present but that could turn out to be wrong. Another way of putting this is: what is fact in high school is often only theory—perhaps well-supported theory but nevertheless only theory—in college. And theories must be treated as such: one must examine the evidence to see how much support it gives the theory, and alternative theories must be examined to see which is better, that is, to see which theory should be believed.

 ## Vocabulary

As you think about this essay, these definitions may be helpful to you:

1. **presupposition**   supposing beforehand
2. **rationality**   reasonableness
3. **hypothesis**   a tentative assumption
4. **conjecture**   a conclusion deduced by guesswork

 ## Discussion Questions

1. What, according to Meiland, do high school students assume about college teaching?
2. What does a college course expect that is different from high school?
3. What does Meiland mean by "a rational justification of belief" when referring to college course work?
4. What is the difference in material being presented by an "authority" versus material presented for "rational justification"?
5. Why is "fact" in high school treated as "belief" in college courses?

 ## How Can These Ideas Apply to You?

1. What were your impressions of the difference between high school course work and college work when you entered college?
2. Have you found first-year courses to be similar to high school courses in the way that Meiland contends?
3. In your experience, does college-level work require you to use evidence to support the factual material you are learning?
4. How has this extended approach to college course work material influenced your way of thinking and learning?

Decoding Your Professors

John N. Gardner

Director, University 101
Vice Chancellor for University Campuses and Continuing Education
Professor of Library and Information Science
University of South Carolina

I went off to college in 1961, at 17 years of age. I went 600 miles from my home in New Canaan, Connecticut, to the oldest college in Ohio, Marietta College. I was homesick for my family and my girlfriend. I turned in a miserable academic performance. When I went home at Thanksgiving (a holiday that, for me, was inappropriately named that year), the news of my midterm grades (three F's, two D's, and one A) had preceded me. The A was in Physical Education, an automatic A for participation in a varsity sport, lightweight crew. There were lots of reasons for my bad grades: I didn't know how to take notes; I lacked proper study habits; I did not seek out professors for help, and I didn't yet know how to relate to them or understand them. No one had taught me how to "decode professors." There isn't enough space in this brief introduction for me to even begin to explain how I turned myself around academically and became a very successful student and leader, but the most important reason for this about face was my relationships with professors. They changed my life for the better and they can change yours, too—if you let them. So let my advice sink in, and you'll have a far richer college experience and a far better life after college.

From years of teaching college students, we have developed many insights into the relationship between student and professor. Little did we suspect, when we were college students, that our professors really had an interest in teaching us something or that they might have appreciated our dropping by for a chat. Office hours, we now know, are for students—and we've often wondered over the years why we weren't smart enough to take advantage of them. We also now know that freshmen who interact with professors outside of class are more likely to become sophomores.

College professors are supposed to be smart, yet some of the things they say and do in class make you wonder. They rush through pages of notes, so it's impossible to remember all the important details. They give too many quizzes and expect too much from you in return. It doesn't matter to them whether it's homecoming weekend, or the big fraternity/sorority rush week, or the day you just have to go home because it's your birthday. They still expect you to be in class, on time, and most importantly, *prepared*! In fact, many of them act as though their class is the only one you're taking.

Do your college professors really understand you? Sure they do (most of them), but if you expect them to act, think, or even dress the way your high school teachers did, you may be in for a rude awakening.

Furthermore, you might be surprised to know that many of your college teachers are extremely interested in your well-being and hope you'll earn high grades in their classes (and believe that you can do so). These same individuals, however, may be quick to disagree with your ideas, ready to correct you when you answer a question in class, and extremely demanding about the amount of work they expect from you. If that scares you as you begin your college career, hold on. Establishing a positive relationship with your college professor, in the way we're about to discuss, can be one of the most rewarding experiences not only of your college years but also of your entire life.

Teachers: People Who Once Were Freshmen

As you warily approach your professors during your first semester in college, remember that they are former freshmen. Your professors are also human beings who respond to many of the same kinds of needs, goals, rewards, aspirations, gestures, and praise that you do. While you need to generate some empathy for them, many of them—despite what you think—have even more empathy for you.

Your college professors are probably teaching because they love their subjects and love to communicate to others what they know best. They certainly did not choose their profession for the money! To find out what kind of people they are, you might begin by studying their offices. Usually you will find them decorated to reflect the interests and personality of each teacher, and you will most certainly find them filled with books. Professors read voraciously, and they like to talk about what they have read. Some may mention articles from the *New York Times* or the *Washington Post*. Others may quote from trade or professional journals, such as *Advertising Age* or the *Chronicle of Higher Education*. Some may speak of travels abroad, or to other parts of the United States, where they have lived, taught, or attended college. If you have lived in the same area most of your life, you can learn much from your college professors about the rest of your country and the world.

Differences Between Professors and High School Teachers

You might be surprised to learn that most of your college professors—unlike your high school teachers—have never taken an education course in their lives. Instead, they chose courses in their academic disciplines that taught them how to acquire new knowledge and to understand that knowledge. They did not learn how to communicate that knowledge to you, or how to entertain you as they did so. In fact, you might find a few professors who would much rather be doing nothing but research, but must teach to justify their salaries. Others have left careers in various fields in order to teach their professions to college students. You'll find lawyers teaching law, physicians teaching medicine, newspaper editors teaching journalism, and corporation executives teaching business management.

Professors who pursued several advanced degrees in graduate schools or spent many years working in a profession have learned the virtues of diligence, patience, and persistence. They know the value of being able to ask about, process, and handle enormous amounts of minute detail, so they'll probably expect you to do the same.

Your professors probably won't spend much time in class teaching you the textbooks, and they won't base their tests exclusively on them, either. If it were enough to teach you the book, professors would not need to work very hard. But your professors have their own ideas about their disciplines, or subjects, and one of their goals is to help you learn as much as you can. This usually means that a textbook is only a support for all else in the course, and you'll probably work harder than you ever did in high school to absorb all the material they give you.

In high school, your teachers filled you with knowledge and information accumulated by others. Their task was simply to pass it on to you. Naturally, your college teachers also want to pass on the knowledge accumulated by others, but many professors feel the need to create new knowledge of their own. At many schools, faculty can only earn tenure if they do such research (more about tenure later in this chapter). As a result, many of them will talk to you about the research they are doing, in the hope that you'll find this interesting and will want to learn more.

Your high school teachers perhaps checked your notebooks to see that they were neat, took attendance regularly, and checked up on you to make certain you were doing all your work. In college, some professors will take roll, but others never will. It isn't that they don't care whether you come or not—they do. But they also feel you should be treated as an adult. They hope, of course, that you're taking adequate notes, but they won't be checking to see that you do. And you do need to take adequate notes because many professors are far more likely to test you on classroom lecture materials than on text materials.

A Belief in Education and Interest in You

To college professors, a solid education is much more than a means of getting a degree and a job. Becoming an educated person is in itself something they prize, and they hope you'll take the same pride in education. Consequently, many professors will be idealistic and not as practical as you might like. You probably can't change that, but you can try to appreciate their zest for knowledge and to understand how vitally it affects their lives.

Many college faculty will take a personal interest in you as a student and as a person. These professors chose teaching because they genuinely wanted to help others. However, they may not take the initiative to ask you to come see them. You will have to do that. Faculty try to treat students as adults. They don't want to baby-sit, but they do appreciate a friendly visit. One of your greatest opportunities for learning in college will come from the kind of one-on-one interaction you can experience with a professor outside the class. As we said before, visiting with professors outside of class enhances your learning and chances of persisting in college. Unlike your high school teachers, professors are required to keep office hours, and that's the time to make an appointment to see them. Don't feel as though you're bothering them. It's part of their job to make time for you.

Why Professors Chose College Teaching

How does one explain what draws an individual to teaching on a college campus? The hours are long, the pay is only fair, and the frustrations are many. Perhaps it begins with a love of the college experience, the professor was once a student, and a desire to someday return to that intellectually and socially stimulating environment. For some, it may involve a desire to learn more about a favorite subject while imparting that knowledge to others. Many professors love research and find it rewarding to uncover new ideas about people and the world. Others are talented in the arts—in writing or music or painting—and want to develop those skills further while helping others develop their skills.

Deep within nearly all college professors is the desire to use their knowledge and experiences to affect the lives of others in a positive way. After all, they were probably affected in the same way by certain professors while they were students. Some professors feel inspired to repay the debt of being helped by professors in their own days as college students. Ask several of your professors why they chose teaching. You'll find as many answers as the number of people you ask.

If your professors don't love what they're teaching, they're probably not very good professors. Often good professors love their subjects so much that in their enthusiasm they may speed up their lectures because they want to tell you so much, and you just can't keep up. That's when you should raise your hand and ask them to slow down. Just because they're rushing through the material doesn't mean they're not willing to listen to you. Many professors get carried away by their own thoughts and must be brought done to earth by a student.

What College Professors Do

One of the most common myths about college professors is that they lead easy lives of quiet contemplation while teaching one or two classes every week. College professors do much more than go to class. In fact, the time they spend in classroom instruction takes up a relatively small part of a typical workweek. The average professor spends between six and fifteen hours in the classroom weekly, compared to the thirty hours or more a high school teacher spends. Yet that same college professor works from sixty to eighty hours a week.

Because they must remain current in their field, professors spend part to that time reading, reading, reading. That leads to additional hours during which they revise and update their class lecture notes. It takes far longer to prepare notes than to deliver them in class. Professors may spend time conducting experiments, reviewing manuscripts, and writing. They may be called upon to speak to community, civic, and professional groups or to assist such groups in the development of a project. They may do consulting for private corporations and government agencies for extra money. They may be writing books, book reviews, journal articles, or papers for delivery at conventions.

When they're not doing any of these things, you'll probably find them advising students. Many spend considerable time in individual and group conferences with students to help them plan their academic programs for the term, reach career decisions, deal with personal problems, or find ways to improve their grades.

And with the time that's left, your professors are asked to perform administrative duties, serve on academic committees, or become involved in special college or university projects. A typical college professor may serve as chairperson of a college advising committee (to improve student advisement), be a member of an awards committee (to nominate and select outstanding students), serve as a faculty senator, or representative, in a university-wide governance system, and be called upon to participate in a special task force to evaluate the current student disciplinary system. When not in the classroom or in the office, professors are still working: behind closed doors in committee sessions or at home grading papers and preparing for tomorrow's classes. To accept this sort of schedule willingly, they must feel strongly about the importance of the college experience.

Making the Most of the Student-Professor Relationship

Remember what we said earlier about professors being people who respond positively to the same things other people do, such as politeness, consideration, tact, a smile, attention, and compliments? If you will remember this, you can do a few simple things to cause your professors to think more positively about you.

First, come to class regularly and be on time. Many students don't do this, so your exceptional behavior will stand out. Take advantage of office hours and see professors when it's appropriate. Realize that professor are not people to be avoided at all costs and that you will not be criticized by your peers if you're seen talking with them. (It's likely that these same peers have already talked with them.) Use office hours to get to know your professors and let them make you a significant person in their lives, too.

What else can you do to make your professors think highly of you? Come to class well groomed and properly dressed. A sloppy appearance suggests you can't be very serious about the lectures and discussions. Read all the assigned material before class. Ask questions frequently, but not to the point of annoyance or distraction. Show interest in the subject. Remember, your professors are extremely interested in their subjects and for that reason they'll appreciate your concern.

Sit near the front of the class. A number of studies have shown that students who do so tend to make better grades. To your professors, this will indicate your heightened interest in their ideas. Never talk or whisper while professors are lecturing. They'll interpret this as an uncaring or even rude gesture, which indeed it is!

Finally, don't hand your professors a lot of "bull." They've been hearing this drivel for years, and can spot phony excuses a mile away. If you're sincere and give honest reasons for missing class or work, they're more likely to respect you for it and may even bend their rules about late work and grade penalties.

Academic Freedom

Academic freedom is a condition and a right most college faculty enjoy at the majority of private and state-supported institutions. Simply put, it is the freedom to pursue intellectual inquiry and research, or to raise questions that are legitimately related to scholarly interests and professions. The concept of academic freedom allows professors to raise controversial issues without risk of losing their jobs. It doesn't give them total immunity from pressure and reprisals, but it does allow them more latitude than your high school teachers had.

Academic freedom is a long-established tradition in American higher education and has its origins in the development of intellectual history, dating back to the Middle Ages. Colleges and universities have found it desirable to promote the advancement of research and knowledge by giving their scholars and professors virtually unlimited freedom of inquiry, as long as human lives, rights, and privacy are not violated. This same assurance of freedom from political intervention and pressure is one of the appealing things to faculty about the collegiate life-style. It allows a professor to enjoy a personal and intellectual freedom not possible in many other professions and opens the door to less conventional thoughts and action.

Such thoughts and actions may surprise and even anger you at times. Your professors occasionally may articulate some ideas and opinions that offend you. You won't like them because they'll be contrary to some of your basic values and beliefs. Professors may insult a politician you admire, may speak with sarcasm about cherished American institutions such as the presidency, or may look with disdain upon organized religion.

Sometimes, they may be doing this just to get a reaction from you. They may believe that, to get you to think, they must disrupt and provoke you out of your "intellectual complacency." On the other hand, your professors may actually believe those statements you find outrageous. You need to realize that professors are highly independent, intellectually and personally, compared to the average American. Since college professors may be free thinkers, you may hear ideas from them that are at variance with many social conventions. This does not mean you must agree with them to get good grades. It does mean, however, that you must understand such views, examine them rationally, and be prepared to defend your own view if you still believe you are correct.

Tenure

The notion of academic freedom is related to something called *tenure*. This is the award a college or university gives to professors once they reach a certain point in their professional development; it promises them lifetime employment. Although untenured faculty also have academic freedom, tenured faculty theoretically have more of it. Tenure, in effect, means that a professor may not be terminated from employment except for these extraordinary situations:

1. *An act of moral turpitude.* Such an act would be a gross violation of the legal code or of any code of conventionally acceptable behavior. As current standards for conventionally accepted behavior become increasingly more tolerant, the range of behaviors involving moral turpitude become narrower.
2. *Insubordination.* Since a professor enjoys academic freedom, it is very difficult to define, let alone prove, insubordination. Few professors, therefore, are terminated for this infraction.

3. *Incompetence.* Once again, who is to prove that the faculty member is incompetent? Obtaining the consensus of one's peers is virtually impossible, although complaints by students may be effective here.
4. *Bona fide reduction in staff.* If your college experiences severe financial hardships, the institution could decide to eliminate faculty positions, departments, or majors, and the reduction in staff might include tenured faculty.

You won't be able to tell if your professors are tenured just by looking at them. The existence of tenure is a support of the general climate of free expression and free inquiry into the pursuit of ideas, which makes higher education an uplifting experience for professors and their students.

Rank

Not all professors are "professors." A subtle yet significant pecking order exists among college professors, reflecting enormous differences in power, authority, prestige, income, and special privileges. Here is how it works.

First, there are instructors and lecturers. Next come assistant professors, followed by associate professors and full professors. Most colleges have probationary periods of employment for faculty that they must complete before applying for promotion to the next highest rank. When promotion comes from assistant to associate professor, it may also include the award of tenure. Full professors generally teach fewer classes, have fewer students, and are more likely to be working with graduate students.

This pecking order may not be important to you at first, but it could become important if you should decide to seek advanced degrees. A recommendation for employment or graduate school from a senior professor can carry more weight than one from a lower ranking professor, especially if your senior professor is well known in the field.

Academic Standards

Although it's difficult to generalize about college professors because they exhibit so many personal and intellectual differences, it's relatively safe to assume that most of them believe in the value of liberal education.

Many people agree that a liberal education is important because it can make you more marketable when you're looking for a job. To your professors, its value goes far beyond that. The word *liberal* is a direct reference to the ability of education to free your mind. Indeed, the word comes from the Latin *libero*, a verb meaning, "to free." The goal of a liberal education is to free you from the biases, superstitions, prejudices, and lack of knowledge that characterized you before you came to college.

To free you of these restraints, it may be necessary to provoke, challenge, and disturb you by presenting you with new ideas, beliefs, and values that differ from your previous perceptions. Keep that in mind the next time your college professors say something that surprises you. In college, as in life, you'll have to learn to tolerate opinions that are vastly different from yours. Note that you need not always accept them, but you should learn to evaluate them for yourself instead of basing your responses on what others have always told you.

Because your professors want you to grow intellectually, they'll probably demand more of you than your high school teachers did. You'll probably have to study more to get good grades, because your professors may be inclined to give fewer A's and more F's than teachers in high school gave. Most college professors believe students who enter college are woefully underprepared to do college work—many through no fault of their own. As a result, they'll challenge you to raise your standards to theirs, instead of lowering theirs to meet yours.

It often comes as a great shock to students who make high grades in high school with little or no studying to find that they must study for hours to earn a high grade on a college exam. As a rule of thumb, you many need to spend two to three hours preparing outside of class for every hour you spend in class. So if you're carrying fifteen hours a semester, you should be spending an additional thirty hours each week studying, for a total workweek of forty-five hours, which is similar to the amount of time you'll be working when you begin your professional career. One of the biggest adjustments high school student have to make in college is simply the greatly increased amount of time they need to spend studying to meet the demands of professors. So even if you think you are studying more now than in high school, it's still probably not enough. Keep trying to increase your study time gradually.

What Professors Want from Their Students

Good professors frequently have students approach them at the end of the term to tell them how much they enjoyed the class. Professors appreciate that, but what they really want to hear is, "I really learned a lot from you and I want to thank you for it." Enjoyment should result from the positive learning experience; it shouldn't result from enjoyment for its own sake. Frankly, the pleasure of learning new ideas should constitute enjoyment in itself, and that is what your professors want to hear. Remember, they're not primarily entertainers but teachers. If they entertain out of proportion to teaching, they may be less than adequate in their profession.

Much has been written about professors who don't really care about students, but are dedicated in their desire to teach them new ideas. It's difficult to see how these two ideas are consistent with one another. Some level of caring must exist before learning can be passed from one individual to another. If you doubt that your professors care about their students, ask them. The question may be revealing to them, and the answer may be revealing to both of you.

Finally, remember that professors will like you more, even though they may not show it, if you participate in class discussion, complete your assignments on time, ask questions during class, make appointments to see them, comment on lecture materials, or simply smile and say "hello" when you meet on campus. They'll appreciate you if you maintain frequent eye contact with them during class, share a story or anecdote, joke with them or the class, and show you realize the value of what they're teaching you.

During the remainder of your life, you'll meet many admirable, stimulating, exciting, unique, remarkable, inspiring, perplexing, frustrating, and challenging individuals. Few will be more complex than your college professors. One or two of your college faculty may help counsel or guide you as you pursue your goals and may indeed affect your entire life significantly. For that reason alone, it pays to get the most out of them during your four years in college, which is probably the most significant period of change in your entire life.

Suggested Activities

1. Interview one or more of your current professors to find out whether they fit the descriptions provided in this chapter. You might ask them how they chose their academic discipline, what motivated them to teach on a college campus, what they regard as the ideal student, and what irritates or bothers them most about college students today. To gain an even more complete picture of college professors, share your interview with other students, and have them share theirs with you.

Why I Don't Let Students Cut My Classes

William R. Brown

William Brown is professor of English at the Philadelphia College of Textiles and Science. In this essay, he presents his opinions on why students cut classes and describes how he arrived at his no-cut policy in his course. The positive results from enforcing his policy are also described.

L ast year I announced to my classes my new policy on absences: None would be allowed, except for illness or personal emergency. Even though this violated the statement on cuts in the student handbook, which allows freshmen cuts each term up to twice the number of class meetings per week and imposes no limit for upperclassmen, my students didn't fuss. They didn't fuss even after they discovered, when I telephoned or sent warning notices through the mail to students who had missed classes, that I meant business.

Part of their acceptance of the policy may have resulted from the career orientation of our college, but I don't think that was the main reason. After I explained the policy, most seemed to recognize that it promoted their own academic interests. It was also a requirement that virtually all of them would be obliged to observe—and would expect others to observe—throughout their working lives. It had to be Woody Allen who said that a major part of making it in life is simply showing up.

I told my classes about recent research, by Howard Schuman and others, indicating that academic success is more closely tied to class attendance than to the amount of time spent studying. I shared my sense of disappointment and personal *affront* when I carefully prepare for a class and a substantial number of students do not attend. I think they got the message that the policy is not arbitrary—that I care about their learning and expect them to care about my professional effort.

I don't claim to have controlled all the variables, but after I instituted the no-cut rule, student performance in my classes improved markedly, not so much in the top rank as at the bottom. In fact, the bottom rank almost disappeared, moving up and swelling the middle range to such an extent that I have reassessed my evaluation methods to differentiate among levels of performance in that range. The implications of so dramatic an improvement are surely worth pondering.

Additional benefits of the policy have been those one would expect to result from a full classroom. Student morale is noticeably higher, as is mine. Discussions are livelier, assignments are generally turned in on time, and very few students miss quizzes.

The mechanics of maintaining the policy kept me a little busier than usual, especially at first, but the results would have justified a lot more effort. I called or mailed notes to several students about their cuts, some more than once. I eventually advised a few with *invincibly* poor attendance to drop my course when it seemed that an unhappy outcome was likely. They did.

No doubt this kind of shepherding is easier in a small college. But it can work almost anyplace where a teacher cares enough about the educational stakes to make it work. The crucial element is caring.

At the first faculty meeting of the year, I confessed what I was doing. After all, I was defying college policy. I told my colleagues—at least those not cutting the meeting—that it rankled me when I had carefully prepared a class and a fifth, a quarter, or a third of the students didn't show. I thought my classes were good, and I *knew* Faulkner, Austen, and Tolstoy were good. What had been lacking in my classes, I said, was a significant proportion of the students. I told my colleagues that I believed my problem was not unique but was true of college classes everywhere, and that I was doing something about it.

Although no one seemed to attach much importance to my ignoring college policy, few of my colleagues gave me active support. Some were agreed that a 25 percent absence rate in a college class was not alarming. Others felt that college students must take responsibility for their studies, and that we should not feel liable for their losses from cut classes. One implied that if students could bag a lot of classes and still pass the course, it reflected badly on the teacher.

If professors have enough drawing power, another said, students will attend their classes. (How do you *parry* that?) Still another pointed out that if the professor covers enough material, there will be no time to waste taking the roll. In a large lecture, someone said, who knows who is there and who isn't? After the meeting, one *wag* told me I should consider using the acronym PAP for my "professional attendance policy," but congratulated me on at least evoking an interesting discussion in a faculty meeting, something rare indeed. It was easy to conclude that most of them preferred not to see a problem—at least their problem—in spotty class attendance.

Why do students cut so frequently? I can cite the immediate causes, but I first want to note the enabling circumstance: They cut because they are allowed to. They cut because of the climate of acceptance that comes from our belief that responsibility can be developed only when one is free, free even to act against personal best interests. That this is a misapplied belief in this case can be easily demonstrated. When substantial numbers of students do not attend, classroom learning is depreciated, student and teacher morale suffer, and academic standards are compromised. Students who miss classes unnecessarily are hurting more than themselves. With our *complicity,* they are undermining what colleges and universities are all about.

Students cut for two general reasons. They have things to do that appear more important than the class, or they wish to avoid what they fear will be painful consequences if they attend. In regard to the first, nursing an illness or attending family weddings or funerals are good excuses for missing a class. But other excuses—the demands of outside jobs, social engagements (including recovering from the night before), completing assignments for other courses—are, at best, questionable.

The other general reason is more disturbing and perhaps less well recognized. A few years ago, I asked several classes what they most disliked about the way courses were taught, and the answer was plain—anything that produced sustained tension or anxiety. I believe cutting is often a result of that aversion. The response of students to feelings of personal inadequacy, fear of humiliation, or a threatening professorial personality or teaching style is often simply to avoid class. This response feeds on itself, as frequent absences make attending even more threatening.

But what accounts for frequent cutting where the teacher tries to make the material interesting, knows the students by name, and approaches them with respect, help, and affability? I accept that question as unanswerable. I simply tell my students: Attend my classes regularly or drop the course. That's the rule.

 ## Vocabulary

As you think about this essay, these definitions may be helpful to you:

1. **affront**   an insult
2. **invincibly**   incapably of being overcome or subdued
3. **parry**   to evade, to shove aside
4. **wag**   joker, smart-aleck
5. **complicity**   association with or participation in

 ## Discussion Questions

1. What, according to Brown, does research indicate about academic success as related to class attendance?
2. What happened after the author instituted his no-cut rule?
3. What benefits did he see after enforcing the policy?
4. What reaction did he get from his colleagues?
5. Why, according to Brown, do students cut classes?

 ## Suggestions for Your Journal

Have you ever cut a class? If so, what were the consequences? If you put yourself in the place of your instructor, how would you be affected by students cutting your class? Do you think students appreciate a teacher who cares enough about them to institute such a policy? For what reasons would you cut a class? Can you answer Professor Brown's "unanswerable" question about why some students cut classes, even when all the positive aspects of the course are in place?

Ideas as Property

Thomas L. Minnick

Thomas L. Minnick, an English teacher who admits to having graded more than 25,000 English composition papers, has served as an expert witness and researcher on issues relating to intellectual property and plagiarism in cases tried in New York, Ohio, and California. In this essay he emphasizes the positive value of ideas and other intellectual creations as property and draws attention to the fact that as property, under the law, ideas can be stolen or mistreated with serious consequences for the thief.

The idea of "property"—that is, something owned by one person or group and therefore *not* owned by anyone else—is among the oldest, most widespread notions that humans share. Even cultures that believe that all things are owned jointly and equally by all members of the society (usually a tribe or clan) also believe that no single individual can claim ownership of those things. For example, because they believe that the land belongs to all, they also regard any individual who claims to own a part of it as violating the property rights of the group. The notions of "thieves" and "theft" depend on the idea of property, since stealing is defined as the act of taking something that does not belong to the thief. The ownership of property is also one of our most important ideas: many of our laws are based on the principle that three rights guaranteed to individuals living in a society are the right to life, the right to liberty, and the right to own property. Thomas Jefferson, writing the Declaration of Independence, paraphrased this already well-established principle when he identified "life, liberty, and the pursuit of happiness" as three *inalienable* rights of Americans.

We take for granted certain categories of property and, along with them, certain kinds of theft or other violations of property rights. For example, if you (or you and your local lending agency together) own a car, then a person who steals your car, drives it carelessly until the fuel is almost gone, then wrecks it, is unquestionably a thief, because he or she has taken your property without your permission and deprived you of it. Even if the car is returned to you no worse for wear, your rights have been violated, and no reasonable person would disagree that a theft has occurred. The same is true if someone takes your watch, your bookbag, your pet, or your Starter jacket identifying your favorite sports team. Furthermore, if someone takes your credit card and buys a substantial amount of merchandise in your name, even if the physical merchandise was never yours (and wouldn't fit you anyway), those items have been stolen from you since your property—in this example, your credit line and the dollars from it that will go to pay the bills—has been taken without your knowledge or approval.

Sometimes it may be less clear that *your ideas are your property*, but that is exactly what they are, and the courts recognize them as such. A specialization in legal studies is the field of intellectual property law, which is based on the premise that an idea belongs to the person who created it, and therefore that any profit, financial or otherwise, derived from that idea also belongs to the originator. The theft of ideas takes many forms. Suppose you design and *patent* an important new drug for the treatment of arthritis and, learning of your research, others market that drug under a different name. Unless you and they have entered into a prior agreement about distributing your drug and sharing the profits, their action violates your rights to your intellectual property. Or again, suppose you write a song, both words and music, and someone else, hearing it, decides the words are effective but that the music is not—then adapts your words to new music of their own. Given adequate evidence to establish your claim of prior ownership, you should be able to show that your intellectual property rights have been violated, and you should further be able to claim a monetary award for damages due to the violation of those rights.

Universities, whose defining reason to exist includes the development and teaching of ideas,[2] have a special stake in the principle that an idea belongs to the person who first conceived it. The integrity of a university depends on a strong belief in this principle, and so universities defend this principle in all they do. For what would a degree from your college or university be worth if students could be caught cheating and nevertheless receive credit for the courses where that offense took place? Undergraduates writing English compositions or research papers for courses in psychology or history, graduate students preparing their master's or doctoral theses, faculty members engaged in leading-edge research— all these participants in the university have a stake in preserving the principle of a creator's right to his or her ideas as property. If they misrepresent themselves as originating ideas that do not belong to them, they are violating the intellectual property rights of others. If they themselves are victims of plagiarists (people who copy their ideas, word-for-word or in paraphrases), then they are deprived of meaningful ownership of what they have created. Even if a particular idea is not worth much money on the open market, the theft of that idea means that the true originator may not receive the *intangible* credit or respect that that idea has earned. So it is essential to the credibility and integrity of a university, and therefore of the degrees that it confers, that it provide the best defense it can for the intellectual property of the members of its community. People who create new ideas should be respected for doing so, and people who claim as theirs those ideas that truly belong to others should be condemned.

Unfortunately, it is part of the nature of ideas that we find it harder to prove ownership of a new idea than, say, of a microwave oven. When someone has stolen your microwave oven, two statements are true: first, you no longer have your microwave, and second, someone else probably does. Ideas are not like that: it is in the nature of ideas that I can tell you my idea, and then you and I both will have it. If I tell you my answer to the third question on our final examination in American history, I will know that answer and so will you. For that matter, I could tell my answer to everyone in our class and we all could produce the same answer on request. And so on: I could tell everyone at my college, or everyone in my state, or everyone in our country, or in the world— and yet I would still have the idea in the same way that I did before, while everyone else also now has it. Moreover, if someone steals your microwave oven, you will probably be able to identify it by brand, size, model number, and condition. If you have had the

---

[2]See the essay "On Academic Freedom" by William H. Halverson and James R. Carter earlier in this chapter—ED.

foresight to mark it as yours—by engraving it with your social security number, for example—then identifying it as your stolen property will be substantially easier. But it is very difficult to mark an idea as yours. Usually the proof of ownership for intellectual property takes the form of a patent or copyright, although it is possible to document prior ownership of an idea in other ways as well.

How can a university protect ideas from thieves? The first step is to make clear to every member of the university that ideas are a kind of property, and that the protection of those ideas really does matter to the well-being of the university. A second step is to teach students at all levels the conventions for acknowledging when they adopt or develop the ideas of someone else. The third is to deal seriously with instances of the theft of ideas, which in an academic setting commonly takes one of two forms—cheating (that is, copying someone else's answers during an examination) and *plagiarism,* the unacknowledged dependence on someone else's ideas in writing, usually in out-of-class assignments. That you are reading this essay is part of your university's effort to make clear that it values and protects ideas as property.

The second step, training in common academic procedures for acknowledging sources, involves learning the accepted forms for footnotes, bibliographies, and citations to other authors in the text of your work. If you have had to write a research paper as a composition exercise in high school or previous college work, then you have probably learned one of the many conventional systems available for acknowledging sources you have used and identifying the specific ideas and language from others that you cite in your own work.[3] What matters is that your reader should be able to tell what ideas are your own original work and what ideas you have adopted or adapted from others. If you quote a section of someone else's writing verbatim, you must enclose the quoted material within quotation marks *and* tell your reader where the original statement appeared. If you rely on someone else's ideas, even if you do not quote them word for word, then a footnote identifying your source and indicating the extent of your indebtedness is appropriate.

The third step a college or university must take to ensure that ideas are credited to their true creators—namely, dealing seriously with instances of the theft of ideas—will be evident in the ways that instructors and the systems of the university react when a case of cheating or plagiarism is suspected. If an instructor suspects that a student has cheated on a test or copied someone else's essay, the easiest action to take will always be no action at all. But would such a lack of action be the right way to proceed? If cheating or plagiarism mean so little that they can be ignored, then the instructor is contributing to the institution's loss of integrity and the weakening of the degree—of *your* degree. Indeed, by such inaction an instructor would become an accessory to the theft. The right way to proceed is to put the investigation of the facts of the alleged case into the authority of a separate group of

---

[3]Perhaps the most widely used guide for authors using footnotes and bibliographies is "Turabian"— which is the shorthand way that writers refer to Kate L. Turabian, *A Manual for Writers of Term Papers, Theses, and Dissertations,* 6th ed. (Chicago: The University of Chicago Press, 1996). Other well-regarded guides of this sort include *MLA Handbook for Writers of Research Papers* (New York: Modern Language Association, 1999); *The Chicago Manual of Style* 14th ed. (Chicago: The University of Chicago Press, 1993); and *Publication Manual* 4th ed. (Washington, D.C.: American Psychological Association, 1994). Your instructor can help you decide among them.

people—often called the Honor Board or the Committee on Academic Misconduct. By hearing many cases of this kind, such a group becomes familiar with the kinds of questions that should be pursued, the kinds of evidence that can be gathered, and the appropriate resolution of the incident. Since effective teachers make a commitment to put forth their own best efforts for their students, those teachers may feel a degree of betrayal when a student knowingly tries to misrepresent someone else's work as his or her own. Therefore, it is usually wiser for a neutral party or group to investigate and *adjudicate* a case of suspected misconduct.

Some schools automatically suspend a student who has been found in violation of the rules on cheating or plagiarizing. Such a suspension may be in effect for a term or several terms, and the student will not be permitted to re-enroll until that assigned time period has passed. Other schools dismiss a student permanently for violating the rules of proper academic conduct. The consequences of academic misconduct can be devastating: law schools, medical schools, and the other professional programs available to you may be permanently closed if your record contains a notation about academic misconduct. You need to know what your college considers to be academic misconduct, and you need to know what the penalties for committing such misconduct can be. At many colleges and universities, students are bound by an "honor code" that requires them to notify instructors of any cheating they may be aware of. In such places, the failure to notify an official about suspected misconduct also qualifies as a violation and is grounds for disciplinary action.

Know the relevant policies at your institution, but do not let the seriousness of those policies paralyze you when you start to write an essay or a research paper for one of your classes. Some students ask, with justification, "How can I be sure that my ideas are original? Surely someone else has had almost every idea before me at some time or another. How can I be safe from misconduct accusations?" When you are told to be original, your teacher does not expect that every idea in your essay will be unique in the history of human thought. But a teacher does have the right to expect that *when you knowingly depend* on the thinking of someone else, you will acknowledge that in the conventional way (using quotation marks, footnotes, and a bibliography). You can express your own original turn of thought by seeing an idea in a new light, or combining ideas that you have not read before in the same combination, or by modifying the acknowledged ideas of someone else with critical commentary or new emphasis, and so on. And just to be sure, if you really have any doubts about the originality of your work, talk to your instructor about them before you turn the work in for a grade.[4]

 ## Vocabulary

As you think about this essay, these definitions may be helpful to you:

1. **inalienable**   incapable of being surrendered or transferred

---

[4] I am pleased to record my gratitude to my colleagues Professor Sara Garnes and Dean Virginia Gordon for their conversations with me about the topic of this essay.

2. **patent**   a license securing for an inventor for a term of years the exclusive right to make, use, or sell an invention
3. **intangible**   not capable of being precisely identified; abstract
4. **plagiarism**   stealing or passing off the ideas or words of another as one's own
5. **adjudicate**   to act as judge

 ## Discussion Questions

1. What is the historical basis for "ownership of property"?
2. How does the author define "ideas as property"? How do ideas and material property differ?
3. Why is the concept of ideas as property so important in a university setting?
4. What steps can be taken by a university to ensure ideas as property are protected, according to the author?
5. What can happen to a student who is found to have cheated or plagiarized?

 ## Suggestions for Your Journal

Find out and write down in your own words your college's policies and procedures for deciding cases of alleged academic misconduct. This exercise is important so that you know what those policies and procedures are: They identify your responsibilities and your rights. Then comment on whether, in your judgment, those policies are justified and those procedures are fair.

WHAT DOES IT MEAN
TO BE AN EDUCATED PERSON?

The academic community describes an educated person as someone who is skilled at critical thinking, ethical reasoning, communication, intellectual inquiry, civic engagement, and interacting with diversity. An educated person also has highly specialized knowledge in a major field of study and the breadth of knowledge to think globally. This list of academic attributes is developed over time and is achieved only though life-long learning.

Mona Patel,
Peer Mentor 09-10
Counseling Graduate
Student

Dear Student,

Freshman year in college is a crucial and invigorating time in your life. It is full of new challenges, experiences, and opportunities. As you begin classes for the first time in college, make sure you learn how to "dig at the roots."

In order to get the most out of college and succeed, class participation and providing your own perspective and analysis are essential. To be an educated person, you must have the ability to think critically! In other words, don't believe everything you read and everything your professors tell you. Learn to make decisions based on your own knowledge, values, and views. You must also pay attention to your own biases. All individuals develop their own attitudes and preferences based on their upbringing, cultural background, what they were taught at home, what they were taught at school, how their parents behaved, the messages they received from their teachers, and where they grew up. Suspend judgment and always be open to listening to the varied and even opposing viewpoints of your classmates, professors, and friends.

Don't be afraid to be independent. You are entitled to your own opinions and deserve to be treated with respect. If everyone in the world shared the same opinion, we would not make progress in fields such as health, medicine, science, technology, law, society, and culture. As Anthony J. D'Angelo wrote in his College Blue Book, "When solving problems, dig at the roots instead of just hacking at the leaves."

Good luck and have fun!

Mona Patel

Purposes
Derek Bok

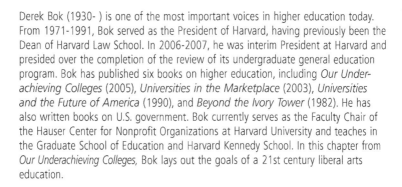

Derek Bok (1930-) is one of the most important voices in higher education today. From 1971-1991, Bok served as the President of Harvard, having previously been the Dean of Harvard Law School. In 2006-2007, he was interim President at Harvard and presided over the completion of the review of its undergraduate general education program. Bok has published six books on higher education, including *Our Under-achieving Colleges* (2005), *Universities in the Marketplace* (2003), *Universities and the Future of America* (1990), and *Beyond the Ivory Tower* (1982). He has also written books on U.S. government. Bok currently serves as the Faculty Chair of the Hauser Center for Nonprofit Organizations at Harvard University and teaches in the Graduate School of Education and Harvard Kennedy School. In this chapter from *Our Underachieving Colleges*, Bok lays out the goals of a 21st century liberal arts education.

Any useful discussion of undergraduate education must begin by making clear what it is that colleges are trying to achieve. As W. B. Carnochan has observed, "Lacking adequate criteria of purpose, we do not know how well our higher education works in practice or even what working well would mean."[1] What, then, should colleges try to have their students take away after four years? How should they help young people to grow and develop during this formative period in their lives?

In pondering these questions, several critics of undergraduate education assume that there must be a *single* overarching purpose to college that faculties have somehow forgotten or willfully ignored. For Bruce Wilshire in *The Moral Collapse of the University*, it is to help students integrate fragmented, specialized fields of knowledge in order to address large questions "about what we are and what we ought to be." [2] For Charles Anderson in *Prescribing the Life of the Mind*, it is "the cultivation of the skills of practical reason."[3] For Bill Readings in *The University in Ruins*, the unifying aim of a college education used to be the interpretation, advancement, and transmission of the "national culture," and it is the demise of this traditional purpose that has left the contemporary university "in ruins," bereft of any animating goal save the vapid claim of "excellence" in all it tries to do.[4]

Nowhere in their writings do the authors make clear why there should be only one dominant purpose for undergraduate education. The very idea seems instantly suspect, since human beings develop intellectually in a number of different ways during their undergraduate years. It is especially implausible in the United States, for American colleges, at least those of the residential variety, to not merely offer courses but also undertake to organize the living arrangements, the recreational and extracurricular activities-indeed, virtually the whole environment in which their students spend four years of their lives. If colleges exercise such a pervasive influence, they should presumably try to help undergraduates develop in even more ways than those fostered by the curriculum alone. Anyone who tries to conflate these forms of growth into a single comprehensive goal is bound to suggest a purpose that is either far too narrow to capture all that colleges should accomplish or far too broad to convey much useful meaning.

Once college faculties look for a series of goals, they will quickly encounter an important threshold problem. According to a school of thought recently expressed by Stanley Fish, the only proper ends of the university are those that involve "the mastery of intellectual and scholarly skills."[5] Fish is not the only professor to hold this view, but his opinion is clearly at odds with the official position of many institutions. College catalogues regularly announce an intention to go beyond intellectual pursuits to nurture such behavioral traits as good moral character, racial tolerance, and a commitment to active citizenship.

Fish's principal argument against trying to develop character or prepare active citizens is that such goals are simply "unworkable." In his words, "There are just too many intervening variables, too many uncontrolled factors that mediate the relationship between what goes on in a classroom and the shape of what is finally a life."[6] Fish believes that universities should confine themselves to what they know how to do. He urges faculty members "to put your students in possession of a set of materials and equip them with a set of skills (interpretive, computational, laboratory, archival) and even perhaps (although this one is really iffy) instill in them the same love of the subject that inspires your pedagogical effort."[7]

In making his argument, Fish commits one of the basic errors identified in the preceding chapter: he equates what an undergraduate education should accomplish with what professors can achieve in their classrooms. This is a cramped and excessively faculty-centered point of view. Colleges can hardly undertake to shape the environment in which their students live, in and out of the classroom, throughout four formative years and then insist that their aims are limited to the things their professors know how to do. By tailoring the role of the college to fit the capabilities and interests of its faculty rather than the needs of its students, Fish overlooks all that admissions policies, residential living arrangements, and extracurricular life can contribute to an undergraduate's development. There is much evidence that these aspects of college do have significant, reasonably foreseeable effects on the attitudes, the values, and even the behavior of students (including their moral and civic behavior). Rather than deal with these findings, Fish commits another error common to faculty debates about undergraduate education.

He is content to rest his case on his own personal observations during 14 years on the Duke University faculty, pointing out that "While Duke is a first-rate institution with many virtues, I saw no evidence whatsoever that its graduates emerged with a highly developed sense of civic responsibility as they rushed off to enter top-10 law schools, medical schools, and business schools."[8]

In fact, researchers have shown that college graduates are much more active civically and politically than those who have not attended college (even after controlling for differences in intelligence, parental education, and socioeconomic background). In fact, political scientists find that formal education is the most important factor in explaining who does or does not go to the polls.[9] Several studies also suggest that certain courses and concentrations, notably in the social sciences, and certain outside activities, such as community service programs, have a positive effect on students' willingness to vote or to work to improve their communities following graduation.[10] Other large-scale studies have found that a variety of extracurricular experiences affect student values in consistent ways. For example, several researchers have concluded that efforts to admit a racially diverse student body and to promote interracial contact through policies on such matters as student living arrangements and racial awareness programs can build greater tolerance. [11] One can surely question such findings or disagree with the methods used in the studies. By ignoring the evidence entirely, however, and relying instead on casual, personal observations, Fish ultimately renders his arguments unconvincing.

Of course, one can accept the possibility of shaping student values and still balk at deliberate efforts to prepare active citizens, build stronger moral character, or promote greater racial tolerance. When colleges seek not merely to sharpen students' minds, but also to improve their behavior, thoughtful faculty members may worry that such intentions smack of human engineering and raise the specter of indoctrination.

Anyone harboring such concerns would only be more troubled after reading essays from faculty members of the left, such as Henry Giroux, Frederic Jameson, or Frank Lentricchia. These authors are explicit about their desire to transform undergraduates into citizens committed to fighting social injustice. Lentricchia plainly acknowledges that "I come down on the side of those who believe that our society is mainly unreasonable and that education should be one of the places where we can get involved in the process of changing it."[12] Literature professor Jameson announces that his purpose is to "make converts" and "form Marxists."[13] According to Giroux, professors should try to change society for the better by engaging their students with "critical pedagogy," that is, "pedagogical practices informed by an ethical stance that contests racism, sexism, class exploitation, and other dehumanizing and exploitative social relations. . . [and that] seeks to celebrate responsible action and strategic risk taking as part of an ongoing struggle to link citizenship to the notion of a democratic public community, civic courage to a shared conception of social justice."[14]

Many people would agree with Giroux's objectives, couched in these terms. Who could be against encouraging students to promote social justice and to oppose "dehumanizing and exploitative social relations"? Who is in favor of "racism, sexism, [and] class exploitation"? But problems start to emerge as one reads further. Behind the protective covering of "social justice" lies a distinct political view of society and a specific program of reform. There are official villains: "corporations have been given too much power in this society, and hence the need for educators and others to address the threat this poses to all facets of public life."[15] Giroux likewise has a specific political agenda: "progressive academics must take seriously the symbolic and pedagogic dimensions of struggle and be able to fight for public services and rights, especially the right to decent health care, education, housing, and work."[16] Apparently, then, faculty members must oppose corporations and promote a progressive welfare state agenda not only as private citizens but through their teaching as well.

Since these political goals are matters of legitimate debate, the vision of a university committed to promoting Giroux's agenda is deeply unsettling.* Could students who disagree with the agenda feel entirely free to express opposing views? Would appointments and promotions committees in Giroux's university evaluate faculty candidates on their intellectual merits or be swayed by how closely the candidates' teaching and writing conformed to his political vision? As Giroux has clearly stated, educators must regard "all calls to depoliticize pedagogy [and presumably scholarship as well] as simply a mask for domination."[17] What he seems to argue is that everything that goes on in a university is inescapably political, that all efforts at neutrality and objectivity are impossible and disingenuous, and that universities should therefore consciously adopt a political agenda and promote it through their teaching and writing.

To be sure, Giroux and others like him often add that students should be free to disagree with their professors. Still, in Giroux's university, one wonders whether undergraduates concerned about their grade point averages will dare to differ with their instructors when they write their papers and take their exams. One also suspects that junior professors of different political persuasions will feel inclined to follow the prevailing party line in their teaching and writing, lest they be deemed expendable when they are considered for tenure. Since Giroux is not alone in his views, one can understand why some professors (and some others as well) might worry about proposals to shape the character and values of students.

Is there any way of promoting certain values and behaviors that does not amount to unacceptable indoctrination? Yes, but the limits need to be clearly defined and carefully circumscribed. Institutional efforts to build character or change behavior should include only goals with which no reasonable person is likely to disagree.** For example, virtually no one would quarrel with attempts to encourage students to be more honest, more scrupulous about keeping promises, more understanding of those of different races, backgrounds, and religions. Nor would anyone in a democracy oppose efforts encouraging undergraduates to vote, inform themselves about public issues, and participate in their communities. It is only when professors use their classrooms to influence *which* promises students keep, *how* they vote, or what kind of community programs they support that their teaching is open to criticism.

Even seemingly unexceptionable goals, of course, raise serious questions at the margin. There are surely *some* cases in which principled people can be excused for not telling the truth or for refusing to vote. That being so, a student should

---

*The problem of indoctrination is not limited to left-wing professors. Well-meaning programs sponsored by a university to improve race or gender relations can easily fall into the hands of officials who announce as fact to incoming freshmen such debatable propositions as "all institutions in America are deeply sexist" or "racism involves only acts of discrimination by whites against minorities." See, far example Charles Alan Kors, "Bad Faith: The Politicization of the University In Loco Parenti,." in Howard Dickman (ed.), The Imperiled Academy (1993), p. 153.

Race and gender can be helpful when they allow open discussion if differences of opinion, potentially unfair practices, misunderstandings, and the like, but dogmatic assertions and indoctrination by persons in authority can be just wrong in the context of promoting understanding among the races or between the sexes as in other academic settings.

**Exceptions may be made far private colleges, such as religiously affiliated institutions, that actively promote a set of special beliefs or behaviors, provided they make this clear to prospective students and their families.

always be free to question principles of behavior both in and out of class, no matter how correct they may seem. Although professors may disagree with students about their views on moral or civic questions, they must never use their power to suppress opposing opinions. Nor should the university use coercive authority to impose its moral or civic principles on its students except where necessary to maintain order, protect persons and property, or uphold the integrity of the academic process (e.g., by punishing cheating or plagiarism). In other words, attempts to shape behavior and character, even for widely accepted ends, should be carried out, insofar as possible, through argument, persuasion, and example, not by force or coercive authority.

Notwithstanding Professor Fish, it is perfectly possible to teach moral reasoning or prepare students to be enlightened citizens without having instructors impose their personal ideologies or policy views on their students. Of course, it is conceivable that instructors will abuse their authority in these ways. All manner of familiar subjects can and occasionally do degenerate into indoctrination in the hands of instructors intent on forcing their own beliefs on students.* Courses on American politics or political philosophy or international economics are obvious examples. Even required courses in English composition are sometimes used to promote a radical political agenda.[18] It would be folly to abolish all courses susceptible to such instruction. Such a response would decimate the curriculum. Rather, the proper course is surely to rally the entire faculty to consider their responsibilities as teachers and to discourage efforts by particular instructors to misuse their positions by trying to indoctrinate students.

To sum up, attempts to prescribe a single overriding aim or to limit the purposes of college to the realm of intellectual development take too narrow a view of the undergraduate experience and threaten to impose a moratorium on efforts to nurture some extremely important human qualities during four formative years of students' lives. Instead, colleges should pursue a variety of purposes, including a carefully circumscribed effort to foster generally accepted values and behaviors, such as honesty and racial tolerance. Within this ample mandate, several aims seem especially important.**

---

*The meaning of indoctrination is not as obvious as it may seem. For example, teachers of "the dismal science" are sometimes accused of indoctrination because they accept the basic assumption of neoclassical economics and do not devote class time to an in-depth discussion of possible alternatives. Similarly, professors of Constitutional law can be said to indoctrinate by refusing to entertain challenges to the legitimacy of the Constitution and the form of government it embodies. Nevertheless, there is a difference between these examples and, say, using a basic writing course to teach students how language is employed to oppress women, minorities, and the poor. In providing instruction on economics or Constitutional law, a college may well decide to offer elective courses in which to consider alternative systems, but it is perfectly legitimate to refuse to use basic courses in these fields for this purpose. In such classes, as currently taught, instructors are not seeking to use the classroom to spread their own private set of controversial beliefs; they are making a commonsense judgment about how best to use scarce class time in a basic course to be of greatest use to the largest number of students. In the writing class, instructors cannot make this claim. Rather, they are taking a required course established for other purposes and deliberately using it to promote their personal political agendas.
**The list that follows does not attempt to include the multitude of purposes that might be appropriate for particular groups of students-learning Russian, for example, or writing poetry, playing football, or acquiring a knowledge of chemistry. The aims described here are those of broad enough applicability to be appropriate for virtually all undergraduates.

The Ability to Communicate

All undergraduates need to develop the capacity to communicate well with various audiences. The ability to write with precision and grace is the most familiar of these competencies, followed by an ability to speak clearly and persuasively. These skills are widely used by students both during college and after. They are essential in civic life and in almost all the careers that students are likely to enter. When asked what they look for in the college graduates they hire, employers repeatedly emphasize the importance of good writing and effective speaking.

Professors have long entertained the hope that students would acquire these skills before coming to college. Efforts were even made more than a century ago to force high schools to do a better job of teaching composition by introducing writing exams for students seeking admission to college.[19] Unfortunately, the wish has never been fulfilled. Freshmen have always arrived on campus deficient in their ability to communicate. They are especially likely to do so now that such a high proportion of young people come to college, often from mediocre schools and from families in which English is not commonly spoken. However welcome or unwelcome the task may be, colleges cannot escape the responsibility of preparing all their undergraduates to speak and write with reasonable precision, clarity, and style.

Critical Thinking

Another aim basic to every college is to enhance the ability of students to think clearly and critically. The importance of this goal is so widely acknowledged that nationwide polls have found that more than 90 percent of faculty members in the United States consider it *the most* important purpose of undergraduate education.[20] In view of the wide variety of interests and backgrounds represented in a typical college faculty, such a strong consensus is impressive.

Defining what critical thinking actually entails, however, is more complicated than many people realize. Some psychologists have invoked a line of thought stretching back to Edward Thorndike's experiments at the beginning of the twentieth century and insisted that there is no such thing as "critical thinking," only an endless series of particular ways to reason about different kinds of problems.[21] There is clearly some truth to this observation. Many subjects are sufficiently complex and unique that no student can think about them productively without first mastering a body of specialized analytic methods and technical knowledge. If all thinking involved such methods, the scope for developing rigorous habits of thought in college would be severely limited, since few undergraduates could acquire enough of the necessary skills and knowledge to address more than a few of these subjects.

Fortunately, many problems arising in everyday life and experience do not require such highly specialized knowledge. Recent research suggests that certain familiar qualities of mind and habits of thought may help resolve such a wide range of problems that every student would benefit from acquiring them.[22] Among these qualities are an ability to recognize and define problems clearly, to identify the arguments and interests on all sides of an issue, to gather relevant facts and appreciate their relevance, to perceive as many plausible solutions as possible, and to exercise good judgment in choosing the best of these alternatives after considering the evidence and using inference, analogy, and other forms of ordinary reasoning to test the cogency of the arguments. These methods will not solve all problems; far from it. But they will solve many and clarify many more, enough to make proficiency in their use well worth the effort.

In addition to these habits of disciplined common sense, certain basic quantitative methods seem applicable to a wide enough range of situations to be valuable for almost all students. For example, a reasonable grasp of statistics and probability may prove useful in thinking about a host of familiar problems, from understanding newspaper articles about risks to personal safety and health to calculating the odds of getting into graduate school or understanding the reliability of opinion polls. A knowledge of mathematics accompanied by practice applying such knowledge to everyday problems and situations can likewise be helpful to students in completing their income tax forms, balancing their budgets, and thinking more rigorously about a variety of complicated subjects. A facility with computers can serve a wide and growing range of purposes in acquiring information and using it to solve problems.

Beyond these few examples, it is hard to think of general problem-solving skills that can be profitably used in enough situations to justify making their study mandatory. Formal logic and advanced calculus, for example, have not proved especially helpful except for solving a limited set of abstract problems.[23] As a result, courses on methods such as these should be available for those who need to learn them, but there is no compelling reason to force every student to master this material.

Moral Reasoning

A related but more controversial aim of college is to help students develop a clearer, stronger set of ethical principles. After decades of neglect, spurred by heated controversies in the 1960s over moral values in public and private life, universities began to offer courses challenging students to think about a variety of practical ethical problems. The growth of these new courses, however, has not persuaded all the skeptics in the faculty. "As for ethics," one sometimes hears, "by the time students begin college, they either have 'em or they don't." According to this line of thought, moral development is the responsibility of parents and schoolteachers, and universities that try to assume the task are destined not to succeed.

Comments of this kind reveal a failure to distinguish between two aspects of ethical behavior. One is the ability to think carefully about moral dilemmas, evaluate the arguments on all sides, and decide on the right thing to do. The other is the desire and self-discipline to put one's conclusions into practice. Parents may have the preeminent role in developing the desire and determination to act responsibly toward others, although, even here, experience teaches that other influences later in life can have an effect. However, when it comes to helping young people to identify ethical problems and to ponder them with care, colleges can certainly make a significant contribution, especially today, when so many students come to college with an easy relativism that clouds their ability to reason about many complex questions, ethical and otherwise.*

Analyzing ethical issues, then, is a form of critical thinking much like other forms that faculties regularly teach. Learning to act on one's beliefs, on the other hand, presents a more formidable challenge that must await further discussion in Chapter 6. For now, the chance to help students learn to identify ethical issues and think about them rigorously is reason enough to include moral education among the aims of college, even if it is not clear whether students will act more ethically as a result. After all, business schools teach students to analyze issues confronting corporations, although one cannot be sure that graduates will have the resolve to act on what they have learned instead of using their powers of rationalization to justify a more expedient course of action. Law schools continue teaching how to reason about legal questions, although they know that students will sometimes ignore the proper answer in order to tell important clients what they want to hear. Much of what faculties teach their undergraduates is conveyed in the faith that most students will use their knowledge and skills for proper ends. There is no reason why colleges should not make the same assumption when they teach students how to think carefully about moral issues.

Preparing Citizens

Another widely neglected aim of liberal education is to prepare students to be informed and active participants in the process of democratic self-government.**

---

*Even those who understand the difference between moral reasoning and the will to act one's beliefs sometimes dismiss the former as relatively unimportant. Gordon Marino, philosophy professor at Saint Olaf College, illustrates this tendency in a recent article in the *Chronicle of Higher Education*. "The fantasy," he declares, "to be that if up-and-coming, accountants just knew a little more about ethics, then they would know better than to falsify their reports so as to drive up the value of company stock. But sheer ignorance is seldom the moral problem. More knowledge is not what is needed. Take it from Kierkegaard: The moral challenge is simply to abide by the knowledge we already have." Gordon Marino, "Before Teaching Ethics, Stop Kidding Yourself," *The Chronicle Review*, 50 *Chronicle of Higher Education* (Feb. 20, 2004), p. 85.

If Professor Marino were correct, one wonders why philosophers spent so much time in years past on practical moral issues. In fact, such questions are often not as simple as he suggests, and the problems have only grown more complicated in recent decades. Today, more than ever before, there is good reason for college graduates to know "a little more about ethics." Modern medicine has created a host of ethical problems that demand the most careful analysis: stem cell research and cloning, for example, not to mention the dilemmas doctors face in deciding whether to withhold the truth from patients or to test new drugs made by companies to which they have financial ties. Lawyers face vexing questions in reconciling their duties to a client with their obligations to court and society. Even accountants will often encounter difficult choices when they discover practices that seem to meet the letter of the accounting rules but arguably raise broader issues of public policy. In all these cases, students need to develop habits of thought that will help them to recognize moral problems when they arise and to reason about them carefully enough to arrive at thoughtful decisions on how to respond.

**Colleges do devote much attention to developing qualities of mind and spirit that can contribute to enlightened citizenship. Critical thinking, racial tolerance, general knowledge indeed, almost everything a college tries to do-can be described as civic education in the broadest possible sense. Far present purposes, however, the term *civic education* is used more narrowly to refer to efforts to give all students the essential knowledge that every citizen needs and to strengthen their commitment to participate effectively in the process of democratic self-govern-

Until the mid-twentieth century in America, educators believed that a sound liberal education would suffice to serve this purpose adequately. During the intervening decades, however, circumstances have changed in important ways that cast serious doubt on this assumption. For one thing, the amount of information citizens need to fulfill their civic duties has become far larger. To understand the broad array of important policy issues and make informed choices among rival candidates, today's voters would need a working knowledge of a vast agenda of complicated subjects, such as healthcare, social security, international relations, and global warming. It is impossible to familiarize students with all these issues, let alone prepare them for the many new questions that will arise during their lifetimes. How to respond to this problem poses an extremely difficult challenge, but one cannot assume that it will be enough merely to offer a traditional liberal education.

In addition, prior to World War II, college students were a small elite, and educators could safely assume that they would take an active part in political and civic life. Now undergraduates in America make up a large share of a generation in which civic apathy is the norm. Young people vote less than any other age group and less than people of their age voted in generations past.[24] For the first time in modern memory, a majority of young Americans turning 18 will have grown up in a home in which no parent has ever voted. In such an environment, one cannot assume that graduates will even bother to go to the polls, let alone play an active part in their communities. Civic education is arguably no longer simply a matter of conveying the knowledge and skills to help students make enlightened judgments about politics and public affairs; colleges must consider whether there is anything they can do to imbue undergraduates with a stronger commitment to fulfill their civic responsibilities.

Living with Diversity

Along with acquiring civic and moral responsibility, undergraduates need to learn to live and work effectively with other people and enter into fulfilling personal relationships. For generations, this part of growing up was taken for granted as a fact of life; it did not entail significant responsibilities for American colleges beyond enacting prohibitions against violence and theft and establishing parietal rules to limit contact between the sexes. In the aftermath of the civil rights revolution, however, blacks, Hispanics, and other minority groups began to enroll in growing numbers on predominantly white campuses, forcing universities to deal with a series of problems and controversies growing out of the troubled history of race in America. The feminist movement and the heightened awareness of subtle and not-so-subtle discriminations against women infused relationships between the sexes with new and urgently felt tensions. Gay rights activists began to assert themselves and urge college administrators to meet the of those with different sexual preferences.

---

ment—as, for example, voters, candidates, public servants, commentators, campaign workers, or simply concerned citizens.

Universities have not been the only institutions to experience these changes. All sorts of organizations find themselves employing a more diverse workforce and offering goods and services to a more heterogeneous set of publics. In this environment, with a population growing steadily more multiracial and a legal system bristling with safeguards for ethnic and religious groups, institutions of every kind expect colleges to prepare their students to work effectively with many different kinds of people. Meanwhile, some intellectuals worry whether a nation divided among so many ethnic and religious groups can hold together as a society, and they look to universities to do their part in fostering tolerance and understanding.

No college can sensibly refrain from doing what it can to help students learn to function successfully in this self-consciously diverse population. Failure to do so would not only seem insensitive to evident needs in the society and workforce; it would ignore deeply felt concerns that exist on every campus. When racial tensions flare, or women angrily protest against sexual violence, or gay students are openly persecuted, campus authorities must respond. They quickly find that merely enacting rules and meting out punishment will not suffice. In one way or another, every college must seek to apply the words of Martin Luther King Jr.: "We have inherited a large house, a great world house, in which we have to live together, black and white, Gentile and Jew, Catholic and Protestant, Moslem and Hindu, a family unduly separated in ideas, culture, and interest, who, because we can never again live apart, must learn somehow to live with each other in peace."[25] The challenge is to determine how to help students learn to live together with understanding and mutual respect while not appearing insensitive to the aggrieved, unfairly accusatory to the majority, or rigidly doctrinaire to the larger society.

Living in a More Global Society

Americans increasingly find themselves affected by circumstances beyond our borders—by other governments, distant cultures, foreign nationals, international crises. Freer trade exposes American workers to overseas economies that can create new jobs or take them away. The lives of ordinary citizens are touched by distant wars, terrorist threats, Middle East oil shortages. Changing methods of communication and travel multiply opportunities for contact across national boundaries. Problems ranging from environmental dangers narcotics trafficking to trade wars and nuclear weapons draw our government into new collaborative relationships with other nations. All these developments suggest that students today will need to know more than earlier generations of undergraduates about international affairs and about other countries and cultures.

Colleges must respond to these challenges, since their graduates are so likely to be involved with other nations and foreign nationals as business executives, public officials, lawyers, or simply citizens. Exactly how to prepare students for such a future, however, poses great difficulties. No one can hope to gain even a rudimentary knowledge of the many nations of the world, each with its own language and culture. Nor can undergraduates foresee in college just which culture and languages will prove important to them after they graduate. No one can predict future events in the international arena with any certainty. Thus the peculiar challenge colleges face is how to construct a foundation of knowledge and understanding that will help their students adapt and respond effectively to whatever international problems and opportunities may confront then in their later lives. More than most of the aims that colleges pursue, this task is novel and remains clouded by uncertainty and confusion.

A Breadth of Interests

Another, more traditional, aim of a college education is to give students the capabilities, knowledge, and breadth of interests to enable them to enjoy full and varied lives. Some of these interests may be intellectual—for example, in history or philosophy. Others may be artistic—understanding and enjoying music, poetry, and painting or actually practicing some form of art as an avocation. Still others may involve engaging in a lifetime sport, such as tennis, swimming, or running. Such a variety of interests brings many blessings. It can help to avoid the dangers of excessive specialization by providing wider perspectives to enlighten judgment. It offers escape from a life too preoccupied with vocational concerns. It supplies the knowledge to understand more of what is occurring in the world, from global warming to presidential campaigns to chronic trade deficits. It furnishes the mind to contemplate the perennial human problems of good and evil, justice and injustice, war and peace. It affords a means for escaping boredom through all manner of absorbing private pursuits.

Although the case for acquiring a breadth of interests and knowledge seems compelling, it is hard to know exactly how colleges should respond. The task may seem manageable on first impression, but only so long as one assumes that students will remember most of what they are taught, especially in their general education classes. Unfortunately, this assumption is patently unrealistic. Most students retain only fragments, and even these will steadily disappear beyond recall if there is no occasion to use them.[26] The limitations of memory are important reason why attempting to compile lists of essential facts and ideas that every student should know is likely to prove a fruitless enterprise. They also cast doubt on ambitious schemes to expose all students to a grand array of courses covering vast areas of human experience.

How, then, should colleges proceed? By trying to awaken interests that will inspire students to continue learning in a variety of fields throughout their lifetimes? By teaching undergraduates basic methods of inquiry that will enable them to explore subjects that might otherwise seem remote and impenetrable? By concentrating on a few fundamental ideas and texts in enough detail that students will conceivably remember much of what they have learned?

There are no easy answers to these questions. That is doubtless one reason why the subject of general education has attracted so much interest since its inception more than a century ago, and why it continues to provoke such heated debates.

Preparing for Work

A last, but still contested, aim of undergraduate education is to prepare students for a career. In his Politics, Aristotle asks, "should the useful in life, or should virtue, or should the higher knowledge be the aim of our training?"[27] Disagreement on this point persists to this day. Humanists have expressed special hostility toward attempts to dilute the liberal arts with courses that prepare students for work. To William Schaefer, former chair of the English department and an academic vice chancellor at the University of California, Los Angeles, "the most critical issue [is] purging the undergraduate curriculum of vocational training."[28] More than 30 years ago, philosopher Robert Paul Wolff also urged that all vocational courses be banished from the curriculum, arguing that such instruction inevitably diverted students from a pure desire to master a subject. Only through an effort to achieve such mastery, he believed, "sharply different from both the dilettante's superficiality and the professional's career commitment, can a young man discover who he is and whom he wants to be."[29]

These opinions seem strangely out of touch with the realities of contemporary American life. For the vast majority of college students, regardless of the college they attend, the undergraduate years are a time when they must choose a vocation. This decision will have a profound effect on their lives, and it is only natural that they should take it seriously and seek whatever help their college can give them. Indeed it is hard to know how any student could truly understand "whom [be wants] to be "*without* thinking carefully about what career to pursue. To make such choices wisely, students need to learn more about the role different professions play in society; the moral dilemmas their members commonly face; the social, psychological, and material rewards they can bring; and the mental, physical, and temporal demands they impose. Surely colleges should do something to help students acquire such knowledge so that they can make informed decisions about a question so vital to their future lives.

In most American colleges, a majority of undergraduates will not merely have to choose a vocation; they will move directly into the workforce and look for a job. For them, college is the last chance to prepare themselves for work by acquiring skills and knowledge of the kind best learned through formal education. Institutions with large numbers of such students can hardly deny them the opportunity. Colleges that did so would soon have to close their doors for lack of enough applicants, and deservedly so, since they might leave their students ill equipped to enter their chosen callings.

Preparing students for a career of course, does not merely mean giving them the essential skills for their first or second jobs. Such a curriculum might have only temporary value and could easily crowd out other important purposes of undergraduate education. Devising a more appropriate preparation, however, presents a number of problems How much time should faculties allot to the purpose in view of the other aims of a college education? How can vocational and liberal arts courses reinforce each other instead of existing in isolation, or even at cross-purposes with one another? Will vocational courses of the traditional kind actually help undergraduates to have a successful career, or will a solid grounding in the liberal arts accomplish more over the long run? These are questions that call for answers from any college with substantial numbers of students moving directly into the workforce. What is not justifiable-nor even practical-is to reject out of hand the very possibility of vocational courses or the legitimacy of preparing students for productive, satisfying careers.

This completes my list of the basic goals of undergraduate education. Although these aims have been treated separately for purposes of clarity, they interact and overlap in many important ways. Courses on moral reasoning help to develop skills in critical thinking and do so using problems that are especially interesting and provocative for many students. Classes in writing can also teach students to think critically and carefully. Courses that prepare students for enlightened citizenship can add breadth to their studies. Conversely, studying moral issues, or living with classmates of different races, or learning about globalization can all help develop more enlightened citizens. These reinforcing qualities do not constitute a problem but an advantage. If particular courses and activities can serve several purposes simultaneously, colleges are more likely to succeed in embracing a number of separate goals within a single four-yea curriculum.

Despite the great variety of American four-year colleges, the aims described here seem suitable not only for all students but for all institutions as well. It is hard to imagine a college that would not want to improve the critical thinking of its undergraduates, enhance their communication skills, broaden their interests, and address in some manner their vocational needs. It is equally hard to understand why every college should not try to improve students' capacity to think carefully about moral questions and to fulfill their responsibilities as citizens. Naturally institutions will differ about how best to pursue these goals. Variations in student bodies, resources, and educational philosophy will dictate different choices. Yet the basic ends to which colleges should direct their efforts seem likely to be and to remain more or less the same.

After reflecting on the purposes just listed, some readers are bound to object that worthy goals have been omitted. How about nurturing powers of imagination and creativity? Fostering leadership ability? Developing judgment and wisdom? These are all valuable aims for any college that is able to pursue them. As the preceding chapter pointed out, however, many faculties have adopted impressive goals without knowing how to achieve them. Such quixotic efforts waste students' time and often leave them disappointed and disillusioned. These are consequences every college should try to avoid. With that cautionary note, the purposes described in this chapter are included not because they are the only important goals that human ingenuity can conceive, but because they are the only worthwhile aims for colleges to pursue that this author is able to recommend with enough confidence and understanding to warrant their inclusion.

NOTES

[1] W.B. Carmochan, *The Battleground of the Curriculum: Liberal Education and American Experience* (1993), p. 126.

[2] Bruce Wilshire, *The Morel Collapse of the University: Professionalism, Purity, and Alienation* (1990), p. xxiv.

[3] Charles Anderson, *Prescribing the Life of the Mind: An Essy on the Aims of Liberal Education, the Competence of Citizens, and the Cultivation of Practical Reason* (1993), p. 4.

[4] Bill Readings, *The University in Ruins* (1996), p. 6.

[5] Stanley Fish, *"Aim Low,"* 49 *Chronicle of Higher Education* (May 16, 2003), p. C5.

[7] Ibid. Fish also suggests that efforts to make students more moral or better citizens might violate the university's neutrality on political issues and hence provoke retaliation from external sources. It strains belief, however, to suppose that society would try to retaliate against a college for encouraging students to vote, or participate in their communities, or keep their word, tell the truth, and refrain from unjustified acts of violence.

[8] Ibid.

[9] Norman Nie, Jane Junn, and Kenneth Stehlik-Barry, *Education and Democratic Citizenship in America* (1996). In the same vein, Robert Putnam has concluded: "Education is by far the strongest correlate that I have discovered of civic engagement in all its forms." 'The Strange Disappearance of Civic America," *The American Prospect* (Winter 1996), pp. 36-37.

[10] See, for example, Alexander W. Astin and Linda J. Sax, "How Undergraduates Are Affected by Service Participation," 39 *Journal of College Student Development* (1998), p. 259.

[11] See, for example, Patricia Gurin, Eric L. Dey, Sylvia Hurtado, and Gerald Gurin. *"Diversity and Higher Education,"* 72 *Harvard Educational Review* (2002), p. 330.

[12] Frank Lentricchia, *Criticism and Social Change* (1983), p.2.

[13] Frederic Jameson, "Marxism and Teaching," 2/3 *New Political Science* (1979/1980), pp. 31, 32.

[14] In Darryl J. Glass and Barbara H. Smith (eds.), *The Politics of Liberal Education* (1992), pp. 128, 135.

[15] Introduction to Henry A. Giroux and Kostas Myrsiades (eds.), *Beyond the Corporate University* (2001), p. 40.

[16] Idem, p. 5.

[17] Idem, p. 8.

[18] See, for example, James A. Berlin, *Rhetoric, Poetics, and Cultures: Refiguring College English Studies* (1996).

[19] See Sharon Crowley, *Composition in the University: Historical and Polemical Essays* (1998), pp. 64-72; Mary Trachsel, *Institutionalizing Literacy* (1992).

[20] See Lion E Gardiner, *Redesigning Higher Education: Producing Dramatic Gains in Student Learning* (1994), p. 2; a later study from 1998-99 found that 99.5 percent of faculty in four-year colleges consider an "ability to think clearly" to be "essential" or "very important," Linda I. Sax, Alexander W. Astin, William S. Korn and Shannon K. Gilmartin, *The American College Teacher: National Norms for the 1989-1999 HERI Faculty Survey* (1999), p. 36.

[21] John E. McPeck, *Critical Thinking and Education* (1981); see also Edward Thorndike, *Principles of Teaching* (1906), especially p. 246.

[22] For example, Gabriel Salomon and David N. Perkins, "Rocky Roads to Transfer: Rethinking Mechanism of a Neglected Phenomenon" 24 *Educational Psychologist* (1989), p. 113; Darrin R Lehman and Richard E. Nisbett, "A Longitudinal Study of the Effects of Undergraduate Training on Reasoning," 26 *Developmental Psychology* (1990), p. 952.

[23] For example, Wilbert J. McKeachie, Paul Patrick, Y. Guang Lin, and David A. F. Smith, *Teaching and Learning in the College Classroom: A Review of the Research Literature* (1986), p. 35; Richard E. Nisbett, Geofftey T Fong, Darrin R. Lehman, and Patricia W. Cheng, "Teaching Reasoning," 238 *Science* (1987), p. 625.

[24] For example, William A. Galston, "Political Knowledge, Political Engagement and Civic Education," 4 *Annual Review of Political Science* (2001), pp. 217-19; see generally Warren E. Miller and J. Merrill Shanks, *The New America Voter* (1996).

[25] Martin Luther King Jr., *Where Do We Go from Here: Chaos or Community?* (1968), p. 167.

[26] "Curricula that emphasize breadth of knowledge may prevent organization of knowledge because there is not enough time to learn anything in depth." John D. Bransford, Ann L. Brown, and Rodney R Cocking (eds.), *How People Learn: Brain, Mind, Experience, and School* (1999), p. 5.

[27] Aristotle, *Politics* (Jowett translation, Book 8, Section 2) (1905), p. 301.

[28] William D. Schaefer, *Education without Compromise: From Chaos to Coherence in Higher Education* (1990), p. 126.

[29] Robert Paul Wolff, *The Ideal of the University* (1969), p. 20.

The Educated Person

Thomas B. Jones

In this reading, Thomas B. Jones, professor at Metropolitan State University in Minnesota, reflects on his experiences as a student and how his college years might have been more valuable.

As you read, think about what Jones' commencement speaker said about the importance of the question, "What is an educated person?" What were the consequences for Professor Jones of never having questioned the prescribed curriculum of his college?

My interest in the educated person question goes back a long way. Just how far back was confirmed the other day when I found a tattered, twenty-year-old file containing my diploma, my transcripts and a list of graduation requirements. These documents took me back to a hot June day in 1964. The day I graduated from college. . .

At 11 A.M., several thousand black-cloaked comrades and I gathered outside the football stadium for the graduation ceremony. Soon we trooped into the stadium and spread over row upon row of folding chairs parked between the 20- and 50-yard lines. Once seated, I started daydreaming, imagining myself quarterbacking a dazzling, length-of-the-field touchdown drive. Unfortunately, the droning of innumerable deans and dignitaries bogged down my football fantasy well short of the goal line.

Frustrated in my make-believe athletic glory, I tried to forget the sweaty heat and tried even harder to focus on the major commencement speaker. Only his final words caught my attention.

He spoke earnestly about the need for students to reflect on the question: "What is an educated person?" He said that answers to that question should be the preface, substance, and measure of an undergraduate education. For those of us planning to continue on in academic life as college faculty, the speaker emphasized that the educated person question should be at the center of our professional lives.

"What the hell is he babbling about," asked one of my friends, still suffering the after effects of the previous night's party. I laughed and said, "I have absolutely no idea."

But that wasn't quite true. I understood much of what the commencement speaker had said, and I took him seriously at that moment because I planned a career in college teaching.

I didn't, however, remember that the university had ever discussed the educated person question with me or any of my classmates. And it seemed odd that the last

Excerpt from "The Educated Person" in *The Educated Person: A Collection of Contemporary American Essays* edited by Thomas B. Jones (St. Paul, MN: Metropolitan State University. Revised edition, 1989, pp. 101-105. Reprinted with permission from Thomas B. Jones, Professor, Metropolitan State University.

formal activity of undergraduate study would be the first mention of this conse-
quential question. If, as the commencement speaker had so strongly suggested, the
question had such importance for higher education, my classmates and I should
have discussed it at some point before we graduated. But we never had.

We had completed our college education without discussing the educated person question, without questioning the rationale behind graduation requirements,
without any process by which to plan out four years of undergraduate study, and
without any standards we understood by which to judge our educational progress. We just drifted from one classroom to another, followed the required paths
toward graduation, and never took responsibility for making our own academic
decisions. Speaking for myself, only by chance did I acquire some of the essential
perspectives I identify now, many years after the fact, as essential for becoming
an educated person.

Of course, the transcript of my college education—a curious jumble of numbers,
course abbreviations, and A, B and Cs—gives the impression that I gained the
depth of breadth of learning so honored by college presidents in their graduation
speeches and fundraising pitches. But I know better. That transcript merely charts
my stumbling, unwitting progress toward graduation.

I know today that I didn't master a number of important subjects and skills
during my undergraduate years. I certainly had but little exposure to interdisciplinary thinking and teaching. I didn't appreciate the values and abilities that survive
the memory of specific course content and give college study its strongest hold
on life. And finally, I couldn't explain to anyone with any measure of confidence
and sophistication exactly why my college education gave me any special claim
to being an educated person.

What if I had confronted the educated person question as an undergraduate
student? Why would it have made a difference?

The process of posing the educated person question and searching for legitimate
answers to it would have been invaluable for me as I started and as I progressed
through college. Digging out the answers would have made it possible for me
to plan my college study with some larger vision—even within the structured
system of graduation requirements I faced. I could have understood better why
certain subjects had to be included in my education. I could have looked for the
understandings and skills in each learning experience that would serve me in
study across the curriculum and in the contexts of life outside the college classroom. I could have tried a wider range of study with my elective choices rather
than building a specialized major and minor. I could have seen more clearly the
relationship between various disciplines and how they can strengthen and enliven
each other. I could have judged the value of my overall college education as well as
the academic reasoning that stood behind it. Most important, I could have known
that becoming an educated person is part of a lifelong process of learning, study,
reflection, experience and action—not just four years of classes.

Activites and Questions for Reflection

1. What is your conception of an educated person as you begin your current studies? To provide information to help you begin defining an educated person, select several people you know, admire, and consider to be educated and ask them how they would describe an educated person. After reflecting on your discussions and your own ideas, write several paragraphs describing your ideal educated person. You may wish to use someone you know as a model, or you may wish to describe an ideal combining characteristics you think are important.

2. Do you see any gaps between your present knowledge and the qualities of the educated person you described? What are they?

A major section of this text will be devoted to readings that explore the ways college can help you become an educated person. Given this knowledge you will not drift from one course to another as in Jones' description of his college experience. You will be able to select and undertake your further college studies with a greater understanding and appreciation of how college can contribute to your development as an educated person.

What Does Society Need From Higher Education?

David R. Pierce

The following two readings address the question, "What does society need from higher education?" Authors Pierce and Atwell carry forward the discussion about educational goals directed toward the common good. In the first reading, David R. Pierce, as President of the American Association of Community Colleges, identifies six needs of society that he believes higher education should meet. Pierce believes that what is good for the workers is good for business, and what is good for the government is good for the citizens. Workers need skills to get good jobs, and businesses need highly skilled workers to maintain their productivity. In a democracy, citizens need to be informed, and the government needs informed citizens.

As you read, think about what Pierce means by each of the social needs he describes.

Although higher education cannot solve all of society's problems, it can act as a resource. Higher education performs certain functions that cannot be done by any other segment of our society. It also supports other institutions, such as government, business, museums, etc., in vital ways.

Society requires the following from higher education:

- To train a skilled, intelligent, creative, and responsible workforce;
- To transmit, sustain, and extend the arts and humanities, the scientific tradition, the historical record, and other aspects of our living culture;
- To support a citizenry that participates responsibly in community affairs including public governance and cares about our country and the world;
- To provide a forum for integrating a multitude of peoples and synthesizing a wealth of ideologies;
- To be a resource for people searching for ideas and information on solving social, economic, political, and scientific problems;
- To give individuals access to lifelong learning in a changing world.

Training a Skilled Workforce

As society increases in complexity, its need for skilled, autonomous workers increases. The pace of change—social, technological, political, and economic—is accelerating, and with it the demand for highly skilled workers. As society moves from a manufacturing and industrial economy to a service and information economy, new skills are required. The information explosion has created a

Excerpt from "What Does Society Need from Higher Education?" in A Wingspread Group on Higher Education. An American Imperative: Higher Expectations in Higher Education (Racine, WI: The Johnson Foundation, 1993), pp. 122-124. Reprinted by permission of the Johnson Foundation, Racine, WI.

demand for people who have not only knowledge, but the resources to gather, analyze, and synthesize information, and technological advances require workers with advanced training in science, mathematics, engineering, technology, and other fields. Our economy will continue to evolve, and higher education must evolve with it, preparing workers for jobs that may not even exist yet. Society, workers, and businesses must be prepared for the unexpected—because that is what will face us in the future. Without workers who have the skills to adapt to new situations, businesses will fail. In addition, workers who lack skills for the future face a cycle of unemployment and despair. Society owes its members more, and it looks to higher education to provide citizens with the tools they require to improve their life situation.

Sustaining a Living Culture

Society does not live by bread alone—it also needs poetry. Preparing people for work gives them the means to live; the traditions and values of our culture give them a reason to live. The visual and performing arts, literature, philosophical and religious traditions, history, and social, physical, and life sciences all have merit aside from their "usefulness" in providing people with work and solving concrete problems. Knowledge, ideas, and creativity are ends in themselves; higher education must help strengthen them. There has been a storm of controversy surrounding this aspect of higher education; at times the battle over the curriculum threatens to turn into a bonfire of humanities. Although higher education has often been criticized during these turbulent times, in a sense the controversy shows that colleges and universities are doing their job. Sustaining a living culture means preserving some old ideas while abandoning others and selecting and incorporating some new ideas while rejecting others. This process cannot and should not be easy, tidy, or painless. But it is necessary.

Supporting Participatory Democracy

If we lived in an authoritarian nation ruled by a small group, society would have much less need for universal education. However, our society requires of citizens that they participate in their own governance. Under a democratic system, the government is only as good as the people who elect it—sometimes worse. If we want a government based upon intelligence, compassion, ethics, and excellence, we must inculcate those values in our future leaders and citizens. Citizens must be aware of the needs and problems of the community so that the political process will be energized to confront the problems. Community colleges can address these issues through programs to inform and educate the citizens, through activities that provide a forum and a voice for the diverse concerns and interests within a community, and through work with other institutions in the community to ensure the interests of all are represented and heard. As Thomas Jefferson said, "If a nation expects to be ignorant and free, in a state of civilization, it expects what never was and never will be."

Integrating Diverse People and Ideologies

As our nation becomes more diverse and our world becomes smaller, society has an ever-greater need to expose all of its members to other cultures and ideologies. To maintain a coherent and peaceful society—both national and global—requires that our people understand and accept one another—even if they do not always agree. The goal is not a homogeneous society, but a respectful one.

Providing Resources for Solving Problems

Like museums and libraries, which often maintain close ties to institutions of higher education, colleges and universities are resources for businesses, government agencies, organizations, and individuals doing research into a wide variety of questions. While our society's technological and scientific progress boggles the mind, our intellectual and spiritual progress has not kept pace with the multitude of social problems that now plague us. Society is in desperate need of assistance in combating poverty, pollution, social unrest, racism, sexism, crime, and many other problems. Higher education, as other segments of society, must do whatever it can to help overcome the many obstacles we face. While higher education cannot take sole responsibility for solving global problems, it can provide valuable resources—such as information, research, and facilities. Even more mundane, local problems faced by small businesses—such as how industrial processes work—and by individuals—such as one person's research into his or her own genealogy—may benefit from the resources available at the average institution of higher education.

Providing Access to Lifelong Learning in a Changing World

This would be a better society if everyone continued to learn. So goes the conventional wisdom. Simply encourage people who want to learn and the battle is nearly won. Well that just isn't so. For one thing, it's a lot tougher to find access to learning than one might think. Barriers to access such as financial constraints, fear, complacency, age, sex or race discrimination are road blocks to learning. The open door of the community college is the access point to postsecondary education for all members of the community. This is often the most meaningful expression of equality in a community. This access must be supported by appropriate financial aid policies. It must be made real by the provision of remediation programs, occupational programs, and transfer programs. Ernest Boyer said that the purpose of education is to "empower individuals to live competently in their communities." That is an appropriate role for higher education; it is an appropriate role for the community college.

Activities and Questions for Reflection

1. Do you understand what Pierce means by moving from a "manufacturing and industrial economy" to a "service and information economy"? How would this affect the planning of a college education intended to prepare you for the future?

2. Pierce believes that sustaining "a living culture" is one of the goals of higher education. Why does he believe that this produces controversy?

3. What did Thomas Jefferson mean when he said that a nation would not be both ignorant and free?

4. What relationship do you see between this reading and the two previous readings in this chapter with respect to the societal expectations of colleges?

5. Do you want to change or expand any of your own college purposes? You might want to review again your own statement of college goals and make any adjustments based on ideas from this reading.

What Does Society Need from Higher Education?

Robert H. Atwell

In the second reading, addressing the question," What does society need form higher education?" Robert H. Atwell, as President of the American Council on Education, identifies three basic needs of society that higher education should meet. He believes providing for these needs is an essential role of higher education in a democratic society, but some persons would disagree with him.

As you read, consider the significance for our society of each of the educational needs Atwell identifies and why they might be controversial.

Most contemporary discussions of society's requirements of higher education begin with economic considerations—most often, the need for colleges and universities to prepare students to work and compete in the global economy of the twenty-first century. We often hear a similarly instrumental approach advocated for university research, that it should be the source of scientific advances and technological development that improve the nation's health and contribute to the strength of its economy.

I take no exception to either of these views, and to one degree or another, have argued them myself. However, for purposes of this brief paper, I want to distinguish between what society *wants* from higher education—a list that seems to expand daily and one that includes many legitimate expectations—and what a base society *needs*. In the latter category I place a set of interrelated roles and functions: the teaching of citizenship and values; the academy as an independent critic of society; and higher education as an agent of social change.

As valuable as these roles and functions are, many members of society would not view them as self-evidently desirable, and some might actively oppose them. Nonetheless, I would maintain that if higher education fails to fulfill these roles and functions, it will undermine both our democratic society and the support on which it depends for its continued vitality.

Teaching Citizenship and Values

Higher education is not value neutral. The essence of liberal learning—what distinguishes higher education from vocational training—is the communication of a basic set of values, including acceptance, understanding, a love of learning, and a devotion to free inquiry and free expression. Debates over the core curriculum or canon often miss the point that liberal learning is fundamentally expansive

Excerpt from "What Does Society Need from Higher Education?" In Wingspread Group on Higher Education. *An American Imperative: Higher Expectations in Higher Education* (Racine, WI: The Johnson Foundation, 1993), pp. 122-124. Reprinted by permission of the Johnson Foundation, Racine, WI.

and inclusive. Much as we might like to reach agreement on a set of facts, ideas, and works, familiarity with which would define and individual as educated, accomplishing such a goal is a hopeless—and perhaps pointless—task. Insistence on its realization often springs from the spirit of ideology rather than inquiry and runs the risk of establishing a totalitarian academic regime with little tolerance for new ideas. Indeed, in an age when the quantity of information is expanding exponentially and coming at us in ever more forms, the importance of inculcating the values named above is greater than ever. Without them, it is impossible for society to sort through its political, economic, and social dilemmas effectively, or humanely. The apportionment of health care, the application of technology, the complexities of international relations—these are but some of the challenges we face now, and will for the foreseeable future, that will test our capacity for rigorous analysis, informed judgment, moral rectitude, and devotion to democratic principles. As daunting and divisive as these challenges are, unless we approach them in this fashion our society risks Yugoslavia of the soul.

The job of colleges and universities, then, is to prepare students to be citizens who can make wise choices and exercise leadership in all spheres of society. Citizenship is not identical to patriotism—at least not the narrow notion of it that we hear expressed too often and that makes it "the last refuge of scoundrels." Citizenship requires active participation in society, in the solution of its problems, what we often now call "service." This concept of citizenship is the basis of President Clinton's call for a national service program; it should be no surprise that it has drawn an enthusiastic response from the nation's youth, as well as many of their elders. It also is behind the explosion of community service activities at colleges and universities through such programs as Campus Compact. These programs are valuable for the benefits they provide to society and the student's understanding of society. They form an important base on which any national effort should build.

Higher Education as an Independent Critic of Society

Colleges and universities often are at their best when they are most annoying, when they stand a little apart from the daily life of society and point out its flaw.

Universities can be catalytic in bringing about positive change. In Eastern Europe, the universities and their students were important engines of the fall of communism in 1989. In our own country, whatever else one might want to say about the 1960s on college campuses, I would argue that universities and their students played a fundamental role in exposing the flaws of American foreign policy and certainly helped to bring about the end of our involvement in Vietnam.

In a larger sense, however, it seems to me that universities have failed in their roles as critics of society. Derek Bok [former president of Harvard University] has pointed out that in teaching and research, universities are responsive to what society chooses to pay for, not what it needs the most. Obviously, our institutions do and will serve society. But I believe more must be done to encourage faculty members and students to assume a critical stance, to use the knowledge and resources assembled on the campus—and the time available to them—to perform this function. Criticism may not be what most citizens and officeholders want to hear, but it is essential to social progress and the functioning of a democratic society.

Higher Education as an Agent of Social Change

Transmitting values and taking a critical stance together constitute a formula for social change. There is no avoiding the fact that colleges and universities have assumed a central position in our society; the position taken and activities engaged in by academic leaders, faculty members, and students have an impact far beyond the boundaries of the campus. I believe all these actors should recognize this fact and act on it for the betterment of society and their own institutions.

Colleges and universities become agents of social change through both their internal and their external activities. Let me cite two examples: diversity and internationalization. By making our campuses—and that includes the curriculum—more inclusive and welcoming to minorities, women, and others who historically have been excluded or neglected, we foster change both within the institution and outside it. Similarly, emphasizing the study of foreign languages and cultures, promotion of increased student exchange, and developing stronger international ties among institutions changes both the campus and the broader society. Again, this is a tricky process and difficulties along the way are inevitable, especially with regard to diversity. But when those difficulties occur, we must resist the rush to regulation, the temptation to believe we can solve all problems by drafting codes and imposing punishments. At the same time, we must be prepared to argue that requiring students to learn about things, ideas, places, and people with which they are unfamiliar is not a penalty but an essential part of a liberal education.

Perhaps John Masefield [an English writer] said it best: "there are few earthly things more splendid than a University. In these days of broken frontiers and collapsing values, when the dams are down and the floods are making misery, when every future looks somewhat grim and every ancient foothold has become something of a quagmire, wherever a University stands, it stands and shines; wherever it exists, the free minds of men [and I would add women], urged on to full and fair inquiry, may still bring wisdom into human affairs."

Activities and Questions for Reflection

1. Would you agree that the needs Atwell identifies as college purposes are important in a democratic society? Why? Or why not?

2. How are Atwell's goals for a college education different from those in the previous two readings relating to the experience of various cultural and ethnic groups in our society?

3. Do the goals you have identified so far for your college education include any related to your role as a member of society? If so, what are they? If not, think about whether you want to add such a goal and how you might state it.

Saved

Malcolm X

Malcom X was born Malcom Little in Omaha, Nebraska, in 1925. After the death of his father, Malcom X became involved with life on the streets, which ultimately led to his imprisonment for burglary. Denouncing his Christian name—his slave name—he took the name "X" and became devoted to the Black Muslim movement headed by Elijah Muhammad. Malcom X's relationship with Eljah led him to become a militant leader of the black revolution. He was preaching the brotherhood of humanity when he was assassinated in 1965. The following is an excerpt from *The Autobiography of Malcom X* where he describes his "homemade education" during the time he spent in prison and his discovery of the power of learning.

Pre-reading Questions

1. What are the denotations and connotations (see the Glossary) of the word "homemade"? How would you personally relate the word "homemade" to the educational process?
2. List the steps you would take if your education were left entirely up to you, without the aid of teachers or parents. What would you do to build your vocabulary, how would you empower yourself as a writer, and how would you develop a thorough knowledge of the world around you?

It was because of my letters that I happened to stumble upon starting to acquire some kind of a homemade education.

I became increasingly frustrated at not being able to express what I wanted to convey in letters that I wrote, especially those to Mr. Elijah Muhammad.* In the street, I had been the most articulate hustler out there—I had commanded attention when I said something. But now, trying to write simple English, I not only wasn't articulate, I wasn't even functional. How would I sound writing in slang, the way I would say it, something such as, "Look, daddy, let me pull your coat about a cat, Elijah Muhammad—."

Many who today hear me somewhere in person, or on television, or those who read something I've said, will think I went to school far beyond the eighth grade. This impression is due entirely to my prison studies.

---

*Elijah Muhammad was a leader of the Black Muslims' Temple of Islam in the 1940s, 1950s, and 1960s.

It had really begun back in the Charlestown Prison, when Bimbi first made me feel envy of his stock of knowledge. Bimbi had always taken charge of any conversations he was in, and I had tried to emulate him. But every book I picked up had few sentences which didn't contain anywhere from one to nearly all of the words that might as well have been in Chinese. When I just skipped those words, of course, I really ended up with little idea of what the book said. So I had come to the Norfolk Prison Colony still going through only book-reading motions. Pretty soon, I would have quit even these motions, unless I had received the motivation that I did.

I saw that the best thing I could do was get hold of a dictionary—to study, to learn some words. I was lucky enough to reason also that I should try to improve my penmanship. It was sad. I couldn't even write in a straight line. It was both ideas together that moved me to request a dictionary along with some tablets and pencils from the Norfolk Prison Colony school.

I spent two days just riffling uncertainly through the dictionary's pages. I'd never realized so many words existed! I don't know which words I needed to learn. Finally, just to start some kind of action, I began copying.

In my slow, painstaking, ragged handwriting, I copied into my tablet everything printed on that first page, down to the punctuation marks.

I believe it took me a day. Then, aloud, I read back, to myself, everything I'd written on the tablet. Over and over, aloud, to myself, I read my own handwriting.

I woke up the next morning, thinking about those words—immensely proud to realize that not only had I written so much at one time, but I'd written words that I never knew were in the world. Moreover, with a little effort, I also could remember what many of these words meant. I reviewed the words whose meanings I didn't remember. Funny thing, from the dictionary first page right now, that "aardvark" springs to my mind. The dictionary had a picture of it, a long-tailed, long-eared, burrowing African mammal, which lives off termites caught by sticking out its tongue as an anteater does for ants.

I was so fascinated that I went on—I copied the dictionary's next page. And the same experience came when I studied that. With every succeeding page, I also learned of people and places and events from history. Actually the dictionary is like a miniature encyclopedia. Finally the dictionary's A section had filled a whole tablet—and I went on into the B's. That was the way I started copying what eventually became the entire dictionary. It went a lot faster after so much practice helped me to pick up handwriting speed. Between what I wrote in my tablet, and writing letters, during the rest of my time in prison I would guess I wrote a million words.

I suppose it was inevitable that as my word-base broadened, I could for the first time pick up a book and read and now begin to understand what the book was saying. Anyone who has read a great deal can imagine the new world that opened. Let me tell you something: from then until I left that prison, in every free moment I had, if I was not reading in the library, I was reading on my bunk. You couldn't have gotten me out of books with a wedge. Between Mr. Muhammad's teachings, my correspondence, my visitors—usually Ella and Reginald—and my reading of books, months passed without my even thinking about being imprisoned. In fact, up to then, I never had been so truly free in my life.

The Norfolk Prison Colony's library was in the school building. A variety of classes was taught there by instructors who came from such places as Harvard and Boston universities. The weekly debates between inmate teams were also held in the school building. You would be astonished to know how worked up convict debaters and audiences would get over subjects like "Should Babies Be Fed Milk?"

Available on the prison library's shelves were books on just about every general subject. Much of the big private collection that Parkhurst had willed to the prison was still in crates and boxes in the back of the library—thousands of old books. Some of them looked ancient: covers faded, old-time parchment-looking binding. Parkhurst, I've mentioned, seemed to have been principally interested in history and religion. He had the money and the special interest to have a lot of books that you wouldn't have in general circulation. Any college library would have been lucky to get that collection.

As you can imagine, especially in a prison where there was heavy emphasis on rehabilitation, an inmate was smiled upon if he demonstrated an unusually intense interest in books. There was a sizable number of well-read inmates, especially the popular debaters. Some were said by many to be practically walking encyclopedias. They were almost celebrities. No university would ask any student to devour literature as I did when this new world opened to me, of being able to read and understand.

I read more in my room than in the library itself. An inmate who was known to read a lot could check out more than the permitted maximum number of books. I preferred reading in the total isolation of my own room.

When I had progressed to really serious reading, every night at about ten p.m. I would be outraged with the "lights out." It always seemed to catch me right in the middle of something engrossing. Fortunately, right outside my door was a corridor light that cast a glow into my room. The glow was enough to read by, once my eyes adjusted to it. So when "lights out" came, I would sit on the floor where I could continue reading in that glow.

At one-hour intervals the night guards paced past every room. Each time I heard the approaching footsteps, I jumped into bed and feigned sleep. And as soon as the guard passed, I got back out of bed onto the floor area of that light-glow, where I would read for another 58 minutes—until the guard approached again. That went on until three or four every morning. Three or four hours of sleep a night was enough for me. Often in the years in the streets I had slept less than that.

The teachings of Mr. Muhammad stressed how history had been "whitened"—when white men had written history books, the black man simply had been left out. Mr. Muhammad couldn't have said anything that would have struck me much harder. I had never forgotten how when my class, me and all of those whites, had studied seventh-grade United States history back in Mason, the history of the Negro had been covered in one paragraph, and the teacher had gotten a big laugh with his joke, "Negroes' feet are so big that when they walk, they leave a hole in the ground."

This is one reason why Mr. Muhammad's teachings spread so swiftly all over the United States, among all Negroes, whether or not they became followers of Mr. Muhammad. The teachings ring true—to every Negro. You can hardly show me a black adult in America—or a white one, for that matter—who knows from the history books anything like the truth about the black man's role. In my own case, once I heard of the "glorious history of the black man," I took special pains to hunt in the library for books that would inform me on details about black history.

I can remember accurately the very first set of books that really impressed me. I have since bought that set of books and I have it at home for my children to read as they grow up. It's called *Wonders of the World*. It's full of pictures of archeological finds, statues that depict, usually, non-European people.

I found books like Will Durant's *Story of Civilization*. I read H. G. Wells' *Outline of History*. *Souls of Black Folk* by W.E.B. Du Bois gave me a glimpse into the black people's history before they came to this country. Carter G. Woodson's *Negro History* opened my eyes about black empires before the black slave was brought to the United States, and the early Negro struggles for freedom.

J. A. Rogers' three volumes of *Sex and Race* told about race-mixing before Christ's time; about Aesop being a black man who told fables; about Egypt's Pharaohs; about the great Coptic Christian Empires; about Ethiopia, the earth's oldest continuous black civilization, as China is the oldest continuous civilization.

Mr. Muhammad's teaching about how the white man had been created led me to *Findings in Genetics* by Gregor Mendel. (The dictionary's G section was where I had learned what "genetics" meant.) I really studied this book by the Austrian monk. Reading it over and over, especially certain sections, helped me to understand that if you started with a black man, a white man could be produced; but starting with a white man, you never could produce a black man—because the white chromosome is recessive. And since no one disputes that there was but one Original Man, the conclusion is clear.

During the last year or so, in the *New York Times*, Arnold Toynbee used the word "bleached" in describing the white man. (His words were: "White [i.e. bleached] human beings of North European origin ...") Toynbee also referred to the European geographic area as only a peninsula of Asia. He said there is no such thing as Europe. And if you look at the globe, you will see for yourself that America is only an extension of Asia. (But at the same time Toynbee is among those who have helped to bleach history. He has written that Africa was the only continent that produced no history. He won't write that again. Every day now, the truth is coming to light.)

I never will forget how shocked I was when I began reading about slavery's total horror. It made such an impact upon me that it later became one of my favorite subjects when I became a minister of Mr. Muhammad's. The world's most monstrous crime, the sin and the blood on the white man's hands, are almost impossible to believe. Books like the one by Frederick Olmstead opened my eyes to the horrors suffered when the slave was landed in the United States. The European woman, *Fannie Kimball*, who had married a Southern white slaveowner, described how human beings were degraded. Of course I read *Uncle Tom's Cabin*. In fact, I believe that's the only novel I have ever read since I started serious reading.

Parkhurst's collection also contained some bound pamphlets of the Abolitionist Anti-Slavery Society of New England. I read descriptions of atrocities, saw those illustrations of black slave women tied up and flogged with whips; of black mothers watching their babies being dragged off, never to be seen by their mothers again;

of dogs after slaves, and of the fugitive slave catchers, evil white men with whips and clubs and chains and guns. I read about the slave preacher Nat Turner, who put the fear of God into the white slavemaster. Nat Turner wasn't going around preaching pie-in-the-sky and "non-violent" freedom for the black man. There in Virginia one night in 1831, Nat and seven other slaves started out at his master's home and through the night they went from one plantation "big house" to the next, killing, until by the next morning 57 white people were dead and Nat had about 70 slaves follow him. White people, terrified for their lives, fled from their homes, locked themselves up in public buildings, hid in the woods, and some even left the state. A small army of soldiers took two months to catch and hang Nat Turner. Somewhere I have read where Nat Turner's example is said to have inspired John Brown to invade Virginia and attack Harper's Ferry nearly thirty years later, with thirteen white men and five Negroes.

I read Herodotus, "the father of History," or, rather, I read about him. And I read the histories of various nations, which opened my eyes gradually, then wider and wider, to how the whole world's white men had indeed acted like devils, pillaging and raping and bleeding and draining the whole world's non-white people. I remember, for instance, books such as Will Durant's *The Story of Oriental Civilization,* and Mahatma Gandhi's accounts of the struggle to drive the British out of India.

Book after book showed me how the white man had brought upon the world's black, brown, red, and yellow peoples every variety of the sufferings of exploitation. I saw how since the sixteenth century, the so-called "Christian trader" white man began to ply the seas in his lust for Asian and African empires, and plunder, and power. I read, I saw, how the white man never has gone among the non-white peoples bearing the Cross in the true manner and spirit of Christ's teachings— meek, humble, and Christlike. ,

I perceived, as I read, how the collective white man had been actually nothing but a piratical opportunist who used Faustian machinations to make his own Christianity his initial wedge in criminal conquests. First, always "religiously," he branded "heathen" and "pagan" labels upon ancient non-white cultures and civilizations. The stage thus set, he then turned upon his non-white victims his weapons of war.

I read how, entering India—half a billion deeply religious brown people—the British white man, by 1759, through promises, trickery and manipulations, controlled much of India through Great Britain's East India Company. The parasitical British administration kept tentacling out to half of the subcontinent. In 1857, some of the desperate people of India finally mutinied—and, excepting the African slave trade, nowhere has history recorded any more unnecessary bestial and ruthless human carnage than the British suppression of the non-white Indian people.

Over 115 million African blacks—close to the 1930's population of the United States—were murdered or enslaved during the slave trade. And I read how when the slave market was glutted, the cannibalistic white powers of Europe next carved up, as their colonies, the richest areas of the black continent. And Europe's chancelleries for the next century played a chess game of naked exploitation and power from Cape Horn to Cairo.

Ten guards and the warden couldn't have torn me out of those books. Not even Elijah Muhammad could have been more eloquent than those books were in providing indisputable proof that the collective white man had acted like a devil in virtually every contact he had with the world's collective non-white man. I listen today to the radio, and watch television, and read the headlines about the collective white man's fear and tension concerning China. When the white man professes ignorance about why the Chinese hate him so, my mind can't help flashing back to what I read, there in prison, about how the blood forebears of this same white man raped China at a time when China was trusting and helpless. Those original white "Christian traders" sent into China millions of pounds of opium. By 1839, so many of the Chinese were addicts that China's desperate government destroyed twenty thousand chests of opium. The first Opium War was promptly declared by the white man. Imagine! Declaring war upon someone who objects to being narcotized! The Chinese were severely beaten, with Chinese-invented gunpowder.

The Treaty of Nanking made China pay the British white man for the destroyed opium: forced open China's major ports to British trade; forced China to abandon Hong Kong; fixed China's import tariffs so low that cheap British articles soon flooded in, maiming China's industrial development.

After a second Opium War, the Tientsin Treaties legalized the ravaging opium trade, legalized a British-French-American control of China's customs. China tried delaying that Treaty's ratification; Peking was looted and burned.

"Kill the foreign white devils!" was the 1901 Chinese war cry in the Boxer Rebellion. Losing again, this time the Chinese were driven from Peking's choicest areas. The vicious, arrogant white man put up the famous signs, "Chinese and dogs not allowed."

Red China after World War 11 closed its doors to the Western white world. Massive Chinese agricultural, scientific, and industrial efforts are described in a book that Life magazine recently published. Some observers inside Red China have reported that the world never has known such a hate-white campaign as is now going on in this non-white country where, present birthrates continuing, in fifty more years Chinese will be half the earth's population. And it seems that some Chinese chickens will soon come home to roost, with China's recent successful nuclear tests.

Let us face reality. We can see in the United Nations a new world order being shaped, along color lines—an alliance among the non-white nations. America's U.N. Ambassador Adlai Stevenson complained not long ago that in the United Nations "a skin game" was being played. He was right. He was facing reality. A "skin game" is being played. But Ambassador Stevenson sounded like Jesse James accusing the marshal of carrying a gun. Because who in the world's history ever has played a worse "skin game" than the white man?

Mr. Muhammad, to whom I was writing daily, had no idea of what a new world had opened up to me through my efforts to document his teachings in books.

When I discovered philosophy, I tried to touch all the landmarks of philosophical development. Gradually, I read most of the old philosophers, Occidental and Oriental. The Oriental philosophers were the ones I came to prefer; finally, my impression was that most Occidental philosophy had largely been borrowed from the Oriental thinkers. Socrates, for instance, traveled in Egypt. Some sources even say that Socrates was initiated into some of the Egyptian mysteries. Obviously Socrates got some of his wisdom among the East's wise men.

I have often reflected upon the new vistas that reading opened to me. I knew right there in prison that reading had changed forever the course of my life. As I see it today, the ability to read awoke inside me some long dormant craving to be mentally alive. I certainly wasn't seeking any degree, the way a college confers a status symbol upon its students. My homemade education gave me, with every additional book that I read, a little bit more sensitivity to the deafness, dumbness, and blindness that was afflicting the black race in America. Not long ago, an English writer telephoned me from London, asking questions. One was, "What's your alma mater?" I told him, "Books." You will never catch me with a free fifteen minutes in which I'm not studying something I feel might be able to help the black man.

Yesterday I spoke in London, and both ways on the plane across the Atlantic I was studying a document about how the United Nations proposes to insure the human rights of the oppressed minorities of the world. The American black man is the world's most shameful case of minority oppression. What makes the black man think of himself as only an internal United States issue is just a catch-phrase, two words, "civil rights." How is the black man going to get "civil rights" before first he wins his human rights? If the American black man will start thinking about his human rights, and then start thinking of himself as part of one of the world's great peoples, he will see he has a case for the United Nations.

I can't think of a better case! Four hundred years of black blood and sweat invested here in America, and the white man still has the black man begging for what every immigrant fresh off the ship can take for granted the minute he walks down the gangplank.

But I'm digressing. I told the Englishman that my alma mater was books, a good library. Every time I catch a plane, I have with me a book that I want to read—and that's a lot of books these days. If I weren't out here every day battling the white man, I could spend the rest of my life reading, just satisfying my curiosity—because you can hardly mention anything I'm not curious about. I don't think anybody ever got more out of going to prison than I did. In fact, prison enabled me to study far more intensively than I would have if my life had gone differently and I had attended some college. I imagine that one of the biggest troubles with colleges is there are too many distractions, too much panty-raiding, fraternities, and boola-boola and all of that. Where else but in a prison could I have attacked my ignorance by being able to study intensely sometimes as much as fifteen hours a day?

 Post-reading Questions

Content

1. What led Malcolm X to improve his vocabulary? That is, what were the initial problems that he had with reading, and how did these lead to his desire to build his vocabulary?
2. What steps did Malcolm X take to build his vocabulary?
3. What were his emotional responses after he copied the first page of the dictionary?
4. How did reading affect Malcolm X's outlook on life?

Strategies and Structures

1. Malcolm X starts many of his paragraphs with the first-person pronoun "I". What effect does this have on the essay, and what does it suggest about the results of education?
2. Malcolm X concludes paragraph 11 by writing "In fact, up to then, I had never been so truly free in my life," referring to his ability to read. How does this concluding statement sum up the value of a homemade, personally tailored education as opposed to the rigid learning methods often used in schools?
3. What transitions lead the reader from one step in Malcolm X's educational process to the next?
4. What phrases does Malcolm X use to keep his writing conversational? Which phrases does he use to suggest that he is educated? What is the effect of balancing these two styles? What does it suggest about the author's personality?

 ## Language and Vocabulary

1. Vocabulary: *articulate, hustler, emulate, riffling, inevitable, bunk*. As Malcolm X did, write down the entire dictionary definitions of the aforementioned words and bring them with you to your group activity.
2. In paragraph 2, Malcolm X suggests that slang cannot be written. Brainstorm a list of your own slang words. Why is slang more effective on the streets or among your peers than it is in an academic setting?

Group Activities

1. Devise some homemade, as opposed to traditional, methods for learning the above vocabulary words. Also devise some homemade study techniques that you can use in your other classes.
2. Today, there is much debate about the education of prisoners. How do you feel about this issue? Should prisoners be educated or simply be punished? In groups, prepare to debate both sides of this issue in a seminar situation.

 ## Writing Activities

1. Write a process essay wherein you explain how to acquire and use common sense to resolve the majority of the problems you encounter in daily life. Make sure that you present your material in clear, sequential steps.
2. Research a current educational program in a local prison. Describe the program in detail, answering such questions as who is involved, what are the benefits and problems, where does the program take place, when is a prisoner or instructor eligible for such a program, why is such a program in place, and how does the program work. Your job is to inform your readers about this program. (Your local research librarian can help you to find out where to get such information.)

Are We Going to Get Smarter?

Roger C. Schank

Roger C. Schank, a leading researcher in artificial intelligence, is the Distinguished Career Professor in the School of Computer Science at Carnegie Mellon, where he is also chair and chief technology officer for the Department of Cognitive Arts.

Is intelligence an absolute? Does mankind get smarter as time goes by? It depends on what you mean by intelligence, of course. Certainly we are getting more knowledgeable. Or at least it seems that way. While the average child has access to a wealth of information, considerably more than was available to children fifty years ago, there are people who claim that our children are not as well educated as they were fifty years ago and that our schools have failed us.

Today, questions about what it means to be intelligent and what it means to be educated are not at the center of our scientific inquiry, nor are they at the center of our popular discourse. Still we live our lives according to implicitly understood ideas about intelligence and about education. Those ideas will be seriously challenged in the next fifty years.

Over ten years ago, I was asked to join the board of editors of *Encyclopaedia Britannica*. The other members were mostly *octogenarians* and mostly humanists. Because I was both a scientist and much younger than everyone else, most of what I said was met with odd stares. When I asked the board if they would be happy to put out an encyclopedia ten times the size of the current one if the costs involved remained the same, they replied that, no, the current encyclopedia had just the right amount of information. I responded that they would be out of business in ten years if that were their belief. They had no idea what I meant—although I tried to explain the coming of what is now called the World Wide Web. At a later meeting, after having heard me make similar assertions about the future, Clifton Fadiman, a literary hero of the 1940s, responded, "I guess we will all have to accept the fact that minds less well educated than our own will soon be in charge of institutions like the encyclopaedia."

The chairman of the board of the *Encyclopaedia Britannica* at the time was the late Mortimer Adler. He was also responsible for a series called The Great Books of the Western World, which was (and is) sold as a set. These books represent all the great written works of the world's wisdom—according to Adler and his colleagues, anyhow—and the series consisted mostly of books written prior to the twentieth century. I asked Adler whether he thought there might be some new books that could be included, and he replied that most of the important thoughts had already been written down.

This idea, that all the great thoughts have already been thought, has been prevalent in the American idea of education and intelligence for a long time. Here are the admission requirements for Harvard College in 1745:

When any Schollar is able to read Tully or such like clasicall Latin Author ex temporare, and make and speake true Latin verse and Prose Suo (ut aiunt) Marte, and decline perfectly the paradigms of Nounes and verbes ine the Greeke tongue, then may hee bee admitted into the Colledge, nor shall any claim admission before such qualification.

What the Great Books series and Harvard of 1745 have in common is an underlying assumption that the study of man and his institutions had been sufficiently mastered in ancient times and therefore education required you to be well read and well versed in the thoughts of those who preceded you. An educated person in this view is one who is able to discuss, with *erudition,* a variety of historical, philosophical, and literary topics. Being educated—and therefore being intelligent—has, for the last century and many centuries before that, been about the accumulation of facts, the ability to quote the ideas of others, and a familiarity with certain ideas. Education has meant accumulating information and intelligence has often meant little more in the popular imagination than the ability to show off what one has accumulated.

But what happens when the facts are in the walls?

Fifty years from now, knowledge will be so easy to acquire that one will be able simply to say aloud whatever one wants to know and hear an instantaneous response from the walls—enhanced by a great deal of technology from the walls, of course. Knowing offhand what Freud had to say about the superego won't mean much when you can turn to the nearest appliance and ask what Freud had to say and hear Freud (or someone who looks and sounds a lot like him) saying it and finding five opposing thought leaders from throughout time ready to propose alternative ideas if you want to hear them and discuss them together.

But is intelligence simply the ability to be informed of answers to your questions, or is it the ability to know what questions to ask? As answers become devalued, questions become more valued. We have lived for a very long time in an answer-based society. Signs of it are everywhere: in the television shows that people watch such as *Jeopardy* and *Who Wants to Be a Millionaire?*; in the games that people play, such as Trivial Pursuit; and most of all in school, where answers are king. Increasingly, the chief concern of our schools is testing. School has become a *regimen* for learning answers rather than learning to inquire.

New technologies will change all this. When the pocket calculator was introduced, people asked whether calculators might as well be used in math tests, since from now on such devices would always be available. As a result, math tests began to focus on more substantive issues than long division. The introduction of artificial intelligence into everyday devices will have the same effect. As machines become omnipresent and able to answer questions about whatever concerns us, the values we place on each individual's being a repository of factual knowledge will diminish. The old idea of school, based on the notion that the most knowledgeable person in town had information to impart and the rest of us were forced to sit and memorize that information, will give way to new ideas of knowledge acquisition. Knowledge will no longer be seen as a commodity to be acquired. Anything obtained easily is devalued in society, and it will be the same with knowledge.

What will be valued will be good questions. *Computers can only take you so far,* we will hear people say.

Imagine the following: You're sitting in your living room, talking with your friend, and an issue comes up between you. You turn to the wall for a response.

"Who was right?" you demand. The wall points out that it has a number of virtual people available to join your conversation. You choose some characters that you have heard about or conversed with before. A lively discussion ensues. Eventually the limits of the computer's collective knowledge are reached. The walls know no more of relevance. "This, then, is an exciting question!" you exclaim. Knowing a good question makes you ready to enter into a discussion with other live humans interested in similar questions. You tell that to the walls, and suddenly the people interested in such questions—those who have gone beyond the software in the same way that you have—are all there in your living room (virtually). In a world where this is possible, what does it mean to be educated? What does it mean to be intelligent?

To think about the education part of that question, we have to ask what a child's life would be like in that world. Fifty years from now school, as we know it, will have atrophied from lack of interest. Why go to school to learn facts, when virtual experiences are readily available and the world's best teachers are virtually available at any moment? Education will mean—even from the age of two—exploring worlds of interest with intelligent guides available to answer your questions and pose new ones. World upon world will open to the child who is curious. Education in such a society will be a matter of what virtual (and later real) worlds you have entered and how much you have learned to do in those worlds.

To Fadiman's remark quoted above, I responded that minds would not be less well educated, just differently educated. In the world of Clifton Fadiman, an educated mind was one that had been trained at Harvard (or its equivalent) and was conversant with the major ideas in Western thought. His idea of education did not include, for example, being able to program in Java, or understanding the basics of neuroscience. In fifty years, there will still be Harvard, but the value of its *imprimatur* will have been altered tremendously.

Education in its deepest sense has always been about doing, rather than about knowing. Many scholars throughout the years have pointed this out, from Aristotle ("For the things we have to learn before we can do them, we learn by doing them") to Galileo ("You cannot teach a man anything; you can only help him discover it within himself") to A. S. Neill ("I hear and I forget; I see and I remember; I do and I understand") to Einstein ("The only source of knowledge is experience"). Nevertheless, schools have ignored this wisdom and chosen—in the words of John Dewey—to "teach by pouring in."

The virtual schools that will arise to take the place of current institutions will attract students less because of the credentials they bestow than because of the experiences they offer. Since these experiences will be there for the taking when a learner decides to learn, most students will start college long before the age of eighteen. Success in various virtual experiences will encourage us to encounter new ones, much as video games do today. Certifying agencies will worry more about what you can do—what virtual merit badges you have achieved—than what courses you have taken.

Fields of endeavor will create experiences in those fields. Instead of Harvard or Columbia offering courses in physics, physicists from around the world will work with virtual-educational–world designers who will build software to create physics experiences. Those experiences will be available to everyone. The old idea that the smartest people were those who received the best grades from schools that tested them to see how well they had learned the lessons will morph into a notion that the smartest students are the ones who pose questions for the software that have to be sent to humans in order to be answered. Intelligence will mean the ability to reach the limits of an educational experience.

Will we collectively be smarter as a society because of all these innovations? In terms of raw capacity for thought, people are as smart now as they ever were or ever will be. But a brilliant cave dweller who had available to him limited knowledge of the world and limited wisdom from the ages, could work only within the *parameters* of the tools he knew. He may have understood the nature of humans and their institutions as well as the Greeks who followed him. But in any absolute sense he wasn't too smart, because there was so much that he hadn't experienced.

Each generation improves on the experiences it opens up to the next. But a leap of tremendous proportions is coming in the next generation. The fact that we still have teachers and classrooms and textbooks will be almost laughable in fifty years. People will look back at us and ask why it took so long for us to change our notions of education, why we thought SAT scores mattered, or why we thought memorizing answers was a mark of intelligence in any way. The notion that education is about indoctrination by the state—an idea boldly stated in the 1700s and little acknowledged today—will seem scary. The governmental control of information—still popular in some countries and still possible in those countries without computer access—will become an archaic notion. Too much experience will be available too readily and too cheaply to prevent anyone from experiencing anything. Governments will have to give up even imagining that they are in the education business, an area they dominate today, and will be unable to control the broad distribution of virtual experiences in much the way that they are failing to control television and computer access in country after country today.

We will begin to understand in the next fifty years that experience and one's ability to extend its range is the ultimate measure of intelligence and the ultimate expression of freedom. The creation of virtual experience will become a major industry; our homes will be dominated by virtual experiences; our schools will have been replaced by them. What we see today in video games and science fiction movies will become our reality. Today, games like EverQuest attract hundreds of thousands of players, who inhabit virtual worlds in an effort to gain status, form relationships, and acquire various virtual objects. These games are so real to the participants that the virtual objects they employ are for sale (for hefty prices) on online auction sites. Some players of these games have a social life entirely based upon them. In the future, these worlds will become much more sophisticated and even more intertwined with the real world.

It is what we can do, not what we know, that will matter in an educational system based on realistic performance environments. The important intellectual issues will revolve around questions arising from the nature of students' interactions in the virtual educational world.

When educational environments demand questions, ask how questions were obtained, and demand to know the experiences that brought on those questions, then the profound change that computers offer will have been realized. We will all be smarter—a great deal smarter—in the sense that we will not be afraid of new experiences. We will know how to find those experiences and will grow from them. Our minds will be differently educated and our intellectual world will be dominated neither by humanists nor by scientists but by experientialists, those who have been there and have become curious as a result.

CHAPTER 4

WHAT IS THE VALUE OF A COLLEGE EDUCATION?

To My Fellow Students:

The purpose of going to college is to graduate with a degree, right? You go in, take the classes you need, pay your tuition and registration fees, and buy numerous stacks of books. What more could there be? Frankly, a lot.

Attaining a college education is more than getting a degree. It's more than attending classes, participating in discussions, and taking your finals. Some might tell you that the purpose of attending college is to guarantee you a higher paying job in your field of interest upon the completion of your degree.

Even if you decide to only earn your bachelor's degree, your education doesn't stop there. To pursue an education is to acknowledge its importance. By pursuing your degree on a campus, you have made a commitment to the values of a college education.

Your education is what you put into it and what you take out of it. The value of your education is based upon what you learn. It's the acceptance of the multitude of different views that surround you on a day-to-day basis, the expansion of your knowledge base, the appreciation of the arts and sciences and the development of your beliefs.

The campus is an important part of your education. It is on this campus that you will grow in ways you did not think were possible. Here is where conflicting ideas will come together and where, for your personal betterment, you will wade through those ideas and opinions and resurface with newfound understanding. A college education cannot happen without a campus. Sure, there are plenty of online colleges where you could attain a degree, but that's all you would get. You would miss the key experience of being part of an academic community where knowledge is constructed not only through reading books, but through face to face social interaction among people.

In the end, the value of your education is what you want from it. I could go on for pages breaking down what you should expect of your education, reasons for completing a degree, and even how to determine which degrees would best suit your needs and interests. But in doing that, would I really be answering the question of what a college education means to you? Would I be able to tell you why you are here and why you wish to pursue a degree? How can anyone tell you how to value your college education? No two people are alike; as such no two college experiences will be the same. As you are unique, so too will your education be.

I wish you the best as you pursue a life of learning and personal development, a path that begins now as you start on the road of higher education.

Best Wishes, Kaely Mullins

Kaely Mullins
Peer Mentor 09, English
and Film Studies Major

"It is not so very important for a person to learn facts. For that he does not really need a college. He can learn them from books. The value of an education in a liberal arts college is not learning of many facts but the training of the mind to think something that cannot be learned from textbooks."

–Albert Einstein

Having a Degree and Being Educated
Edmund D. Pellegrino, M.D.

Edmund D. Pellegrino is professor emeritus of medicine and medical ethics at Georgetown University. This essay was a commencement address given by Dr. Pellegrino at Wilkes College.

Few humans live completely free of illusions. Reality is sometimes just too harsh to bear without them. But comforting as they can be, some illusions are too dangerous to be harbored for very long. Eventually they must meet the test of reality—or we slip into psychosis.

I want to examine a prevalent illusion with you today—one to which you are most susceptible at this moment, namely, that *having* a degree is the same as *being* educated. It is a bit *gauche*, I admit, to ask embarrassing questions at a time of celebration. But your personal happiness and the world you create depend on how well your illusion is brought into focus. And this *emboldens* me to intrude briefly on the satisfaction you justly feel with your academic accomplishment.

The degree you receive today is only a certificate of exposure, not a guarantee of infection. Some may have caught the virus of education, others only a mild case, and still others may be totally immune. To which category do you belong? Should you care? How can you tell?

The illusion of an education has always plagued the honest person. It is particularly seductive in a technological society like ours. We intermingle education with training, and liberal with professional studies, so intimately that they are hard to disentangle. We reward specific skills in politics, sports, business, and academia. We exalt those who can *do* something—those who are experts.

It becomes easy to forget that free and civilized societies are not built on information alone. Primitive and despotic societies have their experts too! Computers and animals can be trained to store and retrieve information, to learn, and even to out-perform us. What they can never do is direct the wise use of their information. They are imprisoned by their programmers and their own expertise. The more intensive that expertise, the more it cages them; the less they can they function outside its restricted perimeter.

In a technological society experts proliferate like toadstools on a damp lawn. Some are genuine. Others are quick studies specializing in the predigestion of other people's thoughts. They crowd the TV screens, the radio waves, the printed page, eager to tell us what to believe and how to live—from sex and politics to religion and international affairs. They manufacture our culture, give us our opinions and our conversational *gambits*.

Now that you have a degree in something, you are in danger of stepping quietly into the cage of your own expertise—leaving everything else to the other experts. Whether they are genuine or phony makes little difference. If you do, you sacrifice the most precious endowment of an education—the freedom to

Reprinted by permission of the author.

make up your own mind—to be an authentic person. Knowledge, as Santayana said, is recognition of something absent. It is a salutation—not an embrace—a beginning, not an end.

You cannot predict when you will be brutally confronted by the falsity of your illusion like the juror who was interviewed following a recent murder trial. He was responding to one of those puerile how-does-it-feel questions that is the trademark of the telecaster's *vacuity*. "Being a juror was a terrible thing," he said. "I had to think like I never thought before. . . . I had to understand words like justice and truth. . . . Why do they make people like us judges?"

This is the pathetic lament of a sincere, sympathetic, but uneducated man. He was surely an expert in something but he could not grapple with the kind of question that separates humans from animals and computers. Justice and truth are awesome questions indeed. But who should answer those questions? Is being a juror another specialty? Do we need a degree in justice and truth? Does not a civilized and democratic society depend upon some common comprehension of what these words mean?

These same questions underlie every important public and private decision— from genetic engineering to nuclear proliferation, from prolonging human life to industrial pollution. They determine *how* we should use our expert knowledge, *whether* we should use it, and *for what* purposes. The welfare of the nation and the world depend on our capacity to think and act rightly— not on the amount of information we have amassed.

To be a juror, to be a person, to live with satisfaction, requires more than a trained mind—it requires an educated one, a mind that does not parrot other men's opinions or values but frames its own, a mind that can resist the potential tyranny of experts, one that can read, write, speak, manipulate symbols, argue, and judge, and whose imagination is as free as its reason.

These attributes are not synonymous with simple exposure to what is *euphemistically* called an education in the humanities or liberal arts, even when these are genuine—as often they are not. That belief only piles one illusion upon another. Rather than courses taken, or degrees conferred, the true tests of an educated mind are in its operations. Let me suggest some questions that indicate whether your mind operates like an educated one—no matter what your major may have been.

First, have you learned how to learn without your teacher? Can you work up a new subject, find the information, separate the relevant from the trivial, and express it in your own language? Can you discern which are your teacher's thoughts and which are your own? Your first freedom must be from the subtle despotism of even a great teacher's ideas.

Second, can you ask critical questions, no matter what subject is before you— those questions that expose a line of argument, evaluate the claims being made upon you, the evidence adduced, the logic employed? Can you sift fact from opinion, the plausible from the proven, the rhetorical from the logical? Can you use skepticism as a constructive tool and not as a refuge for intellectual sloth? Do you apply the same critical rigor to your own thoughts and actions? Or are you merely rearranging your prejudices when you think you are thinking?

Third, do you really understand what you are reading, what people are saying, what words they are using? Is your own language clear, concrete, and concise? Are you acquainted with the literature of your own language—with its structure and nuance?

Fourth, are your actions your own—based in an understanding and commitment to values you can defend? Can you discern the value conflicts underlying personal and public choices and distinguish what is a compromise to principle and what is not? Is your approach to moral judgments reasoned or emotional? When all the facts are in, when the facts are doubtful and action must be taken, can you choose wisely, prudently, and reasonably?

Fifth, can you form your own reasoned judgments about works of art— whether a novel, sonata, sculpture, or painting? Or are you enslaved by the critic, the book reviewer, and the "opinion makers" vacillating with their fads and pretentiousness? Artists try to evoke experiences in us, to transform us as humans. Is your imagination free enough to respond sensitively, or are you among the multitude of those who demand the explicitness of violence, pornography, dialogue—that is the sure sign of a dead imagination and an impoverished creativity?

Sixth, are your political opinions of the same order as your school and athletic loyalties—rooting for your side and ignoring the issues and ideas your side propounds? Free societies need independent voters who look at issues and not labels, who will be loyal to their ideals, not just to parties and factions. Do you make your insight as an expert the measure of social need? There is no illusion more fatal to good government!

If you can answer yes to some of these indicators, then you have imbibed the essence of a liberal education, one which assures that your actions are under the direction of your thought, that you are your own person, no matter what courses you took and what degree you receive today. You will also have achieved what is hoped for you:

> Education is thought of as not just imparting the knowledge of a professional discipline, but also as demonstrating a certain way of life—a way of life which is humane and thoughtful, yet also critical and above all rational.

If your answers are mostly negative (and I hope they are not), then you are in danger of harboring an illusion—one that is dangerous to you and society. The paradox is that the expert too has need of an educated mind. Professional and technical people make value decisions daily. To protect those whose values they affect, to counter the distorted pride of mere information, to use their capabilities for humane ends, experts too must reflect critically on what they do. The liberal arts, precisely because they are not specialties, are the indispensable accoutrements of any mind that claims to be human.

There are two kinds of freedom without which we cannot lead truly human lives. One kind is political and it is guaranteed by the Bill of Rights. The other is intellectual and spiritual and is guaranteed by an education that liberates the mind. Political freedom assures that we can express our opinions freely; a liberal education assures that the opinions we express are free. Each depends so much on the other that to threaten one is to threaten the other.

This is why I vex you with such a serious topic on this very happy occasion. The matter is too important for indifference or comfortable illusions. My hope is that by nettling you a bit I can prevent what is now a harmless illusion from becoming a delusion—firm, fixed belief, impervious either to experience or reason.

May I remind you in closing that the people who made our nation, who endowed it with the practical wisdom that distinguished its history, were people without formal degrees. One of the best among them, Abraham Lincoln, went so far as to say: "No policy that does not rest upon philosophical public opinion can be permanently maintained." Philosophical public opinion is not the work of information or expertise but of an educated mind, one that matches the aim of Wilkes to impart a way of life that is ". . . humane and thoughtful, yet also critical and above all rational."

T. S. Eliot, in his poem "The Dry Salvages," said: "We have had the experience of an education—I hope you have not missed the meaning." You have had the experience of an education—I hope you have not missed the meaning.

 ## Vocabulary

As you think about this essay, these definitions may be helpful to you:

1. **gauche**   (pronounced gosh) lacking social experience or grace
2. **embolden**   to instill with boldness or courage
3. **gambits**   in this essay, remarks intended to start a conversation or make a telling point
4. **vacuity**   the state of being empty or lacking content
5. **euphemistically**   substituting an agreeable or inoffensive expression for one that may offend or suggest something unpleasant

 ## Discussion Questions

1. Why does Dr. Pellegrino think it is an illusion that having a degree and being educated are the same?
2. What is an uneducated person, according to Pellegrino?
3. How does Pellegrino define "knowledge"?
4. List six ways that, according to Pellegrino, the mind works. Why?
5. What are the two kinds of freedom needed to live "truly human lives," according to Pellegrino?

Suggestions for Your Journal

How do you view a college degree? As a piece of paper that can get you a job or as a symbol of the years when you learned to become "educated"? What is your definition of being educated? Do you think it is important to think about how an educated mind works? Why?

What are some specific actions you can take to master the six ways the mind of an educated person operates during your college career? When you graduate, how will you, as Pellegrino states, use your knowledge "to think straight and act rightly," not just use the information you have accumulated in your mind?

The Baccalaureate Degree: What Does It Mean? What Should It Mean?

Howard R. Bowen

The baccalaureate degree, the traditional or historical name for what we now call the bachelor's degree, is awarded following the successful completion of the equivalent of four years of full-time college study or a minimum of 120 semester credits. The bachelor's degree is the oldest college degree and originally consisted almost exclusively of liberal arts studies. Today there are a number of different bachelor's degrees granted by colleges and universities, including the Bachelor of Arts, Bachelor of Science, Bachelor of Professional Studies. Each degree generally provides for various programs of study and for a range of specializations in each program. For example, a Bachelor of Science degree can be earned through a business studies program with a specialization in Accounting or through a natural science program with a specialization in Biology. Some bachelor degrees contain the name of the major in their titles, such as Bachelor of Science in Education.

In the following reading, author Howard R. Bowen, late professor of economics and higher education at Claremont Graduate Center, University of California, described what he viewed as the basic components of a bachelor's degree program that will lead the student to becoming a well-educated person. Bowen uses the terms personal education and practical education to identify the two major parts of his proposed program.

As you read, look for the differences in personal and practical education and for the significance of each in a bachelor's degree program.

The baccalaureate degree signifies many things. It usually refers to four academic years of time served or 120 semester credits earned. For some students, it means a broad liberal education without any training for a specific vocation; for others specialized vocational training with minimal liberal learning. For some students, it means admission at about age 18, immediately after high school graduation; for others it means admission before the completion of high school work or many years beyond the age of 18.

For some it means almost exclusive attention to required studies; for others, unrestricted electives. For some it means full-time studies combined with residence on a campus and participation in a rich extracurricular and social life; for others part-time study with residence off campus and no extracurricular participation. For some it represents the tutelage of renowned professors and access to richly appointed libraries, laboratories, and museums and with commodious recreational and social facilities; for others it represents staff and facilities reeking with poverty.

Excerpt from *American Association for Higher Education Bulletin,* Vol. 34, No. 3, November 1981, pp. 11-15. Reprinted by permission.

Despite the wide range of requirements and conditions under which baccalaureate degrees are earned, there is a certain modal concept of that degree. The
concept is deeply embedded in the traditions of American higher education. In
general, the degree is conceived as representing completion of a four-year program
following upon a high school "preparatory" program. It involves some breadth
of learning among the traditional academic subjects including the sciences, social
studies, and humanities, and some modest specialization in a single field or area.
The specialization may be in an academic field having no career potential other
than teaching the same subject, or it may be in fields such as nursing, engineering,
business, or an allied health profession. Even those vocational fields that demand
most of the student's time, engineering being the prime example, make obeisance
to breadth of learning by requiring students to take a few courses in fields such
as English and economics. The course requirements and the guidance afforded
students, however, usually steer them toward a diversified program intended to
help them become well-educated and cultivated human beings.

The concept of the baccalaureate degree includes not only [the students'] learning of certain subjects, but also their broad emotional and moral development and
their practical competence as citizens and as members of families and organizations. Much emphasis is placed on sound values, aesthetic sensibility, religious
interest, human understanding, physical development, and fruitful leisure. It is
expected that these characteristics will be nurtured partly through the curriculum
and partly through extracurricular facilities, programs, and experiences.

The modal concept of the baccalaureate degree cannot be defined in terms
of a list of courses taken, a major field selected, the amount of time served, the
physical facilities available, or the residential arrangement. In the end, it must
be defined in terms of characteristics imparted to students, that is to say, by the
change in them that occurs from entrance upon a course of study and experiences
and completion of that course of study. The course of study and related experiences need not involve attendance at high school or college. They may be derived
from the educational actives of churches, businesses, the armed services, labor
unions, libraries, the mass media, etc., or may be achieved through experiential
learning and independent study. The object is the well-educated person, not a
particular educational regimen.

These ideas bring us to two of the most difficult questions in educational theory
and practice: What are the characteristics of a well-educated person? How can
one tell whether a particular person or group of people is well-educated?

Characteristics of the Well-Educated Person

I would define a well-educated person as one who had achieved a balanced
combination of personal and practical learning. This level of education could
be achieved through study and other experiences in the traditional educational
system of the United States including the equivalent of the two final years of high
school and four years of college. I do not imply, however, that going to school
and college would be the only means of achieving it. The level of learning I am
suggesting would qualify for a baccalaureate degree regardless of the process by
which it was attained.

The education to achieve this learning would be of two types: personal education by which I mean broad development and fulfillment of the whole person, and practical education by which I mean training for work, family life, politics, consumer choices, health, leisure activities, and other practical affairs. The words personal and practical are akin to but not the same as liberal and vocational. I have deliberately avoided the latter two words because they are hackneyed, ambiguous, and charged with emotion. The distinction between personal and practical education is not clean-cut. The overlap is great. Personal education, though primarily designed to enhance each individual as a person, can have important consequences for work and other practical affairs. Practical education, though primarily designed to enhance specific skills of use in work and other practical affairs, may be influential in the development of the individual personality. Yet the distinction is worth making because of the tendency of the two types of education to get out of balance.

In recent times, for example, practical education, especially that related to future careers, had tended to overwhelm personal education. I do not suggest, however, that practical education is in some sense illegitimate or unnecessary. People understandably want to, and should, prepare themselves, in one way or another, for work and other practical affairs. Each person should find a vocation (in the sense of "calling") through which he or she would be able to contribute to society something of value. The ideal is a reasonable balance between personal and practical education such that the general development of the person is not unduly sacrificed to self-centered pecuniary ends.

Much of practical education is derived from experiences throughout life, and it should not overwhelm personal education during the school years. In achieving the ideal balance, it is necessary to consider the whole of education—from kindergarten through graduate school and beyond including not only school and college but other educational media as well. Some stages or places of education may be more suited to practical education and some more congenial to personal education. It is a balance over a lifetime, not necessarily within each semester of a school or college career, that should be sought.

With these preliminary remarks, let me describe an education that might produce "well-educated people"—of whom I hope there might someday be a great many. Ideally, such an education would be defined in terms of educational achievements or outcomes, rather than specific subjects or operations performed. However, provisionally, one can be more specific by casting the definition in terms of subject, though not necessarily courses. These subjects would constitute a six-year program, two years in high school and four years in college, but building upon a suitable elementary education.

I.   Personal education.
    A.   The common core.
        1.   Language skills including reading, writing, speaking, and, in an era of electronic communication, listening.
        2.   Logic, mathematics, and computer science.
        3.   History.
        4.   Philosophy.
        5.   Religious studies.

6. National and world geography with special reference to peoples, cultures, economics, ecology, and relationships. Perhaps cosmology could be fitted in here.

7. Foreign languages: not required with incentives or encouragement such that a substantial minority of persons would *elect to study them* in some depth *so that the nation could have* contact with many foreign cultures.

8. Educational opportunities: training and guidance related to opportunities and techniques for lifelong educational use of formal adult education, radio, TV, books, magazines, newspapers, libraries, churches, museums, musical organizations, armed forces, workplaces, unions, clubs, experiential learning, and independent study. ("Education is the acquisition of the art of the utilization of knowledge."—A.N. Whitehead.)

9. Career opportunities: the concept of vocation, the world of work, and choice of vocation.

B. Required fields within each of which rather limited choices of specific courses would be permitted. In each field, emphasis would be on fundamental principles, methods, and great issues.

1. Natural sciences.
2. The humanities.
3. The arts.
4. Social studies.

II. Practical education.

Meeting the requirement of major field of study in the sciences and field of study in the sciences and arts which might provide the basis for a vocation or for graduate or professional study leading eventually to a vocation, or preparing for a vocation through undergraduate study, apprenticeship, on-the-job experience and training, etc.

A. Preparing for other practical affairs, such as interpersonal relations, management of personal business, child development, health, consumer choice, and use of leisure.

In defining the kind of education I have in mind in terms of a list of subjects and a specified duration of study, I emphatically do not imply that all learning would take place in schools and colleges. Some of it (or for some students, all of it) might occur elsewhere. Moreover, I do not imply that the various parts of the program would occur in a particular sequence. Personal and practical education might occur at different ages for different individuals. The subjects might be combined or integrated in different ways. A wide range of instructional methods and facilities might be employed. Experimentation with new curricula and modes of learning would be possible. Indeed, diversity would be desirable and essential to fit the education to students of varying backgrounds and interests and to avoid the risk of placing all the educational eggs in one basket. The listing of subjects is intended not to lay down a fixed regimen, but to be specific about the basic ingredients of the education that would be calculated to produce "well-educated people."

Defining education by means of a list of subjects has the merit of specificity but the drawback of not coming to grips with the underlying spirit and purpose of the education. A given set of subjects can be taught and learned with quite different outcomes depending on the basic qualities of mind, character, and temperament that are sought and on the spirit in which the education is conducted. These are reflected especially in the relative emphasis given to positive knowledge and to matters of values and in the kinds of persons serving as exemplars.

 Activities and Questions for Reflection

1. What seem to be the principal differences between associate and bachelor's degree programs other than the length of time required to complete each? What similarities are there?

2. What is the basis for the author's claim that the program he proposes leads to becoming a well-educated person?

3. Does the college in which you are enrolled offer bachelor's degrees? Your college catalog will give you this information including the requirements and degree designations.

4. As you begin, or return to, college at this time, you should consider the appropriateness of a bachelor's degree to achieve your purposes for attending college. Why do you think a bachelor's degree would or would not be appropriate for you?

A New Debate Is Joined Over an Old Question: Is College an Investment or an End in Itself?

James Cicarelli

James Cicarelli is currently dean of the Walter E. Heller College of Business Administration at Roosevelt University in Chicago, Illinois.

In this essay, Cicarelli discusses the objectives of higher education and how to measure its impact on students. He outlines two philosophies and discusses how each is supported by different types of disciplines and institutions.

The seemingly endless debate about higher education is now focusing on the question of what the purpose of higher education is and how best to determine how well colleges and universities are achieving it. Particularly heated right now is the discussion over the pros and cons of so-called value-added *assessment.*

On one side of the debate are proponents of the relatively new view of college as a place where students go to add to their individual reservoirs of information. This philosophy of education emphasizes quantifiable knowledge that can be measured by student performance on nationally standardized tests. The idea is that by testing students before, during, and at the end of their college careers, an institution can discover its educational strengths and weaknesses through "outcomes evaluation"—measuring exactly how much has been added to each student's store of knowledge by the education he or she has received.

On the other side of the debate are those who hold a more traditional view of college as a place where students go to learn to appreciate their cultural heritage, hone their skills in critical thinking and communication, and otherwise transform themselves from self-centered individuals into decent and caring citizens. In this view, the emphasis in college should be more on the development of moral principles than on the accumulation of knowledge, per se. Since that sort of outcome is difficult, if not impossible, to measure, the traditionalist institution looks to "input" rather than "output," measuring success in terms of the variety and depth of experience to which its students have been exposed.

Despite obvious differences, the two philosophies are not mutually exclusive. Actually, both can be seen as variants of "developmentalism," an approach to education concerned with both the content and the cognitive aspects of learning. What set the two views apart are their conflicting methods of assessment, and

Reprinted by permission of the author.

the resulting controversy is going to dominate the discussion of evaluation for the foreseeable future.

While each side aims to improve higher education, both systems have disadvantages that would make them less effective than their proponents promise. For example, it is foolhardy to judge the success of a college education in terms of how much information the students have accumulated, because so much of it is already obsolete by the time they graduate. Students need to learn how to learn and how to teach themselves—talents that are nurtured by the ability to think clearly and read and write effectively, rather than by the mastery of information whose half-life is often measured in months.

On the other hand, it is pretentious to suppose that a college can teach values or should even try to do so. While most people can accept the broad principles embodied in the old Superman motto—"Truth, Justice, and the American Way"— it's difficult to translate them into working precepts. Whose truth? What system of justice? Which American way? Only in a dictatorship is one set of values taught to all. Yet simply exposing students to competing value systems, without discrimination, leads to confusion, if not anarchy.

Contributing to the controversy are the differences between professional, career-oriented education and general, liberal arts education. The former readily lends itself to the value-added approach because a profession is based on a body of knowledge that must be mastered before the student becomes a practitioner. Mastery of factual information can be demonstrated by passing a standardized test. Such a test shows how well an institution has prepared its students for entry into a profession. In other words, it measures the effectiveness of the education provided. Thus, prospective students interested in a particular career might consider such test results when deciding which college to attend. Unfortunately, that is not foolproof.

A decade ago, for example, when the boom in the oil industry led many colleges to expand their geology programs and others to begin new ones, a bachelor's in petroleum engineering was the hottest degree an undergraduate could earn. Today, most of those programs are as inactive as the West Texas oil fields where all the new geologists and engineers were supposed to find work. Educating for a job can produce graduates who are fit for that job and little else. A liberal arts education, on the other hand, can provide students with skills that transcend specific jobs and can be usefully applied in virtually any occupation.

The general-vs.-professional issue is part of the larger question of whether college should be seen as an investment or as an end in itself. Advocates of the value-added philosophy tend to consider higher education an investment, an expenditure of time and resources that should yield a payoff large enough to justify the initial cost. In their view, society invests a great deal in education, in part because of the hope that the schools and colleges will produce productive citizens who will then ensure that the next generation has the wherewithal to renew the investment. Traditionalists are more apt to view higher education as something one acquires for its own sake, not because it may lead to a good job or some other material gain. If it does result in enrichment in monetary as well as intellectual terms, fine; but the purpose of a college education is to make one better, not necessarily richer.

Whatever else is involved in the debate, a big part of it, for me, has to do with romanticism versus realism. My romantic side, the one that envisions college as a mind-expanding experience, sees the value-added philosophy as an educational straitjacket that demands curriculum conformity at the expense of individualism and experimentation. Reducing the purpose of college to producing graduates who can demonstrate their proficiency on national examinations risks our turning out intellectual clones whose creativity and imagination are suppressed, if not obliterated. Only the traditional approach promises to develop free-thinking citizens who cherish liberty and, therefore, are willing to question authority rather than just accept it blindly.

My realistic side, however, characterizes this line of reasoning as so much drivel. The colleges and universities in the United States represent the entire spectrum of values, from secular liberalism to religious fundamentalism. Students are free to choose the institution that best fits their individual preferences, and national value-added tests would not restrict their choice one iota. In fact, such a system would take some of the guesswork out of choosing a college, because it would show prospective students just how well an institution has done in delivering what it promises.

At this point, it's hard to tell how, if at all, the debate will be resolved. Institutions with no national reputation and few resources will probably embrace the value-added philosophy, since they have everything to gain by doing so and little to lose. Conversely, the better-known, better-endowed institutions will tend to stick with tradition, because they have little to gain and a lot to lose. If the students from the nation's top colleges do well on national standardized tests, they will simply be performing as expected. Should they do poorly, however, even in relative terms, their performance would be taken as a sign that the college or university was doing a poor job, and its reputation would suffer accordingly.

The unknown quantity so far is which side the institutions in the middle, the ones with "average" students and reputations and resources, will take in the controversy. They constitute the majority, after all, and it is their response that will determine the outcome of the debate. Should they tilt toward the value-added side, then evaluating educational results by numbers will become an integral part of the American college system. If, however, they stay on the side of tradition, then "value-added" will, like "relevance," become an interesting footnote in the history of higher education.

 Vocabulary

As you think about this essay, these definitions may be helpful to you:

1. **assessment**   a determination of the importance, size, or value
2. **hone**   to make more acute, intense, or effective
3. **traditionalist**   persons who believe an inherited or established patternof thought

4. **developmentalism**   belief in a process of growth, differentiation, or evaluation by successive changes
5. **cognitive**   capable of being reduced to empirical factual knowledge

 ## Discussion Questions

1. What do advocates of the value-added philosophy consider to be the worth
   of a college education?
2. According to Cicarelli, how do traditionalists view higher education?
3. What are the differences between a specific, career-oriented education and a
   general, liberal arts education?
4. How does Cicarelli distinguish between romanticism and realism? Which do
   you think is the better view? Why?
5. Does Cicarelli think the question of value-added assessment will be resolved?
   How?

 ## Suggestions for Your Journal

Write about your current thinking on the major question that Cicarelli addresses:
Do you think of your college education as primarily a way to get a better job, or
do you seek a more general liberal arts education? What factors might change
your thinking on this important question?

You probably have some general education courses to complete as part of
your intended degree program. Do you agree that they will help to make you
knowledgeable about areas of study and thought that you would normally not
be exposed to?

Assume that you have a younger relative or friend who will be entering college next year. Consider writing a journal entry in which you argue for or against
general studies courses using that relative or friend as your primary audience.

Connecting the Dots

Steve Jobs

'You've got to find what you love,' Jobs says
Stanford Report, June 14, 2005

The following is part of the Commencement address at Stanford University by Steve Jobs, CEO of Apple Computer and of Pixar Animation Studios, delivered on June 12, 2005.

Today I want to tell you three stories from my life. That's it. No big deal. Just three stories.

The first story is about connecting the dots.

I dropped out of Reed College after the first 6 months, but then stayed around as a drop-in for another 18 months or so before I really quit. So why did I drop out?

It started before I was born. My biological mother was a young, unwed college graduate student, and she decided to put me up for adoption. She felt very strongly that I should be adopted by college graduates, so everything was all set for me to be adopted at birth by a lawyer and his wife. Except that when I popped out they decided at the last minute that they really wanted a girl. So my parents, who were on a waiting list, got a call in the middle of the night asking: "We have an unexpected baby boy; do you want him?" They said: "Of course." My biological mother later found out that my mother had never graduated from college and that my father had never graduated from high school. She refused to sign the final adoption papers. She only relented a few months later when my parents promised that I would someday go to college.

And 17 years later I did go to college. But I naively chose a college that was almost as expensive as Stanford, and all of my working-class parents' savings were being spent on my college tuition. After six months, I couldn't see the value in it. I had no idea what I wanted to do with my life and no idea how college was going to help me figure it out. And here I was spending all of the money my parents had saved their entire life. So I decided to drop out and trust that it would all work out OK. It was pretty scary at the time, but looking back it was one of the best decisions I ever made. The minute I dropped out I could stop taking the required classes that didn't interest me, and begin dropping in on the ones that looked interesting.

It wasn't all romantic. I didn't have a dorm room, so I slept on the floor in friends' rooms, I returned coke bottles for the 5¢ deposits to buy food with, and I would walk the 7 miles across town every Sunday night to get one good meal a week at the Hare Krishna temple. I loved it. And much of what I stumbled into by following my curiosity and intuition turned out to be priceless later on. Let me give you one example:

Reed College at that time offered perhaps the best calligraphy instruction in the country. Throughout the campus every poster, every label on every drawer, was beautifully hand calligraphed. Because I had dropped out and didn't have to take the normal classes, I decided to take a calligraphy class to learn how to do this. I learned about serif and san serif typefaces, about varying the amount of space between different letter combinations, about what makes great typography great. It was beautiful, historical, artistically subtle in a way that science can't capture, and I found it fascinating.

None of this had even a hope of any practical application in my life. But ten years later, when we were designing the first Macintosh computer, it all came back to me. And we designed it all into the Mac. It was the first computer with beautiful typography. If I had never dropped in on that single course in college, the Mac would have never had multiple typefaces or proportionally spaced fonts. And since Windows just copied the Mac, its likely that no personal computer would have them. If I had never dropped out, I would have never dropped in on this calligraphy class, and personal computers might not have the wonderful typography that they do. Of course it was impossible to connect the dots looking forward when I was in college. But it was very, very clear looking backwards ten years later.

Again, you can't connect the dots looking forward; you can only connect them looking backwards. So you have to trust that the dots will somehow connect in your future. You have to trust in something — your gut, destiny, life, karma, whatever. This approach has never let me down, and it has made all the difference in my life.

The remaining 3 stories can be found at:
http://news.stanford.edu/news/2005/june15/jobs-061505.html
or listen to the speech at
http://www.ted.com/talks/steve_jobs_how_to_live_before_you_die.html

 ## Discussion Questions

1. How do you think "life circumstances" affected Steve Jobs path to college and his experience the first 6 months of college?
2. What do you think Steve Jobs values most about college?
3. Think about how you are approaching each of your courses this term. Is the course a requirement to "get through"? a stepping stone to a career path, or a subject you were curious about?
4. What are you doing now to ensure you will have enough "dots" to connect when you tell the story of your success!?

CHAPTER 5

HOW IS PERSONAL DEVELOPMENT RELATED TO CAREER AND COMMUNITY?

Kimmie Montgomery,
Peer Mentor 08
Pre-Nursing Student

Dear Sac State First Year Students,

Starting college is a huge step. During your freshman year, you are completely immersed into a world very different from what you have experienced before. You will be overwhelmed with financial aid woes, the cost of tuition, the hassle of commuting, crazy dorm life, diets consisting of Easy Mac and Top Ramen, overloaded schedules, intimidating blue books or scantrons, giant lecture halls, and the difficulty of balancing school, work, friends, and family. Here, you will face higher expectations than ever before. But you will also discover a new independence and freedom as you enter an environment where you are treated like a true adult and are able to pursue a wonderful thing called higher education. While we all have a common goal, graduating, you are not here just to get a degree. It is what you go through and experience to obtain this degree that will form your personality and shape your ideas.

I arrived at Sac State eager to learn, excited to make new friends, and terrified of change and challenges. I faced countless difficulties, academically and emotionally, but in the end, I survived. The dedication and resilience that I have gained from relentlessly pursuing my goals are traits invaluable to my chosen career path, Nursing.

I completely immersed myself in campus life, and as a result my college experience has become enriched. I took a volleyball class, became part of a student committee, worked at a hospital emergency room, made friends in all my classes, and studied with them over coffee breaks. While we are here on campus, it is important to make the most of our experience. How do you do this? Do something you are passionate about! Join one of our many student clubs, enroll in a sports kinesiology class, study abroad for a semester, take a student trip with Peak Adventures, get an on-campus job, form study groups within your classes, explore new subjects, become a student leader, or participate in community service; these are all wonderful opportunities that will only enhance your time here at Sacramento State. And since you will be here for four years (some of us more than that), you might as well go for it.

My personal identity, career goals, and view of my place in the community are continually forged by the activities I participate in as a student at Sacramento State. So yes, get your degree! But really, all your hard work is pointless without learning something about yourself, having fun, and making difference, whether its on our campus, in our community, or nationally. So be passionate, enthusiastic, and excited not only about your future when you graduate from Sac State but also about your time spent here as a student; these truly can be the best years of your life if you let them.

Good Luck, Kimmie Montgomery

Strengthening Your Personal Development through Community Engagement

Vanessa Arnaud, Ph.D.

Dr. Vanessa Arnaud is a lecturer at California State University, Sacramento. She teaches in the department of Foreign Languages and Honors Program. Her article urges students to become informed and actively engaged members of society through community engagement. The author explains why community engagement activities can be a powerful force in strengthening a student's personal development.

You have been born into a globally interdependent, pluralistic democracy that is multicultural, multiethnic, and multireligious. You are faced with people who differ from you in language and national origin, in political and sexual orientations, and in privilege and social class. How do you fit into this world of diverse peoples and perspectives? Have you examined your life in light of your surroundings?

Sadly, there are people who live entire lives without reflection. These lives can be filled with trivial choices—of what clothes to buy, what shows to watch—without any effort to shape the form of their life as a whole; without any reflection on life's values and real priorities. "The unexamined life is not worth living," Socrates reminds us. In many ways the unexamined life is not a life at all. It is certainly not something that is yours. It is something that happens to you when you are not paying attention.

One of the most effective ways to explore your life's priorities and values is through *community engagement*, the process of working collaboratively with others for the common good. The CSU Chancellor's Office defines community engagement as "the collaboration between higher education institutions and their larger communities (local, regional/state, national, global) for the mutually beneficial exchange of knowledge and resources in a context of partnership and reciprocity."* You might already be familiar with and/or have participated in different types of community engagement, such as community service. Other examples of community engagement activities include alternative spring breaks, voter registration drives, community-centered forums, community-based research and internships, and service learning, a teaching method that combines meaningful service to the community with curriculum-based learning and reflection.

There is probably no better way for you to clarify what you prioritize or value than by putting yourself in a situation where your assumptions and beliefs are put to the test. Community engagement activities could very well take you out of your

---

*The CSU Chancellor's Office uses the Carnegie Foundation for the Advancement of Teaching and Learning's definition of community engagement: http://www.calstate.edu/cce/about_us/vision.shtml

comfort zone and cause you to stretch yourself and struggle with conflicting issues. You might be surprised to learn about social issues that exist in close proximity to your campus, including poverty, domestic violence, homelessness, challenges faced by non-native English speakers, and violence in schools. The number of campuses with community engagement programs, particularly service-learning programs, has grown tremendously over the last few years. Such reformulation of traditional pedagogies is well underway.

Service learning links classroom-based theory and service practice. If you enroll in a service-learning course, you are expected to make connections between knowledge gained from the academic course and the lessons presented by your service experiences. In this learning context, you are educated by the actions you take. You assume a larger role in the creation and transmission of knowledge in the classroom and beyond. You not only learn from your instructor, fellow classmates, and community partner, but you also teach them. Your professor is no longer the sole source of information, but a facilitator, mentor, or coach in the process of discussion and discovery. This shift of roles in the classroom encourages greater student investment in and ownership of the learning process. It allows students to become aware of themselves as both learner and teacher, responsible and equal partners in a collective process of knowledge creation.

Service learning directly addresses often-raised student questions: What's the point of this class? Why do I have to learn this stuff? Reflection and self-assessment from service-learning experiences are effective vehicles for transforming your perspectives. Service learning lets you see the usefulness of knowledge even as you are developing it. Consequently, these experiences tend to stand out as especially meaningful and transformative. Research has shown that students perform better and invest themselves more fully in the learning process when they are working, not for a teacher, a grade, or even for themselves, but for a larger "real world" audience (Howard, 1998; Gordon, 2000). As one student commented, "People are involved now. You have a responsibility. You don't want to let people down" (Kerrigan, Gelmon & Spring, 2003).

The theories of John Dewey (1938) and Jean Piaget (1952) help explain the effectiveness of experiential learning methods, through which you have direct encounters with the phenomena being studied. Dewey stressed the importance of placing students in real-life experiences for genuine learning. Significantly, for learning to be useful, Dewey felt that the experience must be linked to reflection, a key component of service learning: "Experiential learning takes place when a person involved in an activity looks back and evaluates it, determines what was useful or important to remember, and uses this information to perform another activity" (1938). Piaget's research underlines the importance of direct experiences, and his theory on how children construct meanings as they mature and interact with their environments acknowledges learners as active processors of information. Drawing together Dewey and Piaget's theories, David Kolb (1984) develops the famous experiential learning circle to stress the role experience plays in learning. The learning process is expressed graphically in Figure 1. An individual may enter this cycle at any point, but must complete the entire cycle for effective learning to occur.

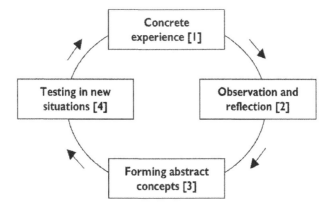

Figure 1 (After David Kolb and Kurt Lewin): This diagram is a version of one included in David Kolb (1984) *Experiential Learning.* http://www.infed.org/foundations/f-explrn.htm

Faculty who incorporate service learning have reported a shift away from a "banking method" of education in which the goal is to deposit knowledge into students, toward a "constructivist" philosophy that encourages students to construct new knowledge and apply that knowledge in meaningful ways. According to Paulo Freire's *Pedagogy of the Oppressed*, knowledge cannot happen with the banking method of teaching where teachers are narrators, and students are passive recorders. Freire defines "knowledge [as] emerg[ing] only through intervention and re-invention, through the restless, impatient, continuing, hopeful inquiry human beings pursue in the world, with the world, and with each other" (1970). Education should be a collaborative process in which teachers and students work together, thereby getting away from the method of lecture-transfer. This can be achieved through dialogue, which has the effect of making the student/teacher relationship reciprocal. In other words, students and teachers become equal participants in educating each other and themselves.

This shift in instruction in service-learning courses has produced noteworthy results. Recent research has proven that service learning increases students' engagement with their studies, the university and the community, and the likelihood of retention into the second year (Gallini & Moely, 2003). Service-learning participants, in comparison with other students, have reported a larger understanding of community issues (Astin & Sax, 1998), greater knowledge and acceptance of diverse races and cultures, and a greater ability to get along with people of different backgrounds (Astin & Sax, 1998; McKenna & Rizzo, 1999). Additionally, they improved their grades, became more motivated, and set more goals (Johnson, Beebe, Mortimer, & Snyder, 1998), not to mention, their self-esteem improved (Giles & Eyler, 1998), and they became less self-centered (Santilli, Falbo, & Harris, 2002).

Many positive outcomes of community engagement are linked directly to the course goals and student learning objectives of your First Year Experience course. Community engagement improves academic skills, such as critical thinking through the ability to connect theory to practice; increases cognitive, social, emotional development; boosts motivation and self-confidence; enhances leadership experience and connection to the community; and helps reduce stereotyping and facilitate racial harmony.

There are many different models of community engagement, ranging from a short-term project to immersion experiences. Despite the varying models, successful community engagement activities emphasize student voice in planning and conducting the undertaking. Students are reported to be more absorbed in the project if they choose the topic, have real responsibilities and challenging tasks, and make important decisions in order for the project to have a positive influence (Morgan & Streb, 2003). Sacramento State has various programs designed to afford you with ample opportunities to have a voice and be involved in the leadership of community engagement activities. A visit to Sacramento State's Community Engagement Center will open the world of possibilities to you: http://www.csus.edu/cec/. You can, for example, participate in Alternative Break where you work on projects throughout the week with organizations such as Sacramento Food Bank & Family Services and Habitat for Humanity. Or you can take part in service projects that address contemporary social issues raised by the One Book program, a campus-wide initiative encouraging all members of the campus to read and discuss a common book. You might even be currently enrolled in a First Year Experience course that has integrated Writing Partners, a program that promotes literacy, enhances awareness of community and educational issues, and exposes K-12 students to college through letter exchanges. Sacramento State has the resources available for you to become actively engaged in real-world lessons about your communities.

For learning to be effective, it must generalize from the college classroom to the world of work and beyond. Being an active participant in your community allows you to discover for yourself the link between subject matter and real-life experience. Involvement and commitment to your community will enhance your understanding of your own personal strengths and weaknesses. This self-awareness could help lead to a better sense of direction in your career development. Students have reported that they used community engagement as an opportunity to make meaning out of their career choices (Kerrigan et al., 2003). You can learn, for example, that a certain aspect of a profession is suited for you. Suppose you've always believed that you wanted to be an accountant, and your service-learning assignment is to help a local nonprofit organization upgrade its accounting system. You discover that what you enjoyed most about the experience was writing user-friendly manuals for client personnel and giving hands-on training to those who would be maintaining the system. Your experience has given you some additional information with which to narrow your career field.

Community engagement provides you with hands-on experience to hone your interpersonal skills and to strengthen communication and listening skills before you begin your career in an increasingly diverse workplace. You will be working in an economy that is global, innovative, fast, and without boundaries. This new economy requires skills and competencies that stretch your capacity to relate to individuals and communities with different values and beliefs. Community engagement provides preparation for career as well as life. Skills learned today could easily be obsolete ten years from now. However, life-long learning continues throughout adulthood. The time, energy, and emotion you invest in understanding your own life, and the ethical dilemmas that confront citizens individually and as members of society, can give purpose and meaning to your everyday actions. Learning that allows you to engage with your own sense of self is vitally important to both intellectual development and the development of your personal values. Community engagement helps to ensure that your college years really do teach you to reflect on the purpose of learning, and on the uses to which you will put your knowledge.

Discussion Questions:

1. Many campuses have community engagement opportunities. Identify some programs on your campus, where you would find information about them, and discuss whether you would like to participate in them.
2. What do you think is the main benefit of service learning for you, for your community partner, and for your instructor?
3. How can community engagement help to clarify your values and personal development?
4. You may have had significant volunteer and/or service-learning experiences. Share your experiences. How have you changed as a result of these experiences?

Suggestions for Your Journal

1. Do you feel that membership or citizenship in a community necessarily includes an obligation to serve others through volunteer work? If so, why is service a necessary aspect of citizenship, and how much is service appropriately expected from community members? If not, why isn't service a necessary component of membership in a community?

References:

Astin, A.W., & Sax, L.J. (1998). How undergraduates are affected by service participation. *Journal of College Student Development, 39* (3), 251-262.

Dewey, J. (1938). *Experience and education.* New York: Collier Books.

Freire, P. (1993). *Pedagogy of the Oppressed.* (M. Ramos, Trans.). New York: Continuum. (Original work published 1970).

Gallini, S., & Moely, B. (2003). Service-Learning and Engagement, Academic Challenge, and Retention. *Michigan Journal of Community Service Learning, 10* (1).

Giles, D.E., Jr., & Eyler, J. (1998). A Service Learning Research Agenda for the Next Five Years. *New Directions for Teaching and Learning, 73,* 65-72.

Gordon, R. (Ed.). (2000). *Problem Based Service Learning: A Fieldguide for Making a Difference in Higher Education.* 2nd ed. New Hampshire: Campus Compact.

Howard, J. (1998). Academic Service Learning: A Counternormative Pedagogy. *New Directions for Teaching and Learning, 73,* 21-29.

Johnson, M.K., Beebe, T., Mortimer, J.T., & Snyder, M. (1998). Volunteerism in adolescence: A process perspective. *Journal of Research on Adolescence, 8,* 309-332.

Kerrigan, S., Gelmon, S., & Spring, A. (2003). The Community as Classroom: Multiple Perspectives on Student Learning. *Metropolitan Universities, 14* (3), 53-67.

Kolb, D.A. (1984). *Experiential Learning: experience as the source of learning and development*. NJ: Prentice-Hall.

McKenna, M.W., & Rizzo, E. (1999). Student perceptions of the "learning" in service-learning courses. In J.R. Ferrari & J.G. Chapman (Eds.), *Educating students to make a difference: Community-based service learning* (pp. 111-123). New York: Haworth Press.

Morgan, W., & Streb, M. (2003). First, Do No Harm: Student Ownership and Service-Learning. *Metropolitan Universities: An International Forum, 14* (3), 36-52.

Piaget, J. (1952). *The origins of intelligence in children*. (M. Cook, Trans.). New York: W.W Norton.

Santilli, J.S., Falbo, M.C., & Harris, J.T. (2002, April). *The role of volunteer services, self perceptions, and relationships with others on prosocial development*. Paper presented at the meeting of the Society for Research on Adolescence, New Orleans, LA.

Developing a Personal System of Values

Richard L. Morrill
PRESIDENT
UNIVERSITY OF RICHMOND

For the past twenty years or more I have had a special interest in the topic of values. My doctoral dissertation involved a comparison of the philosophy of values of two contemporary theorists, one an American and one a Frenchman. Both as a college teacher and in my work as the president of a university, I have continued my studies and reflection, including writing a book on the topic several years ago.

I suppose that some of my interest in the field comes from my own experience as a college student, especially during my first two years. I had been brought up in a conservative home in which standards of personal behavior were tightly enforced. When I went off to college, however, I confronted ways of living that contradicted the ways I had been reared. As I met people who both thought and acted differently with regard to everything from alcohol to personal relationships, it was time to think through the basis for my own positions. Undoubtedly, some of my continuing interest in the topic of values dates to these early personal challenges.

As president of a university, I find that the issue of values continues to be a central one in the experience of most freshmen. For many students the challenges are indistinct and tend to pass quickly, but for others a lengthy and sometimes troubling process of adjustment is set in motion. Experience has taught me that, whatever else, a clear understanding of values and how they function is a crucial first step in making the best ultimate decisions in the values realm. I hope that this brief chapter will contribute toward that end of a better understanding of values.

American society has always shown a particular concern about values. Some would explain this by America's strong religious heritage, while others would relate it to our culture's dominant focus on the rights and happiness of the individual. Whatever the reasons, over the past decade our society has been especially concerned about the uncertain state of American ethics and values. Scandals on Wall Street, sharp divisions over controversial issues such as abortion, deception by TV evangelists, and a preoccupation with material success among many young people are just several of the ways in which our society has recently experienced ethical disorder and a confusion about values.

What Are Values?

Discussions about values often generate more heat than light because the very word *values* means so many different things to different people. For some, values refer to the specific positions that a person might hold on controversial moral question, for example, that capital punishment is right or wrong under various circumstances. To others, values refer more properly to those things most important to a person, such as a good job, a lovely home, nice clothes, a fancy car, and family ties. Another approach to values portrays them more as ideals or goals and uses such abstract nouns as truth, justice, love, peace, success, tolerance, and equality to refer to them. Given this jumble of meanings, let's pause to get our bearings on how best to understand the term values.

When it comes to understanding values in the context of college education, many thinkers would propose that we can best do so by comparing them with other aspects of our ordinary human experience. We use many terms to identify different forms of human thought and behavior: attitudes, feelings, beliefs, ideas, concepts, and, of course, values. When we apply one of these words to ourselves or to other people, we are usually describing some facet of our experience as human beings, often in ways that help us to define our own individuality or the nature of a group or institution. As we talk about the beliefs, feelings, ideas, and attitudes that we hold, we are typically exploring those characteristics that make us who we are and set us apart from other people. In this list of personal characteristics and forms of experience, we often find that our values occupy an important place.

One of the things that many recent thinkers have noticed is that values seem to have a quite different place in our lives than do ideas or feelings. Above all, our values apparently commit us to taking action, to doing something, while the other forms of experience do not necessarily do so. When we truly hold a value, in other words, we act on it. On the other hand, it seems to be perfectly consistent to have ideas, beliefs, attitudes, and feelings that do not lead to any specific action. They may, of course, involve some action but not necessarily. For instance, no contradiction is involved in feeling sad about something but not doing anything about it. We might be watching a television program showing people who are starving in Africa that gives us a feeling of sympathy or regret, but we may never take any action whatsoever based on that feeling. Or perhaps we have the attitude that honesty is the best policy and express that position verbally in many different ways, while at the same time finding ourselves distorting the truth under any number of convenient circumstances.

We can conclude from these cases that attitudes, feelings, beliefs, ideas, and many other forms of experience and behavior do not qualify as genuine values unless they meet some additional tests. As we are trying to learn ever more about who we are, and as the college experience pushes us steadily in the direction of self-knowledge, the ability to find our true values becomes an extremely important consideration. In finding our values, we discover our deeper selves, we come face to face with our identities as unique persons and as responsible agents for our own lives. If our values lead us to do something about them, then our feelings of sympathy may be a genuine value for us to the extent that they motivate us to take an action—for instance, if our feelings of sympathy for starving people cause us to raise funds to help those suffering. Action can take many different forms and should not be thought of only as some form of actual physical motion. Action may be thinking and talking continually about a problem, trying to interest others in it, reading about it, or sending letters to officials regarding it. The basic point is that when we truly hold a value, it leads us to make some impact upon our world.

As we test for the values in our lives, we also look for other characteristics of them. We consider, for example, whether we have accepted our alleged value by choice, whether it is something for which we accept personal responsibility and individual ownership. Many forms of our behavior are the result of things that others have taught us, especially our parents. Many things we have learned from our parents and others close to us will come to count fully as our values, but there is an essential process through which you must fully appropriate those things or beliefs for yourself. You must personally accept or reject something before it can become a value.

Freshmen in college commonly find themselves arguing for political or religious positions, for example, by defending their ideas on the basis that they have always been taught such and such by their parents. A position on politics or religion of this sort may well be a belief but, according to our definition, would not count as a value. Any belief or behavior that is primarily a result of what someone else expects of us without our own active and free choice of it is not a true value for us, whatever else it might be.

Finally, many commentators have noted that our values involve us in a positive relationship with any given line of conduct or behavior. This means that we tend to strongly affirm or prize our values. To one degree or another we become attracted to our values and affected by them. For instance, we might find that our values lead us to take a public stand because we are ready to defend anything that is related to them. We are proud of our values and the choices to which they lead. We also find ourselves ready to sacrifice for them and to establish our priorities around them. Our values have genuine allure and draw forth our loyalties and commitment. Because they hold sway over us, our values can also be a source of judgment when we fail to fully realize them in our daily lives. If truth is one of our values, we know that it can be a stern judge when we fail to live up to its requirements. There is, in other words, a real aura of pressure of "oughtness" surrounding the values that we have chosen for ourselves. In sum, values are those standards of choice that guide individuals and groups toward satisfaction, fulfillment, and meaning. They are present in our lives in those often hidden authorities in the name of which we make our choices and set our course in life.

Discovering Our Values

By the time we start college, most of us have at least a fair sense of what our values are. Yet one of your key tasks during college is to be able to become more conscious and articulate about the values that define your own approach to life. Students typically find the college years to be a time for locating and testing their values by tracing their full implications through comparison with those of other people, by analyzing, and by giving voice to them.

Finding our values is both a simple and a complex task. The place to begin is not with some complex theories about ourselves, but the actual choices that we make in response to life's demands and opportunities. Although the process of discovering values involves many stages and levels of analysis in a task that is never complete for any human being, surely the place to begin is with the actual life that we are living. In this process no one is neutral for no one can escape choices based on values. Everyone has values, although they are held with varying degrees of clarity and commitment.

As one general exercise in discovering our values, let's consider some of the reasons that you have decided to attend college and this particular college. Why are you here? Many students will say that they chose a certain college where they are enrolled because of its academic reputation. Is this true for you and, if so, what do you mean by reputation? Are you interested in the prestige that comes from enrolling in the college? As a value, prestige may signify an interest in high achievement and in meeting demanding standards. Obviously, a value such as prestige can run in many other directions; one important test would be to see whether the weight of the value for you is more at the level of name recognition and "the right label" or whether it represents a commitment to genuine academic distinction. The process of finding values that stand behind our choices is a never-ending one that involves a continuing exploration of our choices and their implications.

Many students say that they have chosen a college because it offers the best opportunity for a good job in the future. Is this true for you? The choice to seek education in terms of its employment benefits suggests any number of possible values. Does this mean that economic security is one of your top values, or does it suggest that you are defining personal success in terms of obtaining wealth? Once again, the point is to examine your actual choice and to move behind or beyond that immediate choice and ask for its implications. How much are you willing to sacrifice to achieve the goals connected with the value? Does the achievement you are seeking bring fulfillment on a short- or long-term basis? How will your obligations to your family and society at large relate to the particular value at hand? Under situations of conflict, what comes first?

As this extended example makes clear, we can put a whole series of questions to ourselves to gain a fuller understanding of the values to which we are committed. We may often begin with some of the tangible and obvious expressions of our choices—such as scholarships received, campus attractiveness, family influence, and reputation, in the case of college—and go from those immediate factors to the deeper reasons that stand behind them. The place to begin is with the concrete forms of our lives and to move to the values that underlie and orient our decision. We are constantly testing ourselves in this process of self-analysis to see whether our choices are motivated by genuine values that involve a consistent pattern of action, of affirmation, and of free choices.

If the test of valuing is met, then we begin to explore the full implications of the value we are committed to. How did we become committed to this value in the first place? How does it relate to other values, since a conflict in values is an ordinary and unavoidable part of our lives? How far are we willing to go in service to this value? What sacrifices do we accept in its name? How do the values we have chosen provide us with a meaning for our future? We are never finished with the effort to give an ever sharper and clearer account of exactly what our values mean and of the implications they have for our lives and those around us.

Through various techniques such as values clarification, you can use simple tests, checklists, and other exercises to get a fuller sense of what your values are.

In one exercise developed by Milton Rokeach in *The Nature of Human Values*, people are asked to rank two different series of values. The first list of eighteen values are intrinsic values that represent the end or purpose of life. The second list of eighteen are more instrumental in nature—they represent ways of behaving that may be necessary to reach a good life. Take some time to carefully rank the values on these two lists from number 1 to 18.

Intrinsic Values

___ A Comfortable Life (a prosperous life)
___ Equality (brotherhood, equal opportunity for all)
___ An Exciting Life (a stimulating, active life)
___ Family Security (taking care of loved ones)
___ Freedom (independence, free choices)
___ Happiness (contentedness)
___ Inner Harmony (freedom from inner conflict)
___ Mature Love (sexual and spiritual intimacy)
___ National Security (protection from attack)
___ Pleasure (an enjoyable, leisurely life)
___ Salvation (deliverance from sin, eternal life)
___ Self-Respect (self-esteem)
___ A Sense of Accomplishment (making a lasting contribution)
___ Social Recognition (respect, admiration)
___ True Friendship (close companionship)
___ Wisdom (a mature understanding of life)
___ A World at Peace (freedom from war and conflict)
___ A World of Beauty (beauty of nature and the arts)

Instrumental Values

___ Ambitious (hard-working, aspiring)
___ Broad-minded (open-minded)
___ Capable (competent, effective)
___ Cheerful (lighthearted, joyful)
___ Clean (neat, tidy)
___ Courageous (standing up for your beliefs)
___ Energetic (active, untiring)
___ Forgiving (willing to pardon others)
___ Helpful (working for the welfare of others)
___ Honest (sincere, truthful)
___ Imaginative (daring, creative)
___ Independent (self-reliant, self-sufficient)
___ Intellectual (intelligent, reflective)
___ Logical (consistent, rational)
___ Loving (affectionate, tender)
___ Obedient (dutiful, respectful)
___ Polite (courteous, well-mannered)
___ Self-Controlled (restrained, self-disciplined)

Other chapters in this book can provide you with a sense of your values as they come into play with reference to specific contexts such as choosing a major or selecting a career. Various exercises can be helpful ice breakers in starting your analysis of values, but ultimately the process of values awareness should become like second nature and be practiced continually.

College and Personal Values

Almost all students find that the college years involve a significant challenge to their existing personal and moral values. The challenge typically comes through friendships and relationships with new people whose backgrounds, ideas, goals, and desires run counter to your own prior experience. This clash with diversity can be unsettling; it may initiate a process of challenge and change in your own values that can be both exciting and threatening.

The encounter with diversity takes many forms, ranging from different habits of studying and sleeping that create conflicts with a roommate to deep philosophical differences over the purposes of life. Many freshmen find some of their most startling challenges in the diverse personal moralities that surround them. Some students have been taught in home or church that the use of alcohol, for example, is wrong and that the abuse of alcohol is deeply sinful. Students with a conservative philosophy on drinking alcohol may find that friends whom they respect and care about use alcohol in many ways that make them uncomfortable.

How do you deal with the circumstances in which you may not approve of some aspects of a friend's way of life? Do you try to change his behavior, make judgments against him, or withdraw from the relationship? Part of the problem is often that the friend demonstrates countless good qualities and values that make the suspect conduct itself seem less significant. In the process your own values may begin to change as a new kind of relativism begins to develop: "I don't choose to do that, but I'm not going to make any judgments against those who do." Much the same pattern of response often develops with reference to sexual involvements. People with one set of standards find themselves friends with others whose behavior is very different than their own. The challenge to a perceived set of moral values can then be severe and result in a lot of personal turmoil.

Outside a detailed knowledge of a concrete set of circumstances, we cannot know which response to a challenge to values is most fitting. Tolerance for others is a central value in our society and a value that often grows through the college experience. On the other hand, it is easy to think of cases in which tolerance can become indulgence of another's destructive tendencies. It is one thing to accept another's liberal but responsible use of alcohol at a party, but quite another to fail to challenge a drunk who plans to drive the car you're about to enter. Sexual intimacy in an enduring relationship is one thing and a series of abusive, one-night stands is quite another. They do not deserve the same response, and a failure to challenge destructive conduct is no sign of friendship.

Are there better and worse ways to deal with these challenges to personal and to moral values? The beginning of an answer, and only the beginning, resides in an awareness of the nature of values themselves. As we saw earlier, true values must be freely chosen by the person and cannot be accepted simply on the authority of another person. After all, the purpose of values is to give meaning to our lives through the choices that we must make. To try to make sense out of the complex circumstances of our own lives by using someone else's values makes little sense and ultimately simply will not work. Thus, in a time of challenge, we must try to find those values that are appropriate to the situation and that offer the prospect of giving that situation purpose and meaning for ourselves. If we tried to apply the values of our friends or parents in a new situation without making them truly our own, the result could produce much unhappiness and failure.

Many people make the mistake of fleeing from the challenge of diversity, of failing to confront the meaning of different moralities. The problem with this strategy is that at some time in their lives, often within a year or two, these people find themselves unable to cope with the next set of challenges to which they are subject. They do not grow as persons because they do not own their values or live out of them. Although only a first step, we must work through challenges to our own moral values by finding answers that truly make sense to us in providing the basis for moving ahead with our own lives. Often our received values prove to be adequate for the diverse experiences at hand, but even the acceptance of traditional answers requires that we make sense of them ourselves.

College and Intellectual Values

In addition to the values that regulate our personal and moral choices there are political, economic, social, religious, and intellectual values. As we involve ourselves in the search for truth and knowledge, a whole set of intellectual values comes into play. These values serve as the standards and authorities guiding our conduct in academic pursuits. Intellectual values such as clarity, accuracy, rigor, and excellence circulate around the fundamental value of truth. One of the most striking transitions that occur during the college years has to do with the way in which a student's understanding of the nature of truth changes.

Many students enter college with the assumption that the purpose of education is to have an unquestioned authority pour truth into the student as an open receptacle. Some students assume that there is a single right answer to every problem and that the teacher or the textbook as authorities will be the source of truth.

Most students soon find, however, that this black-and-white concept of truth is not shared by most college professors. A whole set of intellectual values undergirding most professors' assumptions about truth represent an initial shock to many students. Professors tend to see truth in a much more contextual, flexible, and variable way. It is not that the professor is cynical about the possibility of truth, but rather that the scholar's role is understood as involving a continual, open-ended search for truth. The professor's interest is in asking for as many valid interpretations of the information as can be found, and this search can both confuse and threaten you if you assume that there is but a single, authoritative answer. College teachers ask continually for the reasons that a position is held, for the best arguments for a given point of view, for the assumptions on which a given position is based, and for the evidence that confirms or counts against any given claim.

In all, just as with personal and moral values, college-level education involves the assumption that, as a student, you will become a maker of your own meaning, on your own, with the ultimate responsibility for judgments of truth and error resting in your hands. The whole system of a university's intellectual values—openness, freedom of inquiry, tolerance, rigor, and excellence—is based on this approach and there is no escaping it.

Assessment of Values

We have stressed that the essential first step in developing a values system is for you to become your own maker of meaning whether in the sphere of personal, moral, or intellectual values. But it is only a first step because you must be aware not only of making meaning but also of making a meaning that can lead to a coherent and fulfilling life. As crucial as it is to develop your own values, it is equally important that you find the right values. Little is accomplished if a person develops a genuine system of values that leads to conduct that is egocentric, dishonest, cruel, and irresponsible. It is not enough to own your values; you must think about owning the right values.

The question of the "right" values cannot be given any simple answers. Yet clearly all of us who have accepted life in a democratic society and membership in an academic community such as a college or university are committed to a wide range of significant values. To participate in democratic institutions is to be committed to such values as respect for others, tolerance, equality, liberty, and fairness. Similarly, those who are members of an academic community are usually passionate in the defense of academic freedom, the open search for truth, honesty, and collegiality, civility, and tolerance for dissenting views. In all these fundamental ways there is a substance of values without which we would not be what we are.

Although our participation in a democratic society and in academic communities has settled many of the deepest questions of the nature of the right values, many issues relating to values are open for continuing and legitimate discussion and disagreement. One of the most promising dimensions of an education that effectively addresses values is to give the educated person a process for coming to terms with value choices. The process is similar to the ways in which a good education teaches us to think. That is, an education in values can teach us how to value while leaving to our own independence the actual choices that we will need to make. In teaching us how to value as well as how to think, a good education will help us to be concerned about a series of overarching questions relating to values.

Through a good education you will become sensitive, for example, to whether or not your values are consistent with each other. Where we find cases of unjustified inconsistency, we will know that a contradiction between values can be just as harmful and foolish as a contradiction between ideas. We will also discover that our process for assessing values will make us particularly sensitive to the points at which our values are too limited in scope and fail to provide us with a comprehensive outlook on life. We will learn that our values may work very well within the small circle of our family but tend to produce conflict with individuals with a different background. This will press us to reach for common ground, to try to find those areas of agreement where we can overcome conflict. The pressure always to move outward, to enlarge our circle of association, to move ever more toward the universal sphere of human family beyond all division, beyond all racism, beyond all sexism, is a direction in which we seem always to have to go to find our true and best selves.

So it goes with many other tests by which we can measure the depth, the richness, and the adequacy of our values. We know that many of our choices fail to meet the test that time itself provides, and that partying away precious hours the night before a crucial exam simply fails to meet the test of relative worth. Life teaches us that transient satisfactions and pleasures leave us with little if they rob us of opportunities and accomplishments that may stay with us for a lifetime.

And so it goes. Our life itself is continually giving us tests as to which values will create coherent, consistent, and enduring results that will produce the greatest integrity and the greatest fulfillment of our potential. Just as we can be educated with regard to ways of thinking, so we can be educated with regard to our valuing and our choices. This too is what college is all about, and the opportunity for both personal and intellectual growth is yours. May you seize it and reach your best possibilities by finding and affirming the truest values.

Suggested Activities

1. Do a values survey of a group of your friends (one at a time or in a small group) using the lists of intrinsic and instrumental values included in the article. When you have enough responses, at least twenty, do an analysis of the patterns and frequencies of answers.

2. Share your analysis of the responses with those who participated in the survey. Discuss with the participants the reasons that they ranked the values as they did.

3. Encourage the respondents to assess or test their reasons with reference to others' responses and the criteria of choice discussed in the article—that is, consistency, coherence, comprehensiveness, authenticity.

4. Ask the participants to do the values ranking exercise a second time, and compare the results with the first set of ranking. Try to develop a set of hypotheses about what changes, if any, were the result of the process of the discussion and the assessment of values.

The Developing College Student

Virginia N. Gordon

Virginia N. Gordon, who has been a college teacher and administrator, is best known as a researcher, academic advisor, and counselor for undecided students. She received her Ph.D. in counseling from the Ohio State University.

This essay describes two theoretical perspectives on how students change intellectually and personally during the college years. These theories are based on what students have experienced and related to researchers through personal interviews.

By entering college you begin a very exciting and challenging period in your life. Although it may be difficult for you to imagine now, think about yourself on the day you graduate with a college degree. In addition to being a college graduate, what kind of person will you be? How do you expect to change during your college years?

After careful research, many theorists have described how students change and develop throughout the college experience. Social scientists who have studied college students have discovered some patterns and common themes in the way they change. One such theorist, Professor William Perry, of Harvard University, has studied how college students change intellectually and ethically. He developed a scheme to describe the development of the thinking and reasoning processes that takes place naturally as students mature and grow intellectually. Each phase of this development may be likened to a set of filters through which students see the world around them.

Dualistic students see the world in polar terms; that is, they believe that all questions have a right answer and, therefore, that all answers are either right or wrong. Such students are happiest when they find simplistic answers to their questions about the world, and they want to view their teachers and advisers as experts who can give them the right answer. They believe that hard work and obedience pay off. They depend on others to make important decisions for them. Many freshmen begin their college experience seeing through this dual-istic lens.

As students develop, however, Perry says they become capable of more complex reasoning and dissatisfied with simplistic answers. They are moving into a *"multiplistic"* view of the world. They begin to see and understand cause and effect relationships. Diversity becomes legitimate because they realize that no one has all the answers. They believe everyone has the right to his or her opinion. They still, however, depend on others to make decisions for them. Some freshmen and sophomores view their experiences through this multiplistic lens.

Perry identifies the next phase, "relativism," as the time when students begin to synthesize diverse and complex elements of reasoning. They are able to view

Reprinted by permission of the author.

uncertainty as legitimate. They see *themselves* as the principal agent in decision making and acknowledge that they must not only make their own decisions, but also take responsibility for those decisions, regardless of how well or badly those decisions may turn out. Many juniors and seniors fall into this category of "relativistic" thinkers. Because the emphasis in Perry's system is always on how college students tend to think and reason, his theory is called a theory of *cognitive* development.

For Perry, the most advanced phase of cognitive development is one in which students make a commitment to a personal identity and its content and style. Each develops a sense of being "in" one's self, along with an awareness that growth is always transpiring, that change is inevitable and healthy. Students also make a commitment to a defined career area and are able to develop a lifestyle that is appropriate for them. Many students continue in this state of personal growth and development after college.

Through his theory of cognitive development, Perry helps us understand how students view, react to, and assimilate knowledge as they progress through college. It is important to recognize that while college experiences encourage and foster this development, non-college students also mature and develop in much the same way. (It is also important to remember that any theoretical model, no matter how carefully established, is just that: a model. Judgments about how individuals may be measured against a model require great care. And, as you see later, other models are also well established.)

Perry theorizes that growth occurs in surges, with pauses between the surges when some students might need to detach themselves for a while, while others even retreat to the comfort of their past ways of thinking. Ask five seniors to look back on how they have changed intellectually. While they will be able to reflect on their intellectual development in unique and personal terms, the patterns of growth that Perry describes will usually be evident. However, it sometimes takes courage to confront the risks each forward movement requires. Every student has the freedom to choose what kind of person he or she will become, but the forces of growth, according to Perry, will not be denied.

Developmental Tasks

Another theorist, Arthur Chickering, suggests that college students develop in an orderly way on many dimensions: intellectually, physically, psychologically and socially. He describes several developmental tasks, or "*vectors*," through which students move during their college years. A vector, according to Chickering, is a developmental task that (1) has specific content, (2) shows up at certain times in our lives, and (3) takes two to seven years to resolve. The process is ongoing throughout our lives, and even though we may resolve a task once, it may resurface later. These tasks build on each other; how we resolve one may affect the ones that follow. While these tasks develop in order, they may also be concurrent, so we may be dealing with several at one time. The seven developmental tasks that Chickering has proposed are described next.

1. Achieving Competence

The first task is achieving competence. College students need to achieve competence in several areas: intellectually, physically, and interpersonally. Chickering likens this to a three-tined pitchfork, since all three happen simultaneously.

Intellectual competence involves the skill of using one's mind in "comprehending, analyzing and synthesizing." It means learning how to learn and acquiring knowledge. Most students enroll in college in order to develop intellectual competence. They begin to develop good study habits and the skills of critical thinking and reasoning. They will be able to appreciate and integrate many points of view in their thinking. Ideally, they will enjoy learning for its own sake and feel the excitement of entering new realms of knowledge. Physical competence involves manual skills as well. The recreational value of, and prestige associated with, athletic skills or the creative value of arts and crafts are important to many students. More and more we are concerned that lifelong fitness is important. Recreational skills and interests that one develops in college continue throughout life. Colleges provide many physical facilities for students who seek to develop competency in this area.

Probably the greatest concern of many students is how to develop interpersonal and social competence. They feel a need for communication skills, such as listening and responding appropriately, so they can relate to others individually or in groups. Learning the social graces and how to interact with peers is an important task that most students accomplish early in their college years. Much of this learning happens as a result of observation, feedback from other students, and experience.

When these three competencies are achieved, students feel a *sense* of competence; they sense that they can cope with whatever comes. They are confident of their ability to achieve successfully whatever they set out to do. They respond to new challenges by integrating old learning with new. The task of developing competence is especially important during the freshman year.

2. Managing Emotions

Two major emotional impulses that need to be managed during college are sex and aggression. Maturity implies that legitimate ways have been found to express anger and hate. Sexual impulses are more insistent than ever. Students feel pressured to find answers to questions concerning interpersonal relationships. They move from being controlled by the external rules of their heritage to control by internal norms of self. (Students from rural areas may have different sets of rules, for example, than inner-city students.) Many students are still controlled by the external norms of their peers. Exaggerated displays of emotion are not uncommon: in the past, for example, college students initiated panty raids or held contests for swallowing the greatest number of goldfish.

People often feel boredom, tension and anxiety as normal emotions while their impulsive feelings need to be controlled. Becoming aware of positive emotions such as sympathy, yearning, wonder and awe is also important. Eventually, students learn to be controlled by their own internal set of norms.

Achieving competence in the management of emotions means moving from an awareness of the legitimacy of emotions, to acting on them, to controlling them internally.

3. Moving Through Autonomy Toward Interdependence

Another important task for new college students during the first months of college is to achieve independence. A student may be hesitant to try certain new experiences or to approach new people. Such a student is trying to become independent but, as Chickering says, is like a "hog on ice," a little shaky at first. For probably the first time in their experience, many students may be living with no restraints or outside pressures, with no one to tell them when to study or to be home by 11 o'clock. As they act on their own, they may flounder at first. Beginning students may wonder, for example, why they have so much free time. They attend classes for only three or four hours a day and then may squander the rest of the day—until they realize the importance of quality study time.

The student who achieves *emotional* independence has learned to be free of the continual need for reassurance, affection or approval. Such a student has learned to deal with authority figures and feels comfortable with professors or other very important people on campus. There is less reliance on parents and more on friends and nonparental adults. Achieving *instrumental* independence means students can do things for themselves that parents used to do, such as washing the laundry or managing money. They are able to solve problems and use resources on their own.

When the student finally comes to recognize and accept *inter*dependence, the boundaries of personal choice become clearer and the ranges within which one can give and receive become more settled. Autonomous students feel less need for support from their parents and begin to understand that parents need them as much as they need their parents. They begin to see their parents for what they are: middle-aged people with weaknesses just like themselves. Becoming autonomous is a very important task for freshmen to accomplish.

4. Developing Mature Interpersonal Relationships

Developing mature relationships means that students become less anxious and less defensive, more friendly, spontaneous and respectful. They are more willing to trust and are more independent. They develop the capacity for mature intimacy. They can participate in healthy relationships that incorporate honesty and responsiveness. They finally realize that perfect parents don't exist and that Prince or Princess Charming is not coming to sweep them off their feet. They also have an increased tolerance for people culturally different from themselves. They have acquired increased empathy and altruism and enjoy diversity. They are able to develop mature relationships with many types of people.

5. Establishing Identity

The fifth vector, according to Chickering, is establishing identity. This task is really the sum of the first four vectors: developing competence, managing emotions, developing autonomy through interdependence, and developing mature interpersonal relationships. Success at achieving identity will often hinge on how these former tasks have been accomplished. Studies suggest that students generally achieve a coherent, mature sense of identity during their sophomore or junior years.

In addition to these inner changes, students need to clarify their conceptions of physical needs, personal appearance, and sex-appropriate roles and behavior. They identify a personal lifestyle that is theirs. Once such a sense of identity is achieved, other major vectors may be approached. Establishing an identity is the hinge on which future development depends.

6. Developing Purpose

Developing purpose is the vector related to career choice. The questions to be faced for this vector are not only "Who Am I?" but also "Where Am I Going?" Interests tend to stabilize; vocational exploration becomes a serious task. A general orientation toward a career area is achieved first, and then more specific career decisions are made. Students begin to formulate plans and integrate vocational and lifestyle considerations into those plans. An initial commitment to a career goal is made with the move into adulthood.

7. Developing Integrity

Students also need to clarify a personally valid set of beliefs that have some internal consistency. This happens in three stages, according to Chickering. Their values are first (1) humanized, then (2) personalized, and then (3) their beliefs and actions begin to suit each other. During childhood, students assimilate their parents' values. In college, students begin to examine these inherited values to see if they fit them personally. Some values may be rejected while others may be retained. The student's task is to personalize these values by achieving behavior consistent with them and being willing to stand up for what he or she strongly believes. Such a degree of commitment leads to congruence between one's beliefs and values and one's actions. Standards for assessing personal actions are set and are used as guides for all behavior.

Working through these seven developmental tasks is crucial to the college student's successful passage into mature adulthood. How will you be different on graduation day? I hope that you will have no regrets about missed opportunities to become involved in your own development. The college environment offers an almost unbelievable assortment of opportunities in and outside the classroom. There are many resources, including people, who stand ready to challenge and support you. As you move into the world you will be willing to assert the convictions and values you carefully (and sometimes traumatically) learned during your college years. Knowing that everyone moves through these passages of development and that change is inevitable can help you see the more difficult times as periods of growth. In this way you will be able to react positively and productively.

Vocabulary

As you think about this essay, these definitions may be helpful to you:

1. **dualistic** consisting of two irreducible elements or modes; a way of thinking that sees issues as black or white, rather than as shades of gray
2. **multiplistic**   numerous or various
3. **cognitive**   involving the act of knowing, including both awareness and judgment
4. **vector** a course or direction
5. **instrumental**   serving as a means, agent, or tool; in this essay, instrumental independence is the ability to live and work on your own

 ## Discussion Questions

1. What aspect of student development does Perry's scheme address? What is its primary thesis? Do all students fit these patterns?
2. How does a dualistic student view the world?
3. How does Perry describe commitment, which he considers the most advanced phase of cognitive development? How do you reach commitment?
4. What are the seven developmental tasks of college students as proposed by Chickering? Which are most relevant to first-year, traditional-age college students?
5. What, says Chickering, is required to develop an identity? How are the last two tasks of developing purpose and integrity related to identity?

 ## Suggestions for Your Journal

Sketch your own intellectual development from the time you were a child until now. Where do you think you fit into Perry's scheme? Have you ever consciously experienced a period of intellectual growth? How would you describe it?

Which of Chickering's developmental tasks have you completed? Which will be the most difficult to master?

CHAPTER 6

WHAT IS DIVERSITY AND INTERCULTURAL COMPETENCE?

There are many dimensions of human diversity: age, race, ethnicity, gender, sexual orientation, physical and mental abilities, socioeconomic status, spiritual identity, political ideology, beliefs, and education. People are born with some of these attributes, while others may develop over one's lifetime.

Intercultural competence begins with an individual's perspective on and ability to understand how his or her own culture and identity shapes his or her beliefs and behavior. Over time, competence is developed through thoughtful and effective communication skills and the acquisition of knowledge of and experiences with cultures different from one's own. Intercultural competence is essential for empowering individuals and teams to successfully participate in a rapidly expanding global network.

On October 8, 2008 the Sacramento State Multi-Cultural Center received a donated piece of artwork from Lisa Franklin (Sac State Art student). Lisa together with her parents, Chet and Suzan Young, created this mixed media collage, Evolutionary Transition, for the Multi-Cultural Center.

Conceptualizing the Mural…
The concept for this piece was an evolutionary process birthed in August 2008 by Lisa Franklin, Natchee Blu Barnd, and Charlene Martinez. Lisa initially proposed the idea of creating a conceptual mural that would be a transformation of various colors turning into other colors,

Lisa Franklin,
Art History Major

"I am blessed to be a part of three cultures originating from three different countries; China, Mexico, Italy. My life as a multiethnic, multicultural individual makes a complete revolution around the world.

I wouldn't be here if my ancestors chose not to transition. I wouldn't be here if my parents chose not to evolve. I am transition. I am evolution. I am Evolutionary Transition."

Lisa Franklin

symbolizing the mixing of races/ethnicities. That original idea grew and eventually shifted towards emphasizing four distinct colors that would coalesce into one larger circle in the middle and represent all of our various diversities and intersecting identities. More than just symbolizing ethnic backgrounds, this piece represents our diverse age, gender, class, sexual, and language identities. The colors, textures, and shapes of Evolutionary Transition challenge us to confront the complexities of these individual and collective identities, to own the contradictions of our histories, and to collectively tackle our interconnected social issues.

We hope that this mural stimulates dialogue about our multiple identities and respective places of power, privilege, oppression, and liberation.

The Multi-Cultural Center welcomes these discussions.

Fitting In

Betty LaSere Erickson and Diane Weltner Strommer

Betty LaSere Erickson is an instructional development specialist at the University of Rhode Island and conducts workshops and seminars on college campuses nationwide. Diane Weltner Strommer is former dean of University College and Special Academic Programs at the University of Rhode Island and frequently consults on programs to improve new students' first year. In this essay they draw on their own studies and experience, as well as important research about college students, to point out the importance of "fitting in" to the college environment. They explore the role that a sense of belonging can play for students as they adjust to university life and work.

It's easy to veg out in your room. I know you can't expect people and activities to come to you, but it's hard to be independent and assertive. I want to be involved in the school, but I don't know how.— Freshman

How freshmen elect to spend their time suggests the kind and extent of involvement they have with the college, how well they are fitting in. While more than 80 percent of college-bound seniors still graduate from public high schools enrolling fewer than 500 students,[1] since 1950 most colleges and universities have grown steadily larger, with the average enrollment of all institutions expanding by about 25 percent in the fifteen years between 1970 and 1984.[2] As colleges have grown and become more bureaucratic and complex, freshmen accustomed to a smaller scale find it more difficult to locate a niche, to feel they fit in. Although some schools have instituted strong systems of support for freshmen, on most campuses freshmen are expected to assimilate themselves to the ongoing system as quickly as possible. Nothing much has changed since the Hazen Report of 1968. Then as now colleges can be criticized for doing little, if anything, to maintain the curiosity of freshmen, to stimulate their interest, to expose them to intellectual experiences, or to involve them in college activities.[3]

Although freshmen clearly understand the need to find their place academically as well as socially, the first priority of most is to make new friends with whom to "hang out." Most do so surprisingly quickly, and engaging in "friendly fun" . . . occupies much of their time outside class. Most colleges report a distinct decline in participation in more formalized extracurricular activities. On our campus at the University of Rhode Island, for instance, only 8 percent of the freshmen reported some degree of participation in student clubs or student government in an informal survey taken in 1989. Although freshmen often mention the need to

[1]The College Board. *College Bound Seniors National Report: 1988, Profile of SAT and Achievement Test Takers.* New York: College Entrance Examination Board, 1988.
[2]National Institute of Education. *Involvement in Learning: Realizing the Potential of American Higher Education.* Washington, D.C.: U.S. Department of Education, 1984.
[3]Hazen Foundation, The Committee on the Student in Higher Education. *The Student in Higher Education.* New Haven, Conn.: Hazen Foundation, 1968.
From *Teaching College Freshmen* (pp. 37–41). Copyright 1991, Jossey-Bass Publishers. All rights reserved. Reprinted by permission.

take part in extracurricular activities with great earnestness, as if it were a faintly pleasant duty, their preference during nonworking hours is clearly for more private and casual fun with their peers—parties, pickup games or intramural sports, rock concerts.

Finding a circle of friends and becoming accepted can be particularly difficult for students who do not quite match the campus norm; disabled, minority, international, gay, and older freshmen may all feel particularly alienated and isolated. For minority students and many international students, the painful *disparity* between their college life and home life may increase their sense of isolation. Trying to live in two worlds can be exceedingly difficult. As Marcus Mabry, a black student from New York attending Stanford, writes, "The ache of knowing [my family's] suffering is always there. It has to be kept deep down, or I can't find the logic in studying and partying while people, my people, are being killed by poverty. Ironically, success drives me away from those I most want to help by getting an education."[4]

For minority students, particularly those from disadvantaged backgrounds, the connection to college is often tenuous. They are less likely than majority students to have successful graduates in their immediate or extended families, less likely to have heard that they were expected to be successful in college from others or to have had strong, long-term expectations for themselves, have fewer previous on-campus experiences, and have fewer peers to help them in exploring and adjusting to their new environment or in fitting in.[5]

Although Moffatt reports that during his association with the dorm at Rutgers, blacks and Puerto Ricans "lived reasonably *amiably* among their white peers all year long," he also notes that the minority students did all the adjusting. "They were swamped," he comments, "by the white majority on an 'integrated' floor" and they "lived on the floor in terms of the white majority. None of them were 'threatening.' None of them made much of her or his black or Puerto Rican identity."[6] Another study reports that "the social environments of the large, predominantly white, public universities . . . were problematic even for well-prepared minority students."[7] Minority freshmen may find social support only off campus.

Institutions that expect all adjustment to be on the side of freshmen "limit the range of minority students they can serve responsibly to those who . . . resemble traditional college-goers."[8]

Along with this ever-present assumption that minority students can and will conform to the majority, the past several years have seen a disturbing *resurgence* of racially and ethnically motivated violence and conflict on a number of campuses, demanding that colleges pay serious attention to the climate for minority groups. While middle-class white students usually know they ought to appreciate diver-

---

[4]Mabry, M. "Living in Two Worlds." *Newsweek on Campus,* April 1988, 52.

[5]Attinasi, L. C., Jr. "Getting In: Mexican Americans' Perceptions of University Attendance and the Implications for Freshman Year Persistence." *Journal of Higher Education,* 1989, *60* (3), 247–277.

[6]Moffatt, M. *Coming of Age in New Jersey.* New Brunswick, N.J.: Rutgers University Press, 1989.

[7]Skinner, E. R., and Richardson, R. C. "Making It in a Majority University." *Change,* May/June, 1988, 37–42.

[8]Green, M. F. (ed.). *Minorities on Campus: A Handbook for Enhancing Diversity.* Washington, D.C.: American Council on Education, 1989.

sity, they are in fact often frightened by it, a fear especially apparent as it relates to homosexuality, since being openly *homophobic* is more socially acceptable to peers than is fear of blacks, Hispanics, or Asians.

Typically, therefore, minority freshmen experience an unusual degree of stress as they attempt to fit in, to accommodate: the gay student concealing his or her homosexuality, the black student acting white. In the classroom, faculty create the climate. We know, for instance, not only that overt faculty prejudice "can result in inappropriate racial or ethnic remarks in class or in lowering the performance of alienated or discouraged minority students," but also that "unconscious assumptions that minority students are unable to perform up to par may become self-fulfilling prophecies."[9] Subtle behaviors or different treatment—like calling on students more or less frequently, not asking students the same kinds of questions, not paying the same attention—can create what Hall and Sandler first identified as a "chilly classroom climate" for members of minority groups and women.[10]

Older students, too, need sensitive understanding. As one observes, "Faculty could be more tuned in to the fact that it's not that easy; you're balancing a lot of responsibilities. With age some people find it particularly difficult to admit they need help. Faculty could ask if they need help. And not make up impossible rules. I had one professor who said from the beginning that there would be absolutely no excuses for missing an exam. If you miss an exam, you get a zero. I hardly ever miss a class. But my initial reaction was, what if something happens at home?"

The classroom may be key not only to the successful academic *assimilation* of freshmen, but, interestingly, to their personal growth as well. One somewhat surprising finding of a study designed to determine the benefits of college attendance was that "academic integration" had both direct and indirect effects on freshman-year reports of personal growth.[11] Finding a niche academically, fitting into and succeeding in classes, may have more influence on personal growth, this study suggests, than does fitting in socially. Authors Terenzini and Wright conclude, "Students' integration into the academic systems of an institution may be as important to their personal growth as to their academic and intellectual development. These findings suggest a potential need to rethink campus and departmental orientation programs, many of which focus on introducing students to social, rather than academic, aspects of the collegiate experience. The results also have important implications for faculty members who foster academic integration as they advise students. . . . Finally, the results suggest a coherence and integrity in the developmental process: experiences that promote students' academic or intellectual development also appear to influence students' personal growth."[12]

---

[9]Hall, R. M., and Sandler, B. R. *The Classroom Climate: A Chilly One for Women?* Washington, D.C.: Association of American Colleges, Project on the Status and Education of Women, 1982.
[10]Hall, R. M., and Sandler, B. R. *Out of the Classroom: A Chilly Campus Climate for Women?* Washington, D.C.: Association of American Colleges, Project on the Status and Education of Women, 1984.
[11]Terenzini, P. T. , and Wright, T. M. "Students' Personal Growth During the First Two Years of College." *The Review of Higher Education*, 1987, *10* (3), 259–271.
[12]Ibid., pp. 268, 270.

Vocabulary

As you think about this essay, these definitions may be helpful to you:

1. **disparity**   fundamental difference
2. **amiably**   in a friendly, agreeable manner
3. **resurgence**   state of rising again into life or prominence
4. **homophobic**   irrationally fearing homosexuality
5. **assimilation**   absorbtion into the cultural tradition of a group

 ## Discussion Questions

1. Adapting to a new environment can mean learning to "fit in" to many new situations. Identify some of these situations that are common to most first-year students.
2. Many people regard a new environment as unsettling, but a better way may be to think of each new environment as a new opportunity. How can these different points of view affect students' behavior as they attempt to "fit in"?
3. According to Erickson and Strommer, what special problems do new minority students face when they attempt to fit in at college?
4. In general, what is the role of faculty members in helping students to fit in? Does this have specific implications for minority students?
5. Why do Erikson and Strommer consider the results of the study by Terenzini and Wright to be "somewhat surprising"?

 ## How Can These Ideas Apply to You?

1. Have you found it easy or difficult to fit in to college life? Why? What are you doing to fit in?
2. In your judgment, are Erickson and Strommer correct when they write: "While middle-class white students usually know they ought to appreciate diversity, they are in fact often frightened by it, a fear especially apparent as it relates to homosexuality, since being openly homophobic is more socially acceptable to peers than is fear of blacks, Hispanics, or Asians."? What factors—other than fear—might contribute to students' unwillingness to "appreciate diversity"?
3. Compare your feelings on your first day in college with your feelings today. In what ways have they changed? How did those changes occur?
4. Some adaptations are easier than others. In adjusting to college life, what did you find easiest? Most difficult?

5. Suppose that Terenzini and Wright are correct in their conclusion that learning to fit in academically at college is more important than learning to fit in socially. What steps should you take in order to fit in academically?

Diversity Leads to Discovery
Kim Bancroft and Melinda D. Wilson

Kim Bancroft and Melinda D. Wilson are assistant professors at California State University, Sacramento in the Departments of Teacher Education and Theatre and Dance respectively. This article stems from their shared interest in creating constructive classroom conversations about race and ethnicity.

Question Thyself: Dr. Wilson's Perspective on Diversity

My first year in college, I took two classes—"The Harlem Renaissance" and "Images of Women"—that absolutely blew my mind. I remember reading plays, poems, novels, and articles that challenged not only the way I, at the age of eighteen, viewed African American history, women, and other cultures, but they challenged the way I viewed myself. In these and other classes, I discovered that my thoughts and interests did not always line up exactly with those of my peers. I disagreed with some of what they said. Why was I so different? Was I wrong? Were they right? Could I refute the status quo in class and still get an "A"? I thought I understood where they were coming from, but sometimes I simply did not.

I always looked forward to going to these classes, and some days I left more invigorated than when I arrived. Other days I left infuriated! Storming back across campus one day, I wondered about another student's statement. "What did he mean when he said, 'I wouldn't want to be Black'? How could he say that? Am I a bad thing to be? Why on earth would someone want to be White?!" At the time, I did not realize that my classmate's understanding of what it meant hypothetically to be Black differed from my understanding of what it meant actually to be Black. I did not realize that people, based on their own experiences, read the world (and literature, plays, movies, everyday interactions with other people, etc.) differently. I developed a love-hate relationship with these classes. I loved the material, but I struggled with it because I did not know if I always got the answers to the questions "right."

At the end of the semester, my Images of Women professor announced, "All you have to do in your four years of college is grow intellectually and emotionally." At that moment, I understood perfectly. My task as a college student was to challenge myself and push myself out of my comfort zone. In order for me to grow, I had to first seriously examine myself. Where did my views come from? Second, I had to genuinely consider my peers so I could honestly understand their views as well.

The question, "Who are you?" seems like such a simple thing to ask yourself. However, the answer may be quite complex because you may find it difficult to define yourself as only one thing. Asked another way: Who (or what) *all* are you? I, for example, am a young, African American woman who graduated from two top-twenty universities and now teaches theatre and drama at Sacramento State University. I was born in Louisville, Kentucky, but at this point I have lived in five different states and six different cities, mostly in suburban neighborhoods.

Growing up, I was often the only Black kid in my class. I was also "smart," and it was clear to me that the combination of "Black" and "smart" baffled some of my teachers because Black kids were typically not the smart students. I often sensed that my teachers did not quite know what to do with me, so school tended to bore me. I carry this memory with me today because it reminds me that my Blackness, my race, alone does not define who I am for myself or for other people. When people first see me, they usually see an "African American woman" because my skin tone and gender are visible markers of those social categories. However, my varied experiences with race, class, gender, religion, and age have shaped and continue to shape my identity. In the borrowed words of playwright Amiri Baraka, my identity "changes as I change in a changing world" (Hill, 1994, p. 39). I am not a single label. My identity is diverse.

The word "diversity" literally means variety. When applied to human beings, it defines a myriad of people from several different backgrounds with various interests and abilities who share a community. Often times, when people hear the word "diversity," they tend first to think of the presence of representatives from two groups, so images of opposites like "men and women," "Democrats and Republicans," or "Blacks and Whites" together come to mind. Diversity, however, is not a two-way street that places people in only one of two categories. Diversity integrates overlapping categories of race, age, class, sex, gender, sexual orientation, religion, politics, physical and mental ability, and several additional social factors that define people as both individuals and community members, such as families, congregations, neighborhoods, and universities. Diversity is the merging of your multiple identities that make you an individual. Diversity is also the coming together of multiple individuals to create heterogeneous communities where everyone is not the same.

People often judge others based on stereotypes or generalizations about people or groups based on inaccurate assumptions of others. Allowing a stereotype to determine your opinion of another is like placing that person in a box and not allowing him or her to leave the box. The more you get to know yourself, the more you will discover that you can fit and flourish in multiple boxes.

How do you identify yourself? What does it mean to you to be Black, White, Asian, Latino or mixed? What does it mean to you to be male or female? Do you consider yourself an "adult"? Why or why not? Are there aspects of your identity that you hide from others because you feel embarrassed or ashamed? Your college years will present opportunities for you to explore your own ideas, shape your views, and by extension further develop your self-identity. If you think about how your age, race, class, gender, sex, sexual orientation, abilities and disabilities, religion, etc., all influence your perspective and the choices you make, then you will discover that your life can take several different paths because you have different interests that have been shaped by your life experiences.

Encounter Others Openly: Dr. Bancroft's Perspective on Discovery

Once you feel secure in your own identity, racial, ethnic and other, you may feel less threatened when learning about the experiences of other groups. In fact, you might even feel excited to deepen your knowledge of worlds you have never seen yourself. But what does it take to get there? How do we learn to recognize and then overcome embedded beliefs and reach out intellectually and emotionally to understand the lives of people different from ourselves?

As a white middle class woman, I grew up in a segregated community like so many across the United States in the 1960s and 1970s, segregated due to deeply rooted patterns of residential and employment discrimination. As a result, I had few interactions with people of color, except for the slow integration of our local schools with African American kids who often came from "across town" or the other side of the tracks. Despite an ethic of "we are all equal" promulgated by civil rights leaders such as Martin Luther King Jr., the insults of discrimination were as invisible to me as was my own white middle class privilege (McIntosh, 1998).

Coming to consciousness of racial and ethnic disparities in this country did not come easily for me. The 1980s and 1990s were decades when the continued fervor for equality was no longer just the fodder of large marches and policy battles, but now the skirmishes were also personal, in schools, offices, playing fields, organizations—wherever I encountered people of color who were struggling to expose prejudice, stereotyping and discrimination challenged whites to examine our embedded racism. Rodney King's iconic plea, "Why can't we all just get along?" is now rooted in our social language: What *does* it take to "all get along"?

We have to be willing to listen to how people frame their stories about the forces that have shaped their identities and worldviews. What happens when we have to work in a group—either in a classroom or work setting—with someone whose life experience and/or identity rankles us? For instance, how might you react to the following scenarios if you were one of the people involved?

- Your classmate is an out lesbian, and you have been raised to believe gay people are sinners.
- A liberal co-worker criticizes warfare and unintentionally insults your own experience as a soldier.
- A classmate implies that his family members are undocumented immigrants; you believe those foreigners are taking American jobs.
- The Muslim woman you share a cubicle with covers her head and most of her body; you feel this attire degrades women.
- A classmate discloses that she has a learning disability and gets extra time on exams, but you view this extension as an unfair advantage.
- You insinuate to your African American co-worker that she might have gotten a promotion due to affirmative action; she reacts angrily.

At the heart of much ongoing dissension about racism, sexism, heterosexism, discrimination against disabled people, immigrants or religious minorities is the inability to grasp another's perspective and understand the source of their anger, hurt, or dearly held beliefs. Why do "they" feel or think that way? What meanings can we make of such feelings and values? How can we respect those feelings and values even as they brush up against our own?

For many who grew up in neighborhoods and social groups that reflected their own racial, ethnic or class group, a diverse college setting offers an opportunity to learn about the beliefs and feelings of others as we gain exposure to different groups in classroom conversations (especially when taking General Education requirements aimed at such exposure). We are exposed to the history and struggles of a group, and how each group passes along culture, attitudes, knowledge, and beliefs that stem from a shared experience. Learning about one another's struggles requires listening with an open mind and even an open heart.

Fortunately, the act of listening intently to someone speak about his or her life *also* involves learning about diverse sources of joy—cultural celebrations and traditions, parades and parties, literature and music, ethnic dances and food, religious holidays, ways of communicating outside the mainstream, the stories and humor percolating in other communities. Understanding the *diversity of diversity* discussed at the beginning of this essay includes reveling in the richness of human social life.

Ask the Questions of Yourself and Others to Find the Answers

Our national motto on our currency is *E Pluribus Unum*: Out of Many, One. Becoming unified does not mean we have to lose our individuality. In fact, we can and should celebrate our differences as we learn to negotiate how our differences cause dissension. Just as we cannot understand others until we understand ourselves, we cannot become one as a classroom community, a workplace, a city, a nation until we have delved into and grasped the many lives that make up our society—whether these differences are racial, ethnic, religious, linguistic, cultural, or the other ways in which we are diverse. Generating enough unity to move forward as a national political community requires that ultimately we work together. As we practice that in our classrooms and workplaces, we move beyond complaining about what others believe and do to understanding—we may not agree, but at least we really know where someone is literally coming from.

If you were to go into a room filled with fifty people you did not know, then what would they see when they look at you? A young person? An old person? A man? A Woman? A teenager? A college student? An educated person? A person seeking knowledge? An able-bodied person? A disabled person? A tall person or a short person? Someone with blonde hair and blue eyes or someone with black hair and brown eyes? A sister, a brother, a son? A Baptist, Catholic, Mormon, Buddhist, or none of the above? An Asian American, African American, Latino/a, White American, or some combination thereof? A rich person or someone from a middle or working class background? Would their first impression of you change or be confirmed when you started to speak? Is the way you talk or even dress associated with a certain culture, group of people, or region that might lead people to *assume* that they can define you in a certain way or place you in a particular **paradigm**? If you were to go into a room filled with fifty people that you did not know, then what would you see when you look back at them? If you open your eyes, your ears, and your heart, then you will discover a lot about yourself and others.

References

Hill, E. (1994). Amiri Baraka. In K.A. Berney (Ed.), *Contemporary American Drama-tists*. London: St. James Press. 36-43.

McIntosh, P. (1998). White privilege: Unpacking the invisible knapsack. In E. Lee, D. Menkart, M. Okazawa-Rey (Eds.), *Beyond heroes and holidays*. Washington, D.C.: Network of Educators on the Americas.

 Vocabulary

1. **Paradigm**   a typical example or pattern; archetype

 Discussion Questions

1. How does diversity apply to both individuals and communities?
2. What are some social stereotypes? How do some of these stereotypes make a difference in how you perceive others or others perceive you?
3. Why is it important to discuss diversity, race, and ethnicity?

How Can These Ideas Apply to You?

1. List as many social categories to which you belong as you can. What is your identity? Who are you?
2. Do you self-identify as only one thing? Do others ever attempt to define you are only one thing?
3. How might differences in understanding an individual or communities' identity prove to be problematic? Some scenarios were listed in the article relating to possible points of dissension when people of opposing experiences encounter each other. What problems relating to diversity in our society have you observed or participated in? How were these problems resolved?
4. How are aspects of who you are different from someone else?
5. How can you begin to learn about yourself and others as a way of exploring diversity?

A Racial/Cultural Identity Development Model

Derald Wing Sue and David Sue

Earlier writers (Berry, 1965; Stonequist, 1937) have observed that minority groups share similar patterns of adjustment to cultural oppression. In the past several decades, Asian Americans, Hispanics, and American Indians have experienced sociopolitical identity transformations so that a *Third World consciousness* has emerged with cultural oppression as the common unifying force. As a result of studying these models and integrating them with their own clinical observations, Atkinson, Morten, and Sue (1979, 1989, 1998) proposed a five-stage Minority Identity Development model (MID) in an attempt to pull out common features that cut across the population-specific proposals. D. W. Sue & Sue (1990, 1999) later elaborated on the MID, renaming it the Racial/Cultural Identity Development model (R/CID)) to encompass a broader population. As discussed shortly, this model may be applied to White identity development as well.

The R/CID model proposed here is not a comprehensive theory of personality, but rather a conceptual framework to aid therapists in understanding their culturally different clients' attitudes and behaviors. The model defines five stages of development that oppressed people experience as they struggle to understand themselves in terms of their own culture, the dominant culture, and the oppressive relationship between the two cultures: *conformity, dissonance, resistance and immersion, introspection,* and *integrative awareness*. At each level of identity, four corresponding beliefs and attitudes that may help therapists better understand their minority clients are discussed. These attitudes/beliefs are an integral part of the minority person's identity and are manifest in how he or she views (a) the self, (b) others of the same minority, (c) others of another minority, and (d) majority individuals. Table 8.1 outlines the R/CID model and the interaction of stages with the attitudes and beliefs.

Conformity Stage

Similar to individuals in the pre-encounter stage (W. E. Cross, 1991), minority individuals are distinguished by their unequivocal preference for dominant cultural values over their own. White Americans in the United States represent their reference group, and the identification set is quite strong. Lifestyles, value systems, and cultural/physical characteristics that most resemble White society are highly valued, while those most like their own minority group may be viewed with disdain or may hold low salience for the person. We agree with Cross that minority people at this stage can be oriented toward a pro-American identity without subsequent disdain or negativism toward their own group. Thus, it is possible for a Chinese-American to feel positively about U.S. culture, values, and traditions without evidencing disdain for Chinese culture or feeling negatively about oneself (absence of self-hate). Nevertheless, we believe that they represent a small proportion of persons of color at this stage. Research on their numbers, on how they have handled the social-psychological dynamics of majority-minority relations, on how they have dealt with their minority status and on how they fit into the stage models (progression issues) needs to be conducted.

We believe that the conformity stage continues to be most characterized by individuals who have bought into societal definitions about their minority status in society. Because the conformity stage represents, perhaps, the most damning indictment of White racism, and because it has such a profound negative impact on nearly all minority groups, we spend more time discussing it than the other stages. Let us use a case approach to illustrate the social-psychological dynamics of the conformity process.

Table 8.1 The Racial/Cultural Identity Development Model

Stages of Minority Development Model	Attitude Toward Self	Attitude toward Others of the Same Minority	Attitude toward Others of a Different Minority	Attitude toward Dominant Group
Stage 1 Conformity	Self-depreciating or neutral due to low race salience	Group-depreciating or neutral due to low race salience	Discriminatory or neutral	Group-appreciating
Stage 2 Dissonance and appreciating	Conflict between self-depreciating and group-appreciating	Conflict between group-depreciating views of minority hierarchy and feelings of shared experience	Conflict between dominant-held and group depreciating	Conflict between group-appreciating
Stage 3 Resistance and immersion	Self-appreciating	Group-appreciating experiences and feelings of culturocentrism	Conflict between feelings of empathy for other minority	Group-depreciating
Stage 4 Introspection	Concern with basis of self-appreciation	Concern with nature of unequivocal appreciation	Concern with ethnocentric basis for judging others	Concern with the basis of group-depreciation
Stage 5 Integrative Awareness	Self-appreciating	Group-appreciating	Group-appreciating	Selective appreciation

Source: From Donald R. Atkinson, George Morten, and Derald Wing Sue, *Counseling American Minorities: A Cross Cultural Perspective,* 5th ed. Copyright © 1998 Wm. C. Brown Publishers, Dubuque, IA. All rights reserved. Reprinted by permission.

Who Am I? White or Black

A 17-year-old White high school student, Mary, comes to counseling for help in sorting out her thoughts and feelings concerning an interracial relationship with an African American student. Although she is proud of the relationship and feels that her liberal friends are accepting and envious, Mary's parents are against it. Indeed, the parents have threatened to cut off financial support for her future college education unless she terminates the affair immediately.

During counseling, Mary tells of how she has rid herself of much bigotry and prejudice from the early training of her parents. She joined a circle of friends who were quite liberal in thought and behavior. She recalls how she was both shocked and attracted to her new friends' liberal political beliefs, philosophies, and sexual attitudes. When she first met John, a Black student she was immediately attracted to his apparent confidence and outspokenness. It did not take her long to become sexually involved with him and to enter into an intense relationship. Mary became the talk of her former friends, but she did not seem to care. Indeed, she seemed to enjoy the attention and openly flaunted her relationship in everyone's face.

Because Mary requested couple counseling, the counselor saw them together. John informs the counselor that he came solely to please Mary. He sees few problems in their relationship that cannot be easily resolved. John seems to feel that he has overcome many handicaps in his life and that this represents just another obstacle to be conquered. When asked about his use of the term "handicap," he responds, "It's not easy to be Black, you know. I've proven to my parents and friends in high school, including myself, that I'm worth something. Let them disapprove-I'm going to make it into a good university." Further probing revealed John's resentment over his own parents' disapproval of the relationship. While his relations with them had worsened to the point of near-physical assaults, John continued to bring Mary home. He seemed to take great pride in being seen with a "beautiful blond-haired, blue-eyed White girl."

In a joint session, Mary's desire to continue therapy and John's apparent reluctance becomes obvious. Several times when John mentions the prospect of a "permanent relationship" and their attending the same university, Mary does not seem to respond positively. She does not seem to want to look too far into the future. Mary's constant coolness to the idea and the counselor's attempt to focus on this reluctance anger John greatly. He becomes antagonistic toward the counselor and puts pressure on Mary to terminate this useless talk "crap." However, he continues to come for the weekly sessions. One day his anger boils over, and he accuses the counselor of being biased. Standing up and shouting, John demands to know how the counselor feels about interracial relationships.

There are many approaches to analyzing the above case, but we have chosen to concentrate on the psychological dynamics evidenced by John, the African American student. However, it is clear from a brief reading of this case that both John and Mary are involved in an interracial relationship as a means of rebellion and as attempts to work out personal and group identity issues. In Mary's case, it may be rebellion against conservative parents and parental upbringing, as well as the secondary shock value it has for her former friends and parents (appearing liberal). John's motivation for the relationship is also a form of rebellion. There are many dues in this case to indicate that John identifies with White culture and feels disdain for Black culture. First, he seems to equate his Blackness with a handicap to be overcome. Is it possible that John feels ashamed of who and what he is (Black)? While feeling proud of one's girlfriend is extremely desirable, does Mary's being White, blond-haired, and blue-eyed have special significance? Would John feel equally proud if the woman were beautiful and Black? Being seen in the company of a White woman may represent affirmation to John that he has "made it" in White society. Perhaps he has been sold a false bill of goods and is operating under the belief that White ways are better.

While John's anger in counseling is multidimensional, much of it seems misdirected toward the counselor. John may actually be angry toward Mary because she seems less than committed to a long-term or permanent relationship. Yet to acknowledge that Mary may not want a permanent relationship will threaten the very basis of John's self-deception (that he is not like the other Blacks and is accepted in White society). It is very easy to blame John for his dilemma and to call him an Oreo (Black outside and White inside). However, lest we fall prey to blaming the victim, let us use a wider perspective in analyzing this case.

John (and even Mary) is really a victim of large; social psychological forces operating in our society. The key issue here is the dominant-subordinate relationship between two different cultures (Atkinson, Morten, et al., 1998; Carter, 1995; Freire, 1970; B. Jackson, 1975). It is reasonable to believe that members of one cultural group tend to adjust themselves to the group possessing the greater prestige and power in order to avoid feelings of inferiority. Yet it is exactly this act that creates ambivalence in the minority individual. The pressures for assimilation and acculturation (melting-pot theory) are strong, creating possible culture conflicts. John is the victim of ethnocentric monoculturalism (D. W. Sue et al., 1998): (a) belief in the superiority of one group's cultural heritage—its language, traditions, arts-crafts, and ways of behaving (White) over all others; (b) belief in the inferiority of all other lifestyles (non-White); and (c) the power to impose such standards onto the less powerful group.

The psychological costs of racism on minorities are immense, and John exemplifies this process. Constantly bombarded on all sides by reminders that Whites and their way of life are superior and that all other lifestyles are inferior, many minorities begin to wonder whether they themselves are not somehow inadequate, whether members of their own group are not to blame, and whether subordination and segregation are not justified. K. B. Clark and Clark (1947) first brought this to the attention of social scientists by stating that racism may contribute to a sense of confused self-identity among Black children. In a study of racial awareness and preference among Black and White children, they found that (a) Black children preferred playing with a White doll over a Black one, (b) the Black doll was perceived as being "bad" and (c) approximately one third, when asked to pick the doll that looked like them, picked the White one.

It is unfortunate that the inferior status of minorities is constantly reinforced and perpetuated by the mass media through television, movies, newspapers, radio, books, and magazines. This contributes to widespread stereotypes that tend to trap minority individuals: Blacks are superstitious, childlike, ignorant, fun loving, or dangerous, and criminal; Hispanics are dirty, sneaky, and criminal; Asian

Americans are sneaky, sly, cunning, and passive; Indians are primitive savages. Such portrayals cause widespread harm to the self-esteem of minorities who may incorporate them. That preconceived expectations can set up self-fulfilling prophecies has been demonstrated by Rosenthal and Jacobson (1968). The incorporation of the larger society's standards may lead minority group members to react negatively toward their own racial and cultural heritage. They may become ashamed of who they are, reject their own group identification, and attempt to identify with the desirable "good" White minority. In the *Autobiography of Malcolm X* (A. Haley, 1966), Malcolm X relates how he tried desperately to appear as White as possible. He went to painful lengths to straighten and dye his hair so that he would appear more like White males. It is evident that many minorities do come to accept White standards as a means of measuring physical attractiveness, attractiveness of personality, and social relationships. Such an orientation may lead to the phenomenon of racial self-hatred, in which people dislike themselves for being Asian, Black, Hispanic, or Native American. Like John, individuals operating from the conformity stage experience racial self-hatred and attempt to assimilate and acculturate into White society. People at the conformity stage seem to possess the following characteristics.

1. *Attitudes and beliefs toward the self (self-depreciating attitudes and belief).* Physical and cultural characteristics identified with one's own racial/cultural group are perceived negatively, as something to be avoided, denied, or changed. Physical characteristics (black skin color, "slant shaped eyes" of Asians), traditional modes of dress and appearance, and behavioral characteristics associated with the minority group are a source of shame. There may be attempts to mimic what is perceived as White mannerisms, speech patterns, dress, and goals. Low internal self-esteem is characteristic of the person. The fact that John views his own Blackness as a handicap, something bad, and something to deny is an example of this insidious, but highly damaging, process.

2. *Attitudes and belief toward members of the same minority (group-depreciating attitudes and beliefs).* Majority cultural beliefs and attitudes about the minority group are also held by the person in this stage. These individuals may have internalized the majority of White stereotypes about their group. In the case of Hispanics, for example, the person may believe that members of his or her own group have high rates of unemployment because "they are lazy, uneducated, and unintelligent." Little thought or validity is given to other viewpoints, such as unemployment's being a function of job discrimination, prejudice, racism, unequal opportunities, and inferior education. Because persons in the conformity stage find it psychologically painful to identify with these negative traits, they divorce themselves from their own group. The denial mechanism most commonly used is, 'I'm not like them; I've made it on my own; I'm the exception."

3. *Attitudes and beliefs toward members of different minorities (discriminatory).* Because the conformity-stage person most likely strives for identification with White society, the individual shares similar dominant attitudes and beliefs not only toward his or her own minority group, but toward other minorities as well. Minority groups most similar to White cultural groups are viewed more

favorably, while those most different are viewed less favorably. For example, Asian Americans may be viewed more favorably than African Americans or Latino/Hispanic Americans in some situations. While a stratification probably exists, we caution readers that such a ranking is fraught with hazards and potential political consequences. Such distinctions often manifest themselves in debates over which group is more oppressed and which group has done better than the others. Such debates are counterproductive when used to (a) negate another group's experience of oppression; (b) foster an erroneous belief that hard work alone will result in success in a democratic society; (c) short-change a minority group (i.e., Asian Americans) from receiving the necessary resources in our society, and (d) pit one minority against another (divide and conquer) by holding one group up as an example to others.

4. *Attitude and beliefs toward members of the dominant group (group- appreciating attitude and beliefs).* This stage is characterized by a belief that White cultural, social, and institutional standards are superior. Members of the dominant group are admired respected, and emulated. White people are believed to possess superior intelligence. Some individuals may go to great lengths to appear White. Consider again the example from the *Autobiography of Malcolm X*, in which the main character would straighten his hair and primarily date White women (as in the case of John and the Nisei female student). Reports that Asian women have undergone surgery to reshape their eyes to conform to White female standards of beauty may (but not in all cases) typify this dynamic.

Dissonance Stage

No matter how much one attempts to deny his or her own racial/cultural heritage, an individual will encounter information or experiences that are inconsistent with culturally held beliefs, attitudes, and values. An Asian American who believes that Asians are inhibited, passive, inarticulate, and poor in people relationships may encounter an Asian leader who seems to break these stereotypes (e.g., the Nisei student). A Latino who feels ashamed of his cultural upbringing may encounter another Latino who seems proud of his or her cultural heritage. An African American who believes that race problems are due to laziness, untrustworthiness, or personal inadequacies of his or her own group may suddenly encounter racism on a personal level. Denial begins to break down, which leads to a questioning and challenging of the attitudes/beliefs of the conformity stage. This was clearly what happened when the Nisei Japanese American student encountered discrimination at the restaurant.

In all probability, movement into the dissonance stage is a gradual process. Its very definition indicates that the individual is in conflict between disparate pieces of information or experiences that challenge his or her current self-concept. People generally move into this stage slowly, but a traumatic event may propel some individuals to move into dissonance at a much more rapid pace. W. B. Cross (1971) stated that a monumental event such as the assassination of a major leader like Martin Luther King Jr. can often push people quickly into the ensuing stage.

1. *Attitudes and beliefs toward the self (conflict between self-depreciating and self-appreciating attitudes and beliefs).* There is now a growing sense of personal awareness that racism does exist, that not all aspects of the minority or majority culture are good or bad, and that one cannot escape one's cultural heritage. For the first time the person begins to entertain the possibility of positive attributes in the minority culture and, with it, a sense of pride in self. Feelings of shame and pride are mixed in the individual, and a sense of conflict develops. This conflict is most likely to be brought to the forefront quickly when other members of the minority group may express positive feelings toward the person: "We like you because you are Asian, Black, American Indian, or Latino." At this stage, an important personal question is being asked: "Why should I feel ashamed of who and what I am?"

2. *Attitudes and beliefs toward members of the same minority (conflict between group-depreciating and group-appreciating attitudes and beliefs).* Dominant- held views of minority strengths and weaknesses begin to be questioned as new, contradictory information is received. Certain aspects of the minority culture begin to have appeal. For example, a Latino/Hispanic male who values individualism may marry, have children, and then suddenly realize how Latino cultural values that hold the family as the psychosocial unit possess positive features. Or the minority person may find certain members of his group to be very attractive as friends, colleagues, lovers, and so forth.

3. *Attitudes and beliefs toward members of a different minority (conflict between dominant-held views of minority hierarchy and feelings of shared experience).* Stereotypes associated with other minority groups are questioned, and a growing sense of comradeship with other oppressed groups is felt. It is important to keep in mind, however, that little psychic energy is associated with resolving conflicts with other minority groups. Almost all energies are expended toward resolving conflicts toward the self, the same minority, and the dominant group.

4. *Attitudes and beliefs toward members of the dominant group (conflict between group-appreciating and group-depreciating attitudes).* The person experiences a growing awareness that not all cultural values of the dominant group are beneficial. This is especially true when the minority person experiences personal discrimination. Growing suspicion and some distrust of certain members of the dominant group develops.

Resistance and Immersion Stage

The minority person tends to endorse minority-held views completely and to reject the dominant values of society and culture. The person seems dedicated to reacting against White society and rejects White social, cultural, and institutional standards as having no personal validity. Desire to eliminate oppression of the individual's minority group becomes an important motivation of the individual's behavior. During the resistance and immersion stage, the three most active types of affective feelings are *guilt, shame,* and *anger.* There are considerable feelings of guilt and shame that in the past the minority individual has sold out his or her own racial and cultural group. The feelings of guilt and shame extend to the perception that during this past "sellout" the minority person has been a contributor and participant in the oppression of his or her own group and other minority groups. This is coupled with a strong sense of anger at the oppression and feelings of having been brainwashed by the forces in White society. Anger is directed outwardly in a very strong way toward oppression and racism. Movement into this stage seems to occur for two reasons. First, a resolution of the conflicts and confusions of the previous stage allows greater understanding of social forces (racism, oppression, and discrimination) and his or her role as a victim. Second a personal questioning of why people should feel ashamed of themselves develops. The answer to this question evokes feelings of guilt, shame, and anger.

1. *Attitudes and beliefs toward the self (self-appreciating attitudes and beliefs).* The minority individual at this stage is oriented toward self-discovery of one's own history and culture. There is an active seeking out of information and artifacts that enhance that person's sense of identity and worth. Cultural and racial characteristics that once elicited feelings of shame and disgust become symbols of pride and honor. The individual moves into this stage primarily because he or she asks the question, "Why should I be ashamed of who and what I am?" The original low self-esteem engendered by widespread prejudice and racism that was most characteristic of the conformity stage is now actively challenged in order to raise self-esteem. Phrases such as "Black is beautiful" represent a symbolic relabeling of identity for many Blacks. Racial self-hatred begins to be actively rejected in favor of the other extreme: unbridled racial pride.

2. *Attitudes and beliefs toward members of the same minority (group-appreciating attitudes and beliefs).* The individual experiences a strong sense of identification with and commitment to his or her minority group as enhancing information about the group is acquired. There is a feeling of connectedness with other members of the racial and cultural group, and a strengthening of new identity begins to occur. Members of one's group are admired, respected, and often viewed now as the new reference group or ideal. Cultural values of the minority group are accepted without question. As indicated, the pendulum swings drastically from original identification with White ways to identification in an unquestioning manner with the minority group's ways. Persons in this stage are likely to restrict their interactions as much as possible to members of their own group.

3. *Attitudes and beliefs toward members of a different minority (conflict between feelings of empathy for other minority group experiences and feelings of culturocentrism).* While members at this stage experience a growing sense of comradeship with persons from other minority groups, a strong culturocentrism develops as well. Alliances with other groups tend to be transitory and based on short-term goals or some global shared view of oppression. There is less an attempt to reach out and understand other racial-cultural minority groups and their values and ways, and more a superficial surface feeling of political need. Alliances generally are based on convenience factors or are formed for political reasons

such as combing together as a large group to confront an enemy perceived to be larger.

4. *Attitudes and beliefs toward members of the dominant group (group- depreciating attitudes and beliefs).* The minority individual is likely to perceive the dominant society and culture as an oppressor and as the group most responsible for the current plight of minorities in the United States. Characterized by both withdrawal from the dominant culture and immersion in one's cultural heritage, there is also considerable anger and hostility directed toward White society. There is a feeling of distrust and dislike for all members of the dominant group in an almost global anti-White demonstration and feeling. White people, for example, are not to be trusted because they are the oppressors or enemies. In extreme form, members may advocate complete destruction of the institutions and structures that have been characteristic of White society.

Introspection Stage

Several factors seem to work in unison to move the individual from the resistance and immersion stage into the introspection stage. First, the individual begins to discover that this level of intensity of feelings (anger directed toward White society) is psychologically draining and does not permit one to really devote more crucial energies to understanding themselves or to their own racial-cultural group. The resistance and immersion stage tends to be a reaction against the dominant culture and is not proactive in allowing the individual to use all energies to discover who or what he or she is. Self-definition in the previous stage tends to be reactive (against White racism), and a need for positive self-definition in a proactive sense emerges.

Second, the minority individual experiences feelings of discontent and discomfort with group views that may be quite rigid in the resistance and immersion stage. Often, in order to please the group, the individual is asked to submerge individual autonomy and individual thought in favor of the group good. Many group views may now be seen as conflicting with individual ones. A Latino individual who may form a deep relationship with a White person may experience considerable pressure from his or her culturally similar peers to break off the relationship because that White person is the "enemy." However, the personal experiences of the individual may, in fact, not support this group view.

It is important to note that some clinicians often confuse certain characteristics of the introspective stage with parts of the conformity stage. A minority person from the former stage who speaks against the decisions of his or her group may often appear similar to the conformity person. The dynamics are quite different, however. While the conformity person is motivated by global racial self-hatred, the introspective person has no such global negativism directed at his or her own group.

1. *Attitudes and beliefs toward the self (concern with basis of self-appreciating attitudes and beliefs).* While the person originally in the conformity stage held predominantly to majority group views and notions to the detriment of his or her own minority group, the person now feels that he or she has too rigidly held onto

minority group views and notions in order to submerge personal autonomy. The conflict now becomes quite great in terms of responsibility and allegiance to one's own minority group versus notions of personal independence and autonomy. The person begins to spend more and more time and energy trying to sort out these aspects of self-identity and begins increasingly to demand individual autonomy.

2. *Attitudes and beliefs toward members of the same minority (concern with the unequivocal nature of group appreciation).* While attitudes of identification are continued from the preceding resistance and immersion stage, concern begins to build up regarding the issue of group-usurped individuality. Increasingly, the individual may see his or her own group taking positions that might be considered quite extreme. In addition, there is now increasing resentment over how one's group may attempt to pressure or influence the individual into making decisions that may be inconsistent with the person's values, beliefs, and outlooks. Indeed, it is not unusual for members of a minority group to make it clear to the member that if they do not agree with the group, they are against it. A common ploy used to hold members in line is exemplified in questions such as "How Asian are you?" and "How Black are you?"

3. *Attitudes and beliefs toward members of a different minority (concern with the ethnocentric basis for judging others).* There is now greater uneasiness with culturocentrism, and an attempt is made to reach out to other groups in finding out what types of oppression they experience and how this has been handled. While similarities are important, there is now a movement toward understanding potential differences in oppression that other groups might have experienced.

4. *Attitudes and beliefs toward members of the dominant group (concern with the basis of group depreciation).* The individual experiences conflict between attitudes of complete trust for the dominant society and culture and attitudes of selective trust and distrust according to the dominant individual's demonstrated behaviors and attitudes. Conflict is most likely to occur here because the person begins to recognize that there are many elements in U.S. American culture that are highly functional and desirable, yet there is confusion as to how to incorporate these elements into the minority culture. Would the person's acceptance of certain White cultural values make the person a sellout to his or her own race? There is a lowering of intense feelings of anger and distrust toward the dominant group but a continued attempt to discern elements that are acceptable.

Integrative Awareness Stage

Minority persons in this stage have developed an inner sense of security and now can own and appreciate unique aspects of their culture as well as those in U.S. culture. Minority culture is not necessarily in conflict with White dominant cultural ways. Conflicts and discomforts experienced in the previous stage become resolved, allowing greater individual control and flexibility. There is now the belief there are acceptable and unacceptable aspects in all cultures, and that it is very important for the person to be able to examine and accept or reject those aspects of a culture that are not seen as desirable. At the integrative awareness stage, the minority person has a strong commitment and desire to eliminate all forms of oppression.

1. *Attitudes and beliefs toward the self (self-appreciating attitudes and beliefs).* The culturally diverse individual develops a positive self-image and experiences a strong sense of self-worth and confidence. Not only is there an integrated self-concept that involves racial pride in identity and culture, but the person develops a high sense of autonomy. Indeed, the client becomes bicultural or multicultural without a sense of having "sold out one's integrity." In other words, the person begins to perceive his or her self as an autonomous individual who is unique (individual level of identity), a member of one's own racial-cultural group (group level of identity), a member of a larger society, and a member of the human race (universal level of identity).

2. *Attitudes and beliefs toward members of same minority (group-appreciating attitudes and beliefs).* The individual experiences a strong sense of pride in the group without having to accept group values unequivocally. There is no longer the conflict over disagreeing with group goals and values. Strong feelings of empathy with the group experience are coupled with awareness that each member of the group is also an individual. In addition, tolerant and empathic attitudes are likely to be expressed toward members of one's own group who may be functioning at a less adaptive manner to racism and oppression.

3. *Attitudes and beliefs toward members of a different minority (group- appreciating attitudes).* There is now literally a reaching-out toward different minority groups in order to understand their cultural values and ways of life. There is a strong belief that the more one understands other cultural values and beliefs, the greater is the likelihood of understanding among the various ethnic groups. Support for all oppressed people, regardless of similarity to the individual's minority group, tends to be emphasized.

4. *Attitudes and beliefs toward members of the dominant group (attitudes and beliefs of selective appreciation).* The individual experiences selective trust and liking from members of the dominant group who seek to eliminate oppressive activities of the group. The individual also experiences openness to the constructive elements of the dominant culture. The emphasis here tends to be on the fact that White racism is a sickness in society and that White people are also victims who are also in need of help.

White Privilege: Unpacking the Invisible Knapsack

Peggy McIntosh

Peggy McIntosh is Associate Director of the Wellesley College Center for Research for Women. This essay is excerpted from her working paper, "White Privilege and Male Privilege: A Personal Account of Coming to See Correspondences Through Work in Women's Studies," copyright 1988 by Peggy McIntosh. Available for $4.00 from address below. The paper includes a longer list of privileges. Permission to excerpt or reprint must be obtained from Peggy McInstosh, Wellesley College Center for Research on Woman, Wellesley, MA 02481 781-283-2520, fax 781-283-2504

"I was taught to see racism only in individual acts of meanness, not in invisible systems conferring dominance on my group."

Through work to bring materials from Women's Studies into the rest of the curriculum, I have often noticed men's unwillingness to grant that they are over-privileged, even though they may grant that women are disadvantaged. They may say they will work to improve women's status, in the society, the university, or the curriculum, but they can't or won't support the idea of lessening men's. Denials which amount to taboos surround the subject of advantages which men gain from women's disadvantages. These denials protect male privilege from being fully acknowledged, lessened or ended.

Thinking through unacknowledged male privilege as a phenomenon, I realized that since hierarchies in our society are interlocking, there was most likely a phenomenon of white privilege which was similarly denied and protected. As a white person, I realized I had been taught about racism as something which puts others at a disadvantage, but had been taught not to see one of its corollary aspects, white privilege, which puts me at an advantage.

I think whites are carefully taught not to recognize white privilege, as males are taught not to recognize male privilege. So I have begun in an untutored way to ask what it is like to have white privilege. I have come to see white privilege as an invisible package of unearned assets which I can count on cashing in each day, but about which I was 'meant' to remain oblivious. White privilege is like an invisible weightless knapsack of special provisions, maps, passports, codebooks, visas, clothes, tools and blank checks.

Describing white privilege makes one newly accountable. As we in Women's Studies work to reveal male privilege and ask men to give up some of their power, so one who writes about having white privilege must ask, "Having described it, what will I do to lesson or end it?"

After I realized the extent to which men work from a base of unacknowledged privilege, I understood that much of their oppressiveness was unconscious. Then I remembered the frequent charges from women of color that white women whom they encounter are oppressive. I began to understand why we are justly seen as oppressive, even when we don't see ourselves that way. I began to count the ways in which I enjoy unearned skin privilege and have been conditioned into oblivion about its existence.

My schooling gave me no training in seeing myself as an oppressor, as an unfairly advantaged person, or as a participant in a damaged culture. I was taught to see myself as an individual whose moral state depended on her individual moral will. My schooling followed the pattern my colleague Elizabeth Minnich has pointed out: whites are taught to think of their lives as morally neutral, normative, and average, and also ideal, so that when we work to benefit others, this is seen as work which will allow "them" to be more like "us".

I decided to try to work on myself at least by identifying some of the daily effects of white privilege in my life. I have chosen those conditions which I think in my case *attach somewhat more to skin-color privilege* than to class, religion, ethnic status, or geographical location, though of course all these other factors are intricately intertwined. As far as I can see, my African American co-workers, friends and acquaintances with whom I come into daily or frequent contact in this particular time, place and line of work cannot count on most of the conditions.

1. I can if I wish arrange to be in the company of people of my race most of the time.
2. If I should need to move, I can be pretty sure of renting or purchasing housing in an area which I can afford and in which I would want to live.
3. I can be pretty sure that my neighbors in such a location will be neutral or pleasant to me.
4. I can go shopping alone most of the time, pretty well assured that I will not be followed or harassed.
5. I can turn on the television or open to the front page of the paper and see people of my race widely represented.
6. When I am told about our national heritage or about "civilization," I am shown that people of my color made it what it is.
7. I can be sure that my children will be given curricular materials that testify to the existence of their race.
8. If I want to, I can be pretty sure of finding a publisher for this piece on white privilege.
9. I can go into a music shop and count on finding the music of my race represented, into a supermarket and find the staple foods which fit with my cultural traditions, into a hairdresser's shop and find someone who can cut my hair.
10. Whether I use checks, credit cards, or cash, I can count on my skin color not to work against the appearance of financial reliability.
11. I can arrange to protect my children most of the time from people who might not like them.
12. I can swear, or dress in second hand clothes, or not answer letters, without having people attribute these choices to the bad morals, the poverty, or the illiteracy of my race.

13. I can speak in public to a powerful male group without putting my race on trial.
14. I can do well in a challenging situation without being called a credit to my race.
15. I am never asked to speak for all the people of my racial group.
16. I can remain oblivious of the language and customs of persons of color who constitute the world's majority without feeling in my culture any penalty for such oblivion.
17. I can criticize our government and talk about how much I fear its policies and behavior without being seen as a cultural outsider.
18. I can be pretty sure that if I ask to talk to "the person in charge," I will be facing a person of my race.
19. If a traffic cop pulls me over or if the IRS audits my tax return. I can be sure I haven't been singled out because of my race.
20. I can easily buy posters, postcards, picture books, greeting cards, dolls, toys, and children's magazines featuring people of my race.
21. I can go home from most meetings of organizations I belong to feeling somewhat tied in, rather than isolated, out-of-place, outnumbered, unheard, held at a distance or feared.
22. I can take a job with an affirmative action employer without having coworkers on the job suspect that I got it because of race.
23. I can choose public accommodation without fearing that people of my race cannot get in or will be mistreated in the places I have chosen.
24. I can be sure that if I need legal or medical help, my race will not work against me.
25. If my day, week, or year is going badly, I need not ask of each negative episode or situation whether it has racial overtones.
26. I can choose blemish cover or bandages in "flesh" color and have them more or less match my skin.

I repeatedly forgot each of the realizations on this list until I wrote it down. For me white privilege has turned out to be an elusive and fugitive subject. The pressure to avoid it is great, for in facing it I must give up the myth of meritocracy. If these things are true, this is not such a free country; one's life is not what one makes it; many doors open for certain people through no virtues of their own.

In unpacking this invisible knapsack of white privilege, I have listed conditions of daily experience which I once took for granted. Nor did I think of any of these perquisites as bad for the holder. I now think that we need a more finely differentiated taxonomy of privilege, for some of these varieties are only what one would want for everyone in a just society, and others give licence to be ignorant, oblivious, arrogant and destructive.

I see a pattern running through the matrix of white privilege, a pattern of assumptions which were passed on to me as a white person. There was one main piece of cultural turf; it was my own turf, and I was among those who could control the turf. *My skin color was an asset for any move I was educated to want to make.* I could think of myself as belonging in major ways, and of making social systems work for me. I could freely disparage, fear, neglect, or be oblivious to anything outside of the dominant cultural forms. Being of the main culture, I could also criticize it fairly freely.

In proportion as my racial group was being made confident, comfortable, and oblivious, other groups were likely being made inconfident, uncomfortable, and alienated. Whiteness protected me from many kinds of hostility, distress, and violence, which I was being subtly trained to visit in turn upon people of color.

For this reason, the word "privilege" now seems to me misleading. We usually think of privilege as being a favored state, whether earned or conferred by birth or luck. Yet some of the conditions I have described here work to systematically overempower certain groups. Such privilege simply *confers dominance* because of one's race or sex.

I want, then, to distinguish between earned strength and unearned power conferred systemically. Power from unearned privilege can look like strength when it is in fact permission to escape or to dominate. But not all of the privileges on my list are inevitably damaging. Some, like the expectation that neighbors will be decent to you, or that your race will not count against you in court, should be the norm in a just society. Others, like the privilege to ignore less powerful people, distort the humanity of the holders as well as the ignored groups.

We might at least start by distinguishing between positive advantages which we can work to spread, and negative types of advantages which unless rejected will always reinforce our present hierarchies. For example, the feeling that one belongs within the human circle, as Native Americans say, should not be seen as privilege for a few. Ideally it is an *unearned entitlement*. At present, since only a few have it, it is an *unearned advantage* for them. This paper results from a process of coming to see that some of the power which I originally saw as attendant on being a human being in the U.S. consisted in *unearned advantage* and *conferred dominance.*

I have met very few men who are truly distressed about systemic, unearned male advantage and conferred dominance. And so one question for me and others like me is whether we will be like them, or whether we will get truly distressed, even outraged, about unearned race advantage and conferred dominance and if so, what we will do to lessen them. In any case, we need to do more work in identifying how they actually affect our daily lives. Many, perhaps most, of our white students in the U.S. think that racism doesn't affect them because they are not people of color; they do not see "whiteness" as a racial identity. In addition, since race and sex are not the only advantaging systems at work, we need similarly to examine the daily experience of having age advantage, or ethnic advantage, or physical ability, or advantage related to nationality, religion, or sexual orientation.

Difficulties and dangers surrounding the task of finding parallels are many. Since racism, sexism, and heterosexism are not the same, the advantaging associated with them should not be seen as the same. In addition, it is hard to disentangle aspects of unearned advantage which rest more on social class, economic class, race, religion, sex and ethnic identity than on other factors. Still, all of the oppressions are interlocking, as the Combahee River Collective Statement of 1977 continues to remind us eloquently.

One factor seems clear about all of the interlocking oppressions. They take both active forms which we can see and embedded forms which as a member of the dominant group one is taught not to see. In my class and place, I did not see myself as a racist because I was taught to recognize racism only individual acts of meanness by members of my group, never in invisible systems conferring unsought racial dominance on my group from birth.

Disapproving of the systems won't be enough to change them. I was taught to think that racism could end if white individuals changed their attitudes. [But] a "white" skin in the United States opens many doors for whites whether or not we approve of the way dominance has been conferred on us. Individual acts can palliate, but cannot end, these problems.

To redesign social systems we need first to acknowledge their colossal unseen dimensions. The silences and denials surrounding privilege are the key political tool here. They keep the thinking about equality or equity incomplete, protecting unearned advantage and conferred dominance by making these taboo subjects. Most talk by whites about equal opportunity seem to me now to be about equal opportunity to try to get into a position of dominance while denying that *systems* of dominance exist.

It seems to me that obliviousness about white advantage, like obliviousness about male advantage, is kept strongly inculturated in the United States so as to maintain the myth of meritocracy, the myth that democratic choice is equally available to all. Keeping most people unaware that freedom of confident action is there for just a small number of people props up those in power, and serves to keep power in the hands of the same groups that have most of it already.

Though systemic change takes many decades, there are pressing questions for me and I imagine for some others like me if we raise our daily consciousness on the perquisites of being light-skinned. What will we do with such knowledge? As we know from watching men, it is an open question whether we will choose to use unearned advantage to weaken hidden systems of advantage, and whether we will use any of our arbitrarily-awarded power to try to reconstruct power systems on a broader base.

Privilege Walk

Version B

- Purpose: To provide participants with an opportunity to understand the intricacies of privilege.
- Time: 1 ½ hours
- Note to facilitators: This is a powerful exercise and should be thoroughly discussed afterwards.

1. Participants should be led to the exercise site silently, hand in hand, in a line.
2. At the site, participants can release their hands, but should be instructed to stand shoulder to shoulder in a straight line without speaking.

3. Participants should be instructed to listen carefully to each sentence, and take the step required if the sentence applies to them. They can be told there is a prize at the front of the site that everyone is competing for (optional).
4. If you are short on time, we suggest shortening the number of statements and selecting from the items in underlined type.

Statements:

1. If your ancestors were forced to come to the USA not by choice, take one step back.
2. If your primary ethnic identity is American, take one step forward.
3. If you have ever been called names because of your race, class, ethnicity, gender, or sexual orientation, take one step back.
4. If you grew up in a household with servants (gardeners, housecleaning, etc.) take one step forward.
5. If your parents are educated professionals (doctors, lawyers, etc.) take one step forward.
6. If you were raised in an area where there was prostitution, drug activity, etc., take one step back.
7. If you studied the culture of your ancestors in K-12, take one step forward.
8. If you started school speaking a language other than English, take one step back.
9. If you ever had to skip a meal or go hungry because there was not enough money to buy food when you were growing up, take one step back.
10. If you went on regular family vacations, take one step forward.
11. If one of your parents was unemployed or laid off, not by choice, take one step back.
12. If you attended private school or summer camp growing up, take one step forward.
13. If you have ever been homeless or if your family ever had to move because they could not afford the rent, take one step back.
14. If you have ever been followed in a store or accused of cheating or lying because of your race, ethnicity, gender or sexual orientation, take one step back.
15. If you were told that you were beautiful, smart and capable by your parents, take one step forward.
16. If you were ever discouraged from academics or jobs because of race, class, ethnicity, gender or sexual orientation, take one step back.
17. If you were encouraged to attend college by your parents, take one step forward.
18. If you were raised in a single parent household, take one step back.
19. If your family owned the house where you grew up, take one step forward.
20. If you saw members of your race, ethnic group, gender or sexual orientation well represented in a range of roles on television and the media, take one step forward.
21. If you have ever been offered a good job because of your connection to a friend or family member, take one step forward.

22. If you have inherited or are likely to inherit money or property, take one step forward.
23. If you have to rely primarily on public transportation, take one step back.
24. If you have ever been stopped or questioned by the police because of your race, ethnicity, gender or sexual orientation, take one step back.
25. If you have ever been made uncomfortable by a joke related to your race, ethnicity, gender or sexual orientation but felt unsafe to confront the situation, take one step back.
26. If you have ever been the victim of violence related to your race, ethnicity, gender or sexual orientation, take one step back.
27. If your parents did not grow up in the United States, take one step back.
28. If your parents told you you could be anything you wanted to be, take one step forward.

Processing:
Ask participants to remain in their positions and to look at their position as well as the positions of the other participants.

Ask participants to consider who among them would probably win the prize.

Suggested questions for processing are:

1. What happened?
2. How did this exercise make you feel?
3. What were your thoughts as you did this exercise?
4. What have you learned from this experience?
5. What can you do with this information in the future?

The Face of Racism
Edward A. Delgado-Romero

When thinking of racism, people might imagine the vision of a hooded Ku Klux Klan member lighting a cross, a "skinhead" wearing swastikas, or an angry lynch mob. However, when I think of racism, one image is clear. I learned about racism in the face of my father. I learned hatred, prejudice, and contempt, and, most important, I learned how to turn that racism inward. After many years of self-reflection and healing, I have just begun to understand how deeply racism has affected my attitudes toward others and toward myself. I have begun to understand that racism works on two fronts. One is the overt and obvious racism of the Klan member. The other is the covert and subtle racism that the victim of overt racism begins to internalize, the racism my father taught me.

My father came to this country seeking to escape the personal demons that had haunted him throughout his life. He saw the United States and New York City as a new opportunity, a new beginning. Part of that beginning was rejecting all the things that he had been. My father sought to reinvent himself as an American. In those days, being an American meant being White (some people might argue that this is still true). My father felt he *was* White, because part of his family was descended from Spaniards. Somehow my father thought being Spanish (and therefore European) was better and of higher status than being a South American or a Colombian, and it was certainly better than being *Indio* or native. Our ancestral records show that the Delgado family was a virtuous family with a long tradition in Spain. However, the only records that remain of my ancestors who were native (South) Americans are a few photographs and some of their physical features that were passed along through "blood."

The United States of America taught my father to hate anyone who was not White. Richard Pryor once observed that the first English word that an immigrant is taught is "nigger." Always a quick learner, my father learned to hate "niggers," "gooks," "spics," "wetbacks," and any other "damn immigrant." However, my father soon found out that he was not excluded from the hatred. After days filled with jokes about "green cards" and "drug dealing," my father would return home to his wife and children, full of pent-up rage. We lived in fear of his anger and his explosiveness. My father tried to transform himself yet felt ambivalent about losing his security. Therefore, we were not allowed to speak Spanish to my father, and my mother was not allowed to learn English. By attempting to separate his children from their culture while denying his wife the chance to acculturate, my father replicated his divided psyche. My mother was forced to be the keeper of the culture and language, which she did with incredible bravery and pride. It was through the courage of my mother that I was eventually able to reconnect with my Latino heritage.

My father's drive to be accepted and to be acceptable knew no bounds. I remember one time as a child, we were driving a long distance to go to a restaurant (which was unusual for us). We sat and ate fried chicken and blueberry pie as my father anxiously waited for the owner of the restaurant to come over and acknowledge him. The owner finally did come over, and I remember how proud my father was to meet "a great American." It was only when I was older that I realized that this man was Georgia politician Lester Maddox. Maddox was one of the fiercest opponents of integration during the civil rights era. He was made infamous by keeping a bucket of ax handles by the door of his restaurant as a reminder of the violence that he had threatened to use against any Black person who would try to integrate his home or business. It shocks me to realize how racism had blinded my father to the fact that his fate as an immigrant and a minority group member in the United States was tied to the fate of other minorities.

As hard as he tried to fit in, my father never really succeeded. Often his physical features, his accent, or his clothes would give him away as being different. My father would react violently when confronted with his failure to become one hundred percent American. For example, during an interview for a promotion, the interviewer asked my father about the "good pot" grown in Colombia. At the time my father laughed it off. However, when he returned home he exploded in rage. These explosions became a daily event. My brother, sister, and I were a captive audience. We had no choice but to listen as he would berate us for being worthless. The angrier he became, the more pressure my father would put on us to "be American." We were wildly successful at being American, which only made my father angrier. As I became a teenager, my father became increasingly competitive with and abusive toward me. The fact that I physically resembled him only made things worse. He saw in me things he could never achieve: I spoke English without an accent, was headed toward college, and I dated Caucasian women exclusively.

I learned racism from my father, and just as he had done, I turned it inward. I came to hate the fact that I was Latino, that my parents spoke with an accent, that my skin, although light for a Latino, was darker than it should be. I wanted to be a White Anglo-American, and for many years, I actually thought I was. During my high school and college years I was in deep denial that I was Latino. I believed that America was a "color blind" society that rewarded people solely on the basis of hard work. I remember my Caucasian high school guidance counselor steering me away from minority scholarships for college and telling me "Ed, you want to get in on your own merit." At the time I believed her, and my "own merit" led to my status as a "token" at a predominantly Caucasian college, thousands of dollars in student loans, and 4 more years of denial.

I remember being deeply embarrassed by Latino music, food, customs, and history. My mother would often talk about her home country with pride and fondness. I used to get angry with her because she was being so "un-American." One time, in an attempt to share her culture with me, my mother gave me an expensive recording of Colombian music. I actually had the nerve to give it back to her because I was ashamed of everything Latino. I was particularly ashamed of my Spanish surname because of the way that my peers could mispronounce it in demeaning ways. I became so used to being called names that often I would participate in using ethnic slurs against myself and other minorities. I remember vividly a Latino varsity football player who was proud that his nickname was "Spic." Having a racial slur as a nickname was a badge of honor; it meant he was accepted. As an enthusiastic participant in the ethnic name-calling, I could continue to deny that I was different. The height of my own denial was when I told a Mexican joke to a priest, who was Mexican. The priest laughed, more out of shock than humor. The joke was, quite literally, on both of us. He confronted me, and pointed out that he was Mexican. As I stood in awkward silence, having offended someone I cared about, something began to awaken within me.

I began to realize that I was an impostor and that there was another side of me that I was denying. Although I felt intimidated and uncomfortable around people of color, there was a depth of connection that was missing in most of my relationships. I struggled to make sense of what I was feeling. My longing for connection with other minorities was first manifested in college through my participation in a fraternity. When I joined the fraternity, the membership was almost exclusively White. However, as I was able to influence member selection, the membership became increasingly diverse. I began to surround myself with other people who could understand what it felt like to be of two worlds and never fully at peace in either one. These were my first steps toward healing the racism that I felt inside.

My cultural explorations coincided with the divorce of my parents. My father eventually left our home and emotionally and financially disowned his family. This split helped me to continue the self-exploration and reclamation of my heritage that had begun in college. I learned about my ancestors, their names, and their lives. I learned my full name and the proper way to pronounce it. I was able to become friends with Latino men and Latina women. I asked my mother to give me back the recording of Colombian music I had refused to take from her and asked her to teach me about her culture. My mother saved up her money and took me on a trip to Colombia. I wish that I could say that I found my "home" in Colombia. I wish that I could say that I reconnected with my ancestors on some deep level. However, in Colombia I felt every bit the foreigner that I was. What I gained from my trip to Colombia was an understanding and appreciation for the enormous sacrifice that my mother had made for her children. In Colombia I realized that I was neither fully Colombian nor fully American. I had to find a way to make sense of my divided identity.

Many of my colleagues in psychology say that therapists enter the profession motivated in part by a need to deal with their own issues. As much as I used to argue that I was the exception to the rule, obviously I was not. In an effort to somehow identify, understand, and deal with my issues, I was drawn to graduate study in counseling psychology. I was offered a lucrative fellowship at a major university. However, only one professor (who later became my adviser and mentor) was honest enough to tell me that it was a minority fellowship. Many of the faculty and students saw the minority fellowship as a way for me to cheat the system because they did not think I was "really" a minority. One student explained his belief that I was not a real minority because I did not speak "broken English." The pressure to fit in and deny that I was different was enormous. I was faced with a choice that reminded me of dealing with my father: stay quiet and accept the status quo of the University and the program (basically "pass" as Caucasian) or assert myself and challenge a culturally oppressive system. I wish I could say that I chose to try to change the system simply because it was the moral or just thing to do. However, I think I chose to fight the system because I was tired of being quiet. Multicultural psychology became my passion and the focus of my career. I have my doubts as to how much I was able to change a deeply entrenched racist, sexist, and homophobic system, but I have no doubt that I underwent tremendous personal and professional growth.

As I progressed through my graduate training and into internship, I found that I surrounded myself with other people who could understand what it was like to face overt and covert racism. I formed a supportive network of friends and colleagues of all colors. At first I felt some animosity toward Caucasian people, but a Caucasian friend once pointed out that all people would benefit from being liberated from racism. I found that the term *liberation* captured the essence of what I was searching for: liberation from hatred and racism and, personally, a liberation from the past. I realized that liberation meant letting go of the intense anger and resentment I felt toward my father. My anger toward my father was like wearing a shrinking suit of armor: Although the anger could make me feel powerful and protected, the anger was not letting me grow and, in fact, was starting to choke me. However, I was concerned that, stripped of my armor, I would lose my motivation to fight racism. I was surprised to find that by liberating myself from my father's legacy, I was able to find peace and that from this peace I could generate more energy and motivation to face racism than I had imagined possible.

As I grow older and consider having my own children, I find myself looking in the mirror to see if I can see my father's face. There have been times when I have been both shocked and disappointed to hear his voice angrily coming out of my mouth or have seen my face contorted with his rage. I was surprised to find out that liberation did not mean I could change the facts of my past or get rid of any influence from my father. However, I gained something even more valuable: I learned that because of my experiences, I can understand why someone would be racist. I can understand what it is like to be both a perpetrator and a victim of racism. I have also come to understand that the answer to fighting racism begins with a moral inventory, a fearless look at oneself. I have come to the conclusion that I can never afford myself the luxury of asking the question "Am I racist?" Rather, I need to continually ask myself, "How racist am I?" As I struggle to deal with the reality of racism in my personal and professional life, I will continue to check my mirror and look for the face of racism.

 **Discussion Questions**

1. How does Delgado-Romero's father justify his racism? What do his views tell us about attitudes on race and class in his native Colombian culture?

2.   Delgado-Romero says, "I became so used to being called names that I would often participate in using ethnic slurs against myself and other minorities." Does using the very words that have insulted him give Delgado-Romero a sense of control and/or power in the racial struggle? Have any other groups adopted this approach to confronting discrimination?

3.   "The answer to fighting racism begins with a moral inventory, a fearless look at oneself." How does Delgado-Romero's sense of his own identity influence his view of others? How do these views change over time?

How Does It Feel to Be a Problem?

Moustafa Bayoumi

Prior to 9/11, few White Americans probably understood what it was like for someone to hate you simply because of the group to which you belonged. Bayoumi's personal account of his post-9/11 feelings not only reveals the extent to which racial-ethnic profiling now shapes the experiences of Arab Americans but also examines what it is like to be a target of prejudice and racism.

(NEW YORK CITY, SEPTEMBER 25, 2001)

Thankfully, I was spared any personal loss. Like so many others in the city which I love I have spent much of the past two weeks reeling from the devastation. Mostly this has meant getting back in touch with friends, frantically calling them on the phone, rushing around the city to meet with them to give them a consoling hug, but knowing that really it was me looking for the hug. I dash off simple one-line emails, "let me know you're okay, okay?"

Old friends from around the world responded immediately. An email from Canada asks simply if I am all right. Another arrives from friends in Germany telling me how they remember, during their last visit to see me, the view from the top of the towers. A cousin in Egypt states in awkward English, "I hope this attack will not affect you. We hear that some of the Americans attack Arabs and Muslims. I will feel happy if you be in contact with me."

I am all right, of course, but I am devastated. In the first days, I scoured the lists of the dead and missing hoping not to find any recognizable names, but I come across the name of a three-year-old child, and my heart collapses. I hear my neighbor, who works downtown, arrive home, and I knock on her door.

She tells me how she was chased by a cloud of debris into a building, locked in there for over an hour, and then, like thousands of others, walked home. I can picture her with the masses in the streets, trudging bewildered like refugees, covered in concrete and human dust. Later, I ride the subway and see a full-page picture of the towers on fire with tiny figures in the frame silently diving to their deaths, and I start to cry.

In the following days, I cried a lot. Then, with my friends, I attended a somber peace march in Brooklyn, sponsored by the Arab community. Thousands, overwhelmingly non-Arab and non-Muslim, show up, and I feel buoyed by the support. A reporter from Chile notices my Arab appearance and asks if she can interview me. I talk to her but am inwardly frightened by her locating me so easily among the thousands. Many people are wearing stickers reading: "We Support Our Arab neighbors," which leaves me both happy and, strangely, crushed. Has it really come to this? Now it has become not just a question of whether we—New Yorkers—are so vulnerable as a city but whether we—in the Arab and Muslim communities—are so vulnerable by our appearances. Is our existence so precari-

"How Does it Feel to Be a Problem" by Moustafa Boyoumi From *Amerasia Journal* 27:3 (2001)/28:1 (2002): 69–77. Reprinted by permission.

ous here? I want to show solidarity with the people wearing the sticker, so how can I possibly explain to them how those stickers scare me?

Before September 11, I used to be fond of saying that the relations between the Muslim world and the West have never been at a lower point since the crusades. They have now sunk lower. The English language lexicon is, once again, degraded by war. President George W. Bush's ignorant use of the word "crusade" is but a manifestation. Why don't we ask the Apache what they think of the Apache helicopter? Is there any phrase more disingenuous in the English language than "collateral damage"? . . .

For the first four weeks after the attacks, I felt a bubble of hope in the dark air of New York. The blunt smell of smoke and death that hung in the atmosphere slowed the city down like I had never experienced it before. New York was solemn, lugubrious, and, for once, without a quick comeback. For a moment, it felt that the trauma of suffering—not the exercise of reason, not the belief in any God, not the universal consumption of a fizzy drink, but the simple and tragic reality that it hurts when we feel pain—was understood as the thread that connects all of humanity. From this point, I had hope that a lesson was being learned, that inflicting more misery cannot alleviate the ache of collective pain.

When the bombing began, the bubble burst. Where there was apprehension, now there was relief in the air. It felt like the city was taking a collective sigh, saying to itself that finally, with the bombing, we can get back to our own lives again. With a perverted logic, dropping munitions meant all's right with the world again.

Television, the great mediator, allows the public to feel violence or to abstract it. New Yorkers qualify as human interest. Afghans if they are lucky, get the long shot. In late October, CNN issued a directive to its reporters, for it seems that even a little bit of detached compassion is too much in the media world. "It seems perverse to focus too much on the casualties or hardship of Afghanistan," their leadership explains. "We must talk about how the Taliban is using civilian shields and how the Taliban has harbored the terrorists responsible for killing close to 5,000 innocent people." God forbid, we viewers see the pain ordinary Afghans are forced to endure. CNN must instead issue policy like a nervous state, rather than investigate how cluster bombs, freely dropped in the tens of thousands from the skies, metamorphose into land mines since about 7 percent of these soda-can-sized bombs don't explode on contact. In Canada, in the U.K., across the Arab world, this is becoming an issue. But in the United States, a cluster bomb sounds like a new kind of candy bar.

This is not to say that people in the United States are foolish, but they are by and large woefully underinformed. A study taken during the course of the Gulf War revealed that the more TV one watched, the less one actually knew about the region. In the crash course on Islam that the American public is now receiving, I actually heard a group of well-suited pundits on MSNBC (or its equivalent, I can no longer separate the lame from the loony) ask questions of a Muslim about the basics of the faith, questions like "Now, is there a difference between Moslem and Muslim?' No lie. The USA-Patriot Act, the end of the world as we know it (or at least of judicial review), actually includes the expression "Muslim descent," as if Islam is a chromosome to be marked by the human genome project. About Islam, most people in the United States still know nothing, unlike professional sports, where many are encyclopedias...

For years, the organized Arab American community has been lobbying to be recognized with minority status. The check boxes on application forms have always stared defiantly out at me. Go ahead, try to find yourself, they seem to be taunting me. I search and find that, in the eyes of the government, I am a white man.

It is a strange thing, to be brown in reality and white in bureaucracy. Now, however, it is stranger than ever. Since 1909, when the government began questioning whether Syrian immigrants were of "white" stock (desirable) or Asian stock (excludable), Arab immigrants in this country have had to contend with fitting their mixed hues into the primary colors of the state. As subjects of the Ottoman empire, and thus somehow comingled with Turkish stock (who themselves claim descent from the Caucasues, birthplace of the original white people in nineteenth century thinking, even though the location is Asia Minor), Arabs, Armenians, and other Western Asians caused a good deal of consternation among the legislators of race in this country. Syrians and Palestinians were in 1899 classified as white, but by 1910 they were reclassified as "Asiatics." A South Carolina judge in 1914 wrote that even though Syrians may be white people, they were not "that particular free white person to whom the Act of Congress had donated the privilege of citizenship" (that being reserved exclusively for people of European descent). What is it Du Bois wrote: "How does it feel to be a problem?"

In the twenty-first century, we are back to being white on paper and brown in reality. After the attacks of September 11, the flood to classify Arabs in this country was drowning our community like a break in a dam. This impact? Hundreds of hate crimes, many directed at South Asians and Iranians, whom the perpetrators misidentified as Arab (or, more confusingly, as "Muslim": again as if that were a racial category). In the days following the attack (September 14/15), a Gallup Poll revealed that 49 percent of Americans supported "requiring Arabs, including those who are U.S. citizens, to carry a special ID." Fifty-eight percent also supported "requiring Arabs, including those who are U.S. citizens, to undergo special, more intensive security checks before boarding airplanes in the U.S." Debate rages across the nation as to the legitimacy of using "racial profiling" in these times (overwhelmingly pro). The irony, delicious if it were not so tragic, is that they are racially profiling a people whom they don't even recognize as a race...

From the fall to the fallout, I have been living these days in some kind of limbo. The horrific attacks of September 11 have damaged everyone's sense of security, a principle enshrined in the Universal Declaration of Human Rights, and I wonder if for the first [time] that I can remember in the United States, we can start to reflect on that notion more carefully. All the innocents who have perished in this horrendous crime deserve to be mourned, whether they be the rescue workers, the financiers, the tourists, or the service employees in the buildings. An imam in the city has told me how a local union requested his services for a September 11 memorial of their loss since a quarter of their membership was Muslim. Foreign nationals from over eighty countries lost their lives, and the spectacular nature of the attacks meant that the world could witness the United States' own sense of security crumble with the towers. The tragedy of September 11 is truly of heartbreaking proportions. The question remains whether the United States will understand its feelings of stolen security as a unique circumstance, woven into the familiar narrative of American exceptionalism, or whether the people of this country will begin to see how security of person must be guaranteed for all. Aren't we all in this together?...

Overheard on a city bus, days after the attacks: "They will take them, like they did the Japanese, into camps. I think that's what they're going to do." In *Korematsu v. United States,* the infamous Supreme Court decision on Japanese internment, Justice Black wrote:

> *It is said that we are dealing here with the case of imprisonment of a citizen in a concentration camp solely because of his ancestry, without evidence or inquiry concerning his loyalty and good disposition towards the United States. Our task would be simple, our duty clear, were this a case involving the imprisonment of a loyal citizen in a concentration camp because of racial prejudice. Regardless of the true nature of the assembly and relocation centers—and we deem it unjustifiable to call them concentration camps with all the ugly connotations that term implies—we are dealing specifically with nothing but an exclusion order.*

In this exercise in rationalizing racism, Justice Black's backward logic is underscored by *his* taking offense at the term "concentration camp."

Of course, the Japanese American experience is not far from everyone's mind these days. Two months after the attack on Pearl Harbor, President Roosevelt signed Executive Order 9066, which led to the internment of over 110,000 Americans of Japanese descent. Without any need for evidence, anyone of Japanese ancestry, whether American-born or not, could be rounded up and placed in detention, all of course in the name of democracy and national security. What is less well-known is that in the 1980s, a multi-agency task force of the government, headed by the INS, had plans to round up citizens of seven Arab countries and Iran and place them in a camp in Oakdale, Louisiana, in the event of a war or action in the Middle East.

Will we see the return of the camps? I doubt it. How do you round up some seven or eight million people, geographically and economically dispersed throughout the society in ways people of Japanese descent were not in the 1940s? I suspect that this time we are not in for such measures, but we are already in the middle of something else. Over 1,000 people, most non-citizens, most Arab and Muslim, have been taken into custody under shadowy circumstances reminiscent of the *disappeared* of Argentina. Targeted for their looks, their opinions, or their associations, not one has yet to be indicted on any charge directly related to the attacks of September 11. Now, being Muslim means you are worthy of incarceration. INS administrative courts are the places where much of this happens, since non-citizens are the weakest segment of the population from a judicial point of view. Islam in this scenario becomes both racial and ideological.

In 1920, Attorney General A. Mitchell Palmer launched a nationwide assault on suspected communists and rounded up thousands without any judicial review (this event, an egregious abuse of authority, launched the ACLU). It too was directed mainly at immigrants to this country, and was covert and indiscriminate. This is what Palmer had to say about it: "How the Department of Justice discovered upwards of 60,000 of these organized agitators of the Trotsky doctrine in the United States, is the confidential information upon which the government is now sweeping the nation clean of such alien filth." John Ashcroft may be more circumspect in his language, but what we are facing now is a combination of both Yellow Peril and the Red Scare. Call it the Green Scare if you will, and recognize it is as a perilous path.

 Discussion Questions

1. How did the events of September 11, 2001, now called simply 9/11, redefine Arab Americans as a minority group?
2. How does their experience compare to that of Japanese Americans during World War II? How is it different?

Are There Class Cultures?

Betsy Leondar-Wright

If having a common culture means that the people would recognize each other as similar—might laugh at the same jokes, talk somewhat alike, have a similar range of habits, etc.—then the answer to the question "Are there class cultures?" seems to be "no." We in the US experience the class system in ways so specific to our age, race, geography, religion, ethnicity, and nationality that class alone rarely seems to create that sense of kinship. If poor people from Appalachia and the South Bronx see each other as kin, it's probably as a result of some hard political work to create solidarity, not because of a close cultural similarity.

> *It's easy to fall into stereotypes about people with a particular amount of money or a type of occupation or neighborhood—easy and dangerous.*

In *The Clustering of America,* Michael J. Weiss describes the Claritas Corporation's system of dividing all the zip codes in America into 62 types. The high-priced marketing consultations offered by Claritas promise to predict how the people in any zip code will tend to react to a new product or a politician's slogan, based on their neighborhood type.

For example, the suburban area where I grew up is categorized as "Furs and Station Wagons." Then I went to college and lived in a "Towns and Gowns" area, then moved to a "Bohemian Mix" city neighborhood full of counter-culture folks. I've had community organizing jobs in "Smalltown Downtown," "Emergent Minorities," and "Public Assistance" neighborhoods.

The 62 types are narrow enough that they each have a particular cultural flavor. Most have a predominant race, a predominant age, and/or a predominant source of income. The people in "Shotguns & Pickups" areas, even in different states, might actually recognize each other as kin. The book arranges the types in order of class privilege (by combining median income, education, and home value into a single score). Assuming that Claritas Corporation's research is sound, then it's safe to say that there are approximately 60 class cultures in the United States.

But 60 is an unwieldy number for class analysis. It's an impractical number for the purposes of having discussions about the group dynamics of a mixed group or of organizing solidarity among people of a particular class to press for social change. Two to five would be a much more practical number. But dividing up 280 million Americans into just two to five clumps means that there's going to be a lot of diversity in each clump.

So if class cultures aren't intuitively recognized by the people involved, then it makes sense to step cautiously into generalizing about them. It's easy to fall into stereotypes about people with a particular amount of money or a type of occupation or neighborhood—easy and dangerous. Working-class and poor people in particular don't need any more stereotypes of them, given how negatively they are usually portrayed in the media. Rich people are also usually villains in Hollywood portrayals. Sometimes stereotypes are based on a grain of truth unfairly generalized, but I take it for granted that "smart versus stupid" is not a cultural difference but a stereotype.

The romanticization of working-class people I sometimes hear on the left—they're earthy, warm-hearted people with a natural resistance to oppression—is not universal truth either. Even positive stereotypes are harmful for strategic efforts for social change because our efforts to persuade people will be based on inaccurate understandings of what motivates them. I've heard leftists celebrate economic downturns because they assume that harsher conditions will inevitably cause poor people to rise up in rebellion. That romantic stereotype leads to flawed strategy. The romanticized demonization of all privileged people as coldhearted, uptight betrayers who collude with oppression is similarly untrue. Every class includes people whose relationship to injustice is passive acceptance, enthusiastic collusion, individual gut resistance, or collective organizing.

To avoid stereotypes, we need an experience-based approach that is appropriately cautious. So I'll attempt to stick to generalizations based in a shared experience that socializes people into a class culture.

The clearest examples of a class culture will be families with three or more generations in the same class in the United States. Recent class mobility, recent immigration, and living in the "gray area" between two classes all muddy the waters. Many—perhaps most—people's experience is of a mixed class culture. We will see culture contrasts most clearly if we compare people with long periods in the same class in the same country.

Given all these caveats, are there shared experiences that would define a number of useful class culture distinctions, i.e., significantly less than 60?

Yes, I do believe there are differences of experience that socialize most American people into one of *four* distinct cultural classes: low-income, working-class/ lower middle-class, professional middle-class and owning-class. This set of four class culture categories seems to me to be based on certain material realities. And each one rings true to me from my own experience. My experience is, of course, limited (primarily to progressive activists and three northeast states), so I put the following class culture generalizations forward humbly, generalizing primarily about activists and expecting contradictory evidence from others' experience to enrich them. My goal in risking generalizations is to make visible some class-culture-based coalition behaviors and dynamics that are too often invisible.

Differences between activists steadily employed and those who are not

> *Yes, I do believe there are differences of experience that socialize most American people into one of four distinct cultural classes: low income, working class/lower middle class, professional middle class, and owning class.*

One experience most people have that low-income and owning-class people do not share is this: they expect and have steady employment. Working 35 or more hours a week, 48 or more weeks a year, for 30 or more years—that's what working-

for Low Income:	for Working Class and Middle Class:	for Owning Class:
	STEADY WORK IS	
impossible and/or not expected	inevitable and necessary	optional

class and middle-class men, and in recent decades women too, have been brought up to expect. And that's approximately what the majority of us experience. It's so familiar to us that we forget that not everyone shares our experience. But not everyone does.

For long-term low-income people, steady work is neither possible nor expected. They live outside what economists call "the primary labor market" of steady jobs and patch together an inadequate income from public assistance and temporary, under-the-table, part-time, and/or extremely low-paid jobs.

For owning-class people, defined as those with enough investment income to support them, steady work is optional, just one choice among many. Many are in fact employed, but during their lifetime work fewer hours than working-class and middle-class people. They may travel around for a year or two after college. They may work part-time or run unprofitable businesses doing something they enjoy. Owning-class women are more likely to take extended childrearing leaves.

The class culture of steady workers (in which I include myself) fosters pride in our pragmatism and in our disciplined work habits. And these are indeed gifts to be proud of. But lacking the expectation and experience of steady work leads people to be unconventional and to think outside the box in a way that steady workers often lose.

The very expectation of poverty from generations of low-income living can sometimes make activists bolder and more visionary. My long-time low-income friend Michaelann Bewsee, along with three other welfare recipients, founded an organization 25 years ago. She started ARISE for Social Justice without any funding, and she has stuck with it for all this time, sometimes getting paid, sometimes not. The organization focuses on whatever the low-income people of Springfield, MA, are concerned about, not shying away from controversial and unfundable issues like needle exchanges. I don't know any working-class or middle-class activists who have done the equivalent.

I do, however, know owning-class activists who have done the equivalent, including in my very own workplace. United for a Fair Economy was the brainchild of an owning-class white man, Chuck Collins. Chuck has been the originator of some of UFE's most original programs. He comes into the office with a dozen new ideas every week, some wacky, but some brilliant. I, a child of money-anxious Depression-era parents, come into the office every morning worrying about the length of my task list and how I'll get everything done. It's not that I'm not creative at work, but my creativity usually comes out as solving a problem, not as dreaming up something new. Chuck grew up with different expectations than I did about how constrained his life would be, and this freed him up to be a visionary. There are working-class and middle-class visionaries, to be sure, but they are going against their class culture far more than low-income and owning-class visionaries are.

Of course, most activists who don't expect to be steadily employed aren't visionaries and don't start organizations, but even so, they tend to be less bound by convention and less deterred by difficulty than steadily employed people. Often when I've felt taken aback by low-income or owning-class activists, it has been because they seem undeterred not just by difficulty, but by impossibility. Middle-class activists often take the necessity of pragmatic compromise for granted, but low-income activists often resist compromise.

When middle-class and working-class people work with low-income or own-ing-class people, we steady workers find ourselves frequently in the roles of the pragmatist bringing things down to what's realistic. This pragmatic role can add some helpful realism but also an unhelpful wet blanket.

In my organizing experience, the tensions between working-class and low-income people—the groups writer Barbara Jensen calls "settled living" and "hard living" working-class people—arise over issues of conventional and unconventional behavior. When I worked as a tenant organizer, there were chronic tensions between the steadily employed or retired tenants and the long-time unemployed or errati-cally employed tenants on public assistance. The former saw the latter as breaking the rules and getting away with it, and frequently expressed resentment.

And as a welfare rights advocate, I often encountered hostility among steadily employed working-class people towards welfare recipients—not just among socially conservative people, but also among people progressive on most other issues, including African Americans and former short-term welfare recipients.

A lot of the confusion about class on the left comes from not understanding this class-cultural difference between long-time low-income people and long-time steadily employed people. Often anyone with less than middle-class privilege is clumped together under the labels "working class" or "poor." In part this clumping is done for the progressive goal of valuing poor people and promot-ing solidarity among all less privileged people. But it doesn't serve our cause to obscure real differences and real antagonisms just because our opponents might misuse them.

Differences between low-income and owning-class activists

What does it do to the culture when everyone has money or lack money? It adds or removes a sense of efficacy and entitlement.

Perhaps it seems strange to find similarities in class groups at the polar ends. Can low-income and owning-class people really have cultural traits in common? Both are more commonly unconventional, eccentric, visionary, undeterred by impossibil-ity, and/or impractical than steadily employed people—but what happens to their visions is very different because of their vastly different resources and status.

What does it do to the culture when everyone has money or lacks money? It adds or removes a sense of efficacy and entitlement. A low-income activist once told me, "Being rich means that everything works." When the car breaks down, they fix it or buy a new one. Owning-class people, especially white men, can assume that society will respond to their needs and desires.

Constrained, Discouraged, Low Income	Working Class and Middle Class, steadily employed,	Entitled, Owning Class:
more unconventional	more conventional and pragmatic	more conventional

Being poor, on the other hand, means that things don't reliably work. One thing I've learned from my colleagues living in poverty is that they spend an appalling amount of time dealing with crises and chaos: moving frequently, avoiding creditors, dealing with transportation breakdowns, crawling through the welfare bureaucracy, and dealing with sick or disabled or addicted family members, arrested and imprisoned family members, depressed or mentally ill family members, violent family members, evicted or just plain broke family members. It takes a lot of resourcefulness just to get through a day.

The psychological effects of constant crisis vary, but I've heard several poor people describe the same feeling: a discouragement that anything can change, resisted mightily but too often leeching all hope out of the spirit. I've also met angry low-income activists propelled by rage to speak out against conditions harming their families, but a sense of efficacy is a hard-won rarity. Low-income activists tend to see-saw between being lifted up into action by rage and dreams and being sunk low in discouragement over personal crises and hopelessness.

It's important not to romanticize poverty. I've said that in my experience low-income people are more likely to be unconventional dreamers, but most don't have the time, energy, or hope to launch their dreams in any major, outward way. More common are inner dreams—religious, romantic, artistic, or philosophical—with at most small-scale outward expressions. Buying lottery tickets may be the most common expression of a dream. Lower-income people spend more money on gambling than higher-income people, and it usually impoverishes them further. And some ways of being unconventional are, of course, destructive and illegal.

But it's also important not to assume that hardship empties people's minds and hearts. Tracy Chapman may be indulging in wishful thinking when she says, "They're talking about a revolution, standing in the unemployment line or those armies of salvation." But it's true that people waiting for the buses, waiting in soup kitchen lines, and waiting out prison sentences are not zombies. They don't feel less, don't think less than people who are better off.

When owning-class people act on their visions, they have the resources to create them in a bigger way. Here's a portrait of many progressive owning-class people I've known: By carefully investing a small inheritance and living simply, they can travel around for years filming footage for the independent documentary of their dreams. Others are writing books, painting, giving away healing services, or starting "businesses" with little likelihood of breaking even.

Contrast all these creative people with this story: An alcoholic and mentally ill woman volunteered for my affordable housing group. Her rent took up virtually all of her SSI check, so she had almost zero discretionary income. But some of it went for a pair of white sneakers and a set of washable markers. Every day she would come in with a new design drawn on the sneaker tops. Sometimes we made her day by ooh-ing and ahh-ing over her new shoe painting.

Both spending years gathering footage for an independent movie and painting a new design on your shoes every day are ways of expressing dreams that might be unlikely behavior in working-class and middle-class adults. But one has a wider audience than the other, one paints on a bigger canvas than the other.

Owning-class people may get lost and confused deciding among their options, they may do things in ungrounded ways, they may sink into addictions where their money keeps them from hitting bottom. But when they do decide to express their dream, they have a far greater sense of efficacy than do low-income dreamers, especially if they're male. There's a positive aspect to this—it would be wonderful if all human beings felt empowered to express their dreams and had the resources to do it—but there's a negative side as well.

Owning-class people can often self-fund their dreams, and so they get less feedback and have fewer external constraints from funders and collaborators. This freedom can lead to delusions of grandeur, particularly among men, a belief that one's own project is better or more important than it is, and an unrealistic expectation chat others will fill one's needs. I would sum up their positive sense of empowerment and their negative sense of arrogance with the term "entitlement." Low income activists' good ideas too often go nowhere: owning class activists' bad ideas too often don't flop.

So there are discouraged unconventional people constrained to paint on a small canvas at one end of the class spectrum, and entitled unconventional people painting on a big canvas at the other end.

Class Cultures Comparison

Hand-out by Barbara Jensen and Jack Metzgar at a workshop on class cultures at the 2003 conference of the Working-Class Studies Program at Youngstown State University.

PROFESSIONAL MIDDLE CLASS	WORKING CLASS
DOING & BECOMING	**BEING & BELONGING**
• achievement-oriented	• character-oriented
• future-oriented	• present-oriented
• life as transformative	• life as a tangled web of relationships
• status concerns	• anti-status
• individualistic	• solidaristic
UNINTENDED HOMOGENEITY	**UNAVOIDABLE DIVERSITY**
• more cosmopolitan	• more parochial
• weaker loyalties to persons, places, groups, institutional affiliations	• stronger loyalties to persons, places, groups, institutional affiliations
BEST RESULT:	**BEST RESULT:**
• individual achievement has positive human impact	• secure community
WORST RESULT:	**WORST RESULT:**
• the lonely individual	• unachieved potential

Differences between working-class/lower-middle-class and professional middle-class activists

I've proposed the experience or lack of steady employment as a dividing line between class cultures. But what divides steadily employed people into different class cultures? Is there a common experience that socializes more and less privileged people differently, one that has enough of a material base to cause class-cultural differences consistent across race, religion, and geographical boundaries?

Yes. I think one life experience is key: the expectation of and experience of four years of residential college.

Going away to college is an assumed rite of passage for more privileged middle-class kids, those with parents in professional and managerial occupations. It's an experience that professional middle-class people share with owning-class people, and it helps connect them in a common privileged worldview.

Class-Culture Aspects of Labor/Environmental Conflicts

For his book Coalitions Across the Class Divide, Fred Rose did participatory research with union members and middle-class environmentalists and came up with a description of their cultural differences similar to that of Jensen/Metzgar and my own. Playing power politics to advance shared interests makes sense from a rooted, working-class life experience. Individuals voluntarily coming together due to their shared values in order to educate the public—this makes sense from an unrooted, middle-class life experience. From his interviews with timber workers and environmentalists locked in conflict over old-growth forests in the Northwest, he concludes:

Loggers and environmentalists come from alien realities, and each side misinterprets the other through its own cultural framework… Laborers must conform to work rules and the pace of production. Unions confront this external power by organizing workers' ability to deprive management of their labor… While the working class is regulated by externally imposed rewards and punishments, the middle class internalizes the rules that regulate their lives. Personal goals and ambitions to succeed are developed early and pursued without supervision. In the workplace, outcomes are rewarded rather than tasks being monitored. People choose to work for causes that provide a sense of identity, purpose and value… Relations with family members, peers in school and work, and neighbors tend to be inherited in working-class communities. By contrast the middle class defines itself by its activities and accomplishments… Because of these class-based cultural differences, working- and middle-class movements have difficulty perceiving their common interests and working together… Working-class unions and middle-class environmentalists seek change differently. The working class seeks to build power to confront external threats, while the middle class hopes to change people's motivations, ideas, and morality.

How does going away to college change someone? First and most basically, it means leaving home and spending four years with a large group of age peers.

Others enroll in college as well, of course. But living at home, taking community college courses while working and/or parenting, is not the same total

Low Income	Working Class and Lower Middle Class	Professional/Managerial Middle Class College Graduates

immersion experience as four-year residential college. As bell hooks, Barbara Jensen, and others have written, residential college is perceived as crossing a class boundary for many working-class and lower-middle-class kids who are the first in their families to go to college. People who have left home, lived on campus, been full-time students, and earned BA or BS degrees afterwards recognize each other as culturally similar, whether old or young, rural or urban, middle-class or owning-class, white or people of color.

How does going away to college change someone? First and most basically, it means leaving home and spending four years with a large group of age peers. It also means an immersion into abstract thinking and book learning. It means having a flexible, self-coordinated schedule with some free time. And, of course, it opens up options in professions that incorporate abstract thinking and flexible schedules.

College, whether residential or not, tends to have a homogenizing, assimilating effect. It typically means exposure to a rational secular worldview; in fact, college graduates are less religious on average than working-class people.

"Rooted" and "unrooted" are terms that sum up these differences. US-born working-class people are more likely to live where they grew up or, if they moved, to have moved as a family, not solo. They are more likely to live near extended family and to have more frequent contact with the older generations of their family—their ancestral roots. (Of course, this isn't true of working-class solo immigrants, who have been uprooted from their entire society.) There has been more geographic mobility in recent decades, but a working-class young adult is likely to have been raised and socialized by traditionally rooted people, whether stability is his or her own experience or not. Working-class and lower-middle-class people are also more likely to have strong ethnic and/or religious identities.

Besides these obvious kinds of roots, working-class and lower-middle-class people tend to have a pragmatic knowledge rooted primarily in heir own experience (as opposed to book learning). They also tend to be rooted in the sense of having their time constrained by work schedules imposed by others. With fewer options, they are often rooted as in "stuck," unable to leave an undesirable job or neighborhood.

Professional middle-class people and owning-class people, on the other hand, tend to be "unrooted" because prior generations may have left behind distinct ethnic cultures. Then they unroot themselves further by leaving their families to go to college, often never returning to their hometowns. Professional middle-class work schedules are more mobile, less defined by schedules set by others. They have more options and can more easily move on to a new job or home. Professional middle-class people also unroot their minds by filling them with book knowledge that exceeds and supercedes their own lived experience.

Professional middle-class kids are each other's competitors to get into college, and then are age-segregated for four years with peers who are also competitors

Low Income	Working Class and Lower Middle Class	Professional Middle Class	Owning Class
Thinking outside the box, less convention-bound, but discouraged by hardship	Rooted, pragmatic steady workers	Unrooted, competitive steady workers	Entitled, unrooted, thinking outside the box, less convention-bound

for professional success. Self-worth among college-educated middle-class people often rests on feeling smarter than other people—a major obstacle to cross-class alliance building!

Combining the gifts of all class cultures

Each of these class cultures was formed as a creative coping mechanism in social conditions that were oppressive to varying degrees, and each gives gifts and has limitations. None should be regarded as the ideal. The current class situation does not encourage the best in any of us to thrive. For the liberal assimilation worldview, the goal is to make low-income people more similar to middle-class people. But in fact, the process of humanization is just as rocky a path for more privileged people.

Our movements will be stronger if they include the strengths of each class culture. Rather than reacting with judgment to activists of other class backgrounds, we should develop an attitude of welcoming gifts and giving a hand with limitations in order to make collaboration possible. Hearing each other's stories and understanding the experiences that formed each other's class cultures will enable us to become better cross-class bridgers.

However, if activists treat everyone as "equal," without recognizing institutional advantages and disadvantages, we will replicate society's class and race oppression in our movements. To be able to organize successfully, low income and working-class activists need more of the resources they are short on: money, decision-making power, skills, and information. Middle-class and owning-class activist need to share their resources aid learn to follow the leadership of those without class privilege. And we need to realize that our motivation to be allies is not some kind of nice political correctness, but rather to increase the size and effectiveness of the movements we care about.

> *Our movements will be stronger if they include the strengths of each class culture. Rather than reacting with judgment to activists of other class backgrounds, we should develop an attitude of welcoming gifts and giving a hand with limitations in order to make collaboration possible.*

Growing Up with Two Moms

Megan McGuire

Megan McGuire, an 18-year-old student-at Mills College at the time she wrote this essay for the November 4, 1996, issue of *Newsweek* magazine, examines her child-hood embarrassment that her mother was a lesbian. She hid the truth from friends and lied about her mother, but in retrospect, she is proud of her family.

Pre-reading Questions

1. Do you think that gay parents can do as good a job at raising children as straight parents can? Why or why not?
2. Did you ever feel that you needed to hide the truth about your family from your immediate friends and acquaintances? Jot down your response to this question in your writing log or journal.

1   When I was growing up, the words "fag" and "queer" and "dyke" were every-where, even though we lived in a relatively tolerant community, Cambridge, Mass. I even used them myself to put down someone I didn't like. If you were a fag or a dyke, you were an outcast. All that changed when I was 12. My mother had a friend, Barb, who started spending the night, though she lived minutes away. One night when Barb wasn't there, I asked my mother, "Are you gay?" I can only remember the "yes"—and the crying. All I could think was that she couldn't be gay. It wasn't fair. She was one of "those" people.

2   I always thought my family was normal. By the time I was 5, my mother and father no longer lived together. My brother and I split our time between our parents. My father remarried, and my mother dated men. We assumed our parents were straight. That's all you see on TV.

3   As it turned out, we didn't have a stereotypical family. The years after my mother came out to me were very difficult for me and my brother. We had just moved from Washington, D.C. We had to start over, and at the same time we had to lie about our mom. In school I wanted to be liked, so I laughed at the jokes about gays. I had yet to figure out how to make a friend I could trust with my secret. I wasn't ready to talk about my family because I wasn't ready to deal with it myself.

4   High school was the hardest. I was into all kinds of clubs, but I was afraid everything I had gained socially would disappear if anyone ever found out that while they went home after volleyball practice to their Brady Bunch dinners with Mom and Dad, I went home to two moms. My brother and I would never allow Mom and Barb to walk together or sit next to each other in a restaurant. We wouldn't have people spend the night; if we did have friends over, we would hide the gay literature and family pictures. When a friend asked about the pink triangle on our car, my brother told him it was a used car and we hadn't had time to take the sticker off. We lived like this for three years, until we moved to a house with a basement apartment. We told our friends Barb lived there. It was really a guest room.

5   Ironically, our home life then was really the same as a straight family's. We had family meetings, fights, trips and dinners. My brother and I came to accept Barb as a parent. There were things she could never have with us the way our mother did. But she helped support us while my mother got her Ph.D in public health. And she pushed my brother and me to succeed in school, just like a mom.

6   With the help of a really great counselor and a friend who had a "it's not a big deal and I knew anyway" attitude, I started to become more comfortable with my two-mom family. The spring of my junior year, a local newspaper interviewed me for an article on gay families. I was relieved, but also afraid. The day the article appeared was incredibly tense. I felt like everyone was looking at me and talking about me. One kid said to my brother, "I saw the article, you fag." My brother told him to get lost. Some people avoided me, but most kids were curious about my family. People asked if I was gay. I chose not to answer; as teenagers, most of us can't explain the feelings in our minds and bodies.

7   Last year, in my final year of high school, I decided to speak at our school's National Coming Out Day. Sitting up front were my best friend, my mother, my brother and my counselor, Al. That day was the best. I no longer had to laugh at the jokes or keep a secret. I hoped I was making a path for others like me: a kid with a gay parent, scared and feeling alone. After my speech, I lost some friends and people made remarks that hurt. But that only made me stronger. The hardest thing to deal with is other people's ignorance, not the family part. That's just like any other family.

 Post-reading Questions

Content

1. What was the cause of McGuire's discomfort and embarrassment as a child?
2. When was her mother's sexual orientation hardest on her? Why?
3. What was McGuire's home life like? Did it really differ that much from the home life of her friends? Explain.
4. At what point in her life did McGuire come to terms with her "two moms"?
5. After the speech she gave at her school's National Corning Out Day, how did some of her friends treat her? What did McGuire realize about them?

Strategies and Structures

1. In addition to using cause and effect to describe her childhood with "two mothers," what other literary technique does McGuire use to develop her essay?
2. How does the tone reflect the author's attitude, and what purpose does this serve?

3. Why is the testimonial approach to McGuire's essay so appropriate to her subject matter? What might have been lost if she had opted to discuss "growing up with two moms" from a strictly scientific point of view?

4. Explain what you consider to be the most thought provoking part of McGuire's essay.

5. To what extent do you believe that the length of McGuire's essay is sufficient to analyze her subject matter? Do you believe more detail or further exposition would have added to her discussion? Why or why not? How?

 ## Language and Vocabulary

1. Vocabulary: *fag, queer, dyke, gay, stereotypical.* What is "pejorative language"? Look up the word "pejorative" in your dictionary as well as in your thesaurus. What are the denotative and connotative meanings of a pejorative word? How are most of the vocabulary terms above pejorative?

2. How does the author's simple word choice lend clarity to the real focus of McGuire's essay (a girl growing up with two mothers)?

Group Activities

1. Break into groups and brainstorm as many pejorative terms for as many groups of individuals as you can. What pejorative terms, for instance, refer to straight people, to men, to women, to people of color, to politicians, and so on?

2. Have all groups go to the library and make a copy of the articles on gay families in the November 4, 1996, issue of *Newsweek* magazine (the source of Megan McGuire's article). After reading each article, do some additional research on (1) what growing up in a gay family can or might be like and (2) the future probability of the social acceptance of gay families. Finally, divide think that gay couples should have the right to adopt children and those who oppose granting gay couples such a right. Debate both sides of the issue, attempting to clearly distinguish between social prejudice, beliefs about traditional families, and the idea that gay people can be as good at parenting as straight people can.

 ## Writing Activities

1. Construct an essay where you examine the cause(s) of discomfort for children who grow up in a single parent, a two-mother, or two-father family and the positive or negative effect(s) of such an upbringing. Providing plenty of representative examples that justify your claims will be an essential part of your essay.

What Could I Know of Racism?

Joy E. Weeber

Joy Weeber was a graduate student in a doctoral program in psychology at North Carolina State in Raleigh.

What could I know of racism, being a middle-class, college-educated White woman. What could I know of the pain of being rendered invisible because of a single characteristic? What could I know of having the complexity of myself, a Dutch American from a large extended family living around the world, reduced to that feature which marks me as "different" from the dominant culture? What could I know of being denied entrance to public facilities or required to sit in segregated places because of that characteristic? What could I know of being forced to use a back service entrance, like a second-class citizen? What could I know about being told that if I "work hard enough" I could make it, although getting in the front door for an interview seems an impossibility? What could I know about having to endure painful procedures to make my appearance more acceptable? What could I know of being charged a higher price for services because of the way I look? What could I know about not being able to ride a bus with dignity? What could I know of having a hard time finding a place to live because of housing discrimination or being unable to visit in the homes of my classmates? What could I know of growing up in a society that never portrays my people with positive images in the media, except for those exceptional, inspirational heroes who have more than made it? What could I know of being viewed as less intelligent simply because of the way I look? What could I know of being educated in a segregated school setting, not expected to amount to much and denied opportunities because of it? What could I know of being thought of as less than acceptable because of the way that I speak? What could I know of having to work twice as hard as others just to prove I am as good as they are? What could I know of being viewed as a charity case, rather than one who possesses civil rights?

I can know the pain of all of these things because I am disabled. My disabled brothers and sisters and I experience such acts of discrimination on a daily basis, and the pain these encounters cause is the same pain that racism causes people of color. It is the pain caused by the unconscious beliefs of a society that assumes everyone is, or should be, "normal" (i.e., White and very able-bodied). It is the pain caused by the assumption that everyone should be capable of total independence and "pulling themselves up by their own bootstraps." It is a belief in the superiority of being nondisabled that assumes everyone who is disabled wishes they could be nondisabled—at any cost. In the disability community, we call this "ableism," a form of prejudice and bigotry that marks us as less than those who are nondisabled. In this narrative, I use language the disability community claims in naming its own lived experience. And although it may not be "politically correct," it is meant as a true reflection of how many of us view ourselves and our lives as members of the disability community.

Ableism causes pain because it convinces us that there is something fundamentally wrong with us, that we are not acceptable just as we are. After all, we are the ones who are "defective," with bodies, speech, hearing, vision and emotional or cognitive functioning to be fixed by doctors and therapists. Ableism also causes pain to nondisabled people who are unprepared to deal with their own vulnerability and mortality when accidents and aging require that they do so. I did not understand the pain these attitudes had caused me until I was 35, despite having lived with the effects of polio since I was an infant. Until then, I did not know that I had spent my entire life trying to prove how I had "overcome" my polio, which is no more possible than overcoming being female or African American! I did not understand that these ableist attitudes and acts devalued my body and denied an essential element of who I am.

I only began to understand all of this when I read an essay, "The Myth of the Perfect Body," by Roberta Galler (1984),[13] who also had polio as a child. I felt as if I were reading my own diary! I was not an alien; I had a disability! I was the "supercrip" she wrote about, the defiant opposite of the pathetic cripple I had been made so deathly afraid of being. I had spent enormous amounts of my energy proving how "able" I was, to counter society's belief that I am "unable." I thought I had "passed" as normal in my nondisabled world (despite my crutches and braces), because I was often "complimented" by strangers and friends who "did not think of me as handicapped." Only when I read this woman's words did I begin to understand how my life had been shaped by living with a disability, even though my family and I had not been able to acknowledge that it existed! Only then did I begin to understand how my sense of self had been constructed by how my body had been touched, treated, and talked about by those who had been my "caregivers." Only then did I begin to understand how my life had been lived as an outsider, struggling unconsciously for acceptance.

Throughout my childhood, I had successfully resisted sincerely religious strangers' urgings for me to get "healed," people who thought of me as sick and infirm. Although these encounters left me feeling violated and nauseated, I knew I was fine and intact the way I was! Why did they think I was sick? I lived in a tight-knit community that accepted me as a whole person; they did not see me as sick. Not once had I been stopped from living life fully by anyone's low expectations, fear, or lack of imagination in how to change the world to meet my needs. I had been allowed to participate on my terms and discover my own physical limitations. My parents understood the stigma that society places on people with disabilities and were determined to nurture a sense of self that could deflect such negativity.

And yet, at the age of 10, I was marked as "other" by a diagnosis of scoliosis, found to be "defective" with a curving spine and weak leg muscles, and in need of" corrective" surgery. Thus began my searing journey into a medical world that

---

[13]R. Galler, "The Myth of the Perfect Body," in C. Vance (ed.), *Pleasure and Danger: Exploring Female Sexuality* (Boston: Routledge and Kegan Paul, 1984), pp. 165–172.

would teach me well what it really means to be disabled in this society! It was a world that taught me I was invisible, a defective body part to be talked about as if not connected to a lonely, hurting child. It was a world that taught me I had to be tough to survive, cut off from the emotional support of my family for all but 2 hour visits a week. It was a world that taught me that it was okay for others to inflict pain on me—if their goal was to make me more "normal." This world taught me that what I felt or wanted had nothing to do with what happened to my body, that it was okay to publicly strip children and parade their defects in front of strangers. The result of seven surgeries and innumerable scars was a girl who was numb, disconnected from both body and soul. I was fragmented and lost to a family who had no clue of my inner devastation. The emotional isolation of the hospital followed me home, as I heard in my family's lack of understanding that something was "wrong" with how I responded to life—emotionally, psychologically, spiritually, and politically!

My response to the horror of those years was to make myself outdo everyone, need help from no one, and take care of everyone else's needs. I was constantly proving I was the "exception," not one of those dependent cripples society cannot tolerate. Never mind that I spent my entire adult life struggling with devastating bouts of exhaustion-induced depression—although others only ever saw my bright, cheerful self. Never mind that I was alone, unable to sustain any vital romantic relationships, ever untouchable and independent. I became the angry one who spoke out against social injustice and felt the sexism in our community and family. I was the one who felt the arrogance and violence of racism. I was the one who felt the fragmentation of only seeking spiritual and physical sustenance, while psychological and emotional needs went unacknowledged. Being alone in the hospital, and the thought of seeking the company of those who might share them never crossed my mind.

At no time did I connect my different ways of perceiving and responding to the world with my experience of living with a disability. I couldn't. There was no disabled person in my world to help me understand that my empathy for those who suffered from injustice or were devalued because of race was rooted in my own experience of being devalued because of my disability. In the 7 years since my first encounter with a disabled person who understood, I have never felt alone. I have come to know the healing of belonging, of being understood without a word in a community of people who validate my feelings. I did not know how fragmented I was, and I needed other disabled people to teach me to love myself wholly! I had needed them to teach me how to embrace that part of myself that society so devalues. I needed them to show me the commonalities between our experiences of ableism and others' experiences of racism. I needed them to give words to the feelings I had never had reflected back to my self in my nondisabled world.

Most of us with disabilities learn to survive alone and silently in our nondisabled families and worlds, never knowing a disability community exists. I was the only disabled person in my family, my community, schools, and my adult social world. As a child, I had learned an aversion to the company of other disabled people because they were associated with being "defective" and stigmatized, and I was neither of those! My only experiences with other disabled people had been in situations in which nondisabled professionals "medicalized" our lives, defining us negatively. I even had my own turn at working in such settings, "helping" others in sheltered workshops and group homes, although always quitting for emotional reasons I only now understand. I had never been in an environment in which disabled people defined themselves in their own terms and celebrated their uniqueness. And now, in the written words and in the company of disabled people, I have found brothers and sisters who are teaching me that there are powerful ways of dealing with the pain of being "other." They are helping me find the words to express what I have always "known" in my body, but had no language to express.

James Baldwin (1972) wrote that "to be liberated from the stigma of blackness by embracing it, is to cease, forever, one's interior argument and collaboration with the authors of one's degradation (p. 190)."[14] It has been my experience that learning to embrace my whole self, disability and all, was not a task I could do alone. I needed the support and guidance of others who not only had lived my experience but also had ceased their internal collaboration with the negative voices of society. It is the same process that bell hooks (1989) speaks of in *Talking Back: Thinking Feminist, Thinking Black*,[15] as the need to "decolonialize" one's mind by rooting out all that does not honor one's own experience. I have found that in addition to decolonializing my mind, I have also needed to decolonialize my body. I have had to cease my interior argument with society's negative messages that I am not as good as everybody else by no longer pushing my body beyond its limits. As I have learned to listen to my body's limits, honoring them as a source of wisdom and strength, I have experienced the healing and liberation of the embrace, and I have begun to thrive.

A most profound way that I have begun to thrive is that I no longer require that I spend most of my energy walking to get around—I have begun to use a scooter for mobility. What an act of liberation—and resistance—this has been! I felt like a bird let out of a cage, the first time I used one! I could go and go and not be exhausted! I was able to fully participate in the conference I was attending, rather that just be dully present. To choose to use a scooter, when I can still walk, flies in the face of all the "wisdom" of those without disabilities. We are taught that to walk, no matter how distorted or exhausting it is, is far more virtuous than using a chair— because it is closer to "normal." Never mind that my galumphing polio-gait twists my muscles into iron-like sinew that only the hardiest of masseuses can "unknot." Never mind that my shoulders and hands, never meant for walking, have their future usefulness limited by 40 years of misuse on crutches. To choose to use a scooter also places me squarely in that stigmatized group of "pitiful unfortunates" who are "confined" to their chairs. It removes me from the ranks of "overcomers," such as Franklin Delano Roosevelt, Wilma Rudolph, or Helen Keller, whom society mistakenly believes actually "got over" their disabilities. My using a scooter is an act that scares my family. They are afraid that somehow giving up walking will make me give up—period! It makes them think that I am losing ground, becoming dependent on the scooter, when they and society need me to act as if I am strong and virile. Only now that I am embracing my limitations do I know how I spent much life-energy protecting my family from them. I rarely slowed them down or

---

[14]J. Baldwin, *No Name in the Street* (New York: Doubleday, 1972).
[15]b. hooks, *Talking Back: Thinking Feminist, Thinking Black* (Boston, MA: South End Press, 1989).

burdened them with feelings they could not understand. Only now can I celebrate my unavoidable need for interdependence in a society that oppresses everyone with its unattainable standard of independence!

Traditionally, families are taught by professionals that their child's disability is an individual functional problem that can only be remedied by individualized medical interventions. And so it remains the focus of many families to adapt their child to a society that needs them to be "normal." The larger social and cultural oppression that some of those interventions represent is only now being raised by those of us, former disabled children who question the extreme and painful measures taken to "fix" us, measures that went beyond what may have been truly needed to ensure our full, unique development. In my scooter, I am choosing now to live by other values—the values of the disability community that require society to adapt to our needs rather than vice versa.

In using my scooter, I experience the full range of the disability experience, including those aspects I avoided when I thought I was "passing" as normal. In my scooter, I experience being denied access to places walking people enter without a thought, because they are inaccessible. In my scooter, I am eligible to use service entrances near stinking dumpsters and seating at public events that is segregated from my walking companions. Seated in my scooter, I am even more invisible to those who could never look the walking-me in the eye—an averted gaze not even required to obliterate my presence. In my scooter, I cannot visit some friends' homes because of stairs or use their bathrooms because of narrow doors. The very cost of my scooter includes a sizable "crip tax"—as the sum of its component parts is far less costly than its hefty price tag in the inflated (and captive) medical equipment market. In my scooter, I don't have full assurance that I will even be able to get on public transportation, much less treated with dignity when I do. In my scooter I feel the insult of those telethon hosts who want to paint my life as pathetic, not livable, unless I am cured. In my scooter, I know that I am viewed as far less able, needing public assistance rather than ramps and power doors to get into job interviews. Although my speech was not affected by polio, my scooter provides further reason to dismiss me, as society dismisses my brothers and sisters who use voice synthesizers to communicate their artistic vision of the world. In my scooter, I am inextricably and unavoidably a member of the disability community, with all the pain and privileges associated with that membership.

I am proud to have found my way home to the disability community. I am now able to "hang out on the porch" and hear stories from the elders of how their visions of equal justice for all took shape, how legislation acknowledging our civil rights was passed. And although it is true that we continue to struggle to define our own lives and live it on our own terms, we have also begun to create a culture that brings us together and celebrates our unique ways of being in the world. I am moved when I hear poetry that speaks my truth and read books that truly reflect my life experiences. I am healed when I see unflinchingly honest performances dealing with the reality and pain caused by ableism. I now know that I have indeed experienced the pain of ableism and I know why I felt the pain of racism when I had words for neither. I now also know the liberating power of embracing my disability and of celebrating who I am because of it.

Discussion Questions

1. Describe the elements of society that caused Weeber to feel that her life had been "lived as an outsider, struggling unconsciously for acceptance." How does Weeber's experience as a disabled person parallel that of other marginalized populations?

2. How does Weeber's experience as a disabled person enrich her life? Why does her decision to embrace her limitations introduce tensions into her interactions with her family?

3. Does Weeber's eventual connection to the disabled community change her view of herself and mold her values? How important is it to have friends and role models who share your life experience?

"We Will All Be Minorities"
Ronald Takaki

Ronald Takaki, Ph.D. (1939–2009) was a world-renowned scholar in ethnic studies and our nation's diversity. Dr. Takaki spent 36 years of his academic tenure with the Ethnic Studies Department at the University of California, Berkeley. The following excerpt is the closing article from his American Book Award winning *A Different Mirror: A History of Multicultural America* (Revised edition). A detailed biography and list of accomplishments can be found at the following URL: http://ethnicstudies.berkeley.edu/story.php?id=5

On a Monday morning in June 1997, I was writing in my study at home when I received a call from Doris Matsui, an assistant to President Bill Clinton. She told me that the president wanted me to come to Washington to help him write a major speech on race. "He would like to take the national dialogue on race beyond the black/white binary," she said. "So it's very important for you to be here." Within hours, I was flying to Washington.

The next day, at the White House, President Clinton facilitated the meeting of a small gathering of civil rights leaders and intellectuals. After raising my hand, I said: "I think your speech is timely. Sometime in the twenty-first century, whites will become a minority in the U.S. population. They already are in California. So when you come to my state to give your speech, you will be a minority." Then I tried to crack a joke: "Welcome to the club, Mr. President." Instantly, he winked at me: "Yes, I know! Why do you think I am doing all of this?" "Yes," I answered, "we will all be minorities."

That Saturday, President Clinton gave his address, "One America in the Twenty-first Century: The President's Initiative on Race." To the graduating class of the University of California at San Diego, he declared: "A half-century from now, when your own grandchildren are in college, there will be no majority race in America." He then presented highlights from our multicultural past:

> Consider this: we were born with a Declaration of Independence which asserted that we were all created equal and a Constitution that enshrined slavery. We fought a bloody civil war to abolish slavery and preserve the union, but we remained a house divided and unequal by law for another century. We advanced across the continent in the name of freedom, yet in so doing we pushed Native Americans off their land, often crushing their culture and their livelihood. In World War II, Japanese Americans fought valiantly for freedom in Europe, taking great casualties, while at home their families were herded into internment camps. The famed Tuskegee Airmen lost none of the bombers they guarded during the war, but their African American heritage cost them a lot of rights when they came back home in peace.

In his conclusion, President Clinton identified the challenge we faced: "More than 30 years ago, at the high tide of the civil rights movement, the Kerner Commission said we were becoming two Americas, one white, one black, separate but unequal. Today, we face a different choice: will we become not two, but many

Americas, separate, unequal and isolated? Or will we draw strength from all our people and the ancient faith in the quality of human dignity, to become the world's first truly multiracial democracy?"[1]

The future is in our hands. The choices we make will be influenced by whether our memory of the past is the Master Narrative of American History or the narrative of "a different mirror." A history that leaves out minorities reinforces separation, but an inclusive history bridges the divide.

We have the opportunity to redefine the "errand into the wilderness"—to write our own ending to Shakespeare's play about America. The bard need not be prophetic, for we have the advantage of hindsight: we know what happened not only to Prospero but also to Caliban in American history.

This epic story was illuminated by Herman Melville in his great American novel *Moby-Dick*. The crew of the *Pequod* represents the races and cultures of the world. On deck, Captain Ahab and his officers are all white men. Below deck, there are whites like Ishmael, Africans like Daggoo, Pacific Islanders like Queequeg, American Indians like Tashtego, and Asians like Fedallah. There is a noble class unity among the workers: they possess "democratic dignity," and an "ethereal light" shines on the "workman's arm."[2]

On their voyage through history, the people on board the *Pequod* known as America found their paths crisscrossing one another in events and developments such as Bacon's Rebellion, the Market Revolution, the Civil War, and World War II. Their lives and cultures have swirled together in the settling and building of America from the first meeting of Powhatans and English on the Virginia shore to the last Mexican immigrants crossing the border.

Together, they have been creating what Gloria Anzaldúa calls a "borderland"— a place where "two or more cultures edge each other, where people of different races occupy the same territory." How can all of us meet on communal ground? "The struggle," Anzaldúa responds, "is inner: Chicano, *indio*, American Indian, *mojado, mexicano*, immigrant Latino, Anglo in power, working class Anglo, Black, Asian—our psyches resemble the border-towns and are populated by the same people.... Awareness of our situation must come before inner changes, which in turn come before changes in society."[3]

Such awareness must come from a "re-visioned" history. What Gloria Steinem termed "revolution from within" must ultimately be grounded in "unlearning" much of what we have been told about America's past and substituting a more inclusive and accurate history of all the peoples of America.[4]

A cutting edge of this "unlearning" can be found on the continent's western shore. "California, and especially Los Angeles, a gateway to both Asia and Latin

---

[1]President Bill Clinton, "One America in the Twenty-first Century: The President's Initiative on Race" (Washington, D.C., White House, June 16,1997). On July 10, Minyon Moore, deputy assistant to the president for political affairs, wrote to me: "Thank you for the valuable input you provided President Clinton in preparation for his speech on Race and Reconciliation in San Diego. The ideas you shared with the President meant a great deal to him."

[2]Herman Melville, *Moby-Dick* (Boston, 1956; originally published in 1851), pp. 105, 182, 253, 322–323.

[3]Gloria Anzaldua, *Borderlands, La Frontera: The New Mestiza*: (San Francisco, 1987), first page of preface, p. 87.

[4]Gloria Steinem, *Revolution from Within* (Boston, 1990), p, 107.

America," Carlos Fuentes observed, "poses the universal question of the coming century: how do we deal with the Other?"[5]

Asked whether California, with its multiethnic society, represented the America of the twenty-first century, Alice Walker replied: "If that's not the future reality of the United States, there won't be any United States, because that's who we are." Walker's own ancestry is a combination of Native American, African American, and European American.[6]

King of golf Tiger Woods is a mixture of different races. "All the media try to put black in him," protested his mother, Kultida Woods. "Why don't they ask who half of Tiger is from? In the United States, one little part black is all black. Nobody wants to listen to me. I've been trying to explain to people, but they don't understand. To say he is 100 percent black is to deny his heritage. To deny his grandmother and grandfather. To deny me!" Tiger Woods himself declared to the media: "My parents have taught me to always be proud of my ethnic background. Yes, I am the product of two great cultures, one African American and the other Asian. On my father's side I'm African American. On my mother's side I am Thai. Truthfully, I feel very fortunate, and equally proud to be both African American and Asian."[7]

Barack Obama is proud of his biracial identity. "We've got a tragic history when it comes to race in this country," he said, noting "pent-up anger and mistrust and bitterness." "I continue to believe that this country wants to move beyond these kinds of things." Pointing out that his father is black and his mother white, he declared: "Born into a diverse family, I have little pieces of America all in me."

One of those "pieces" is Asian American. Obama was born and raised in Hawaii, the only state with an Asian-American majority. His stepfather, Lolo Soetoro, was Indonesian; his half-sister, Maya Soetoro-Ng, is married to a Chinese Canadian. Obama's legislative director is Chris Lu, the daughter of Chinese immigrants. "A lot of aspects of the senator's story will be recognizable to many Asian Americans," she said. "He talks about feeling somewhat of an outsider, about coming to terms with his self-identity, about figuring out how to reconcile the values from his unique heritage with those of the larger U.S. society. These are tensions and conflicts that play out in the lives of all children of immigrants."[8]

Native-American writer Paula Gunn Allen prizes the "little pieces" in herself— American Indian, Scotch, Jewish, and Lebanese. "Just people from everywhere are related to me by blood," she explained, "and so that's why I say I'm a multicultural event. It's beautiful, it's a rainbow. It reflects light, and I think that's what a person like me can do."[9] Imagine what "light" a "multicultural event" called America can reflect.

---

[5]Carlos Fuentes, *The Buried Mirror: Reflections on Spain and the New World.* (New York, 1992), p. 348.
[6]Reese Erlich, "Alice's Wonderland," an interview with Alice Walker, Image, *San Francisco Examiner*, July 19, 1992, p. 12.
[7]Greg Mayeda, "Golf Phenomenon Asserts Mixed Race Identity," *What's Hapa'ning: The Hapa Issues Forum Newsletter*, vol. 3, no. 2, summer 1995 (Berkeley, Calif.).
[8]Johanna Neuman, "Obama Decries Rash of Divisive Campaigning," *San Francisco Chronicle*, March 16, 2008; Jeff Yang, "Another First for Obama If Elected?" *San Francisco Chronicle*, July 21, 2008.
[9]Paula Gunn Allen, interview, in Laura Coltelli (ed.), *Winged. Words: American Indian Writers Speak* (Lincoln, Neb., 1990), p. 17.

America's dilemma has been the denial of our immensely varied selves. Asked whether she had a specific proposal for improving the current racial climate in America, Toni Morrison answered: "Everybody remembers the first time they were taught that part of the human race was Other. That's a trauma. It's as though I told you that your left hand is not part of your body."[10]

We need not repeat what Prospero did to Caliban. Instead, we can heed the lesson of Black Elk. In his vision of the "whole hoop of the world," the Sioux holy man saw "in a sacred manner the shapes of all things in the spirit, and the shape of all shapes as they must live together like one being." The "sacred hoop" of his people was "one of many hoops that made one circle, wide as daylight and as starlight, and in the center grew one mighty flowering tree to shelter all the children of one mother and one father."[11] Today, we need to stop denying our wholeness as members of one humanity as well as one nation.

We originally came from many different shores, and our diversity has been at the center of the making of America. Composed of many colors and cultures, we have been "singing with open mouths their strong melodious songs" from the tobacco fields of Virginia, the textile mills of Lowell, the "Trail of Tears," the cotton fields of Mississippi, the battlefields of the Civil War, the Indian reservations of South Dakota, the railroad tracks in the Sierras of California, the snow-covered ground of Wounded Knee, the garment factories of the Lower East Side, the canefields of Hawaii, the internment camp of Manzanar, South Central Los Angeles, the Lincoln Memorial in Washington, D.C., and a thousand other places.[12]

Signs of our ethnic diversity can also be found across America—Ellis Island, Angel Island, Chinatown, Harlem, South Boston, the Lower East Side, places with Spanish names like Los Angeles and San Antonio or Indian names like Massachusetts and Iowa. Much of what is familiar in America's cultural landscape has ethnic origins. The Bing cherry was developed by an early Chinese immigrant named Ah Bing. American Indians were cultivating corn, potatoes, tomatoes, and tobacco long before the arrival of Columbus. The term "okay" was derived from the Choctaw word, *oke,* meaning "it is so." There is evidence indicating that the name "Yankee" came from Indian terms for the English—from *eankke* in Cherokee and *Yankwis* in Delaware. Jazz and blues as well as rock and roll have African-American origins. The "Forty-Niners" of the gold rush learned mining techniques from the Mexicans; American cowboys acquired herding skills from Mexican *vaqueros* and adopted their range terms—such as "lariat" from *la reata,* "lasso" from *lazo,* and "stampede" from *estampida.* Songs like "God Bless America," "Easter Parade," and "White Christmas" were written by a Russian-Jewish immigrant named Israel Baline, more popularly known as Irving Berlin.[13]

---

[10]Interview with Toni Morrison, *Time,* May 22, 1989, p. 121.
[11]John G. Neihardt (ed.), *Black Elk Speaks: Being the Life Story of a Holy Man of the Oglala Sioux* (Lincoln, Neb., 1988), p. 43.
[12]Walt Whitman, Leaves of Grass and Selected Prose (New York 1958), p. 10.
[13]Ronald Takaki, *Strangers from a Different Shore: A History of Asian Americans* (Boston, 1989), pp. 88-89; Jack Weatherford, *Native Roots: How the Indians Enriched America* (New York, 1991), pp. 210, 212; Carey McWilliams, *North from Mexico: The Spanish-Speaking People of the United States* (New York, 1968), p. 154; Stephan Thernstrom (ed.), *Harvard Encyclopedia of American Ethnic Groups* (Cambridge, Mass., 1980), p. 22; Howard Sachar, *A History of the Jews in America* (New York, 1992), p. 367.

Like Caliban and Stephano, marginalized minorities have been chanting, "Freedom, highday! highday, freedom! freedom, highday, freedom!" They have been singing: "We shall overcome. We shall overcome." While their struggle must continue, they have won a multitude of victories—the abolishing of slavery, the integrating of the U.S. Armed Forces, the outlawing of segregated schooling for Mexican Americans and African Americans, the ending of Jim Crow in the South, the extending of naturalized citizenship to all immigrants regardless of race, the overturning of anti-miscegenation laws, the guaranteeing of voting rights for minorities, the reopening of immigration from Asia, the granting of redress and reparations to Japanese internees, and the awakening of America to our amazing diversity. Indeed, in many significant ways, we have "overcome."

What does the future hold for America? Over one hundred years ago, Herman Melville wrote: America is not a nation "so much as a world." In this new society, the "prejudices of national dislikes" could be "forever extinguished." Walt Whitman chimed: All of us belonged to "a teeming Nation of nations" where "all races and cultures" could be "accepted" and "saluted," not "controlled or placed in hierarchy," and all could be welcomed—"Chinese, Irish, German, pauper or not, criminal or not—all, all, without exceptions." "Of every hue and caste am I, I resist any thing better than my own diversity."[14]

"The problem of the twentieth century," as W. E. B. Du Bois observed, was "the problem of the color line." However, the promise of: the twenty-first century is the promise of the changing colors of the American people. Demography is redefining who is an American. The time has come for us to embrace our varied selves. A new America is approaching, a society where diversity is destiny. How can we prepare ourselves for this "brave new world that has such people in't"? Here, history matters. Offering our "mystic chords of memory" more inclusively, *A Different Mirror* tells the story of America as a diversely peopled nation, "dedicated to the proposition that all men are created equal." Woven into the multicultural tapestry of our national narrative is the fervent and felicitous message of Langston Hughes: "Let America be America again.... Let America be the dream the dreamers dreamed... [where] equality is in the air we breathe."[15]

 ## Discussion Questions

1. As our nation becomes more multi-ethnic and there ceases to be a majority of any racial group, do you think it is possible to achieve harmony in our society?

---

[14]Herman Melville. *Redburn* (Chicago, 1969; originally published in 1849), p. 169; also quoted in Henry Louis Gates, Jr., *Loose Canons: Notes on the Culture Wars* (New York, 1992), pp. 116–117; Walt Whitman, *Leaves of Grass and Selected Prose* (New York, 1958), pp. 284. 9, 10, 38.
[15]W. E. B. Du Bois, *The Souls of Black Folk: Essays and Sketches* (New York, 1965), p. v; Abraham Lincoln, "First Inaugural Address," in *The Annals of America*, vol. 9, *1861–1865: The Crisis of the Union* (Chicago, 1968), p. 255; Abraham Lincoln, "The Gettysburg Address," in ibid. pp. 462–463; Langston Hughes, "Let America Be America Again," in Langston Hughes and Arna Bontemps (eds.), *The Poetry of the Negro, 1746–1949* (Garden City, N.Y, 1951), p. 106.

2. In a multi-ethnic society, should individual groups maintain their cultural practices and values, or does doing so make it harder for diverse groups to coexist?

3. Do you think that the increased population numbers for people of color means that those traditionally under-represented groups will have increased access to power, or will white Americans continue to receive a disproportionately large share of economic and governmental influence?

Selected Bibliography

Davis, S., Jenkings, G. & Hunt, R. (2002). *The pact: Three young men make a promise and fulfill a dream*. New York, NY: Riverhead Books.

Dawkins, P.A. (2001). Apologizing for being a black male. In J. Ferrante & P. Brown, Jr. (Eds.), *The social construction of race and ethnicity in the United States* (2nd ed., pp. 68-69). Upper Saddle River, NJ: Prentice-Hall, Inc.

Delpit, L. (2008). No Kinda Sense. In A. Knepler, E. Knepler, & M. Knepler (Eds.), *Crossing cultures: Readings for composition* (7th ed., pp. 108-120). Boston, MA: Houghton Mifflin.

Jones-Deweever, A.A. & Hartmann, H. (2009). Abandoned before the storms: The glaring disaster of gender, race, and class disparities in the Gulf. In E. Higginbotham & M. L. Andersen (Eds.), *Race and ethnicity in society: The changing landscape* (2nd ed., pp. 249-259). Belmont, CA: Wadsworth, Cengage Learning.

Lorde, A. (2007). Women redefining difference. In M. L. Andersen & P. H. Collins (Eds.), *Race, class, and gender: An anthology* (6th ed., pp. 52-59). Belmont, CA: Thomson Wadsworth.

Obama, B. (2004). *Dreams from my father: A story of race and inheritance*. New York, NY: Three Rivers Press.

Shapiro, T.M. (2007). The hidden cost of being African American. In M. L. Andersen & P. H. Collins (Eds.), *Race, class, and gender: An anthology* (6th ed., pp. 127-135). Belmont, CA: Thomson Wadsworth.

Staples, B. (2008). Night Walker. In A. Knepler, E. Knepler, & M. Knepler (Eds.), *Crossing cultures: Readings for composition* (7th ed., pp. 256-259). Boston, MA: Houghton Mifflin.

Tatum, B.V. (2007). Defining racism: "Can we talk?" In P. S. Rothenberg (Ed.), *Race, class, and gender in the United States: An integrated study* (7th ed., pp. 123-130). New York, NY: Worth Publishers.

Ugwu-Oju, D. (2001). What will my mother say. In J. Ferrante & P. Brown, Jr. (Eds.), *The social construction of race and ethnicity in the United States* (2nd ed., pp. 63-67). Upper Saddle River, NJ: Prentice-Hall, Inc.

WHAT IS YOUR ACADEMIC PLAN?

What comes to mind most often when thinking about academic planning are:

Courses: Electives - general education -
            major courses - prerequisite courses

Questions: What should you take next term?
            Is it time to declare or change your major?
            Who do I ask for help?

Greg Wheeler,
Associate Dean
Undergraduate Studies

Dear First-Year Students,

I am very pleased to have this chance to write to you. Many of you are not sure what you want your future to look like. What will you do? Where will you live? How will your education prepare you for your future? Some of you feel sure of the answers to these questions, but it is likely that your answers will change. Many sources tell us that new information is accumulating at a staggering rate. Each year brings new technology and new possibilities. Richard Riley, a former United States Secretary of Education, said, "We are currently preparing students for jobs that don't yet exist, using technologies that haven't been invented, in order to solve problems that we don't even know are problems yet." In this context, what should your education at Sacramento State provide?

Until recently general education and vocational education have been considered two parts of a good university education. A student, merely wanting a job, could take vocational training and get good jobs in some fields. The broader education offered by a university might include art for the science major, philosophy for the kinesiology major, or English for the math major, and was not always considered important to begin or maintain a career. That long-held belief has changed. It is general education that prepares you to be flexible in a changing world. It is general education that allows you to discover new talents and explore new opportunities. While the need for a focused major has not been eliminated, it is clear that in most professions the liberally educated individual will always have the advantage.

At Sacramento State, what we call general education makes up about 40 % of the course work you will be required to take. It is a mix of courses from across the departmental boundaries. There are over 400 General Education courses to choose from. You will find information and skills to lead you into your future. Embrace the opportunity.

By enrolling in First Year Seminar, you took a critical step in answering the questions I posed at the beginning of this letter. Not only will you learn the meaning of a university education, but you will discover important pathways to the success you seek. Pay attention!

The First Year Seminar is your chance to start an exciting new phase of your education. Over the last ten years, we have shown that students who give serious effort to this course have a much deeper understanding of General Education, become familiar with the resources available to them, and are better prepared to plan their education. These students graduate with higher grade-point averages and graduate sooner than students who don't take the course.

Many people in our world will never get the chance to receive the education that lies ahead of you at this university. Let me end with a quote from the General Education/Graduation Requirements Policies Committee. "This is your opportunity to lay the foundation for the rest of your life and to define yourself as an educated member of the human community." Go for it!

Greg Wheeler,
Associate Dean, Undergraduate Studies, Retired

Major Decisions

James Tunstead Burtchaell

Father James Burtchaell, professor emeritus of Theology at the University of Notre Dame, served as provost for many years. While holding that title, which in a university is normally the position of chief academic officer and ranks just below the president, Burtchaell lived in student residence halls and saw firsthand the student concerns that he discusses in this reading. Although many colleges strive to get students to decide on a major early, often before being admitted, Notre Dame in Burtchaell's time told students that, as first-year students, they could specify an intent but not declare a major. This essay explains why.

More than two out of every three undergraduates at this university change majors between the time they are accepted and the time they graduate. A good number change two or three times. Any decision that has so many students second-guessing must be tricky, and it is.

The difficulty comes from several directions. First, there are so many options that you had no opportunity to sample in high school. Everyone has some experience studying literature, mathematics, French and physics, but no high school in the country offers electrical engineering. Nor can you get a running start in microbiology or finance or metallurgy or philosophy. More than half of the disciplines we offer are new to you. So how can you have a responsibly cultivated preference early enough to select one as your principal interest here?

Another difficulty is pressure. Some students get pretty clear advice from their parents about what a sensible major would be. Most of that advice tends to have something to do with earning a living after college. And much of it is bad advice.

In the old days there were parents who threatened to cut off tuition money unless their child studied the subject they thought was right. That rarely happens today, but there is another kind of pressure that may be worse. There are few students at Notre Dame whose parents didn't make sacrifices for them to be here. And most students are backed by parents who didn't have, or weren't free to accept, the kind of education they worked hard to provide their children. The result: Most people on this campus walk around with an abiding and compelling sense of gratitude to their parents.

For every student here whose parents have told him what to study, there are a hundred whose parents never breathed a word of instruction on the matter. But most of those hundred, in the privacy of their hearts, want to make a choice that will satisfy their parents. They are drawn to major in subjects their parents can see as oriented toward a useful future. One somehow feels it would be ungrateful to receive a first-rate university education and not put it to maximum use from the start. That is a more *insidious* and damaging form of pressure precisely because there is nothing the parents can do to change it. They had nothing to do with imposing it.

In addition, high school counselors often talk to seniors in a way that is excessively career oriented. They make the student aware, even before s/he sets foot on a college campus, that s/he is going to higher studies with an eye toward an eventual profession or job. The message is that it is wasteful to spend four years without any clear idea of where all that expensive study is leading.

Students also have a tendency, especially in their early years at college, to feel crowded by competition. Most freshmen look up and down the corridor the first week they're here and feel intimidated. Everyone they encounter seems to have been a valedictorian, student council president, all-state breast-stroke champion, published poet.

I exaggerate, of course, but most people here *are* used to being at the head of the line. That is how you got here. Now you are at a place with a lot of others who were at the head of *their* lines, and there just isn't room for all of you at the top of this class. So you tend to figure that your choice of study here will have to be canny and careful if it's going to make you competitive with such bright and aggressive classmates.

After a few years you discover everyone else is as normal as you, but by then you've begun to worry that since Notre Dame accepted you it must be a second-rate institution. There are all those other more talented people out there at better places who, when they emerge, are going to have a running start on you. So your choice of what to study is fretful because you have these other, more quick-witted people to compete with.

Those are three difficulties that most of you have to cope with: the subjects are so unknown, the choice is so pressured, and the competition is so strong. Unfortunately these difficulties cause students to stumble into a few classical misunderstandings, which in turn lead them to wrong decisions about their major.

The first misunderstanding is to confuse education with training. An institution that offers you training is trying to provide you with the information and skills you need for a specific career. A law school must acquaint you with how to interview clients, how to plead before a court, and how to draw up proper legal documents. A welding academy will teach you the materials and methods of the trade. Advanced training in computing will prepare you not simply to program, but to create software, to understand the mysteries of central processing, and then to grasp the theoretical underpinnings of applied mathematics.

All of that is training: specific knowledge needed for specific professional or skilled work. It is not education.

Education is the opportunity, through studying a variety of subjects, to gain the information and the dexterity to use your wits and your expression. Education prepares you to *be* someone more than to *do* something. Education is what prepares you to hear more when you listen, to reach deeper when you think, to say more when you speak.

Education is quite different from training, which prepares you in advance to do the tasks that are well known in a given job. Education prepares you in advance to see beneath and beyond what is well known. The principal value that an educated person brings to her career is intelligence. What one wants of an educated person, beyond his skills, is the ability to see into problems that cannot be foreseen. A welder must know in advance all the techniques he has to use, but a banker or a physician or a teacher or a member of the city council is expected to move beyond previous experience and apply his wits to the heart of new problems.

A good university such as this one will give you quite a few skills and a broad grounding of information. But we do not exist to teach skills to undergraduates; we do that in our graduate and professional programs. The result of a college education should be a person whose mind is enlivened and whose imagination is limber. England's Robert Benchley put it in his own peculiar and wise way:

"Gentlemen: You are now about to embark upon a course of studies which will occupy you for several years. Together they form a noble adventure. But I would like to remind you of an important point. Some of you, when you go down from the University, will go into the Church, or to the Bar, or to the House of Commons, or to the Home Civil Service, to the Indian or Colonial Services, or into various professions. Some may go into the Army, some into industry and commerce, some may become country gentlemen. A few—I hope very few— will become teachers or *dons*.

"Let me make this clear to you. Except for the last category, nothing that you will learn in the course of your studies will be of the slightest possible use to you in after life, save only this: That if you work hard and intelligently you should be able to detect when a man is talking rot, and that in my view is the main, if not the sole, purpose of education."

People fortunate and qualified enough to receive a university education will make their living by their wits. You will be served less by what you *have* learned than by what you *can* learn.

The good thing about education is that it matters hardly at all what subjects you choose to study. You can be educated in any discipline because there is no direct connection between an educational subject and a specific career. So never ask what you can *do* with your major.

This touches on the second classical misunderstanding that has led so many students astray. The choice of a major is not the choice of a career. Undergraduates are not making lifetime decisions. When they imagine they are, it can be paralyzing.

As you know, Notre Dame has delaying tactics to slow you down in the selection of a major. Before coming here most of you speculated about your eventual career, and then about what course of study you would select. You arrived here ready to declare a major, but the Freshman Year of Studies would not allow that. The most you were permitted was to designate an "intent." We wanted you to get the maximum exposure and experience here, and a year or two more of self-knowledge, so that your intellectual curiosity and interests could ripen and the decision would be more sound, more considered.

Let me say a bit about that. Some talents show themselves early in life. If you are an excellent athlete, you already have the coordination and stamina and pleasure from sports in your early teens. Nobody suddenly develops into a star athlete in his/her 30s. The same is true for mathematical ability. If you are good at quantitative understanding, you are already good at it in junior high school; in fact, you tend toward high achievement in math and other related subjects. You know science is your strong suit, and you come to college aware that you will study science and excel in it. Then things go wrong. Physics will begin to bore some of you. You will conceal from your parents that you signed up for a few extra theology courses, and you'll write poetry by flashlight under the covers at night. You may plug on and earn good grades, but with less and less appetite. It is *disconcerting* to develop a new range of interests when your track record of achievement and satisfaction is so definitely in another direction. But that is what happens when a new range of talent begins to mature and to rival other talents that had declared themselves earlier. No one tells you in advance that philosophical thinking matures later than mathematical thinking. The choice of a major needs to be slowed down to allow you to get confirmation of your emergent strong interests and abilities.

But even then, near the close of your sophomore year, you are only choosing a major, not a career. Still more developments and experiences will come. Fixing on a lifetime career when you are a sophomore in college is like getting engaged at 14.

What you study here may have little necessary connection with what you will do later. We give baccalaureate degrees in about 40 disciplines and in many combinations of subjects. But people graduate in philosophy and end up lawyers. They study mechanical engineering and end up as business executives. They get degrees in English and go to medical school, do art history and run the family business, choose chemistry and go into politics. They major in sociology and become priests. They finish in accountancy with their CPAs and choose to be homemakers and mothers.

Even if they emerge from a program most students would consider a direct pipeline to a specific profession—architecture, for example—they are really much more free than you would suppose. Do you know how many people with degrees in architecture practice architecture? About half. So consider yourself enhanced, rather than caught, by what you choose to study. You are not making a lifetime decision, you are making a decision for the next two or three years . . . or until you change that decision.

This is not to say that there should be no natural growth from study to career. It does imply, however, that educated people have such enormous advantage and versatility that they retain a basic freedom to do whatever they please in life. To have graduated in any discipline that Notre Dame offers in no way forecloses career possibilities. It has become increasingly the case that you will enter a career that requires or provides specific training. About 60 to 70 percent of you will go on to graduate or professional schools; others to corporate training programs. Do not suffer a failure of nerve by imagining that you are more attractive to employers if you have more advanced professional training. For then you will forfeit the unrepeatable and more valuable opportunity to get an education first.

You have talents that will be enormously attractive to employers, talents so superior that you are free to make your living by your wits, your versatility of understanding, your imagination. Don't double-think the future.

The temptation is to figure out your career and then choose the studies that lead up to it. That is exactly the wrong way round. You are not ready to choose a career, except in the most tentative and speculative way. You are barely ready to choose a major. Select what you want to study with the belief that it will lead you to the point of deciding—well, not quite your career, but what you will do after graduation. What educates you best is not what you figure will lead somewhere, but what you now believe will give you most enjoyment. Pick your major on the pleasure principle, for what you most enjoy studying will draw your mind in the liveliest way to being educated.

If you want to study medieval history, don't fret about what you can do with it. You are not at a trade school. If you want to study marketing, do it because you find marketing the most fascinating subject we offer. If you came to Notre Dame determined to become a physician but in your freshman year you couldn't stand math and you failed chemistry and you threw up over your laboratory frog, there's a message there. It's not that you are incapable of becoming a doctor, but that the kind of disciplines that govern a doctor's work do not really appeal to your appetite. If in the meantime drama has caught your eye, then make that your choice and let the future handle itself. Or, more accurately, let it help you to become more qualified to determine the future. If throughout the course of four years you progressively follow your intellectual nose into what fascinates you most, when you emerge you will be in a much wiser position to choose the threshold of the proper career than you were at the start.

In the meantime don't feel pushed to make the decision prematurely. Our curriculum is versatile enough that the decision can be reviewed and postponed and changed. I am not arguing for indecision or instability. I am merely pleading for a sense of freedom, a certain responsible recklessness about study, that too many students feel guilty about having.

Let me put it this way. Imagine you are told now that on graduation day you will die. It will be painless and gentle; you will slowly and beautifully fade, right here on the main quad, with family and roommates gathered round, the Glee Club singing under the trees, and *Father Hesburgh* giving you a potent final blessing. Knowing of your death now—realizing that whatever your major is, it can never lead you into a career but will be only for your pleasure and fascination—would it make any difference what you choose to study in the interim? If it would, then you ought to change. Ironically, what you then choose will lead you, by steady and proper pacing, into the most reliable future.

It is essential to realize that any major can lead to any career, and that the best major is the one you choose with no lookout out of the corner of your eye to where it will lead.

Once that is cleared up, the difficulties are less difficult. Yes, most of the majors possible here are subjects you cannot have studied before. So use the first and especially the second year to explore. Use the freedom the curriculum provides. Far too many men and women graduate from here and come to this regret: If they had it to do over again, or had had the nerve earlier, they would study another subject.

As for the pressure from parents whose approval you seek, remember: If you are mature enough to undertake university studies, you have to be mature enough to choose those studies. You might choose unwisely, but it should be your choice.

Parents who virtually demand what their children will study at college are misguided and, fortunately, rare. I think parents ought to have the freedom to suggest or lobby for a choice of major, but you take away your parents' freedom if you transform their cue into a command. Parents ought to be able to promote an idea without children complaining they are being forced or browbeaten. If your parents do suggest a course of study, give it serious thought, but don't pretend you owe it to them to follow their recommendation.

And don't get up a guilt if you choose another major because you may in fact be trying to make *them* feel guilty for something they never did.

And if you feel tempted to make a curriculum choice to gain your parents' respect: don't. If you have anything to be grateful for, it is that your parents have wanted you to get the best education within your reach and theirs, precisely so that you could and would make these kinds of decisions responsibly for your own satisfaction. If they didn't want you to develop independent judgment, they would have kept you home.

How can you choose your major to sidestep most of the rush-hour traffic of competition? By ignoring competition. Only about 40 percent of your fellow Americans manage to enroll in college, and only about half of those graduate. Virtually all of you at this University will complete your degree requirements. That puts you among the top fifth of all people your age. And among that 20 percent, only the most highly qualified are competitive for admission to a university like Notre Dame, which means you have educational opportunities that rank you among the top one or two percent in the country.

It makes one feel uneasy to hear such talk of exclusiveness, but these are simple facts. So when you get uneasy because everyone in the corridor seems pretty swift of mind, calm down. You are moving among classmates who have the same advantaged education you have, who have been *sieved* through highly selective admission processes. After a while they may begin to look ordinary enough, but they aren't. And you aren't. The older one gets and the more experience one accumulates, the more clear it becomes that the number of really quick-minded people is small. You wonder how the world gets by with so few. Rather than imagining yourself as part of a large, capable crowd trying to crush through a narrow doorway of opportunity, it is more realistic to understand you are advantaged to an embarrassing degree, and there aren't nearly enough of you to go around.

To select a major program of study wisely, you need not figure out what other people want of you. You need to figure out what you want. And that's not easy. It requires much self-knowledge.

But that is both what education gives and what education requires. William Johnson Cory, a Cambridge man, expressed impatience when critics complained that English schools were offering an education that was not useful enough. Education was not supposed to be useful, he retorted.

"You are not engaged so much in acquiring knowledge as in making mental efforts under criticism," he continued. "A certain amount of knowledge you can indeed with average faculties acquire so as to retain; nor need you regret the hours that you spent on much that is forgotten, for the shadow of lost knowledge at least protects you from many illusions.

"But you go to a great school, not for knowledge so much as for arts and habits; for the habit of attention, for the art of expression, for the art of assuming at a moment's notice a new intellectual posture, for the art of entering quickly into another person's thoughts, for the habit of submitting to censure and refutation, for the art of indicating assent or dissent in graduated terms, for the habit of regarding minute points of accuracy, for the habit of working out what is possible in a given time, for taste, for discrimination, for mental courage and mental soberness.

"Above all, you go to a great school for self-knowledge."

There are crucial freedoms that others can neither keep from us nor give to us. We must take possession of them ourselves. The sense of freedom that leads one to follow his or her own sensible instincts into a major course of study, confident that if one does that, then—and only then—will one be ready to make other even more crucial decisions: that is the sense of freedom I urge upon you before it is too late, and even before it is too early. Go ahead.

And after you have made your choice, remember that your major is only a minor portion of your higher education. You are invited—prodded—to surround and enliven your mind with elective courses. Relish them. The instructors in your discipline believe that you can never study enough of it, and some of us would advise you to take every elective our discipline has to offer. That is because we hanker to have our students love what we love, and this tempts us to tempt you to forgo your education and begin training in our field. Instead, browse in the clover.

When I was an undergraduate in philosophy, we were directed to read only primary sources; only the great thinkers, not the secondary folks who wrote textbooks about them. Excellent. But in retrospect, the good times were the hundreds of hours when I got lost in the stacks of the library and read my fascinated way through an education that no one had planned, but was lavishly provided.

Your duty is to enjoy. Nothing you might do could be more useful.

Vocabulary

As you think about this essay, these definitions—and one identification—may be helpful to you:

1. **insidious**   harmful but enticing or having a gradual but cumulative effect
2. **dons**   the British educational system's equivalent for college teachers
3. **disconcerting**   unsettling or emotionally disturbing
4. **Father Hesburgh**   for more than twenty years, the legendary president of the University of Notre Dame
5. **sieved**   filtered

Discussion Questions

1. What are the three difficulties that cause undergraduates to make wrong initial decisions about a major?
2. For Burtchaell, what distinguishes training from education? Give some examples of your own for training.
3. According to Burtchaell, what should a "good university" provide its students?

4. Based on your experience and that of your friends, is Burtchaell correct in saying that new students have insufficient information to select a major?

5. Burtchaell's final two sentences may have surprised you. Did you expect a serious teacher to draw this conclusion? How does he justify it?

 ## Suggestions for Your Journal

Write about how you chose your academic major. If you have not decided on a major yet, discuss why you have not done so.

What is your reaction to Burtchaell's ideas about not putting pressure on students to make a choice too soon in their first year? Do you agree that choosing a major is not necessarily choosing a career? Why?

Do you agree or disagree with Burtchaell that choosing a major should be done on the "pleasure principle"? Why?

College Major Doesn't Mean All That Much

William Raspberry

William Raspberry is a widely syndicated columnist who works with the *Washington Post* Writers Group. In this brief essay, which was first published as one of his regular columns, he stepped away from his usual commentary on the Washington scene and grew more personal as he counseled his daughter about approaching the question of what college major to select.

Soon to every fledgling student
Comes the moment to decide.
But since Angela's a freshman,
My advice is: let it ride.

With apologies to James Russell Lowell, that is pretty much my counsel to my daughter, who is about to begin her first year in college. Soon enough, she'll have to face the sophomore necessity of choosing a major—whether or not she's decided on a career. In the meantime, I tell her, don't worry about it.

A part of the reason for my advice is the memory of my own struggle to decide on a major. I eventually had four of them, none of which related to what was to become my career. But the more important reason is my conclusion, regularly reinforced, that majors just don't matter that much. The latest reinforcement is from John Willson, a history professor at Michigan's Hillsdale College, who having heard once too often the question, "But what do I do with a history major?" has decided to do what he can to put his students at ease.

"Every sophomore has a majoring frenzy," he wrote in a campus publication. "It is typical for sophomores to say, 'I want to be an anchorman. Therefore, I will major in journalism. Where do I sign up?' They act like they have had a blow to the *solar plexus* when I say, (a) Hillsdale has no major in journalism, and (b) if we did, it would no more make you an anchorman than a major in English makes you an Englishman."

But rather than simply repeating what professionals already know, or urging colleges to dispense with the requirement for declaring a major, Willson has reduced his advice to a set of rules and principles.

The first, which college students often find incredible, is that aside from such vocational courses as engineering or computer science, any relationship between majors and careers is largely incidental. Physics majors are hardly more likely to become physicists than business majors to become *entrepreneurs*.

The rule that derives from this principle: If you wanted your major to be practical, you should have gone to the General Motors Institute.

The second principle is that students (and colleges) should delay the necessity of choosing for as long as practicable. "Most students (and even more parents) have rather vague notions of what the subject of any given subject is. . . . Talk with your parents, but don't let parents, teachers, media experts, television evangelists or fraternity brothers pressure you into a majoring frenzy before you know what the major is all about." In short: All things being equal, it is best to know what you are talking about, which may even prevent majoring frenzies.

The third is a quote from the Rev. James T. Burtchaell (writing in *Notre Dame* magazine): "Pick your major on the pleasure principle, for what you most enjoy studying will draw your mind in the liveliest way to being educated." It's good advice, and not only for students at small liberal arts colleges. A few years ago, the University of Virginia published a booklet, "Life after Liberal Arts," based on a survey of 2,000 alumni of its college of arts and sciences. The finding: 91 percent of the respondents not only believe that liberal arts prepared them for fulfilling careers but would also not hesitate to recommend liberal arts majors to students considering those same careers. The "winning combination" derived from the Virginia survey: a liberal arts foundation, *complemented* with career-related experience and personal initiative.

Colleges aren't assembly lines that, after four years, automatically deposit students into *lucrative* careers. What is far likelier is a series of false starts followed by the discovery of a satisfying career. In the Virginia survey, for example, only 16 percent reported being happy with their first jobs.

Willson's advice, the results of the Virginia survey, and my advice to Angela come down to the same thing: Major in getting an education.

 ## Vocabulary

As you think about this essay, these definitions may be helpful to you:

1. **fledgling** a bird at about the age it learns to fly; here, metaphorically, someone getting ready to start independent living

2. **solar plexus** a *plexus* is a gathering or network of nerves, and the solar plexus is located in the abdomen; a blow to the solar plexus will cause the victim to double over in pain

3. **entrepreneurs** people who start and maintain businesses, taking the risk for the sake of possible profit

4. **complemented** not *complimented* or *flattered* but completed and perfected by something else

5. **lucrative** profitable

 ## Discussion Questions

1. What reasons does William Raspberry give for his assertion that your choice of a major is not as important as many college students think?

2. How do you react to Raspberry's thesis that any relationship between majors and careers is "largely incidental?" Why is this perceived connection made by so many students?

 Suggestions for Your Journal

Raspberry and Burtchaell clearly agree on some important points about selecting a college major. What argument does Raspberry add to the discussion that Burtchaell does not mention? Which author do you find more persuasive? Why?

Fourteen Ways of Looking at Electives

Thomas L. Minnick

Thomas L. Minnick is Special Assistant to the Vice Provost of Minority Affairs and former associate dean of University College at The Ohio State University, where he completed his bachelor's, master's, and doctoral degrees in English. He is a specialist in the English Bible and the writings of William Blake. In this essay, he encourages you to think before you schedule your electives so that they can complement your required course work by helping you to achieve some of your goals for college study.

Electives are what is left over for you to take once you deduct all your required courses.

Typically, a college degree is made up primarily of several kinds of requirements. These may include courses required of all students, no matter what degree they may have decided to seek; such university-wide requirements are often called "core" or "general education" requirements. They are likely to include some basic mathematics, one or more courses in college-level English composition, and several courses distributed among the social sciences, sciences, and humanities. Does everyone at your institution need to take some history? Then history is probably a general education or "core" requirement for your institution, whether you are working toward a bachelor's degree at a university with an extensive graduate program or toward an associate's degree at a community college.

Additionally, you are likely to have to complete some courses that everyone in your degree program needs to take. For example, students working toward a degree in engineering, no matter what area of specialization, all typically need to have at least a year of college physics, mathematics through differential equations, some basic course work in engineering graphics, mechanics, and chemistry. Similarly, business students are all required to study economics (both "micro" and "macro"), accounting, statistics, marketing, finance, and the like. Requirements shared by everyone aiming toward a specific degree are usually called "program requirements" or "degree requirements."

A third kind of required course work is that which you complete for your major. Major requirements might include an introductory survey course (or a series of them), usually taken by first- or second-year students while they learn the dimensions and variety of the major field. English majors are likely to be required to take a survey of American literature and another of British literature, for example. In some colleges they may be required to have a course in research methods for English majors. And some majors require that everyone in the program complete a senior year "capstone" course that puts—or attempts to put—all their previous major work into a *coherent* perspective.

Once you add up all these kinds of requirements (general education, college, and major), you are likely to find that there are still some classes you need to take to complete your degree. At the university where I work, which follows the quarter system and sets 196 quarter credit hours as the minimum for an undergraduate degree, the university-wide general education core and the college/program requirements usually total about 100 credits. Major programs vary dramatically but average about 45 credit hours. Deduct 145 from 196 and you get 41 credit hours (or eight to ten classes) that are not specified. For these, which are "electives," our students can take just about anything they like. This essay is about some ways you can use these extra classes to your advantage.

1. To explore possible majors. Many students enter college without knowing what they want to study for a major. An undecided student can use elective hours to explore several possible major programs, usually by taking the appropriate introductory survey classes. Do you think you might like Forestry? Sign up for a basic introduction to the field and find out through that class whether you really have an interest and/or an aptitude for it.

2. To serve as a cushion. This use of electives is closely related to (1) above. Suppose you started college as an engineering major and then discovered that you lack the commitment or the focus to be an engineer, so you change programs to business. You will probably have taken some classes in your first term (engineering graphics, for example) that are not required in your new major. Electives allow you to move from one major to another without losing useful credits: in this example, the engineering graphics class will still count toward graduation, and it served the purpose of helping you make a sound decision on a new major. Electives give you flexibility—within reasoned limits—to change from one program to another without losing credits or unduly prolonging your degree work.

3. To develop a focus or cluster outside your major. Perhaps you don't really want to be limited to a single concentration. If your college does not provide for dual majors or minors, or if you don't want to complete *all* the work for a second major but would like an additional focus to your degree, electives can provide the way. Imagine that you have decided to major in Elementary Education but you also have an interest in the History of Art. Using your electives, you can build your own concentration in art history by taking the courses in that area that attract you. In this way you may be able to select your art history classes more freely than a formal major might allow—limiting yourself to national schools (American painting) or individual styles (contemporary art) that you really like, while official majors may need to follow a strictly prescribed *regimen* of courses.

4. To explore your career options. Nationally, one of the most frequently selected electives is the career exploration course. Such courses usually fall into one of two categories—fairly general in approach and scope, or quite specific. A general approach can help you assess your personal characteristics, such as your interests, abilities, values, and goals. It can also help you explore educational and occupational fields that might match your personal interests and strengths. Some courses include information about techniques for writing your resume and for presenting yourself effectively in job interviews. These general career courses can teach you career decision-making strategies that will be useful throughout your life. The other, more specific type of career course is often limited to specific career opportunities in the area (or areas) related to the department teaching the class: "Careers in Agriculture" would be such a course that focuses on, and discusses in very specific detail, the career options available to people with a specific kind of education. Such a course typically provides very helpful information about specific employers who look for and hire graduates with a particular educational and career background. Career information courses—whether general or specific—can help you enhance your understanding of who you are in relation to your academic major and related career opportunities and, in so doing, prepare you for the work world.

5. To enhance your marketability. A popular use many students make of their electives is to build a business focus—even if they are not pursuing a business degree. Suppose you are an English major who likes and knows something about computers. By adding several advanced computer science courses to your English major, you become more competitive for job offers that want a liberally educated student with added skills. Your focus might take the form of several courses from a single department (a number of marketing classes, for example), or several related classes from a variety of departments (a marketing class, a course in beginning accounting, a class in business management, a course in personnel issues). A business major might like to take classes in the language and culture of a specific part of the world in order to be better prepared to do business with that part of the globe.

6. To develop a talent you have neglected. Are you good at singing or playing a musical instrument? Perhaps you don't want to major in that area, but it would be a shame to give up that *expertise* or let it *languish* while you complete your undergraduate studies. Take a class in singing, or join one of your college's choral or instrumental groups. Register for drawing or painting, or making pottery, or creating art on the computer. Sign up for a basic photography class. Electives can allow you to pursue and develop interests and talents that you do not plan to turn into a major, but that you should not neglect. Because the credit you earn with electives counts toward your graduation, you do not need to feel that courses you take just because you want to are wasted.

7. To get, or stay, fit. I am often surprised by the number of college students I talk with who participated strenuously in high school sports. Both men and women find physical exercise and competition to be challenging and exciting. Yet often, when such students get to college, they neglect their interests in being fit, largely, I think, because they equate college courses with "serious" work and sports with play. However, getting fit and staying fit are lifelong activities that help you to work and think better. They also promote a healthful lifestyle because people who have worked to keep fit as a rule avoid destructive activities like drinking alcohol to excess and smoking. If your college has a good physical education facility and offers you courses in activities you have never tried, take a few elective credits to learn and practice some of these activities—martial arts, for example, or caving, or whitewater rafting, or working out on the high ropes. And all these physical activities can be great for helping to cope with the stress of college work.

8. To develop skills in leisure time activities. Once you begin your career, your work will take up much of your life, but it will always be important for you to make time for enriching activities—especially when you are away from the stimulus of a learning environment. Develop the habit of reserving time for thoughtful entertainment. Electives may provide just the opportunity you need to learn more about theater, fine art, music, and similar interests. Do you like jazz? Check your school's course catalogue to see if there are classes in American music, or nonwestern music, that might help you to better understand the origins and history of jazz. Do you like attending plays? Take an introductory theater course, or take an acting class and try out your talents in a learning setting, or sign up to help build scenery and earn college credit while learning more about the technical details of putting on a performance.

9. To learn to help others. Most universities provide courses, often for modest amounts of credit, in such helpful skills as first aid and cardiopulmonary resuscitation (commonly abbreviated to "CPR"). These skills can help you in getting summer work. More important, knowing how to help others in an emergency can actually save a life—maybe even your own. Less dramatic but also very helpful are opportunities to provide tutoring and similar assistance to others at your university or in your neighborhood. Interested? Ask your adviser if there is a program where you can tutor underprivileged kids or read a textbook for a blind student or help in adaptive physical education for disabled students. These experiences can teach you a great deal about yourself and may provide some of the greatest personal rewards of your college experience.

10. To learn life-skills that will be useful later. For example, many business schools provide a "service course" (so named because they teach it as a service to students from outside their own college) about basic financial matters, like establishing credit, managing your income, buying a home, planning for financial independence, selecting basic insurance, and the like. Courses in family financial planning for nonbusiness majors are likely to accentuate the practical and introduce theory only when absolutely necessary. Many other departments offer the chance to learn material that will have lifelong practical value. Basic courses in public speaking and communicating effectively in small groups apply to almost every later career; go to the Communications Department to find them. Most sociology departments offer a class in the varieties of modern marriage, or the sociology of the family—with obvious utility for later experience.

11. To learn to understand and appreciate different cultures. Studying other cultures can help you prepare for working with people from those cultures in your life after college. Many American cities in the south and west—Dallas, Los Angeles, Miami—already have no dominant majority group, only larger or smaller minorities. Even if you plan to live in a largely *homogeneous* small town, chances are you will be doing business with, or your children will need to do business with, the larger multicultural world. If you find that a little frightening, take a class about other cultures and you may find it exciting instead. Check with the appropriate language departments, and you are likely to find some classes taught in English that will help you understand the patterns and values of cultures different from your own.

12. To learn study and time management skills. Most two- and four-year colleges now provide organized help for students who need better study habits. This need is not restricted to students who did less than well in high school. Often, good students could earn better than average grades in high school with only modest investments of study time—and have consequently developed weak study habits that need to improve in the face of more difficult, more rapid college instruction. Would you like to read with greater comprehension? Could you manage your time better than you do? Check with your adviser for information about classes that teach effective study skills, time management, and related learning skills. Even if these are offered *without* credit, and so are not technically "elective hours," consider them carefully, since they can greatly improve the quality of your work as a student.

13. To develop leadership skills. Usually students turn to their extracurricular experiences (student government, interest clubs, other campus associations) for training in leadership. But there is a significant body of writings about various leadership qualities and styles, and your institution is likely to offer at least one credit-bearing class in leadership. Such courses are often taught as "laboratory courses"—that is, you get practical training in a hands-on way. If you are aiming toward a professional career in a management position, you ought to get some experience in leadership, and such a course may be your best route toward it.

14. To take some courses just because you will enjoy them. In the best of all possible worlds, every class you take would be one that you love to attend, and I hope that many of your required courses—in general education, in classes that relate to your degree program, and certainly in your major—fit this description. But in the real world we are bound to spend our time in, you may find yourself required to take some classes you enroll in only because they are required. If you anticipate that such a course is coming up next term, you may successfully balance it with an elective class that you take just because you want to take it: perhaps you've already had the instructor, and you really enjoyed his or her previous course, or perhaps you've always had a hobby of reading about a specific area, so taking a course in it as an elective would help round out your knowledge of that field.

How can you select classes for Use Number 14? I encourage my advisees to imagine that they have just won the state lottery (tonight at $35 million!) and have spent a chunk of it having fun—traveling the world, buying your parents a mansion and each of your friends an expensive car. Eventually, you tire of doing nothing, however nicely you can now afford to do it, and you realize the permanent attraction of learning. In such a case, what courses would you take? Assuming you do not financially *need* a degree, you could just take the classes you want. If you were free in this way, what classes would you sign up for? Make a list of them, then sign up for them as electives!

Vocabulary

As you think about this essay, these definitions may be helpful to you:

1. **coherent**   consistent
2. **regimen**   a systematic plan
3. **expertise**   the skill of an expert
4. **languish**   to be or become weak or enervated
5. **homogeneous**   of the same or similar kind or nature

 Discussion Questions

1. How are electives defined in this reading? How do they fit into the general structure of degree requirements?

2. What kind of electives can enhance your chances of finding a satisfying career?

3. Through what kind of electives can you acquire skills and knowledge that may be useful for your future leisure time activities?

4. Although taking extra courses in your major is not listed as a way to use elective hours, would this use of courses be a way to increase your mastery of the subject? Why or why not is this a good idea?

5. How can you expand your understanding and appreciation of other cultures through electives? Why is this a particularly good use of electives today?

 Suggestions for Your Journal

What has been your impression of the function of electives in the curriculum? Which of the 14 reasons for selecting electives appeal to you the most? Why? Look at the list of courses in your college's catalogue. If you could select any courses to take just for fun (and not worry about a grade), which would you choose? Why? What does this tell you about your choice of major?

It's Okay to be Undeclared

Julie Collier, M.S. and Al Levin, Ed.D.

Today's college graduates face a totally different world than previous generations. Technology and globalization, including digitization and the outsourcing of routine tasks, have created a new economic landscape and changed the way organizations do business. The "information highway" has fostered a new interconnectedness between markets and nations. Sophisticated software, video conferencing and faster travel have facilitated business transactions and partnerships unthinkable even fifteen years ago. According to Stephen Banick, author of *The Student Guide to the Coolest New Jobs and Hottest New Industries*, a graduate starting work today could have an employer in Japan, a boss in Germany, and meet virtually with teammates in cities across the globe.

These changes call for a new approach to career planning. Students have more occupational options than ever before and need more time to sort out the numerous possibilities. We used to believe that it was best to make up your mind as quickly as possible, even before you had really considered very many options. Now is actually a great time to review the advantages of being undeclared during your first two years of college. Perhaps being undeclared could be redefined as the best choice in a world where what you learn today could quickly become out-of-date.

There's more than one "right" career for you.

In actuality, everyone should consider several careers. With the significant changes in the economy today, the possibility exists that you may change careers several times during your lifetime. Sticking to one career for life may have been feasible for your grandparents or your parents; however, it is no longer feasible in this new career climate. Advances in technology and the marketplace mean new occupations are created and existing occupations disappear often faster than anyone can predict.

A wiser choice is to build flexibility into your career planning. The recent career planning book *Luck is No Accident* (written by Sacramento State Professor Al Levin and Stanford Professor John Krumboltz) warns individuals about the dangers of foreclosing too early on a career decision. In the process of narrowing down your options, you may miss a golden opportunity. The authors suggest instead of saying to yourself, "I am going to become a doctor," try saying, "I want to explore a career in medicine. I'll give it my best shot. If I get any better ideas along the way, I'll stay flexible." *A college major does not seal your fate.* Consider it the first decision of many in a series of decisions you will make about your career and life.

Successful people remain open-minded and adaptable throughout their careers.

In reality, only a small percentage of people end up in a career they've planned from a young age. The book *Road Trip Nation* profiles many successful people, the majority of whom tried a variety of occupations before landing on their present career. You can access hundreds of the *Road Trip Nation* interviews on DVD at the Sac State Career Center. You can also visit the RTN web site: www.roadtripnation.com.

Making an informed decision-in and out of the classroom

Many college counselors and faculty encourage students to explore majors and careers during the first two years of college. This is a great time to take classes you are interested in and learn about occupational fields. Talking with professors, participating in student clubs, volunteering, or participating in an internship are all ways of learning more about yourself and your interests. External pressure from peers, parents and the media to make a quick decision sometimes causes students stress. However, if you are taking action and trying out different experiences you will have the perfect answer when family members or friends ask, "What are you majoring in?" Take this opportunity to tell them about the activities you are engaging in to explore different majors and careers rather than naming one limited occupational area you might not know much about.

The story of Alicia, a second semester sophomore, illustrates how getting involved can prove invaluable in the career decision-making process. Upon entering college, Alicia took as many science classes as possible in preparation for medical school. Outside of classes, she was a member of the speech and debate team and a women's service fraternity. She also had a part time job working with children at an after-school program where she tutored math and taught nutrition. Nearing her junior year, Alicia realized that even though she did well in her biology courses, her real passion was in public speaking and helping children learn about their health. With the help of a career counselor, she switched her major to communications with a specialization in public relations and is hoping to become the director of a children's health organization.

Remember, it's okay to try something and decide you want to change direction. Some 65% of college students in the U.S. change their major at least once. Sometimes the only way to find out about a subject is to jump in and try it out. It might take two semesters of chemistry to realize whether it's a good fit for you or not. But how would you have known if you hadn't tried it out first?

You can do most anything with a liberal arts degree.

People with liberal arts degrees such as English, Music, and History are employed in all kinds of different fields including law, medicine, business, and technology. Many employers appreciate the problem-solving skills, communication skills, and versatility liberal arts graduates bring to the workplace. Changes in the economy such as downsizing have resulted in a need for workers with a well-rounded skill set. So-called "soft-skills," such as the ability to communicate or work with a team, are more important than ever in a workplace that is increasingly global and diverse.

Learning how to learn—one of the key skills of the 21st century.

In his book, *The World is Flat*, Thomas Friedman discusses the importance of *"learning how to learn."* In a "flat" world, he says, the ability to absorb new information and to become skilled in the process of learning "is an ability every worker should cultivate in an age when parts or all of many jobs are constantly going to be exposed to digitization, automation, and outsourcing, and where new jobs, and whole new industries, will be churned up faster and faster. In such a world, it is not only what you know but how you learn that will set you apart because what you know today will be out-of-date sooner than you think."

Take action now and get involved

It's very difficult to make a good decision about your academic major by sitting alone on the couch trying to figure everything out in your head. Instead, we're recommending that you take action now and get involved. So it's okay to be undeclared as long as you participate in such activities as taking different classes, volunteering, joining a student club, studying abroad, or obtaining a summer internship. You can obviously learn a great deal about your interests in the classroom, but remember that the classroom isn't the only place to learn. Engaging in various activities in and out of the classroom is a proven method for making the best possible decisions about your major and your career.

CHAPTER 8

HOW IS YOUR COLLEGE EDUCATION RELATED TO WORK AND CAREER?

Jennifer Santos,
Alumna 2007
Communication
Studies Major

Dear Future Fellow Alumni,

I am proud to say that I am an Alumna of Sacramento State University. Without my college experience I would not be the woman I am today, and I am forever grateful for my experience at the University. To put it simply, I learned a lot. I learned about the world, society, politics, and most importantly I learned about myself. My journey through college was not a straight paved road; instead it was full of curves, speed bumps, rest stops, and dead ends. However, it was a really fun road trip! On this journey I learned lessons that helped shape me into the student and woman I am today. Here are a few that had the greatest effect on me:

1. The power of discovery.

There is so much to discover in college. Everything from a new sport, new friends, new talents and new cultures to answering the big question we all ask ourselves. Who am I? My journey has brought me both closer and farther from the answer. Ultimately I learned not to be afraid to try new things since they lead to discovering things about myself and the world around me.

2. Not everyone is from your backyard.

When I first came to college, I knew that I would meet new people. But I completely under-estimated the meaning of "new". I am from a small town, and the majority of its residents share the same cultural background and economic standing. I never truly understood how big the world really was until I moved away. At Sacramento State I met people who had different religious practices, different economic standings, different sexual orientations, different ages, different hobbies, and spoke different languages. College showed me how diverse the world is, and I began to realize that most people didn't go to a private school, live in a rural town, attend a small high school, go to the same churches, shop at the same stores, or like the same movies that I did. For the first time I was intrigued by culture and I embraced it.

3. No one else is responsible for you, but you.

Throughout my journey I made some mistakes. I took the wrong classes, got a few bad grades, scored low on a few tests, and missed a few deadlines. At first I tried to find some way to avoid the consequences of those mistakes, and I made every excuse possible. But what I came to learn is that there is no way around consequences. I encourage you to examine your level of responsibility for your education. Learning how to be fully aware of your responsibilities will result in a successful college experience.

These were just a few of the many lessons that I learned. By embracing discovery and trying new things, I learned that I had an interest in event planning and enrolled in an internship, which directly led to a job after college. By embracing the diversity around me, I became a more cultivated and well-rounded person which aids me personally and professionally. By learning how to take responsibility for myself, I was a successful student which led to the final goal, graduation.

I encourage you to take this time and cherish it, learn from your mistakes, and learn your own lessons. Like mine, I hope your journey is full of curves and speed bumps; it serves for a much more interesting ride!

Sincerely,
Jennifer Santos
Class of 2007

The College Dropout Boom

David Leonhardt

Journalist David Leonhardt has reported elsewhere that "At the most selective private universities across the country, more fathers of freshmen are doctors than are hourly workers, teachers, clergy members, farmers or members of the military-combined." In this essay he explores the many challenges students from working-class and lower-income families encounter not just in getting into college but in staying there through graduation. As Leonhardt shows us in this essay, while colleges have made great strides in recruiting and admitting students from diverse racial and ethnic backgrounds, they are only beginning to acknowledge and address the issues involved in recruiting and retaining students from diverse economic backgrounds.

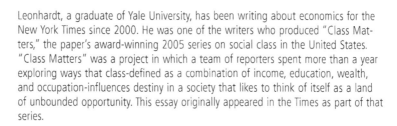

Leonhardt, a graduate of Yale University, has been writing about economics for the New York Times since 2000. He was one of the writers who produced "Class Matters," the paper's award-winning 2005 series on social class in the United States. "Class Matters" was a project in which a team of reporters spent more than a year exploring ways that class-defined as a combination of income, education, wealth, and occupation-influences destiny in a society that likes to think of itself as a land of unbounded opportunity. This essay originally appeared in the Times as part of that series.

1   One of the biggest decisions Andy Blevins has ever made, and one of the few he now regrets, never seemed like much of a decision at all. It just felt like the natural thing to do.

2   In the summer of 1995, he was moving boxes of soup cans, paper towels, and dog food across the floor of a supermarket warehouse, one of the biggest buildings in the area of southwest Virginia surrounding the town of Chilhowie. The heat was brutal. The job had sounded impossible when he arrived fresh off his first year of college, looking to make some summer money, still a skinny teenager with sandy blond hair and a narrow, freckled face.

3   But hard work done well was something he understood, even if he was the first college boy in his family. Soon he was making bonuses on top of his $6.75 an hour, more money than either of his parents made. His girlfriend was around, and so were his hometown buddies. Andy acted more outgoing with them, more relaxed. People in Chilhowie noticed that.

4   It was just about the perfect summer. So the thought crossed his mind: maybe it did not have to end. Maybe he would take a break from college and keep working. He had been getting Cs and Ds, and college never felt like home, anyway.

5   "I enjoyed working hard, getting the job done, getting a paycheck," Blevins recalled. "I just knew I didn't want to quit."

6   So he quit college instead, and with that, Andy Blevins joined one of the largest and fastest-growing groups of young adults in America. He became a college dropout, though non-graduate may be the more precise term.

7   Many people like him plan to return to get their degrees, even if few actually do. Almost one in three Americans in their mid-twenties now fall into this group, up from one in five in the late 1960s, when the Census Bureau began keeping such data. Most come from poor and working-class families.

8   The phenomenon has been largely overlooked in the glare of positive news about the country's gains in education. Going to college has become the norm throughout most of the United States, even in many places where college was once considered an exotic destination-places like Chilhowie, an Appalachian hamlet with a simple brick downtown. At elite universities, classrooms are filled with women, blacks, Jews, and Latinos, groups largely excluded two generations ago. The American system of higher learning seems to have become a great equalizer.

9   In fact, though, colleges have come to reinforce many of the advantages of birth. On campuses that enroll poorer students, graduation rates are often low. And at institutions where nearly everyone graduates—small colleges like Colgate, major state institutions like the University of Colorado, and elite private universities like Stanford—more students today come from the top of the nation's income ladder than they did two decades ago.

10   Only 41 percent of low-income students entering a four-year college managed to graduate within five years, the U.S. Department of Education found in a 2004 study, but 66 percent of high-income students did. That gap had grown over recent years.

11   "We need to recognize that the most serious domestic problem in the United States today is the widening gap between the children of the rich and the children of the poor," Lawrence H. Summers, the president of Harvard, said when announcing in 2004 that Harvard would give full scholarships to all its lowest-income students. "And education is the most powerful weapon we have to address that problem."

12   There is certainly much to celebrate about higher education today. Many more students from all classes are getting four-year degrees and reaping their benefits. But those broad gains mask the fact that poor and working-class students have nevertheless been falling behind; for them, not having a degree remains the norm.

13   That loss of ground is all the more significant because a college education matters much more now than it once did. A bachelor's degree, not a year or two of courses, tends to determine a person's place in today's globalized, computerized economy. College graduates have received steady pay increases over the past two decades, while the pay of everyone else has risen little more than the rate of inflation.

14   As a result, despite one of the great education explosions in modem history, economic mobility-moving from one income group to another over the course of a lifetime-has stopped rising, researchers say. Some recent studies suggest that it has declined over the last generation.

15   Put another way, children seem to he following the paths of their parents more than they once did. Grades and test scores, rather than privilege,

determine success today, but that success is largely being passed down from one generation to the next. A nation that believes that everyone should have a fair shake finds itself with a kind of inherited meritocracy.

16   In this system, the students at the best colleges may be diverse—male and female and of various colors, religions, and hometowns—but they tend to share an upper-middle-class upbringing. An old joke that Harvard's idea of diversity is putting a rich kid from California in the same room as a rich kid from New York is truer today than ever; Harvard has more students from California than it did in years past and just as big a share of upper-income students.

17   Students like these remain in college because they can hardly imagine doing otherwise. Their parents, understanding the importance of a bachelor's degree, spent hours reading to them, researching school districts, and making it clear to them that they simply must graduate from college.

18   Andy Blevins says that he too knows the importance of a degree, but that he did not while growing up, and not even in his year at Radford University, sixty-six miles up the interstate from Chilhowie. Ten years after trading college for the warehouse, Blevins, who is twenty-nine, spends his days at the same supermarket company. He has worked his way up to produce buyer, earning $35,000 a year with health benefits and a 401(k) plan. He is on a path typical for someone who attended college without getting a four-year degree. Men in their early forties in this category made an average of $42,000 in 2000. Those with a four-year degree made $65,000.

19   Still boyish-looking but no longer rail thin, Blevins says he has many reasons to be happy. He lives with his wife, Karla, and their son, Lucas, in a small blue-and-yellow house at the end of a cul-de-sac in the middle of a stunningly picturesque Appalachian valley. He plays golf with some of the same friends who made him want to stay around Chilhowie.

20   But he does think about what might have been, about what he could be doing if he had the degree. As it is, he always feels as if he is on thin ice. Were he to lose his job, he says, everything could slip away with it. What kind of job could a guy without a college degree get? One night, while talking to his wife about his life, he used the word "trapped."

21   "Looking back, I wish I had gotten that degree," Blevins said in his soft-spoken lilt. "Four years seemed like a thousand years then. But I wish I would have just put in my four years."

The Barriers

22   Why so many low-income students fall from the college ranks is a question without a simple answer. Many high schools do a poor job of preparing teenagers for college. Many of the colleges where lower-income students tend to enroll have limited resources and offer a narrow range of majors, leaving some students disenchanted and unwilling to continue.

23   Then there is the cost. Tuition bills scare some students from even applying and leave others with years of debt. To Blevins, like many other students of limited means, every week of going to classes seemed like another week of losing money—money that might have been made at a job.

24   "The system makes a false promise to students," said John T. Casteen III, the president of the University of Virginia, himself the son of a Virginia shipyard worker.

25   Colleges, Casteen said, present themselves as meritocracies in which academic ability and hard work are always rewarded. In fact, he said, many working class students face obstacles they cannot overcome on their own.

26   For much of his fifteen years as Virginia's president, Casteen has focused on raising money and expanding the university, the most prestigious in the state. In the meantime, students with backgrounds like his have become ever scarcer on campus. The university's genteel nickname, the Cavaliers, and its aristocratic sword-crossed coat of arms seem appropriate today. No flagship state university has a smaller proportion of low-income students than Virginia. Just 8 percent of undergraduates in 2004 came from families in the bottom half of the income distribution, down from 11 percent a decade earlier.

27   That change sneaked up on him, Casteen said, and he had spent a good part of the previous year trying to prevent it from becoming part of his legacy. Starting with the fall 2005 freshman class, the university will charge no tuition and require no loans for students whose parents make less than twice the poverty level, or about $37,700 a year for a family of four. The university has also increased financial aid to middle-income students.

28   To Casteen, these are steps to remove what he describes as "artificial barriers" to a college education placed in the way of otherwise deserving students. Doing so "is a fundamental obligation of a free culture," he said.

29   But the deterrents to a degree can also be homegrown. Many low-income teenagers know few people who have made it through college. A majority of the non-graduates are young men, and some come from towns where the factory work ethic, to get working as soon as possible, remains strong, even if the factories themselves are vanishing. Whatever the reasons, college just does not feel normal.

30   "You get there and you start to struggle," said Leanna Blevins, Andy's older sister, who did get a bachelor's degree and then went on to earn a Ph.D. at Virginia studying the college experiences of poor students. "And at home your parents are trying to be supportive and say, 'Well, if you're not happy, if it's not right for you, come back home. It's okay.' And they think they're doing the right thing. But they don't know that maybe what the student needs is to hear them say, 'Stick it out just one semester. You can do it. Just stay there. Come home on the weekend, but stick it out."

31   Today, Leanna, petite and high-energy, is helping to start a new college a few hours' drive from Chilhowie for low-income students. Her brother said he had daydreamed about attending it and had talked to her about how he might return to college.

32   For her part, Leanna says, she has daydreamed about having a life that would seem as natural as her brother's, a life in which she would not feel like an outsider in her hometown. Once, when a high school teacher asked students to list their goals for the next decade, she wrote, "having a college degree" and "not being married."

33   "I think my family probably thinks I'm liberal," Leanna, who is now married, said with a laugh, "that I've just been educated too much and I'm gettin' above my raisin'."

34   Her brother said that he just wanted more control over his life, not a new one. At a time when many people complain of scattered lives, Andy Blevins can stand in one spot—his church parking lot, next to a graveyard—and take in much of his world. "That's my parents' house," he said one day, pointing to a sliver of roof visible over a hill. "That's my uncle's trailer. My grandfather is buried here. I'll probably be buried here."

Taking Class into Account

35   Opening up colleges to new kinds of students has generally meant one thing over the last generation: affirmative action. Intended to right the wrongs of years of exclusion, the programs have swelled the number of women, blacks, and Latinos on campuses. But affirmative action was never supposed to address broad economic inequities, just the ones that stem from specific kinds of discrimination.

36   That is now beginning to change. Like Virginia, a handful of other colleges are not only increasing financial aid but also promising to give weight to economic class in granting admissions. They say they want to make an effort to admit more low-income students, just as they now do for minorities and children of alumni.

37   "The great colleges and universities were designed to provide for mobility, to seek out talent," said Anthony W. Marx, President of Amherst College. "If we are blind to the educational disadvantages associated with need, we will simply replicate these disadvantages while appearing to make decisions based on merit."

38   With several populous states having already banned race-based preferences and the United States Supreme Court suggesting that it may outlaw such programs in a couple of decades, the future of affirmative action may well revolve around economics. Polls consistently show that programs based on class backgrounds have wider support than those based on race.

39   The explosion in the number of non-graduates has also begun to get the attention of policy makers. In 2005, New York became one of a small group of states to tie college financing more closely to graduation rates, rewarding colleges more for moving students along than for simply admitting them. Nowhere is the stratification of education more vivid than in Virginia, where Thomas Jefferson once tried, and failed, to set up the nation's first public high schools. At a modest high school in the Tidewater city of Portsmouth, not far from John Casteen's boyhood home, a guidance-office wall filled with college pennants does not include one from rarefied Virginia. The colleges whose pennants are up—Old Dominion University and others that seem in the realm of the possible—have far lower graduation rates.

40   Across the country, the upper middle class so dominates elite universities that high-income students, on average, actually get slightly more financial aid from colleges than low-income students do. These elite colleges are so

expensive that even many high-income students receive large grants. In the early 1990s, by contrast, poorer students got 50 percent more aid on average than the wealthier ones, according to the College Board, the organization that runs the SAT entrance exams.

41   At the other end of the spectrum are community colleges, the two-year institutions that are intended to be feeders for four-year colleges. In nearly every one are tales of academic success against tremendous odds: a battered wife or a combat veteran or a laid off worker on the way to a better life. But overall, community colleges tend to be places where dreams are put on hold.

42   Most people who enroll say they plan to get a four-year degree eventually; few actually do. Full-time jobs, commutes, and children or parents who need care often get in the way. One recent national survey found that about 75 percent of students enrolling in community colleges said they hoped to transfer to a four-year institution. But only 17 percent of those who had entered in the mid-1990s made the switch within five years, according to a separate study. The rest were out working or still studying toward the two year degree.

43   "We here in Virginia do a good job of getting them in," said Glenn Dubois, Chancellor of the Virginia Community College System and himself a community college graduate. "We have to get better in getting them out."

"I Wear a Tie Every Day"

44 College degree or not, Andy Blevins has the kind of life that many Americans say they aspire to. He fills it with family, friends, church, and a five-handicap golf game. He does not sit in traffic commuting to an office park. He does not talk wistfully of a relocated brother or best friend he sees only twice a year. He does not worry about who will care for his son while he works and his wife attends community college to become a physical therapist. His grandparents down the street watch Lucas, just as they took care of Andy and his two sisters when they were children. When he comes home from work, it is his turn to play with Lucas, tossing him into the air and rolling around on the floor with him and a stuffed elephant.

45   Blevins also sings in a quartet called the Gospel Gentlemen. One member is his brother-in-law; another lives on his street. In the long white van the group owns, they wind their way along mountain roads on their way to singing dates at local church functions, sometimes harmonizing, sometimes ribbing one another or talking about where to buy golf equipment.

46   Inside the churches, the other singers often talk to the audience between songs, about God or a grandmother or what a song means to them. Blevins rarely does, but his shyness fades once he is back in the van with his friends.

47   At the warehouse, he is usually the first to arrive, around 6:30 in the morning. The grandson of a coal miner, he takes pride, he says, in having moved up to become a supermarket buyer. He decides which bananas, grapes, onions, and potatoes the company will sell and makes sure that there is always enough. Most people with his job have graduated from college.

48   "I'm pretty fortunate to not have a degree but have a job where I wear a tie every day," he said.

49   He worries about how long it will last, though, mindful of what happened to his father, Dwight, a decade ago. A high school graduate, Dwight Blevins was laid off from his own warehouse job and ended up with another one that paid less and offered a smaller pension.

50   "A lot of places, they're not looking that you're trained in something," Andy Blevins said one evening, sitting on his back porch. "They just want you to have a degree."

51   Figuring out how to get one is the core quandary facing the nation's college non-graduates. Many seem to want one. In a *New York Times* poll, 43 percent of them called it essential to success, while 42 percent of college graduates and 32 percent of high school dropouts did. This in itself is a change from the days when "college boy" was an insult in many working-class neighborhoods. But once students take a break—the phrase that many use instead of "drop out"—the ideal can quickly give way to reality. Family and work can make a return to school seem even harder than finishing it in the first place.

52   After dropping out of Radford, Andy Blevins enrolled part-time in a community college, trying to juggle work and studies. He lasted a year. From time to time in the decade since, he has thought about giving it another try. But then he has wondered if that would be crazy. He works every third Saturday, and his phone rings on Sundays when there is a problem with the supply of potatoes or apples. "It never ends," he said. "There's never a lull."

53   To spend more time with Lucas, Blevins has already cut back on his singing. If he took night classes, he said, when would he ever see his little boy? Anyway, he said, it would take years to get a degree part-time. To him, it is a tug-of-war between living in the present and sacrificing for the future.

Few Breaks for the Needy

54   The college admissions system often seems ruthlessly meritocratic. Yes, children of alumni still have an advantage. But many other pillars of the old system—the polite rejections of women or blacks, the spots reserved for graduates of Choate and Exeter—have crumbled.

55   This was the meritocracy John Casteen described when he greeted the parents of freshmen in a University of Virginia lecture hall in the late summer of 2004. Hailing from all fifty states and fifty-two foreign countries, the students were more intelligent and better prepared than he and his classmates had been, he told the parents in his quiet, deep voice. The class included seventeen students with a perfect SAT score.

56   If anything, children of privilege think that the system has moved so far from its old-boy history that they are now at a disadvantage when they apply, because colleges are trying to diversify their student rolls. To get into a good college, the sons and daughters of the upper middle class often talk of needing a higher SAT score than, say, an applicant who grew up on a farm, in a ghetto, or in a factory town. Some state legislators from northern Virginia's affluent suburbs have argued that this is a form of geographic discrimination and have quixotically proposed bills to outlaw it.

57   But the conventional wisdom is not quite right. The elite colleges have not been giving much of a break to the low-income students who apply.

When William G. Bowen, a former president of Princeton, looked at admissions records recently, he found that if test scores were equal a low-income student had no better chance than a high-income one of getting into a group of nineteen colleges, including Harvard, Yale, Princeton, Williams, and Virginia. Athletes, legacy applicants, and minority students all got in with lower scores on average. Poorer students did not.

58   The findings befuddled many administrators, who insist that admissions officers have tried to give poorer applicants a leg up. To emphasize the point, Virginia announced in the spring of 2005 that it was changing its admissions policy from "need blind"—a term long used to assure applicants that they would not be punished for seeking financial aid—to "need conscious." Administrators at Amherst and Harvard have also recently said that they would redouble their efforts to take into account the obstacles students have overcome.

59   "The same score reflects more ability when you come from a less fortunate background," Lawrence Summers, the president of Harvard, said. "You haven't had a chance to take the test-prep course. You went to a school that didn't do as good a job coaching you for the test. You came from a home without the same opportunities for learning."'

60   But it is probably not a coincidence that elite colleges have not yet turned this sentiment into action. Admitting large numbers of low-income students could bring clear complications. Too many in a freshman class would probably lower the college's average SAT score, thereby damaging its ranking by *U.S. News & World Report*, a leading arbiter of academic prestige. Some colleges, like Emory University in Atlanta, have climbed fast in the rankings over precisely the same period in which their percentage of low-income students has tumbled. The math is simple: when a college goes looking for applicants with high SAT scores, it is far more likely to find them among well-off teenagers.

61   More spots for low-income applicants might also mean fewer for the children of alumni, who make up the fund-raising base for universities. More generous financial aid policies will probably lead to higher tuition for those students who can afford the list price. Higher tuition, lower ranking, tougher admission requirements: these do not make for an easy marketing pitch to alumni clubs around the country. But Casteen and his colleagues are going ahead, saying the pendulum has swung too far in one direction.

62   That was the mission of John Blackburn, Virginia's easygoing admissions dean, when he rented a car and took to the road in the spring of 2005. Blackburn thought of the trip as a reprise of the drives Casteen took twenty-five years earlier, when he was the admissions dean, traveling to churches and community centers to persuade black parents that the university was finally interested in their children.

63   One Monday night, Blackburn came to Big Stone Gap, in a mostly poor corner of the state not far from Andy Blevins's town. A community college there was holding a college fair, and Blackburn set up a table in a hallway, draping it with the University of Virginia's blue and orange flag.

64   As students came by, Blackburn would explain Virginia's new admissions and financial aid policies. But he soon realized that the Virginia name might have been scaring off the very people his pitch was intended for. Most of the students who did approach the table showed little interest in the financial

aid and expressed little need for it. One man walked up to Blackburn and introduced his son as an aspiring doctor. The father was an ophthalmologist. Other doctors came by, too. So did some lawyers.

65   "You can't just raise the UVA flag," Blackburn said, packing up his materials at the end of the night, "and expect a lot of low-income kids to come out."

66   When the applications started arriving in his office, there seemed to be no increase in those from low-income students. So Blackburn extended the deadline two weeks for everybody, and his colleagues also helped some applicants with the maze of financial aid forms. Of 3,100 incoming freshmen, it now seems that about 180 will qualify for the new financial aid program, up from 130 who would have done so the year before. It is not a huge number, but Virginia administrators call it a start.

A Big Decision

67   On a still-dark February morning, with the winter's heaviest snowfall on the ground, Andy Blevins scraped off his Jeep and began his daily drive to the supermarket warehouse. As he passed the home of Mike Nash, his neighbor and fellow gospel singer, he noticed that the car was still in the driveway. For Nash, a school counselor and the only college graduate in the singing group, this was a snow day.

68   Blevins later sat down with his calendar and counted to 280: the number of days he had worked last year. Two hundred and eighty days—six days a week most of the time— without ever really knowing what the future would hold.

69   "I just realized I'm going to have to do something about this," he said, "because it's never going to end."

70   In the weeks afterward, his daydreaming about college and his conversations about it with his sister Leanna turned into serious research. He requested his transcripts from Radford and from Virginia Highlands Community College and figured out that he had about a year's worth of credits. He also talked to Leanna about how he could become an elementary school teacher. He always felt that he could relate to children, he said. The job would take up 180 days, not 280. Teachers do not usually get laid off or lose their pensions or have to take a big pay cut to find new work.

71   So the decision was made. Andy Blevins says he will return to Virginia Highlands, taking classes at night; the Gospel Gentlemen are no longer booking performances. After a year, he plans to take classes by video and on the Web that are offered at the community college but run by Old Dominion, a Norfolk, Virginia, university with a big group of working-class students.

72   "I don't like classes, but I've gotten so motivated to go back to school," Blevins said. "I don't want to, but, then again, I do."

73   He thinks he can get his bachelor's degree in three years. If he gets it at all, he will have defied the odds.

Exercises

Some of the Issues

1. Why does Leonhardt write that Andy Blevins's decision didn't really seem like a decision, but rather it "just felt like that natural thing to do" (paragraph 1)?
2. In paragraph 6, Leonhardt states that Blevins is part of "one of the largest and fastest-growing groups of young adults in America." To what does he attribute this growing rate of college dropouts?
3. In what ways, according to Leonhardt, have "colleges come to reinforce many of the advantages of birth?" How has college become not necessarily the "great equalizer" it was once hoped to be (paragraphs 8-9)?
4. Leonhardt asserts that a "college education matters much more now than it once did" (paragraph 13). Based on your own experience and what others have told you (your parents, teachers, school counselors, or peers) do you find this to be true?
5. How does Leonhardt question American concepts of diversity?
6. What reasons does Leonhardt give for the disproportionate number of low-income students who drop out of college (paragraphs 22-23)?
7. What changes has John T. Casteen III, the president of the University of Virginia, implemented and why? Are other universities following his lead?
8. What are some of the ways policy makers are beginning to address issues of college retention (paragraph 39)? Do the policies, such as the one initiated in New York State, seem important to you?
9. What are Andy Blevins's concerns about his own life and future? How does his own family history contribute to his fears?
10. What is the difference between a "need blind" and a "need conscious" admissions policy (paragraph 58)?
11. What are some of the "problems" that could potentially be brought on by admitting low-income students (paragraph 60)?
12. Leonhardt's article first appeared in the *New York Times* in a series dedicated to examining the subject of class in the United States. To what extent do you feel Americans talk openly about class? Do you think this is a subject that needs more or less attention here in the United States?

The Way We Are Told

13. What is the effect of Leonhardt's opening paragraphs? How do they set up the subject of the article?
14. Leonhardt interweaves information about college and class with Blevins's story. Is this an effective way to approach the subject? Would he have benefited from focusing on a number of examples in more detail?
15. How would you characterize the author's tone at the end of the essay? Is it consistent with his tone throughout?

Some Subjects for Writing

16. What factors led you to choose to go to college? What do you expect to get from your college experience? Did you, or do you still, have any reservations about your decision? Write a narrative in which you explain your own decision to attend college and analyze your reasons for doing so. If you do not want to write about your own experience, interview two or three peers who come from different backgrounds about their experience (you do not have to use their real names). You may also choose to use your own experience and compare it to that of your peers.

17. What, in your opinion, can or should be done to encourage more low-income students to go to or stay in college? Drawing from your own experience, along with ideas from Leonhardt's article as well as other readings, write an essay in which you present two to four possible ways to address the issue. Be sure to use specific examples to back up your point.

18. With the help of your instructor, research the retention rates at your own college. How many students leave after their first or second year? How many eventually graduate? What factors, if any, appear to determine who stays and who leaves? Has your school done anything to raise the rates of retention? Using the information you find, along with your own experience and that of your peers, write a paper in which you analyze your school's success in retaining students and helping them finish college.

Rigor Redefined

Tony Wagner

Even our "best" schools are failing to prepare students for 21st-century careers and citizenship.

Tony Wagner is Codirector of the Change Leadership Group at the Harvard Graduate School of Education; tony_wagner@harvard.edu; www.schoolchange.org. The themes of this article are discussed more fully in his book *The Global Achievement Gap: Why Even Our Best Schools Don't Teach the New Survival Skills Our Children Need—and What We Can Do About It* (Basic Books, 2008).

In the new global economy, with many jobs being either automated or *"off-shored,"* what skills will students need to build successful careers? What skills will they need to be good citizens? Are these two education goals in conflict?

To examine these questions, I conducted research beginning with conversations with several hundred business, nonprofit, *philanthropic*, and education leaders. With a clearer picture of the skills young people need, I then set out to learn whether U.S. schools are teaching and testing the skills that matter most. I observed classrooms in some of the nation's most highly regarded suburban schools to find out whether our "best" was, in fact, good enough for our children's future. What I discovered on this journey may surprise you.

The Schooling Students Need

One of my first conversations was with Clay Parker, president of the Chemical Management Division of BOC Edwards—a company that, among other things, makes machines and supplies chemicals for the manufacture of *microelectronics* devices. He's an engineer by training and the head of a technical business, so when I asked him about the skills he looks for when he hires young people, I was taken aback by his answer.

"First and foremost, I look for someone who asks good questions," Parker responded. "We can teach them the technical stuff, but we can't teach them how to ask good questions—how to think."

"What other skills are you looking for?" I asked, expecting that he'd jump quickly to content expertise.

"I want people who can engage in good discussion—who can look me in the eye and have a give and take. All of our work is done in teams. You have to know how to work well with others. But you also have to know how to engage customers—to find out what their needs are. If you can't engage others, then you won't learn what you need to know."

I initially doubted whether Parker's views were representative of business leaders in general. But after interviewing leaders in settings from Apple to Uni-

October 2008 | Volume 66 | Number 2
Expecting Excellence Pages 20-25

lever to the U.S. Army and reviewing the research on workplace skills, I came to understand that the world of work has changed profoundly.

Today's students need to master seven survival skills to thrive in the new world of work. And these skills are the same ones that will enable students to become productive citizens who contribute to solving some of the most pressing issues we face in the 21st century.

1. Critical Thinking and Problem Solving

To compete in the new global economy, companies need their workers to think about how to continuously improve their products, processes, or services. Over and over, executives told me that the heart of critical thinking and problem solving is the ability to ask the right questions. As one senior executive from Dell said, "Yesterday's answers won't solve today's problems."

Ellen Kumata, managing partner at Cambria Associates, explained the extraordinary pressures on leaders today. "The challenge is this: How do you do things that haven't been done before, where you have to rethink or think anew? It's not incremental improvement any more. The markets are changing too fast."

2. Collaboration and Leadership

Teamwork is no longer just about working with others in your building. Christie Pedra, CEO of Siemens, explained, "Technology has allowed for virtual teams. We have teams working on major infrastructure projects that are all over the U.S. On other projects, you're working with people all around the world on solving a software problem. Every week they're on a variety of conference calls; they're doing Web casts; they're doing net meetings."

Mike Summers, vice president for Global Talent Management at Dell, said that his greatest concern was young people's lack of leadership skills. "Kids just out of school have an amazing lack of preparedness in general leadership skills and collaborative skills," he explained. "They lack the ability to influence."

3. Agility and Adaptability

Clay Parker explained that anyone who works at BOC Edwards today "has to think, be flexible, change, and use a variety of tools to solve new problems. We change what we do all the time. I can guarantee the job I hire someone to do will change or may not exist in the future, so this is why adaptability and learning skills are more important than technical skills."

4. Initiative and Entrepreneurialism

Mark Chandler, senior vice president and general counsel at Cisco, was one of the strongest proponents of initiative: "I say to my employees, if you try five things and get all five of them right, you may be failing. If you try 10 things, and get eight of them right, you're a hero. You'll never be blamed for failing to reach a stretch goal, but you will be blamed for not trying. One of the problems of a large company is risk aversion. Our challenge is how to create an entrepreneurial culture in a larger organization."

5. Effective Oral and Written Communication

Mike Summers of Dell said, "We are routinely surprised at the difficulty some young people have in communicating: verbal skills, written skills, presentation skills. They have difficulty being clear and concise; it's hard for them to create focus, energy, and passion around the points they want to make. If you're talking to an exec, the first thing you'll get asked if you haven't made it perfectly clear in the first 60 seconds of your presentation is, 'What do you want me to take away from this meeting?' They don't know how to answer that question."

Summers and other leaders from various companies were not necessarily complaining about young people's poor grammar, punctuation, or spelling—the things we spend so much time teaching and testing in our schools. Although writing and speaking correctly are obviously important, the complaints I heard most frequently were about fuzzy thinking and young people not knowing how to write with a real voice.

6. Accessing and Analyzing Information

Employees in the 21st century have to manage an astronomical amount of information daily. As Mike Summers told me, "There is so much information available that it is almost too much, and if people aren't prepared to process the information effectively it almost freezes them in their steps."

It's not only the sheer quantity of information that represents a challenge, but also how rapidly the information is changing. Quick—how many planets are there? In the early 1990s, I heard then–Harvard University president Neil Rudenstine say in a speech that the half-life of knowledge in the humanities is 10 years, and in math and science, it's only two or three years. I wonder what he would say it is today.

7. Curiosity and Imagination

Mike Summers told me, "People who've learned to ask great questions and have learned to be inquisitive are the ones who move the fastest in our environment because they solve the biggest problems in ways that have the most impact on innovation."

Daniel Pink, the author of *A Whole New Mind,* observes that with increasing abundance, people want unique products and services: "For businesses it's no longer enough to create a product that's reasonably priced and adequately functional. It must also be beautiful, unique, and meaningful."[1] Pink notes that developing young people's capacities for imagination, creativity, and empathy will be increasingly important for maintaining the United States' competitive advantage in the future.

The Schooling Students Get

I've spent time observing in classrooms across the United States for more than 20 years. Here is a sampling of what I've seen recently. These examples come from secondary honors and advanced placement (AP) classes in three school systems that enjoy excellent reputations because of their high test scores.

AP Chemistry

Students work in groups of two and three mixing chemicals according to directions written on the chalkboard. Once the mixtures are prepared, students heat the concoction with Bunsen burners. According to the directions on the board, they are supposed to record their observations on a worksheet.

I watch a group of three young men whose mixture is giving off a thin spiral of smoke as it's being heated—something that none of the other students' beakers are doing. One student looks back at the chalkboard and then at his notes. Then all three stop what they are doing, apparently waiting for the teacher to come help them.

"What's happening to your mixture?" I ask the group.

"Dunno," one mutters. "We must have mixed it up wrong."

"What's your hypothesis about what happened—why it's smoking?"

The three look at one another blankly, and the student who has been doing all the speaking looks at me and shrugs.

AP U.S. Government

The teacher is reviewing answers to a sample test that the class took the previous day. The test contains 80 multiple-choice questions related to the functions and branches of the federal government.

When he's finished, he says "OK, now let's look at some sample free-response questions from previous years' AP exams." He flips the overhead projector on and reads from the text of a transparency: "Give three reasons why the Iron Triangle may be criticized as undemocratic. How would you answer this question?"

No one replies.

"OK, who can give me a definition of the Iron Triangle?"

A student pipes up, "The military-industrial-congressional complex."

"OK, so what would be three reasons why it would be considered undemocratic?" The teacher calls on a student in the front row who has his hand half raised, and he answers the question in a voice that we can't hear over the hum of the projector's fan.

"Good. Now let's look at another one." The teacher flips another transparency onto the projector. "Now this question is about bureaucracy. Let me tell you how to answer this one. . . ."

AP English

The teacher explains that the class is going to review students' literature notes for the advanced placement exam next week. The seven students are deeply slouched in their chairs, arranged in a semicircle around the teacher's desk.

The teacher asks, "Now what is Virginia Woolf saying about the balance between an independent life versus a social life?"

Students ruffle through their notebooks. Finally, a young woman, reading from her notes, answers, "Mrs. Ramsey sought meaning from social interactions."

"Yes, that's right. Now what about Lily, the artist? How did she construct meaning?"

"Through her painting," another student mumbles, her face scrunched close to her notes.

"So what is Woolf saying about the choices these two women have made, and what each has sacrificed?"

No reply. The teacher sighs, gets up, goes to the board, and begins writing.

A Rare Class

Once in a great while, I observe a class in which a teacher is using academic content to develop students' core competencies. In such a class, the contrast with the others is stark.

At the beginning of the period in an Algebra II class, the teacher writes a problem on the board. He turns to the students, who are sitting in desks arranged in squares of four that face one another. "You haven't seen this kind of problem before," he explains. "Solving it will require you to use concepts from both geometry and algebra. Each group will try to develop at least two different ways to solve this problem. After all the groups have finished, I'll randomly choose someone from each group who will write one of your proofs on the board, and I'll ask that person to explain the process your group used."

The groups quickly go to work. Animated discussion takes place as students pull the problem apart and talk about different ways to solve it. While they work, the teacher circulates from group to group. When a student asks a question, the teacher responds with another question: "Have you considered . . .?" "Why did you assume that?" or simply "Have you asked someone in your group?"

What makes this an effective lesson—a lesson in which students are learning a number of the seven survival skills while also mastering academic content? First, students are given a complex, multi-step problem that is different from any they've seen in the past. To solve it, they have to apply critical-thinking and problem-solving skills and call on previously acquired knowledge from both geometry and algebra. Mere memorization won't get them far. Second, they have to find two ways to solve the problem, which requires initiative and imagination. Third, they have to explain their proofs using effective communication skills. Fourth, the teacher does not spoon-feed students the answers. He uses questions to push students' thinking and build their tolerance for ambiguity. Finally, because the teacher announces in advance that he'll randomly call on a student to show how the group solved the problem, each student in every group is held accountable. Success requires teamwork.

Rigor for the 21st Century

Across the United States, I see schools that are succeeding at making adequate yearly progress but failing our students. Increasingly, there is only one curriculum: test prep. Of the hundreds of classes that I've observed in recent years, fewer than 1 in 20 were engaged in instruction designed to teach students to think instead of merely drilling for the test.

To teach and test the skills that our students need, we must first redefine excellent instruction. It is not a checklist of teacher behaviors and a model lesson that covers content standards. It is working with colleagues to ensure that all students master the skills they need to succeed as lifelong learners, workers, and citizens. I have yet to talk to a recent graduate, college teacher, community leader, or business leader who said that not knowing enough academic content was a problem. In my interviews, everyone stressed the importance of critical thinking, communication skills, and collaboration.

We need to use academic content to teach the seven survival skills every day, at every grade level, and in every class. And we need to insist on a combination of locally developed assessments and new nationally *normed*, online tests—such as the College and Work Readiness Assessment (www.cae.org)—that measure students' analytic-reasoning, critical-thinking, problem-solving, and writing skills.

It's time to hold ourselves and all of our students to a new and higher standard of rigor, defined according to 21st-century criteria. It's time for our profession to advocate for accountability systems that will enable us to teach and test the skills that matter most. Our students' futures are at stake.

Endnote

1. Pink, D. (2005). *A whole new mind: Moving from the information age to the conceptual age.* New York: Riverhead Books, pp. 32–33.

 ## Vocabulary

off-shored
philanthropic
microelectronics
Entrepreneurialism
normed

 ## Questions

1. Business leaders said they want "someone who asks good questions" and can work well with others on a team. How do these attributes and the 7 "survival skills" compare and contrast with the attributes of an educated person described in Chapter 3? Draw a chart to illustrate your thinking.
2. In the AP English class the teacher says "let me tell you how to answer this one". Explain why this style of instruction does or does not support the development of the 7 survival skills or attributes of an educated person.

Using the Decision-Making Process To Choose a College Major and Career Path

Debra Marcus, M.S., & David McVey, M.S.
Career Counselors, Sacramento State University

Students make decisions every day. Choosing a major and/or a career field essentially involves the decision-making process. The effectiveness of choosing a major and career field can be greatly influenced by the information available to you at the point of decision-making and the effectiveness of your decision-making relies on accurate and up-to-date information. Give due time to gathering information about yourself, college majors, and the world of work as you go through the process of choosing a major and/or career field.

Recent research indicates that it is typical for undergraduates to "try out" four or five majors before deciding which one best fits their needs. If you have not selected a major, or you are uncomfortable with the major you are currently in, you are not alone.

A common myth about selecting an academic major is that the major you choose must relate to a specific field. The reality is that a bachelor's degree prepares you for many different career paths. Some majors are more directly linked to specific career options, while others are less directly related. For example, a Nursing major will most likely seek work in the field of nursing or a closely related healthcare position. However, a Sociology major may work as a caseworker, a manager, a claims representative or a marketing manager.

There are many factors that influence your choice of major and/or career field. Family and cultural influences, economic trends, skill preferences, peer pressure, personal values, work values, interests, personality, health considerations, natural talents, and aptitude can all influence career and education decisions. Most people experience some level of apprehension when making a decision. It is, alternatively, an opportunity to learn more about ourselves each time we go through the decision-making process.

People use many different strategies when making decisions, sometimes without enough forethought. Often we let other people decide for us or make decisions according to someone else's suggestions. Have you ever procrastinated or got so lost in the details that you had difficulty making any decision at all? Moreover, some of us use our gut feeling when making decisions, risking making a decision before gathering all the needed information. Finally, we may decide based upon an alternative that involves the least amount of stress.

All of us have used some or all of the above decision-making strategies during our lifetimes. Sometimes the decision-making strategy we use interferes or prevents us from making positive decisions, making decisions in a timely manner, or making the "right" decision. Most importantly, it is important to understand that not everyone makes decisions in the same ways. There is no single method of decision-making that is right for everyone.

The following is a 6-Step Decision-Making Model that may be a helpful outline to follow as you begin the process of making educational and career decisions.

Step 1: Identify the Decision(s) To Be Made

Before you begin gathering information, it is important to have a clear understanding of what it is you are trying to decide. When entering college, some typical considerations might include:

- What should I major in?
- How does my major relate to the world of work?
- Should I select a minor to compliment my major?
- What are my educational goals?
- Which G.E. courses offer good introductions to various majors/fields?
- How does my choice of major relate to my career goals?
- What are my career goals?

Step 2: Get to Know Yourself

Before you select a major, choose a field or career or decide whether you would like to go to graduate school, it is important to develop a sense of who you are— your interests, values, skills, and personality. Some questions you might wish to consider are:

Interests:
- What brings you joy?
- What do you spend your time thinking or reading about?
- What activities or classes do you really like?
- What types of people do you like to be around?
- What energizes you – think about activities you have seen, heard, or participated in?
- What is your earliest recollection of what you wanted to be when you "grew up? How does it relate to what you are thinking about now?

Skills:
- What activities do you enjoyed doing?
- What are your strengths?
- What do you least enjoy doing?
- Which skills and abilities would you most enjoy using at work or in school?
- What skills would you enjoy using that you still need to acquire?
- What are your natural talents?

Values:
- What characteristics need to be present in your ideal job or career?
- How does the way you live your life relate to your choice of major or career field?
- What motivates you?

- What are the five most important things in your life; how do you prioritize them?
- How would others describe you?
- What would others say you value?

Personality:

- Describe your attitude?
- How would others describe your personal qualities?
- Do you prefer to work alone or with others?
- How does your personality relate to your choice of major and/or career field?
- Do you prefer working with people, data or things?
- What type of people do you feel most comfortable being around?

Step 3: Begin to Identify Options (Career Exploration)

Exploring the world of work and academic majors includes gathering information about ideas you are already considering as well as learning about new ideas and options you may not have considered. Information is empowering. There are many sources of information about college majors and careers. Utilize resources in the Career Center to learn the various strategies for researching college majors and the world of work.

- Are you creating time to research occupational and major information?
- Have you identified several options based upon what you have learned about yourself?
- Are you able to write down options you are considering in your choice of major or career field?
- As you gather occupational and major information, what additional alternatives have you discovered?

Step 4: Factors Influencing Decisions

As you begin the process of deciding on an education and career path, you may experience factors, both positive and negative, that impact your ability to identify options, choose among alternatives, make a decision, or follow through with a plan. The staff in the Career Center are available to assist you with identifying factors that are impacting your education and career decisions.

- What internal and external factors are present that influence your decisions or your choice of alternatives?
- What has been your experience with making decisions in the past?
- What decisions have you made in the past?
- How did you make those decisions?
- What resources helped you?
- What did you learn from your decisions?

Step 5: Identify Your Options

After you have competed your career and/or educational research, the next step is to make a list of options, including alternative options, for each decision to be made.

- Are you able to assess the possible outcomes or consequences for the decisions to be made?
- Have you identified the pros and cons of each alternative, while also considering the factors influencing your decision?
- Are you able to identify your best possible alternative(s)?
- Have you gathered enough information to evaluate your options?
- Have you been able to evaluate the information/resources presently available?
- Are there any new alternatives/options that you are able to identify from the new information?

Step 6: Design a Course of Action To Implement the Decision(s)

Based upon the information you have gathered, the last step is to choose among several options. If needed, the Career Center can assist you in narrowing your options and developing a plan of action. Once you have narrowed your options and decided on a course of action, it is helpful to identify the action steps that are necessary for you to accomplish your goal(s). Be sure and consider several alternatives or back-up plans for the primary decision you will be making.

- Have you outlined a plan of action?
- Are you able to identify action steps to implement your decision?
- Have you identified a timeline for your plan of action, including deadline dates?
- Are there any internal and/or external obstacles to implementing your decision?
- Are you able to identify how you plan to overcome them?
- Remember to reflect and evaluate throughout the implementation of your decision.

    Good job! You have gone through the process of making an educational and/or career decision. Remember, everyone makes decisions differently. This 6-step method is just one way to make education and/or career decisions.

Questions about using the decision-making process to choose a college major and career path:

1. Describe some of the ways you have made decisions in the past.
2. Which parts of the 6-step decision-making model are your favorite and why?
3. What is the most difficult aspect of making decisions about your major and/or career path?

4. What are some of the resources you can use to help you decide about majors and career fields?
5. Have you experienced a "roadblock" or what felt like an obstacle in decisions you have considered in your past? What did you learn from that experience and how did you maneuver around the "roadblock"?
6. What would you recommend to freshmen who are in the process of making decisions about their major and/or career path?

Job Search: Chance or Plan?

Mark R. Ballard

Formerly the director of career services in a liberal arts college, Mark Ballard is currently director of human resources development at Victoria's Secret Catalogue, where he continues his work in career planning and organizational career development. In this essay, Ballard offers some excellent advice for initiating the job-search process and delineates specific career-planning tasks for each year of student life. He believes his advice, if followed, will generate good job prospects upon graduation.

I want to tell you about Terry—the alumnus who "chanced" his career. His story can provide important insights for your own career planning.

Terry was a popular student in high school, was involved in many activities, and graduated in the top 25 percent of his class. Terry could hardly wait to leave his hometown to become a college student at the university. His academic performance was quite respectable. He could not believe how quickly the years passed. They elapsed so fast that he did not get involved in any structured *co-curricular* activities because he was "too busy" with school, sports, and friends. For spending money, Terry worked, but his employment experience, for the most part, consisted of being a lifeguard during the summers at his hometown pool and a cashier in a fast-food restaurant.

The quarter before Terry was slated to graduate, he decided to visit the Career Services Office. (He remembered hearing about this resource in his freshman orientation class.) Terry eagerly signed up for several on-campus interviews with companies that came to campus to interview students.

Terry bought a suit, had someone prepare a resume for him, and interviewed with several company representatives. He was confident that he presented himself well in the interviews and would most assuredly get an offer from one of the employers with whom he interviewed. After all, he had never had difficulty finding part-time jobs.

Graduation came and went for Terry. Summer came, and Terry began to panic. Mid-summer, Terry returned to Career Services since the anticipated job offers did not materialize out of his interviews. Terry came back to the office looking for additional companies who were coming on campus to interview students and alumni. But there were none during the summer, since companies who do come to college campuses to interview students generally complete their hiring visits during April. Terry was unaware of this fact since he did not attend the on-campus interviewing orientation session: he was "too busy." Terry left the office disappointed, failing to take advantage of the many other employment resources. He vowed to return "sometime," but he never got around to it.

In the follow-up questionnaire mailed to alumni six months after graduation, we received a letter from Terry. Good news: he had landed a job! Well, maybe not good news. The job, which he stumbled on by "accident," was not the kind

Reprinted by permission of the author.

of position Terry thought he would land with a college degree. Sadly, his college education would not be fully utilized, and his salary was not comparable to similar college graduates.

Here's the moral of Terry's tale: Finding meaningful employment *commensurate* with one's educational level is not an event that occurs at the end of one's final term in college. It is a process that begins early in one's collegiate career. Making the transition from academics to the work world does not begin with writing a resume, buying a new suit, or getting that first job interview. It begins with thought, research, and goal setting.

To secure employment upon graduation, begin with the process of self-assessment. As a part of this process, you need to be able to answer such questions as, "What do I want to do for work?" and "Where do I want to do it?" In other words, what are your abilities, strengths, assets, gifts, talents? What is it that you are interested in, enjoy, are curious about, are motivated by, or get pleasure from? What are your values—those needs that you want satisfied by your work (recognition, independence, money, prestige, social status, uncovering knowledge)? What are the job tasks or activities of the careers that you are considering, the types of organizations that employ individuals in these occupations, the job outlook/forecast, salary ranges, entrance requirements, and lifestyle issues associated with the vocations you are considering? What are the steps necessary to undertake the decision-making process related to your career? Do you know where to go to find out how to write a resume, interview for job offers, and to learn strategies to find jobs? If you can answer these questions, you will increase your prospects for success in the job search.

As an entering student, you may find it easy to say: "I'll deal with those job-related questions and issues during my senior year, or when I'm ready to graduate." "It's too early now." "I don't have time." "I'm just a freshman." "I'll figure it out. After all, I figured out how to apply to and get accepted to college."

But consider the following. Suppose you were to interview today for the job of your dreams, and the interviewer said to you, "Tell me about yourself and why you want this job. You have thirty minutes. I'll begin timing when you begin talking." How would you respond? What would you say? That is a common opening statement for an employer to make in a job interview.

To land the job of your dreams, you will first need to know about yourself. Do not confuse starting the process with implementing your career decision. You don't need to choose a career now, just to begin to think about, and to get actively involved in, the process during your early years of college. That way, early in your senior year, you can reflect on the self-assessment and the career exploration tasks that you addressed and the career decision that you made early in your college years. Your senior year is also the time for you to focus attention on *transitional* issues that will take you from academics to the work world, or on to graduate or professional school. Career planning is working through the many tasks associated with finding employment through planning—rather than through chance.

Career planning is the developmental, systematic process of:

1. learning about yourself (for example, your interests, abilities, and values),

2. identifying occupations that correspond to your assessment of self,

3. exploring the occupations that you are considering,

4. selecting an occupation to pursue,

5. readying yourself for the job search process (resume and application letter writing, job interview skill development, job finding techniques and strategy knowledge), and

6. securing satisfying employment.

Does it seem that the process of career planning could be simplified by proceeding directly to step six—finding a job upon graduation? If so, remember Terry. That is exactly what he did. He jumped into the job search without establishing the foundation of the first five stages. He landed a job, but a job in the ranks of the underemployed, and that can have *ramifications* for a lifetime.

Your career process will be easier if you fully use the career planning and placement services provided at your university. There, staff members can help you answer the all too familiar question, "What can I do with a major in . . . ?" and assist you in finding purposeful, gratifying employment.

As a career services professional, I have worked with thousands of students, employers, and alumni. When I survey employers and alumni for their perspective on how students can best prepare themselves to make the transition from academics to the work world, they usually give five recommendations for students entering a university.

1. Choose a major in a subject that interests you—one that really gets you excited. Do not rely on your parents, peers, or counselors to make the choice for you regarding your academic major or the occupation to pursue. Make the decision yourself. As a related note, given the difficulty of predicting which skills will be in demand even five years from now, not to mention in a lifetime, your best career preparation is one that emphasizes broad skills (for example, social, communication, analytical, logical, leadership, human relations), intellectual curiosity, and knowledge of how to learn.

2. Strive for a rigorous academic program and high grades. Yes, grades are important to employers. Job candidates are often rejected from interviews due to low GPAs.

3. Develop your leadership, communication, human relations, and time management skills by taking active roles of responsibility in student organizations and activities. This involvement will provide you with an opportunity to put knowledge from the classroom into practice.

4. Get career-related experience prior to graduation (through part-time positions, *cooperative education,* internships, and volunteer work). The benefits of such experience go well beyond making money. You will have a chance to sample a variety of jobs and work settings, make valuable contacts with professionals for future networking, develop self-confidence, and gain insight when choosing elective courses in your academic program.

5. Use the career planning and placement services on campus early in your academic experience to help you with your career decision making and your job search. By doing so, you can get a head start on your employment future.

You can take the above recommendations a step further by following a year-by-year plan for your job search. Use this scheme as a general strategy to increase the likelihood of your landing the job of your dreams upon graduation.

As a Freshman . . .

The goal of your freshman year should be to learn as much as you can about yourself and the relationship this information has to careers. Consider the following:

In your academic course work, use the required general education courses and other college courses to help you explore your potential. You might wish to take courses and explore subjects that have always been of interest to you but that you never before had an opportunity to take.

Visit the career services office on your campus and get acquainted with the services and resources of that office. Your academic adviser can direct you to the right place.

Explore your interests, abilities, and values. Identify appropriate career choices by using the computerized career guidance systems (DISCOVER and SIGI-PLUS are two that are commonly available), meeting with a staff member of the career services office for a career counseling session, attending any career awareness workshops offered on campus and sharing your goals with your academic adviser.

Find out about cooperative education and internship opportunities through your intended college of graduation.

Analyze job descriptions in the career services office and ask yourself how these positions fit with your identity profile.

Begin investigating and getting involved in at least one of the student organizations and activities on campus to develop your leadership, communication, human relations, and time management skills.

Find a summer job that will provide you with an opportunity to learn or refine skills that will be attractive to a prospective employer (e.g., communication, responsibility, ethical decision making, and human relations—learning to work with individuals of differing backgrounds).

As a Sophomore . . .

During your sophomore year, your goal should be to concentrate on identifying careers that appeal to you and to begin testing them out.

Use the career books and other references in the career office and elsewhere on campus to research career options.

Learn to begin the process of informational interviewing—contacting and talking with people employed in fields you are considering. For example, if you are interested in chemistry, dietetics, or nutrition as a major, consider conducting an informational interview with a nutritional researcher at an area business or hospital. Career services staff members can help you identify professionals working in occupations that are of interest to you.

Take active roles of responsibility in clubs, organizations, and activities.

Cultivate relationships with faculty, counselors, and others who can help in answering questions that relate to careers and the relationship of course work to careers.

Take time to attend the "career days" held on campus and in the area. These events provide you with the opportunity to meet representatives from major U.S. organizations. Be sure to ask about cooperative education and internship opportunities.

Find out about summer internships and cooperative education opportunities through the career services office.

Begin developing a resume as well as job interviewing skills. Workshops on these topics are conducted regularly through many career services offices.

As a Junior . . .

During your junior year, your goal should be to obtain career-related experience.

Prepare for the job search by attending workshops and individual counseling sessions on resume writing, application letter writing, job search strategies, and interviewing skills.

Develop a network of contacts in the field of your choice through continued informational interviewing, involvement in professional associations, and cooperative education or internships.

Continue to attend the "career days" held on the campus and in the area. Continue to ask the company representatives about internships and cooperative education opportunities.

Research job leads and make initial contacts early in winter for sources of possible employment that have some relationship to your tentative career choice. Gather letters of recommendation written on your behalf from past employers, current employers, professors, teaching associates—professionals who can vouch for your skills and abilities. Open a credentials file if your career services office has such a service.

As a Senior . . .

Your senior year is the culmination of your college education and is the launching pad for your future. Your goal is to secure satisfying employment or to get accepted to graduate or professional school if your career interest indicates the need for an advanced degree.

Learn the procedures for interviewing with the various career placement offices on campus should you wish to interview with organizations that come on campus to interview graduating students.

Research the organizations with which you wish to interview by using the career services office's company literature libraries.

Attend "career day" events that are held on the campus and in the area and actively participate by distributing resumes to the company representatives and telling them about who you are and the type of position you are seeking.

Interview for jobs during the year with employers who come on campus through the career services office. Note: they are not likely to be there during the summer. (Remember Terry's disappointment?)

Continue collecting letters of recommendation written on your behalf by people who can attest to your skills and abilities. Keep these letters on file in your college's career services office.

Explore, in consultation with career services personnel, other strategies to find employment for your field of interest, such as using the many job listings that are published through career services offices, making use of computerized listings of positions, enrolling in national employment databases through career services offices, and learning the process of networking (getting involved with professionals in the field you wish to enter and learning where the hidden job market is). **The best job search strategy is to use a variety of job search strategies simultaneously; do not rely solely on one strategy to find employment.**

Choosing a career and finding a professional job take a lot of time and effort. You need to find out as much as you can about what interests you, what you do well, and what you want out of life. Even after you have decided on your career direction, you will find a wide range of job options available to you. There may be occupations that you have never even heard of that would suit your education, interests, values, and abilities perfectly. It is important to find out about them as early as possible. By waiting too long to begin proper planning and preparation for a successful career, you run the risk of embarking on the job search scene unaware of what field to pursue, getting frustrated, giving in, giving up, and taking any job you are offered.

The staff members of your career services office can help you with every phase of the career planning and employment process. It is not a magical, quick process, and the staff will not find a job for you. What you can expect, however, are informed professionals who will guide your career decision making and your job search process.

The valuable information you will receive from these offices will prove beneficial to you for the rest of your life. Make a commitment to get a head start on your career. Visit your career services office today. You owe it to yourself.

Vocabulary

As you think about this essay, these definitions may be helpful to you:

1. **co-curricular** being outside of but complementary to the regular curriculum
2. **commensurate** equal in measure or extent
3. **transitional** in the process of passing from one state, stage, or place to another
4. **ramifications** consequences or outgrowths
5. **cooperative education** a program that combines academic studies with actual work experience

Discussion Questions

1. What is the first important step in the job search process, according to Ballard?
2. What would you tell an employer about yourself in thirty minutes during a job interview?
3. What are the six steps that Ballard outlines to systematically begin the career planning process?
4. What type of work experiences can students engage in prior to graduation?
5. What are some strategies students can use during their first year to enhance the career planning process? As sophomores? Juniors? Seniors?

 ## Suggestions for Your Journal

Describe your dream job. Where would it be? What tasks would you be involved with all day? How would it fulfill your work values? How would it affect your family? How could it affect your lifestyle? Paint a picture of what a typical day would be like.

Which of the tasks or activities on Ballard's list for the first-year college student have you accomplished? What specific steps can you take to complete them by the end of the year?

Discuss the differences between the practical suggestions for career planning in this reading and the ones suggested by Burtchaell in Chapter 7. How can you accomplish both?

School's Out: One Young Man Puzzles Over His Future Without College

Laura Sessions Stepp

Laura Sessions Stepp is a *Washington Post* staff writer.

"You see these clothes I'm wearing?" he asks. "I bought them. These shoes I'm wearing? I bought them. That car out there? I'm paying for it."

Critical Thinking Points: *As You Read*

1. What are some stereotypes about high school students who choose not to go to college? Where do those stereotypes come from?

2. What kind of town does Ben Farmer live in? How does that influence him and his choices?

3. Keep a list of reasons you feel Ben did not go to college.

Ben Farmer at 19, steering his silver Camaro Z28 down Main Street on a Friday night, glances at the Dairy Freeze and thinks about the buddies he graduated from high school with last year. They're off at college, probably partying tonight, the beer, the girls, at Virginia Tech, Radford, wherever.

He passes a karate studio, beauty supply store and boarded-up movie theater with a marquee begging passersby to "Shop Altavista First."

He could be at college. He had the grades, he's got the brains, but here he is, listening to the cough in his 330-horsepower engine and worrying about his spark plugs.

"There was a lot of unknowns about college," he says after he thinks about it. "It was going to be this big, tough, hard, hard time in which all you'd do is write papers, which I don't like to do." So for now he assembles air conditioning ducts in a factory, for $7 an hour, which is as much as his mother makes in her new job at the bank, her first sit-down job in all the years she's been raising him.

Nobody in his family ever went to any kind of college. His mom wanted him to go. She helped him with the application and the financial aid forms. But he didn't go, he took a $7 job in a town with a lot of $7 jobs, a little river town in central Virginia, where the Southern railroad met the Norfolk and Western, spawning a furniture factory, textile mill and other small manufacturers.

Ten to 12 hours a day, he hammers sheet metal, then goes home to shower off the dirt and fibers. Some nights he heads out to the driving range to hit golf balls. Weekends, he drives over to South Boston to watch guys do what he would like most to do, race stock cars. He has thought about signing on with a NASCAR pit crew, a great job except you're never home.

Altavista is home. He knows everybody, he's already got a job, and now he's met a girl, named Apryl East. He's having visions of a little house one day with a two-car garage, "going to work and going on vacation, not worrying where your next meal is coming from."

So now he's thinking of asking his boss at Moore's, an electrical and mechanical construction firm, if the company will pay him to take night classes at the local community college and then move him indoors to a better-paying job, a sit-down job. Apryl, who goes to Virginia Tech, encourages this line of thinking.

The fall after Ben and 70 others graduated from the local high school, 2.5 million American seniors enrolled in either a two-year or a four-year college.

Almost a million did not. They were overwhelmingly poor, male and white. Much to the surprise of social scientists who traditionally have looked for educational problems among minorities, low-income black and Hispanic men are more likely to go to college right out of high school than white guys like Ben. So are young women of any back- ground. If Ben had a twin sister, she'd likely be enrolled.

There are Ben Farmers all over: in the coal towns of Pennsylvania, the suburban sprawl west of Sacramento and especially in the rural South. They've always been there, hidden in the pockets of America where they pump gas, assemble machine parts and put their pay on the family's kitchen table. They do work that needs to be done—building houses, running backhoes, riveting airplanes, surveying land and fixing the BMWs of upscale college types who occasionally might call them rednecks. America might well lose all its advanced-degree business school graduates with less pain than it would lose these young men.

They're proud of the work they do. At the same time, they've found it harder and harder to acquire full-time jobs with decent pay increases and good health insurance. Their earnings, adjusted for inflation, have fallen or stalled. Altavista, population 3,400, has several thousand people commuting there to work, so there are jobs. But fewer and fewer: Altavista has lost 1,300 jobs in a little over a year.

Other young Altavista men in Ben's position fear they're headed nowhere in a society that prefers paper-pushers to pipe fitters. They don't want to manage accounts payable for a living, or scan X-rays for cancerous tumors. They're proud of doing hard, physical work. But people around them say that white-collar jobs, available only with a college diploma, are the only way to win at life. This attitude, says Patricia Gandara, a professor of education at the University of California, Davis, can make these young white men feel invisible.

"Latinos and African Americans have horrendous problems, too, but at least they have a group identity," says Gandara, who studies low- income, primarily minority youths. "These poor white males don't know where in the culture they fit. Some are really alienated and angry."

Ken Gray, a professor of workforce education at Pennsylvania State University, worries about them, too. "No one's interested in the Bubbas," he says.

Ben is no Bubba, more an easygoing, smart kid with a goatee and a vague future. Off work, he wears American Eagle polo shirts, khakis and Nike sandals.

"You see these clothes I'm wearing?" he asks. "I bought them. These shoes I'm wearing? I bought them. That car out there? I'm paying for it." It's a matter of pride and obligation that richer people can't understand.

He has friends whose parents pay their school expenses, their apartment rent. One of his pals lives off campus in a nice two-bedroom apartment with a big leather couch and an air hockey table.

"On some days I wish I were him," Ben says. On other days? All he'll say about his buddy is this: "If you asked him how much his cell phone bill is, he wouldn't know."

Ben's a guy whose mother taught him to "always keep good credit and pay your bills on time." You get his drift.

His father, Walter, a truck driver who left Ben and Ben's mom when Ben was 3, hasn't played much of a role in his life. But Walter's parents, Marvin and Frances, sure have. Until his early teens, he'd spend the school months in Altavista with his mom, Patsy Moore, and all summer with Marvin and Frances, big NASCAR fans who followed the circuit.

"I think I disappointed Granny the most not going to college, and Mom second," he says.

His mom, eating dinner with Ben in his favorite restaurant, El Cazador, says she's still wondering why he didn't go to college. Hasn't he learned from her example?

Researchers would say that some kids never want to venture much farther along life's path than did the people they know and love best. Moore, a sweet woman of 42, doesn't understand this, as she explains to Ben over a taco salad that he helped her choose.

"You've seen me struggle from week to week," she says. "You can't want that."

No, he doesn't want that. But what does he want? More pressing still, what can he realistically expect to attain?

Ben has loved hot rods since he was a baby. He ran Matchbox cars over his grandmother's rug for hours at a time before he could walk, and as he got older he took up dirt bikes with a bunch of boys his age who lived in the country near his granny.

"We stayed outside all the time," he recalls.

As they got older, their little group carved a dirt track in woods of scrub pine and began racing cars and trucks. Ben's two best friends eventually acquired race cars and the gang started spending time at Big Daddy's South Boston Speedway, a NASCAR-sanctioned short track. Ben began to dream of becoming another Tony Stewart or a pit crew chief.

His teachers couldn't understand this fascination. He's such a good student, they'd sigh, as if you couldn't be interested in both math and Chevys, which happen to have a serious relationship through mechanical engineering. He pulled down A's and B's in high school, taking calculus and Latin. But his teachers didn't foresee a career in engineering, they just seemed to see a car-crazy kid.

One problem they didn't count on: His friends' families all had more money than his, and to dress the way they did and do the things they did, Ben had to get a job.

So at age fifteen he found one at the Amoco Food Shop south of town. He stopped playing high school basketball and started stocking shelves. Making money became something of an obsession. Not big money, though. That would have required college.

When Ben's friends started talking about four-year colleges, Ben would go silent. When they took the SAT in their junior year, Ben didn't. "I thought to myself, where would I find the money?"

His mom encouraged him to try a two-year school, and so he got an application to Danville Community College. But his heart wasn't in it. The message of his guidance counselor and some of his teachers, he says, was that four-year colleges or universities were the only goal worth aiming for.

Those who hold bachelor's degrees have a hard time understanding why anyone wouldn't want one. At Ben's high school, administrators took pride in the fact that they send proportionately more graduates to four-year colleges than other schools in the area. They talked about former students who chose Columbia, Duke or the University of Virginia. For Ben, even $8,000 to $10,000 a year for in-state tuition, room and board didn't seem in the cards.

Other young men in Ben's position report similar experiences.

"They were good at giving out papers to kids going to college, but didn't pay no attention to students going to community college," says Jason Spence, who makes bulletproof vests on the night shift at BGF Industries. Jason and Ben both remember sitting through school assemblies where the same students won award after award, scholarship after scholarship—to four-year schools.

Ben's mother recognized she needed someone to help jump-start her son, but when she sought out school authorities, she says, she received only an offhand kind of attention.

I'd never done this before. They told me I could take Ben to Danville and Lynchburg. It wasn't very helpful."

Ben says he asked at school if, on career day, organizers could bring in someone who worked in the racing industry. With several local drivers around, it would have been easy to find someone, but nothing happened.

"You feel like kind of an outsider," he says.

He might not have felt that way a decade ago, because young men and young women here could still come right out of high school and go to work for family-run industries offering decent starting wages and chances for promotion. They didn't need higher education to enjoy job security at places like Lane Furniture, famous for its cedar chests. But once the Lane family lost direct control of the company in the late 1980s, things started to change. Gradually the manufacturing of cedar chests and dining sets moved to the cheap labor market of China, and fewer and fewer workers filled the million-square-foot brick and wood complex that had dominated, indeed was, AltaVista's skyline.

Last year, on Aug. 31, the last hope chest rolled off the assembly line. Other industries in the area started folding or cutting back, and by this past spring, the unemployment rate in central Virginia had hit a 10-year high. When a health supplements lab in town advertised for 40 new jobs, the cars lined up for interviews the first morning snaked for blocks through town.

Ben worried about his mother—she'd get a job, then be laid off under a last-hired, first-fired policy. "She's had a string of bad luck," he says. Rather then head for college in the hope of improving their chances for a good job, Ben and other young men like him sought out jobs right away that offered health insurance, pension plans and savings programs.

Max Everhart, who lives around the corner from Ben, was one of them. Also a bright young man, he went to work at a machine bearings plant for $10 an hour plus benefits. "It's a good job," Max says. "I'm lucky to have it."

Ben felt the same way when he got hired four months ago at Moore's. With 300 employees, it's one of the few companies in town that is growing. In its vast, open garage he bends, shapes and glues ducts with men like Smoky Hudson and Melvin Mann, who have been doing this kind of work for 30 years. He has learned to respect them.

These guys "really work for their money," he says. "They get their hands dirty."

T.O. Rowland, a 33-year-old welder at Moore's, tells Ben he earns as much money as his wife, a schoolteacher with a master's degree. This makes Ben wonder again: Why do people make such a big deal over college?

This is a question that resonates only in some quarters of the educational establishment. Ken Gray, the Penn State professor, says: "The real opportunities for youth are grossly distorted by colleges. Seventy-one percent of jobs don't require anything beyond a high school education."

But that doesn't mean people can't or shouldn't keep learning, acquiring new skills. In Altavista, Central Virginia Community College runs a satellite center in the former Lane executive building here. The idea is to reach people in high-layoff areas. Center director Linda Rodriguez says the response from older workers, especially older female workers, has been terrific.

But young men like Ben aren't coming in.

When she approached high school authorities about coming to visit classes, she was met with some of the same lack of enthusiasm for community college that Ben's mom did. School authorities said there was no time in the calendar for her visits-the students were too busy taking tests-and offered a one-time assembly instead.

One evening last winter, as Ben arrived at the Amoco store to start his shift, the store manager pushed a paper napkin over to him across the counter. "Someone left this for you," he said.

On the napkin next to the beef jerky, the name Apryl East was scribbled along with a phone number. Ben smiled, remembering the blonde with the cornflower-blue eyes and infectious laugh who had stopped by a couple of weeks earlier. She was after him. Sweet.

Eight months later, the blonde is riding with him in his Camaro as they return from a football game between his old high school and hers in nearby Gretna, where she led cheers and played piccolo in the marching band. Now she's a senior at Virginia Tech, planning on teaching elementary school.

Apryl swears that her best friend left the napkin without her knowledge. Ben doesn't know whether to believe her but he also doesn't care.

He eventually did call her, they went out to a movie. Now a wallet photo of the two of them is propped next to the odometer in his beloved car.

Increasingly, their conversation involves the years to come, and tonight is no exception. Ben ran into a guy at the game whose girlfriend is taking courses in motorcar management at a community college.

"That kinda makes me want to try it," he tells Apryl.

He could choose to stay on at Moore's and go to school at the same time, "maybe get a job on computers" at Moore's. He also has had a couple of conversations with NASCAR driver Stacy Compton. Perhaps, while he's still young, he should just chuck everything—except Apryl— and enlist Compton's help signing on with a racing crew. The sponsors and money for his own car might follow.

"I am so not sure," he says.

Apryl has accepted his confusion, for now.

"I'd like you to go to college," she tells Ben, "but it's okay with me if you don't." Her three best friends are all at different universities. But neither her dad, a supervisor at Moore's, nor her mom, a secretary in a printing shop, attended college, and they've been happy together. From what she has observed at home, college isn't crucial to the married life she dreams of.

What is important, she has told Ben gently, is that he get his behind in gear. He can always try one avenue and move to another if he doesn't like it. He's not yet 20, she reminds him.

Where will he find the motivation?

"From me," she says. She laughs but she's serious. "I'm going to get out of college, come back home and tell him to do it. I can be his little mentor."

A few hours before Ben picks her up for the game, over lunch at a downtown diner, she admits that when she learned that Ben wasn't in college, "I was shocked. I told my mom he didn't get the right kind of guidance."

So why does she stick with him? "He's got a great personality. He's funny." Unlike her previous boyfriend, "he treats me well. Oh, and another thing I like about him? My dad and he have bonded. He says when we have kids, he wants to be the kind of dad he never had."

She takes a breath, then adds, "Ben's everything I ever wanted." She laughs again, then cups her hand over her mouth as if she has revealed just a little too much.

CRITICAL THINKING POINTS: *AFTER YOU'VE READ*

1. Do you have any friends who are not in college? Is it difficult to explain to them what it is like? Why or why not?

2. If you could predict a future for Apryl and Ben, what might it be? Why?

3. If you were going to give Ben some advice, what would it be?

SOME POSSIBILITIES FOR WRITING

1. Compare and contrast your life now to the life you might have had if you had not gone to college.

2. In so many ways, Ben is a product of the environment and people around him. Imitating the "feature reporter" tone of this essay, write a similar one with you as the subject.

3. "No one's interested in the Bubbas," this essay asserts. Is that true? Why do you think the way you do?

CHAPTER 9

WHAT HAPPENS AFTER COLLEGE?

What happens after college? I wouldn't consider myself an expert on the subject, but I don't think there is anyone out there who knows exactly where their life is going to take them once they finish their undergraduate education. Life after college is filled with a lot of uncertainties, just like the uncertainties that you may be facing now in your first semester. One of the biggest uncertainties is your career. We all hope that we will land jobs in the field that we spent years studying, but that isn't always going to be the case. I earned my Bachelors of Science in Recreation Administration. My field of study prepared me for a managerial role in the tourism and hospitality industry. However, after graduation, I didn't find myself managing a five-star resort in the Bahamas; I found myself working for Sacramento State as an admissions and outreach counselor. I didn't even know that higher education would be field that I would enjoy, but it turned out to be something that I definitely have a passion for.

The best thing that you can do, in spite of all the uncertainties, is to pursue experiences that make you happy because that will make the transition much easier. It can be pretty terrifying graduating from college and tackling all the challenges that the real world throws at you. As much as you learn in college, there is still so much to learn after. There will be all sorts of trials and tribulations for you to overcome as you take the independence you had as a college student to an entirely new level. Life after college can be a difficult chapter for you to write, but with all the unknowns and challenges that will face you, you do have one advantage that you can bank on, and that is your college degree. The education you receive will serve as a valuable contribution to your success. We all write our definition of success, much in the way that we all write our own chapter on what happens after college.

Justin Gomez

Justin Gomez,
Alumnus 2008 Recreation
Administration Major

Job Outlook for College Graduates

Jill N. Lacey and Olivia Crosby

You've heard it again and again: Having a college degree leads to higher earnings and more career opportunities. But is it true?

For the most part, it is. When it comes to paychecks and prospects, conventional wisdom is right. On average, college graduates earn more money, experience less unemployment, and have a wider variety of career options than other workers do. A college degree also makes it easier to enter many of the fastest growing, highest paying occupations. In some occupations, in fact, having a degree is the only way to get your start.

According to statistics and projections from the U.S. Bureau of Labor Statistics (BLS), college graduates will continue to have bright prospects. Data consistently show that workers who have a bachelor's or graduate degree have higher earnings and lower unemployment than workers who have less education. And between 2002 and 2012, more than 14 million job openings are projected to be filled by workers who have a bachelor's or graduate degree and who are entering an occupation for the first time.

A college education can be costly, of course, in terms of both time and money. But the rewards can be bigger than the sacrifices if a degree helps you to qualify for occupations that interest you...

In this article, a college graduate is defined as a person who has a bachelor's, master's or doctoral (Ph.D.) degree or a professional degree, such as one in law or medicine...

College Graduates: In Demand and Doing Well

More people are going to college now than ever before, in part because of the career advantages that a college degree confers. College-educated workers' higher earnings and lower unemployment are good reasons to go to college, and these benefits are also evidence of the demand for college graduates. Higher earnings show that employers are willing to pay more to have college graduates work for them. And lower unemployment means that college graduates are more likely to find a job when they want one.

More people going to college

The number of people who have a college degree has been increasing steadily. According to Current Population Survey data, the number of people aged 25 and older who have a college degree grew from 35 million to 52 million between

"Job Outlook for College Graduates" by Jill N. Lacey and Olivia Crosby, *Occupational Outlook Quarterly*, Winter 2004-05.

1992 and 2004, an increase of almost 50 percent. By mid-2004, nearly 28 percent of people aged 25 and older had a bachelor's or graduate degree. (See chart 1).

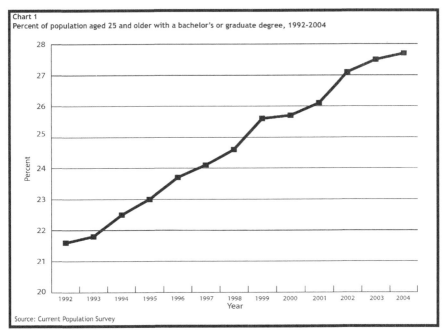

Chart 1
Percent of population aged 25 and older with a bachelor's or graduate degree, 1992-2004

Source: Current Population Survey

Percent of population aged 25 and older with a bachelor's or graduated degree, 1992-2004

Higher earnings, lower unemployment

As a whole, college-educated workers earn more money than workers who have less education. In 2003, workers who had a bachelor's degree had median weekly earnings of $900, compared with $554 a week for high school graduates—that's a difference of $346 per week, or a 62 percent jump in median earnings. (Median earnings show that half of the workers in the educational category earned more than that amount, and half earned less.)

For workers who had a master's, doctoral, or professional degree, median earnings were even higher. In addition to earning more money, workers who had more education were also less likely to be unemployed. Chart 2 shows the median earnings and unemployment rates for workers at various levels of educational attainment.

Taken together, higher earnings and more regular employment amount to large differences in income over a lifetime.

Higher earnings for workers who have a college degree are part of a long term trend. Even when adjusted for inflation, the wages of college-educated workers have been rising over the past decade. (See chart 3.) Moreover, the earnings for the college-educated workers have been increasing faster than the earnings for workers who do not have a bachelor's degree.

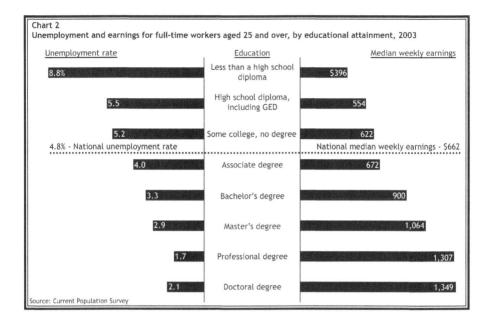

Chart 2
Unemployment and earnings for full-time workers aged 25 and over, by educational attainment, 2003

Unemployment rate	Education	Median weekly earnings
8.8%	Less than a high school diploma	$396
5.5	High school diploma, including GED	554
5.2	Some college, no degree	622
4.8% - National unemployment rate		National median weekly earnings - $662
4.0	Associate degree	672
3.3	Bachelor's degree	900
2.9	Master's degree	1,064
1.7	Professional degree	1,307
2.1	Doctoral degree	1,349

Source: Current Population Survey

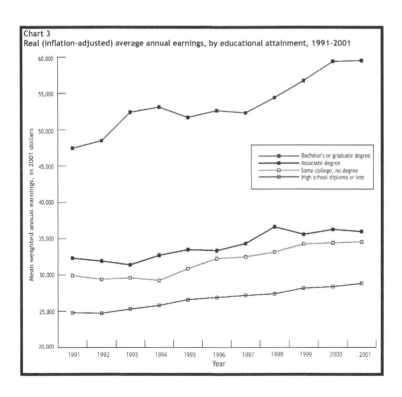

Chart 3
Real (inflation-adjusted) average annual earnings, by educational attainment, 1991-2001

Legend:
- Bachelor's or graduate degree
- Associate degree
- Some college, no degree
- High school diploma or less

(Y-axis: Mean weighted annual earnings, in 2001 dollars; X-axis: Year, 1991–2001)

The trouble with averages

Statistics about college graduates paint a rosy—and numerically accurate—picture of overall employment. But the data are based on college graduates as a whole. For every graduate who earns more than the median, another earns less. And while unemployment rates are low overall, many college graduates sometimes have trouble finding work, especially if they wait for the type of job they want.

The career prospects of individuals depend on many factors besides having a college degree. These factors include the local job market, the type of degree they have, their level of experience and skill, and the occupation they are trying to enter.

Openings and Where They Will Be

Between 2002 and 2012, BLS projects 56 million job openings for workers who are entering an occupation for the first time. Of these, at least 14 million are expected to be filled by college-educated workers. More than half of these openings are expected to come from the need to fill newly created jobs.

The remaining openings for college-educated workers are projected to come from the need to replace workers who leave an occupation permanently. With many of today's college-educated workers poised to retire, replacement needs are expected to be great, especially in large occupations.

In some occupations, most workers have bachelor's or graduate degrees. In other occupations, education levels are more varied.

Many of the occupations that are expected to have the most openings for college graduates are in the business, computers and engineering, education, counseling, and healthcare fields.

"Pure college" occupations

For this analysis, it is assumed that each future job opening will be for a college-educated worker. In these "pure college" occupations, at least 60 percent of current workers aged 25-44 have a bachelor's or graduate degree, fewer than 20 percent have a high school diploma or less education, and fewer than 20 percent have some college courses but less education than a bachelor's degree. Even if some workers do not have a bachelor's or graduate degree, all openings are counted as being for college-educated workers because that most accurately reflects the job market new workers face...

BLS projects that pure-college occupations will provide about 6.8 million openings over the 2002-12 decade for college graduates who are entering an occupation for the first time. Chart 4 shows the 20 pure-college occupations expected to provide the most openings during the projections decade. Like nearly all pure-college occupations, all but one of the occupations on the chart have earnings above $27,380, the 2002 median for all workers.

Despite high numbers of job openings, jobseekers can face strong competition when trying to enter some occupations, such as public relations specialists or management analysts. Because these occupations offer high earnings and prestige and because workers can qualify with many different college majors, the number of qualified workers who want these jobs could be greater than the number of openings. Analyses of job competition are possible for a few occupations, ones for which there is anecdotal evidence or for which other data exist. To qualify for many of the occupations shown on chart 4, workers need more than a bachelor's degree. In three of the occupations—lawyers, physicians and surgeons, and pharmacists—a professional degree is required. Similarly, physical therapists now train for their occupation only in a master's or doctoral degree program.

In other occupations, educational requirements are more flexible. About one-fourth of management analysts have a master's degree, for example, but many analysts do not have education beyond a bachelor's degree. School teachers, too, often have a graduate degree, but many teachers earn that degree after they begin their careers; while employed, they take graduate-level courses to gain skills, qualify for higher salaries, and maintain certification. In many occupations, employment and advancement opportunities improve with attainment of a graduate degree, even when one is not required for career entry.

Education level often determines the type of work a person can do within an occupation. Psychologists, for example, usually need a doctoral degree to do

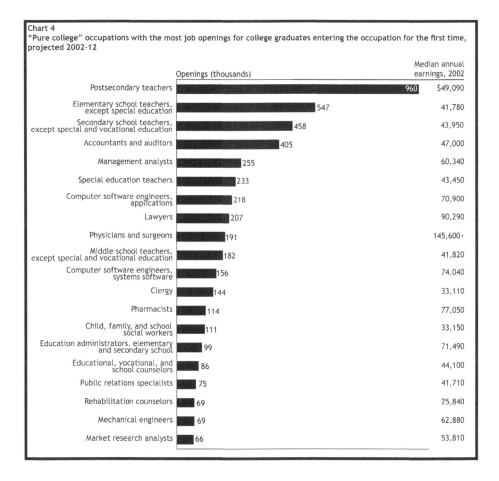

Chart 4
"Pure college" occupations with the most job openings for college graduates entering the occupation for the first time, projected 2002-12

	Openings (thousands)	Median annual earnings, 2002
Postsecondary teachers	960	$49,090
Elementary school teachers, except special education	547	41,780
Secondary school teachers, except special and vocational education	458	43,950
Accountants and auditors	405	47,000
Management analysts	255	60,340
Special education teachers	233	43,450
Computer software engineers, applications	218	70,900
Lawyers	207	90,290
Physicians and surgeons	191	145,600+
Middle school teachers, except special and vocational education	182	41,820
Computer software engineers, systems software	156	74,040
Clergy	144	33,110
Pharmacists	114	77,050
Child, family, and school social workers	111	33,150
Education administrators, elementary and secondary school	99	71,490
Educational, vocational, and school counselors	86	44,100
Public relations specialists	75	41,710
Rehabilitation counselors	69	25,840
Mechanical engineers	69	62,880
Market research analysts	66	53,810

independent, clinical work, but some school psychologists do not need this level of education. Social workers can get some jobs with a bachelor's degree, but to work in a clinical setting, they often need a graduate degree.

"Mixed education" occupations

Many college graduates work in occupations that employ workers who have a variety of education levels. Over the 2002-12 decade, about 23 million openings are projected to be in occupations in which the number of college-educated workers is significant—20 percent or more—but for which college is not the only level of education workers have. For example, of the 1.1 million job openings projected for registered nurses, over 650,000 are projected to be filled by bachelor's or graduate degree holders based on current educational attainment patterns. Overall, of the 23 million job openings in these "mixed education" occupations, BLS expects 7.5 million to be filled by college graduates.

Chart 5 shows the mixed education occupations that are expected to provide the most openings over the projections decade for college graduates who are entering an occupation for the first time. In several of these occupations, such as registered nurses, police and sheriff's patrol officers, and wholesale and manufacturing sales representatives, the education levels of workers have been rising. When hiring workers, some employers prefer their new employees to be college graduates, even though many existing workers do not have a degree.

Sometimes, as is often the case for preschool teachers and social and human service assistants, having a degree benefits workers beyond helping them get the job. It may qualify workers to take on more complex tasks in the occupation, for example, or increase workers' opportunities for advancement and responsibility.

In other occupations—such as retail salesperson and customer service representatives—workers from every education level are represented even though most qualify after a few weeks or months of on-the-job training. A degree is not required, and many college graduates choose these occupations for reasons unrelated to education or training, such as plentiful opportunities or flexible hours.

Mixed-education occupations make it difficult to measure with certainty the demand for college graduates. Defining a college-level occupation is highly subjective. Some openings in an occupation might require a degree; for other openings, a degree might be useful; and for still other openings, a degree might not make much of a difference.

Occupations with increasing demand: Trends and themes

As a whole, occupations that employ mostly college graduates are expected to gain new jobs faster than other types of occupations. Between 2002 and 2012, pure-college occupations are projected to grow 22 percent overall, considerably faster than the 15-percent average growth projected for all occupations. Eighteen of the 20 pure-college occupations in chart 4 are projected to grow faster than the 15-percent average for all occupations.

Looking at job growth is important because occupations that are gaining jobs quickly are, in effect, showing rapidly increasing demand for workers. Some of

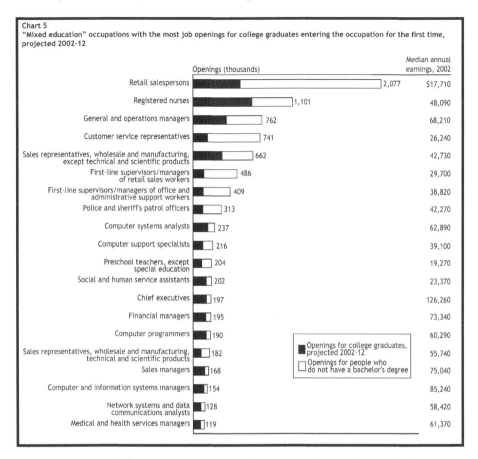

Chart 5
"Mixed education" occupations with the most job openings for college graduates entering the occupation for the first time, projected 2002-12

	Openings (thousands)	Median annual earnings, 2002
Retail salespersons	2,077	$17,710
Registered nurses	1,101	48,090
General and operations managers	762	68,210
Customer service representatives	741	26,240
Sales representatives, wholesale and manufacturing, except technical and scientific products	662	42,730
First-line supervisors/managers of retail sales workers	486	29,700
First-line supervisors/managers of office and administrative support workers	409	38,820
Police and sheriff's patrol officers	313	42,270
Computer systems analysts	237	62,890
Computer support specialists	216	39,100
Preschool teachers, except special education	204	19,270
Social and human service assistants	202	23,370
Chief executives	197	126,260
Financial managers	195	73,340
Computer programmers	190	60,290
Sales representatives, wholesale and manufacturing, technical and scientific products	182	55,740
Sales managers	168	75,040
Computer and information systems managers	154	85,240
Network systems and data communications analysts	128	58,420
Medical and health services managers	119	61,370

■ Openings for college graduates, projected 2002-12
□ Openings for people who do not have a bachelor's degree

the economic trends that are creating growth in pure-college and mixed-education occupations are described below by career field.

Business, finance, and sales. The growing complexity of business is expected to increase the demand for college graduates in business and financial occupations. More workers will be needed to manage rising personal incomes, increased regulation of financial activity, and growing competition among businesses.

Sales occupations are expected to grow along with the overall economy. Although numerous workers in these occupations do not have a college degree, many others do. Having a degree is especially valued in occupations involving sales of complex scientific or technical products.

Computers and engineering. The demand for new products and new technology is expected to continue to drive growth in computer and engineering occupations. Occupations in emerging engineering specialties, including biotechnology and environmental engineering, are expected to gain jobs rapidly over the projections decade. However, these specialties are expected to remain small and provide fewer openings than larger engineering specialties, such as mechanical and computer engineering.

Counseling, social service and psychology. Numerous social trends are projected to increase the number of counselors, social workers, and psychologists needed over the 2002-12 decade. More schools are hiring trained counselors. At the same time, more people are seeking counseling for family problems, substance abuse, and mental disorders. And to ease overcrowding at prisons, many offenders are being sent instead to rehabilitation facilities—where counselors, social workers, and psychologists are employed to assist them.

Education. Most opportunities in the field of education will come from the need to replace the many teachers and administrators who are expected to retire over the 2002-12 decade. But additional positions are projected because of efforts to reduce class sizes and because of increasing enrollment at colleges and universities.

Healthcare. As the population ages, the need for healthcare will increase, fueling the need for more healthcare practitioners. Moreover, improvements in medical technology will create more medical and rehabilitative treatments. Those treatments are prescribed and often administered by workers who have a college degree.

How These Numbers Were Developed

There are many ways to measure job outlook by education, and each method has both strengths and limitations. This analysis focuses on future job openings because job openings show how many new workers will be able to enter an occupation.

Deciding which job openings will be filled by college graduates was more complicated. Counselors and jobseekers often ask which occupations are "college level." But answering that question is difficult because workers in most occupations come from many different educational backgrounds. This analysis used the education levels of current workers as an objective way to account for this variation.

Like any analysis based on projections and estimates, however, this one has limitations to its accuracy. Understanding these limitations will help readers to better use the results.

Methods used

To estimate the demand for college graduates between 2002 and 2012, BLS analysts got specific. First, they projected the number of job openings for workers entering each of more than 500 occupations over the decade. Next, analysts estimated how many of those openings would be filled by college graduates.

Measuring job openings. Job openings come from two sources: The need to fill newly created jobs and the need to replace workers who retire or leave an occupation permanently for other reasons.

To estimate the number of newly created jobs, analysts projected how much each occupation would grow or decline between 2002 and 2012. An occupation might gain jobs for many reasons. Sometimes, the demand for a specific good or service creates the need for additional workers in an occupation, such as when an increased use of computer software creates a greater need for software engineers. The way a good service is provided can also lead to more jobs in an occupation.

Rather than relying solely on teachers and administrators to guide and educate students, for example, more schools are hiring counselors and psychologists, creating more openings for those workers. In the same way, a decrease in the demand for a good or service or a change in production methods can reduce the number of jobs and openings in an occupation.

The second source of job openings is replacement needs. To estimate how many workers will need to be replaced during the projections decade, BLS analysts studied the ages of current workers and the length of time that workers in each occupation usually remain. In occupations that require high levels of training, workers tend to stay longer. In other occupations, especially those that have shorter trainings periods, workers tend to leave or retire more quickly.

Job openings for college graduates. After analysts projected the number of job openings for workers entering an occupation, they estimated how many of those openings would be for college graduates. Using information from 2000, 2001, and 2002 Current Population Survey data, analysts classified current workers' educational attainment into one of three categories: A high school diploma or less, some college but no bachelor's or graduate degree, or a bachelor's or graduate degree. If at least 20 percent of workers in an occupation belonged to a given educational category, that level was deemed significant. Expected openings were divided among each of these significant education categories, according to how common each category was.

For example, the occupation of administrative services managers includes workers in each educational category. About 23 percent have a high school diploma or less, 37 percent have some college coursework or an associate degree but no bachelor's degree, and 41 percent have a bachelor's or graduate degree. Projected openings were divided among the education categories using those percentages.

For some occupations, a bachelor's or graduate degree was the only education level common enough to be significant. At least 60 percent of workers in the occupation were college graduates. And fewer than 20 percent of workers belonged to the other two educational categories. In these 115 "pure college" occupations, every projected opening was considered to be for a college graduate.

In addition to using the three educational attainment categories, this article provides specific information about the types of degrees commonly required in some occupations. This type of information comes from the occupational analyses conducted for the *Occupational Outlook Handbook*.

Earnings data. This analysis uses earnings data from two surveys: The Current Population Survey and the Occupational Employment Statistics survey. Earnings data from the Current Population Survey, which includes information about workers' education levels, were used to compare earnings by education. Earnings data from the Occupational Employment Statistics survey, which is more comprehensive, provide median earnings for an occupation as a world.

The two surveys are different. The Current Population Survey is a household survey that asks workers themselves to give earnings, occupational, and other types of information; it includes self-employed workers. The Occupational Employment Statistics survey, an establishment survey, asks employers to provide earnings and occupational information about their workers; it does not include the self-employed.

Limitations of the data

To measure job openings for college graduates, BLS analysts needed to make assumptions about the future. First, analysts assumed that the education levels in each occupation would remain roughly the same over the 2002-12 decade. In reality, the educational characteristics of some occupations change over time. Many occupations—such as registered nurses and police officers—have had a gradual increase in the number of workers who have a bachelor's degree.

Analysts also ignored education levels that were uncommon in an occupation; as stated previously, at least 20 percent of workers in an occupation had to have a given level of education for it to be considered significant. So, for example, even though almost 17 percent of engineering technicians have a college degree, none of that occupation's projected openings were counted as openings for college graduates.

Another limitation of this study is that it focuses on the number of job openings projected in an occupation. But job openings give only a partial view of the prospects that workers can expect. The number of people who will compete for those openings is also important. For most occupations, however, BLS analysts do not have enough information to analyze the competition for jobs.

Finally, the accuracy of this study is limited by its use of survey data. Surveys are always subject to some error because not every worker is counted and because the information gathered is sometimes incorrect. In addition, the education levels of many occupations could not be determined with statistical accuracy because the number of workers surveyed was too small. In those cases, analysts substituted the education levels of similar occupations or groups of occupations that had larger numbers of workers.

Even with its assumptions and limitations, however, there is evidence that estimating future job openings using the analysis described here produces accurate results. When existing jobs are separated into educational categories in such a way, the results closely match current numbers.

 Reflection Questions

1. In this reading the average earnings of individuals with a college education are compared with those of individuals who did not go to college. It also points out that college graduates have less unemployment. Did this surprise you? Why or why not?
2. Can you think of an instance when it would not be "valuable" to attend college?
3. What do the authors mean by "pure college" occupations? In the past, these same jobs may have been held by individuals without a college degree. Why

do you think this has changed? Do you agree that now these jobs should require a degree?

4. Other than monetary, what other benefits might one realize from going to college?

5. In the future, the jobs that are now in demand might change. What might account for this change?

Work and Personal Satisfaction

Martin E. P. Seligman

Seligman is the Fox Leadership Professor of Psychology at the University of Pennsylvania where he has pioneered the study of "Positive Psychology." Unlike some past practices in psychology that have focused on mental illness and abnormality, Positive Psychology studies the ways happy and mentally healthy people maintain their happiness and mental health. Thus, Dr. Seligman studies positive emotion, positive character traits, and positive institutions. When, in 1996, he was elected President of the American Psychological Association, by the largest vote in modem history, his goal was to join practice and science together to "make the world a happier place." His best-selling books include *Learned Optimism* (1991), and *Authentic Happiness* (2002). For more information on his ideas and to take the "Signature Strengths" Survey referred to in this reading visit www.authentichappiness.org.

Work life is undergoing a sea change in the wealthiest nations. Money, amazingly, is losing its power. The stark findings about life satisfaction detailed in Chapter 4—that beyond the safety net, more money adds little or nothing to subjective well-being—are starting to sink in. While real income in America has risen 16 percent in the last thirty years, the percentage of people who describe themselves as "very happy" has fallen from 36 to 29 percent. "Money really cannot buy happiness," declared the *New York Times*. But when employees catch up with the *Times* and figure out that raises, promotions, and overtime pay buy not one whit of increased life satisfaction, what then? Why will a qualified individual choose one job over another? What will cause an employee to be steadfastly loyal to the company he or she works for? For what incentive will a worker pour heart and soul into making a quality product?

Our economy is rapidly changing from a money economy to a satisfaction economy. These trends go up and down (when jobs are scarcer, personal satisfaction has a somewhat lesser weight; when jobs are abundant, personal satisfaction counts for more), but the trend for two decades is decidedly in favor of personal satisfaction. Law is now the most highly paid profession in America, having surpassed medicine during the 1990s. Yet the major New York law firms now spend more on retention than on recruitment, as their young associates—and even the partners—are leaving law in droves for work that makes them happier. The lure of a lifetime of great riches at the end of several years of grueling eighty-hour weeks as a lowly associate has lost much of its power. The newly minted coin of this realm is life satisfaction. Millions of Americans are staring at their jobs and asking, "Does my work have to be this unsatisfying? What can I do about it?" My answer is that your work can be much more satisfying than it is now, and that by using your signature strengths at work more often, you should be able to recraft your job to make it so.

This chapter lays out the idea that to maximize work satisfaction, you need to use the signature strengths you found in the last chapter on the job, preferably every day. This is just as deep a truth for secretaries and for lawyers and for nurses as it is for CEOs. Recrafting your job to deploy your strengths and virtues every day not only makes work more enjoyable, but transmogrifies a routine job or a stalled career into a calling. A calling is the most satisfying form of work because, as a gratification, it is done for its own sake rather than for the material benefits it brings. Enjoying the resulting state of flow on the job will soon, I predict, overtake material reward as the principal reason for working. Corporations that promote this state for their employees will overtake corporations that rely only on monetary reward. Even more significantly, with life and liberty now covered minimally well, we are about to witness a politics that goes beyond the safety net and takes the pursuit of happiness very seriously indeed.

I'm sure you are skeptical. What, money lose its power in a capitalistic economy? Dream on! I would remind you about another "impossible" sea change that swept education forty years ago. When I went to school (a military one at that), and for generations before, education was based on humiliation. The dunce cap, the paddle, and the F were the big guns in the arsenal of teachers. These went the way of the wooly mammoth and the dodo, and did so astonishingly quickly. They disappeared because educators discovered a better route to learning: rewarding strengths, kindly mentoring, delving deeply into one subject rather than memorizing a panoply of facts, emotional attachment of the student to a teacher or a topic, and individualized attention. There is also a better route to high productivity than money, and that is what this chapter is about. "Royal flush!" I shouted into Bob's ear as I hovered over his body. "Seven card stud, high-low!" He didn't move. I lifted his muscular right leg by the ankle and let it drop with a thud on the bed. No reaction.

"Fold!" I shouted. Nothing.

I had played poker with Bob Miller every Tuesday night for the past twenty-five years. Bob was a runner; when he retired as a teacher of American history, he took a year off to run around the world. He once told me he would sooner lose his eyes than his legs. I had been surprised when, on a crisp October morning two weeks before, he showed up at my house with his collection of tennis rackets and presented them to my children. Even at eighty-one, he was a fanatical tennis player, and giving away his rackets was disquieting, even ominous.

October was his favorite month. He would run through the Adirondacks, never missing a run up Gore Mountain, religiously return to Philadelphia each Tuesday evening at 7:30 sharp, and then run off before dawn the next morning for the gold- and red-leaved mountains. This time he didn't make it. A truck hit him during the early hours of the morning in Lancaster County, Pennsylvania, and now he was lying unconscious in the Coatesville hospital. He had been in a coma for three days.

"Can we have your consent to take Mr. Miller off life support?" his neurologist asked me. "You are, according to his attorney, his closest friend, and we haven't been able to reach any of his relatives." As the enormity of what she was saying slowly seeped in, I noticed an overweight man in hospital whites out of the corner of my eye. He had removed the bedpan, and then he unobtrusively started to adjust the pictures on the walls. He eyed a snow scene critically, straightened it, and then stepped back and eyed it again, dissatisfied. I had noticed him doing much the same thing the day before, and I was happy to let my mind drift away from the subject at hand and to turn my attention to this strange orderly.

"I can see you need to think this over," the neurologist said, noticing my glazed look, and she left. I pitched myself into the lone chair and watched the orderly. He took the snow scene down and put the calendar from the back wall in its place. He eyed that critically, took it down, and then reached into a large brown grocery bag. From his shopping bag emerged a Monet water-lily print. Up it went where the snow scene and the calendar had been. Out came two large Winslow Homer seascapes. These he affixed to the wall beyond the foot of Bob's bed. Finally he went to the wall on Bob's right side. Down came a black and white photo of San Francisco, and up went a color photo of the Peace rose.

"May I ask what you're doing?" I inquired mildly.

"My job? I'm an orderly on this floor," he answered. "But I bring in new prints and photos every week. You see, I'm responsible for the health of all these patients. Take Mr. Miller here. He hasn't woken up since they brought him in, but when he does, I want to make sure he sees beautiful things right away."

This orderly at the Coatesville hospital (preoccupied, I never learned his name) did not define his work as the emptying of bedpans or the swabbing of trays, but as protecting the health of his patients and procuring objects to fill this difficult time of their lives with beauty. He may have held a lowly job, but he recrafted it into a high calling.

How does a person frame work in relation to the rest of life? Scholars distinguish three-kinds of "work orientation": a job, a career, and a calling. You do a *job* for the paycheck at the end of the week. You do not seek other rewards from it. It is just a means to another end (like leisure, or supporting your family), and when the wage stops, you quit. A career entails a deeper personal investment in work. You mark your achievements through money, but also through advancement. Each promotion brings you higher prestige and more power, as well as a raise. Law firm associates become partners, assistant professors become associate professors, and middle managers advance to vice-presidencies. When the promotions stop—when you "top out"—alienation starts, and you begin to look elsewhere for gratification and meaning.

A *calling* (or vocation) is a passionate commitment to work for its own sake. Individuals with a calling see their work as contributing to the greater good, to something larger than they are, and hence the religious connotation is entirely appropriate. The work is fulfilling in its own right, without regard for money or for advancement. When the money stops and the promotions end, the work goes on. Traditionally, callings were reserved to very prestigious and rarified work—priests, supreme court justices, physicians, and scientists. But there has been an important discovery in this field: any job can become a calling, and any calling can become a job. "A physician who views the work as a Job and is simply interested in making a good income does not have a Calling, while a garbage collector who sees the work as making the world a cleaner, healthier place could have a Calling."

Amy Wrzesniewski (pronounced rez-NESkee), a professor of business at New York University, and her colleagues are the scientists who made this important discovery. They studied twenty-eight hospital cleaners, each having the same official job description. The cleaners who see their job as a calling craft their work to make it meaningful. They see themselves as critical in healing patients, they time their work to be maximally efficient, they anticipate the needs of the doctors and the nurses in order to allow them to spend more of their time healing, and they add tasks to their assignments (such as brightening patients' days, just as the Coatesville orderly did). The cleaners in the job group see their work as simply cleaning up rooms.

Let's now find out how you see your own work.

Work-Life Survey

Please read all three paragraphs below. Indicate how much you are like A, B, or C.

Ms. A works primarily to earn enough money to support her life outside of her job. If she was financially secure, she would no longer continue with her current line of work, but would really rather do something else instead. Ms. A's job is basically a necessity of life, a lot like breathing or sleeping. She often wishes the time would pass more quickly at work. She greatly anticipates weekends and vacations. If Ms. A lived her life over again, she probably would not go into the same line of work. She would not encourage her friends and children to enter her line of work. Ms. A is very eager to retire.

Ms. B basically enjoys her work, but does not expect to be in her current job five yeas from now. Instead, she plans to move on to a better, higher-level job. She has several goals for her future pertaining to the positions she would eventually like to hold. Sometimes her work seems like a waste of time, but she knows she must do sufficiently well in her current position in order to move on. Ms. B can't wait to get a promotion. For her, a promotion means recognition of her good work, and is a sign of her success in competition with her coworkers.

Ms. C's work is one of the most important parts of her life. She is very pleased that she is in this line of work. Because what she does for a living is a vital part of who she is, it is one of the first things she tells people about herself. She tends to take her work home with her, and on vacations, too. The majority of her friends are from her place of employment, and she belongs to several organizations and clubs pertaining to her work. Ms. C feels good about her work because she loves it, and because she thinks it makes the world a better place. She would encourage her friends and children to enter her line of work. Ms. C would be pretty upset if she were forced to stop working, and she is not particularly looking forward to retirement.

How much are you like Ms. A?

Very much____ Somewhat____ A little____ Not at all_____

How much are you like Ms. B?

Very much____ Somewhat____ A little____Not at all_____

How much are you like Ms. C?

Very much____Somewhat____A little_____ Not at all____

Now please rate your satisfaction with your job on a scale of 1 to 7, where 1 = completely dissatisfied, 4 = neither satisfied or dissatisfied, and 7 = completely satisfied.____

Scoring: The first paragraph describes a Job, the second a Career and the third a Calling. To score the relevance of each paragraph, very much=3, somewhat=2, a little=1 and not at all = 0

If you see your work as a calling like Ms. C in the third paragraph (with a rating of that paragraph 2 or higher), and if you are satisfied with work (with your satisfaction 5 or greater), more power to you. If not, you should know how others have recrafted their work. The same cleavage between jobs and callings that holds among hospital cleaners also holds among secretaries, engineers, nurses, kitchen workers, and hair-cutters. The key is not finding the right job, it is finding a job you can make right through recrafting.

Haircutters

Cutting another person's hair has always been rather more than a mechanical task. Over the last two decades, many haircutters in the big cities of America have recrafted their jobs to highlight its intimate, interpersonal nature. The hairdresser expands the relational boundaries by first making personal disclosures about herself. She then asks her clients personal questions and cold-shoulders clients who refuse to disclose. Unpleasant clients are "fired." The job has been recrafted into a more enjoyable one by adding intimacy.

Nurses

The profit-oriented system of hospital care that has evolved recently in America puts pressure on nurses to make their care routinized and mechanical. This is anathema to the tradition of nursing. Some nurses have reacted by crafting a pocket of care around their patients. These nurses pay close attention to the patient's world and tell the rest of the team about these seemingly unimportant details. They ask family members about the patients' lives, involve them in the process of recovery, and use this to boost the morale of the patients.

Kitchen Workers

More and more restaurant cooks have transformed their identity from preparers of food to culinary artists. These chefs try to make the food as beautiful possible. In composing a meal, they use shortcuts to change the number of tasks, but they also concentrate on the dish and the meal as a whole rather than the mechanics of the elements of each dish. They have recrafted their job from sometimes mechanical to one that is streamlined and aesthetic.

There is something deeper going on in these examples than activist members of particular professions merely making their otherwise dull jobs less mechanical and routine, more social, more holistic, and more aesthetically appealing. Rather, I believe that the key to recrafting their jobs is to make them into callings. Being called to a line of work, however, is more than just hearing a voice proclaiming that the world would be served well by your entering a particular field. The good of humankind would be served by more relief workers for refugees, more designers of educational software, more counterterrorists, more nanotechnologists, and more truly caring waiters, for that matter. But none of these may call to you, because a calling must engage your signature strengths. Conversely, passions like stamp collecting or tango dancing may use your signature strengths, but they are not callings—which, by definition, require service to a greater good in addition to passionate commitment.

> *"He's drunk and mean," whispered a frightened Sophia to her eight-year-old brother, Dominick (who has asked me not to use his real name). "Look what he's doing to Mommy out there."*
>
> *Sophie and Dom were scrubbing the dishes in the cramped kitchen of their parents' small restaurant. The year was 1947, the place was Wheeling, West Virginia, and the life was hard-scrabble. Dom's father had come home from the war a broken man, and the family was toiling together from dawn to midnight just to get by.*
>
> *Out at the cash register, a drunken customer—unshaven, foul-mouthed, and huge, at least to Dom—was hulking over his mother, complaining about the food. "That tasted more like rat than pork. And the beer. . ." he shouted angrily as he grabbed the woman's shoulder.*
>
> *Without thinking, Dom propelled himself out of the kitchen and stood protectively between his mother and the customer. "How can I help you, sir?"*
>
> *". . . was warm and the potatoes were cold . . ."*
>
> *"You're absolutely right, and my mother and I are very sorry. You see it's only the four of us trying our best, and tonight we just could not keep up. We really want you to come back, so you will see that we can do a better job for you. Please let us pick up your check now and offer you a bottle of wine on us when you return to us again."*
>
> *"Well, it's hard to argue with this little kid . . . thanks." And off he went, very pleased with himself and not displeased with the restaurant.*

Thirty years later, Dominick confided to me that after that encounter his parents always gave him the difficult customers to wait on—and that he loved doing it. From 1947 on, Dom's parents knew that they had a prodigy in the family. Dom possessed one signature strength precociously and in extraordinary degree: social intelligence. He could read the desires, needs, and emotions of others with uncanny accuracy. He could pull exactly the right words to say out of the air like magic. When situations became more heated, Dom became cooler and more skilled, while others would-be mediators typically aggravated the situation. Dom's parents nurtured this strength, and Dom began to lead his life around it, carving out a vocation that called on his social intelligence each day.

With this level of social intelligence, Dom might have become a great head-waiter, or diplomat, or director of personnel for a major corporation. But he has two other signature strengths: love of learning and leadership. He designed his life's work to exploit this combination. Today, at age sixty-two, Dominick is the most skilled diplomat that I know in the American scientific community. He was one of America's leading professors of sociology, but was nabbed as provost by an Ivy League university when he was only in his late thirties. He then became a university president.

His almost invisible hand can be detected in many of the major movements in European and American social science, and I think of him as the Henry Kissinger of academia. When you are in Dominick's presence, he makes you feel that you are the most important person in his world, and remarkably, he does this without any tinge of ingratiation that might otherwise arouse your distrust. Whenever

I have had unusually tricky human-relations problems at work, it is his advice
I seek out. What transforms Dominick's work from a very successful career to
a calling is the fact that what he does summons the use of his three signature
strengths virtually every day.

If you can find a way to use your signature strengths at work often, and you
also see your work as contributing to the greater good, you have a calling. Your
job is transformed from a burdensome means into a gratification. The best understood aspect of happiness during the workday is having flow—feeling completely
at home within yourself when you work.

Over the last three decades, Mike Csikszentmihalyi, whom you met in Chapter
7, has moved this elusive state all the way from the darkness into the penumbra
of science and then to the very borders of the light, for everyone to understand
and even practice. Flow, you will remember, is a positive emotion about the present with no conscious thought or feeling attached. Mike has found out who has
it a lot (working-class and upper-middle-class teenagers, for example) and who
doesn't have much of it (very poor and very rich teenagers). He has delineated
the conditions under which it occurs, and he has linked these to satisfying work.
Flow cannot be sustained through an entire eight-hour workday; rather, under
the best of circumstances, flow visits you for a few minutes on several occasions.
Flow occurs when the challenges you face perfectly mesh with your abilities
to meet them. When you recognize that these abilities include not merely your
talents but your strengths and virtues, the implications for what work to choose
or how to recraft it become clear.

Having any choice at all about what work we do, and about how we go about
that work, is something new under the sun. For scores of millennia, children
were just little apprentices to what their parents did, preparing to take over that
work as adults. From time out of memory until today, by age two, an Inuit boy
has a toy bow to play with, so that by age four he is able to shoot a ptarmigan;
by age six, a rabbit; and by puberty, a seal or even a caribou. His sister follows
the prescribed path for girls: she joins other females in cooking, curing hides,
sewing, and minding babies.

This pattern changed starting in sixteenth-century Europe. Young people in
droves begin to abandon the farms and flock to the cities to take advantage of
the burgeoning wealth and other temptations of city life. Over the course of three
centuries girls as young as twelve and boys from age fourteen migrated to the city
for service jobs: laundresses, porters, or domestic cleaning. The magnetic attraction
of the city for young people was action and choice, and not the least significant
of the choices was about a line of work. As the cities expanded and diversified,
the opportunity for myriad different lines of work expanded in lockstep. The
agricultural parent-child job cycle shattered; upward (and downward) mobility
increased, and class barriers were strained to the breaking point.

Fast forward to twenty-first century America: Life is all about choice. There
are hundreds of brands of beer. There are literally millions of different cars available, taking all the permutations of accessories into account—no more are the
black Model T, the white icebox, and jeans only in dark blue. Have you, like me,
stood paralyzed in front of the stunning variety on the breakfast cereal shelves
lately, unable to find your own brand of choice? I just wanted Quaker Oats, the
old-fashioned shot-from-a-gun kind, but I couldn't find it.

Freedom of choice has been good politics for two centuries and is now a big business, not just for consumer goods but for structuring the very jobs themselves. In the low-unemployment economy America has been enjoying for twenty years, the majority of young people emerging from college have considerable choice about their careers. Adolescence, a concept not yet invented and so unavailable to the twelve- and fourteen-year-olds of the sixteenth century, is now a prolonged dance about the two most momentous choices in life: which mate, and which job. Few young people now adopt one of their parents' lines of work. More than 60 percent continue their education after high school, and college education—which used to be considered rounding, liberal, and gentlemanly—is now openly centered on vocational choices like business or banking or medicine (and less openly centered on the choice of a mate).

Work can be prime time for flow because, unlike leisure, it builds many of the conditions of flow into itself. There are usually clear goals and rules of performance. There is frequent feedback about how well or poorly we are doing. Work usually encourages concentration and minimizes distractions, and in many cases it matches the difficulties to your talents and even your strengths. As a result, people often feel more engaged at work than they do at home.

John Hope Franklin, the distinguished historian, said, "You could say that I worked every minute of my life, or you could say with equal justice that I never worked a day. I have always subscribed to the expression 'Thank God it's Friday,' because to me Friday means I can work for the next two days without interruption." It misses the mark to see Professor Franklin as a workaholic. Rather, he gives voice to a common sentiment among high-powered academics and businesspeople that is, worth looking at closely. Franklin spent his Mondays through Fridays as a professor, and there is every reason to think he was good at it: teaching, administration, scholarship, and colleagueship all went very well. These call on some of Franklin's strengths—kindness and leadership—but they do not call enough on his signature strengths: originality and love of learning. There is more flow at home, reading and writing, than at work because the opportunity to use his very highest strengths is greatest on weekends.

The inventor and holder of hundreds of patents, Jacob Rabinow at age eighty-three told Mike Csikszentdmlyi, "You have to be willing to pull the ideas because you're interested . . . [P]eople like myself like to do it. It's fun to come up with an idea, and if nobody wants it, I don't give a damn. It's just fun to come up with something strange and different." The major discovery about flow at work is not the unsurprising fact that people with great jobs—inventors, sculptors, supreme court justices, and historians—experience a lot of it. It is rather that the rest of us experience it as well, and that we can recraft our more mundane work to enjoy it more frequently.

To measure the amount of flow, Mike pioneered the experience sampling method (ESM), which is now used widely around the world. As mentioned in Chapter 7, the ESM gives people a pager or Palm Pilot that goes off at random times (two hours apart on average), all day and all evening. When the signal sounds, the person writes down what she is doing, where she is, and whom she is with, then rates the contents of her consciousness numerically: how happy she is, how much she is concentrating, how high her self-esteem is, and so on. The focus of this research is the condition under which flow happens.

Americans surprisingly have considerably more flow at work than in leisure time. In one study of 824 American teenagers, Mike dissected free time into its active versus passive components. Games and hobbies are active and produce flow 39 percent of the time, and produce the negative emotion of apathy 17 percent of the time. Watching television and listening to music, in contrast, are passive and produce flow only 14 percent of the time while producing apathy 37 percent of the time. The mood state Americans are in, on average, when watching television is mildly depressed. So there is a great deal to be said for active as opposed to passive use of our free time. As Mike reminds us, "Gregor Mendel did his famous genetic experiments as a hobby; Benjamin Franklin was led by interest, not a job description, to grind lenses and experiment with lightning rods; [and] Emily Dickinson wrote her superb poetry to create order in her own life."

In an economy of surplus and little unemployment what job a qualified person chooses will depend increasingly on how much flow they engage at work, and less on small (or even sizable) differences in pay. How to choose or recraft your work to produce more flow is not a mystery. Flow occurs when the challenges—big ones as well as the daily issues that you face—mesh well with your abilities. My recipe for more flow is as follows:

- Identify your signature strengths.
- Choose work that lets you use them every day.
- Recraft your present work to use your signature strengths more.
- If you are the employer, choose employees whose signature strengths mesh with the work they will do. If you are a manager, make room to allow employees to recraft the work within the bounds of your goals.

What Students Must Know to Succeed in the 21st Century

Donna Uchida

Donna Uchida is a communications officer for Levi Strauss in San Francisco. The Council of 55 to which she refers in this essay is a group of advisers from varied fields— education, business, government, psychology, sociology, demography, and others. These experts participated in a study that asked, "What do students need to know in order to succeed in the 21st century?" This reading summarizes their conclusions and relates them to the academic content that students need to master for success in the foreseeable future.

What will students need to know to be well-educated for the 21st century? According to the Council of 55, here are some essential elements necessary to the content of education:

1. Use of math, logic, and reasoning skills; functional and operational literacy; and an understanding of statistics. Jan Mokros, writing in *Math Textbooks: Where Is Math?*, notes that the term "mathematics" comes from "a family of Greek words denoting to learn or search for meaning." Mokros objects to many math textbooks because "students who use them never have a chance to gather, describe, summarize, and interpret real data for themselves."

"Math must also be viewed as a language and as a way of communicating or making sense of the world," according to Stephanie Pace Marshall, executive director of the Illinois Mathematics and Science Academy. "Math is a language of relationships, patterns, and connection," she adds. "This is the mathematics we must teach."

The National Council of Teachers of Mathematics has led a pioneering effort to establish standards for the teaching of math. As with any standards, they should guide schools in developing and judging the content, teaching, and evaluation of math curriculum. An understanding of math concepts, computation, and problem solving is essential to a truly literate person.

Math is one way to generate thinking and reasoning skills among students. Performance-based assessments that ask students to reveal how they arrived at answers to math problems can also give students practice in reaching logical conclusions.

As part of the Math Counts program, *USA Today* published a poster showing a front page of the newspaper and highlighting how some knowledge of statistics was necessary to understand nearly every article. Students will need to know not only how to interpret statistics, but also how to determine their authenticity. They also will need to be able to use legitimate statistics to build a case for their ideas. In addition, well-educated students must be able to sort out and evaluate mounds of evidence bombarding them from an expanding number of sources, ranging from textbooks to the Internet. . . .

Teaching thinking and reasoning skills goes far beyond math. It is a part of every discipline, from writing to studying the causes and the effects of historic events. "Reasoning is not a separate category of learning. It is integral to any lesson, any exercise, and any educational experience," says Mary Bicouvaris, the 1989 National Teacher of the Year, who currently is associate professor of education at Christopher Newport University in Newport News, Virginia.

2. Critical interpersonal skills, including speaking, listening, and the ability to be part of a team. "Interpersonal skills include more than speaking and listening. Students need the ability to work collaboratively with different people," says Anne Campbell. Campbell is a former Nebraska Commissioner of Education and served as a member of the National Commission on Excellence in Education, which developed the 1983 report, "A Nation at Risk."

The ability to work with and communicate effectively with others was an overarching issue in this study. In fact, it placed as an essential part of knowledge, skills, and behaviors.

The Council of 55 made several points about the importance of this critical body of knowledge and cluster of skills. "Respect for other opinions and perspectives is increasingly vital in a more demographically diverse society," says Michael Usdan, president of the Institute for Educational Leadership. "More emphasis needs to be placed on achieving these skills through the teaching of core subject areas," adds Chris Pipho, director of state/clearinghouse services for the Education Commission of the States.

The bottom line for some Council members was that interpersonal and communication skills are at the front line of "getting you hired or fired." Others emphasized that the classroom should be a laboratory for collaborative decision making and team building, urging principals and teachers to model the behavior by collaborating. One panelist remarked, "Students will not buy into the 'do as I say, not as I do' *syndrome.*"

3. Effective information accessing and processing skills using technology. The spotlight of the nation and much of the world is focused on more effectively accessing the *plethora* of information that is virtually at our fingertips. Concern continues to grow about an expanding gulf that may divide the information rich and the information poor. Education cannot stop with simply helping students learn to access information. Students also will need to understand how to process and use the volumes of often conflicting information that will reach them each and every day. "Everyone says you must be able to read," says Marvin Cetron, president of Forecasting International and a chief advisor for this study. "It's more important for us to understand that we now have videodiscs; we have tools we can use interactively. Now, with technology, you can learn by seeing and doing."

Some students will be expected to create new technologies. Others will be expected to explain technology in plain language. Thus, both technical and communication skills will continue to be valued simultaneously.

"We need more effective training for teachers to emphasize information accessing and processing, plus we need to ensure that all students have access to technology," says Mary Hatwood Futrell, dean of the George Washington University Graduate School of Education and Human Development, and a former president of the National Education Association.

Of course, both the technological tools and the knowledge and skills needed to use them are essential to education for the 21st century. "Education at all levels will require large increases in funding to provide the equipment and training for teachers to meet the demand for technology in the curriculum," according to Jack Dulaney, superintendent of the Monongalis County Schools in West Virginia. "This may require asking more businesses to become involved." Adds Marshall, "We must go beyond information accessing to include information creation and knowledge development."

4. Writing skills to enable students to communicate effectively.

Writing is one of the essential elements of literacy. It is a key to effective communication, and the very act of writing demands thinking and reasoning. Writing helps individuals develop initiative as they sort through ideas, organize thoughts, and draw parallels. It develops courage, since sharing ideas leaves them open to the scrutiny of others. Writing also has been shown to contribute to even better reading skills.

Writes Kathryn Au, an education psychologist with the Kamehameha School in Honolulu, Hawaii, "If we want students to become good readers and writers, we need to involve them in the full processes of reading and writing. We should have them read literature and write for a variety of purposes, just as we want them to do in real life."

The National Council of Teachers of English has done extensive research on effectively teaching students to write. While debate continues over the importance of mechanics vs. free and creative writing, the fact remains that both are important. Ultimately, students need to be able to write to inform, to persuade, to express, and perhaps even to entertain. . . .

We should keep in mind that language itself evolves, and so do writing styles. Members of the Council of 55 suggested continuing in-depth training for teachers, coupled with providing students with sound materials and practical experiences in writing. They also emphasized the need for students to be able to write creatively and scientifically and to be able to use tools such as hardware and software to assist them in writing, editing, and rewriting (often considered among the most important steps in the writing process). . . .

5. Knowledge of American history and government to function in a democratic society and an understanding of issues surrounding patriotism. "Becoming involved in our representative democracy is critical for our nation's future," said Thomas Shannon, executive director of the National School Boards Association. "When students get involved, theory touches reality," he added.

Indeed the best way to learn about civics is to become a part of it. Of course, a knowledge of history and government is key to avoiding pitfalls of the past. . . .

During 1995, the Center for Civic Education, working with a number of other groups, released standards focusing on five significant questions:

1. What are civic life, politics, and government?
2. What are the foundations of the American political system?
3. How does the government established by the Constitution embody the purposes, values, and principles of American democracy?

4. What is the relationship of the United States to other nations and to world affairs?

5. What are the roles of the citizen in American democracy?

These questions, plus a framework found in a report on those standards, "We the People . . . the Citizens and the Constitution," are essential touchstones for developing effective programs to teach students about their government and to guide them in the teaching of history. Of course, state and local history as well as family and recent history are important in connecting with the continuum of social, political, and economic development.

In "Education for Democracy," a joint project of the American Federation of Teachers, the Educational Excellence Network, and Freedom House, three convictions were presented for "schools to purposely impart the ideals of a free society." They are: "First, that democracy is the worthiest form of human government conceived. Second, that we cannot take its survival or its spread—or its perfection in practice—for granted. Third, that democracy's survival depends upon our transmitting to each new generation the political vision of liberty and equality that unites us as Americans."

The National Council for the Social Studies and other subject area organizations have intensified their focus on preparing students to function in a free and democratic society. The issue of patriotism raised several comments among members of the Council of 55. "It is important that students have knowledge about the democratic process and not just blind patriotism," emphasized former superintendent K. Jesse Kobayashi.

Panel members also appealed for integration in the teaching of history, government, geography, and other social sciences to show how they all are related and interconnected.

6. Scientific knowledge base, including applied science. "One cannot just learn *about* science," says Marshall. "Science is the active engagement with the physical world. It is risk, experimentation, failure, and discovery. It must be *experienced.*"

Scientific discovery and the practical and commercial applications of discoveries have brought profound changes to the nation and the world. Most would agree that leadership in science is directly connected to our nation's capacity to maintain a sound economy and may even determine whether the nation or the planet will survive. Therefore, science education, from knowledge about scientific principles, to applied science, to an understanding that over time, evidence may suggest new theories, is essential. . . .

"All of our children and young adults, not just those preparing to be professional scientists, must have an understanding of scientific ways of thinking and science knowledge in order to function in an information age," writes Mary Lewis Sivertsen in *Transforming Ideas for Teaching and Learning Science,* published by the U.S. Department of Education. "Equally important is the ability for all citizens to make good decisions using a basic understanding of the science and technology behind the various social issues affecting their lives."

As superintendent of the Princeton, New Jersey, Public Schools, Paul Houston, currently executive director of the American Association of School Administrators, worked with a community planning group that discussed whether technology drives values or vice versa. Their answer was that technology does drive values. For example, our abilities to extend life through technology and medicine are increasing, which leads to questions about how we define "life," the morality of *euthanasia*, and more. Therefore, as science and technology are applied in real-world situations, ethics and values must be developed to guide their use. . . .

In her report, Sivertsen notes that science has remained a relatively low priority in elementary schools, yet the elementary grades are a critical time for capturing children's interest. "If students are not encouraged to follow their curiosity about the natural world in the primary grades, waiting to teach science on a regular basis in grade four may be too late. Data show that many children tend to lose interest in science at about the fourth grade," she says.

Percy Bates, director of Programs for Educational Opportunity at the University of Michigan School of Education, says that "for too long the field of science has seemed to be reserved only for the bright, the smart, the elite in our schools." In an Equity Coalition article, "Science Education and Equity," Bates cites evidence from the National Center for Educational Statistics, dated June 1992, showing that "Boys and girls are virtually even in math and science achievement in the third and seventh grades. However, by the eleventh grade boys achieve at a much higher level than girls." He encourages the "removal of all barriers in the field of science. Evidence shows that not only gender, but race, ethnicity, and socioeconomic class (SES) are acting as gatekeepers to becoming a scientist." . . .

7. An understanding of history of the world and world affairs. As much as some people would like to think of their nation as an island detached from the rest of the world, it is simply no longer possible to maintain that separation. Political, technological, sociological, economic, and environmental issues jump both natural and political borders. They affect us all. Therefore, students need to understand world history and world affairs.

An understanding of world history and world affairs could help today's students avoid future Holocausts or explore how various nations might become allies in conquering disease or reaching into inner, outer, and cyberspace.

Tom Maes, superintendent of the Adams County School District #1 in suburban Denver, Colorado, believes, "Like languages, the lack of world history has serious implications for world markets." Adds NSBA's Shannon: "Patriotism, founded on pride in our national, political culture, traditions, and institutions is clearly important. But this does not mean that knowledge, respect and appreciation of other cultures and nationalities should be *sloughed*. We are in a mutually interdependent world and must get along—but not at the price of surrendering our own values." Students need to be grounded in the cultures of other peoples, if only to understand them and to maintain peace in an interdependent world.

8. Multicultural understanding, including insights into diversity and the need for an international perspective. The world has become more interrelated as satellites, cyberspace, and jet travel bring people and nations closer together. Communication transcends political boundaries. Our nation, too, has become more cosmopolitan as new waves of immigrants come to America. In fact, except for Native Americans, the United States is a land of immigrants. All are seeking common as well as divergent purposes in a free and democratic society. Now, more than ever, an understanding of diversity is key. In the future it will only become more important.

The ability to work in collaboration with different people is critical, says Richard Warner, principal of Fargo South High School in North Dakota. "Different people means not only color, but gender, nationality, religion, and political persuasion," he adds. "The basic need is for understanding our dependency on each other," says California superintendent K. Jesse Kobayashi.

Other members of the panel also called for not only the teaching of multicultural understanding but also the modeling of it in every school and community.

Properly managed, diversity can enrich. Not properly managed, it can divide. The key is education.

9. Knowledge of foreign languages. "How can we provide a sound education and compete in world markets without learning foreign languages?" asks Maes. For that matter, how can we make ourselves understood if we aren't able to communicate in languages of the world marketplace? How can we be sure we aren't being taken advantage of because we don't understand the conversations taking place around us? How can we fully enjoy the history and culture of other nations or of the immigrants who come to this country without an understanding of other languages? These are questions demanding our attention as we approach the 21st century.

The stories are legion. Businesspeople from other countries come to the United States and speak our language. Americans go to other countries and need interpreters. As businesses become increasingly multinational and as nations pool resources to collaborate on global issues, such as the environment, the lack of ability to communicate in other languages becomes an even more costly barrier.

10. Knowledge of world geography. Similarly, a lack of knowledge about geography will be a barrier to understanding our shrinking universe.

Anthony R. DeSouza, in "Time for Geography: The New National Standards," writes: "By the year 2000, planet Earth will be more crowded, the physical environment more threatened, natural resources more depleted, the global economy more competitive, world events more interconnected, human life more complex, and the need for people to have a solid grasp of geography even more essential."

He adds, "By learning geography thoroughly, students come to understand the connections and relationships among themselves and people, places, cultures, and economies across the world."

An Integrated Curriculum

While the Council of 55 identified fairly specific disciplines or bodies of knowledge that will be required for students to thrive in the 21st century, members of the council also made clear that the curriculum should be integrated across disciplines. "Perhaps history, government, geography, and other social sciences need to be integrated," Dulaney suggests. "This will show students the connections and interrelationships."

"It seems that with the emphasis on an integrated curriculum across disciplines as well as the need for students to learn to work collaboratively, this will lead to a new curriculum of the 21st century," says J.C. Sparkman, former executive vice president of Tele-Communications, Inc. (TCI) of Denver. . . .

Vocabulary

As you think about this essay, these definitions may be helpful to you:

1. **syndrome**   a medical term referring to a number of symptoms that, when they occur together, characterize a specific disease
2. **plethora**   excessive in number; overabundant
3. **euthanasia**   the act or method of causing a painless death, often to protect against suffering
4. **slough** [pronounced sluff]   as a verb, to shed or get rid of

Discussion Questions

1. What is the purpose behind Uchida's frequent quotations from members of the Council of 55?
2. Are there any kinds of knowledge that surprised you by being included on this list? Are there any important omissions that you can think of?
3. How would you rank these ten kinds of knowledge from most important to least important? If you need to put some of them together into categories, feel free to do so, but explain why you think they fit together.
4. Uchida lists the ability to get along with others (Item 2) as an "academic content" area. Is it? Why or why not?

How Can These Ideas Apply to You?

1. One way to understand the ten categories in this reading is to think of them as goals for your own education. Select the one or two that will be the hardest for you to attain, and explain what about you or about the goals you select make them especially difficult.
2. The Council of 55 identified kinds of knowledge other than academic content that, in their view, students in the 21st century need to learn. Can you suggest what some of them might be?
3. Select one of these areas and explain what you can do to master the knowledge in it that you need for success in the 21st century.

Postgraduate Paralysis

Mary Sherry

Mary Sherry owns a firm that publishes research reports for architects and real estate developers. In this essay, which first appeared in *Newsweek* magazine, Sherry offers a parent's perspective on an offspring's job search. When she realized her daughter was looking for a career, not a job, her perspective on how to help changed.

Thousands of college graduates took their diplomas this year in fear or even embarrassment. They were not proud of themselves, nor eager to take on the real world. Instead, they thought of themselves as failures. These are the graduates who have not been offered fat salaries and generous benefits. They are the ones who won't be going to work as lawyers, investment bankers and engineers. They have taken the right courses, gotten good grades and gone through some on-campus job interviews. But because they weren't offered the perfect job—no, that exciting career—seemingly guaranteed to all those who make the right moves, they are sitting at home, victims of postgraduate paralysis.

This may come as a surprise to anyone who has read about the fabulous job offers tendered to recent graduates. However, those of us who are parents of children in this age group know that such offers are relatively rare and that many liberal arts students graduate with the belief that the work world may not have a place for them.

Consider my daughter; she graduated from college with a degree in economics two years ago. She was offered a job by a *recruiter* who came to her campus—but it was with a trucking firm in South Carolina, as a dispatch-management trainee. She turned it down. It was her parents' first clue that she had a problem.

It seems economists don't work for trucking firms. Nor do Midwestern children want to live in the South before they become arthritic. Yet even at home in Minneapolis, our daughter couldn't seem to find anything to apply for. Her father told her to make the rounds of the personnel agencies. But she was so horrified by the *demeaning* atmosphere at one that she refused to visit any others.

Then one day, when she was looking at the Sunday paper and complaining that there was nothing in it, I told her that there had to be something. "Look at this," I commanded. "And this! And this!" I circled a number of jobs in the first two columns I skimmed. But Maureen protested: "I don't want to be an administrative assistant."

It was then that her father and I realized that she had been looking in the paper for a career, not a job. And ever since, we have watched the children of friends suffer from this same *delusion*. No one, it seems, has told them that a career is an *evolutionary* process.

When I graduated from college 25 years ago, I never expected to find a job that was in itself a career. In those days, we were told we knew nothing, but that upon graduation we would have the tools to learn. And learn we did—on the job. I began

Reprinted from *Newsweek* by permission of the author.

by doing grunt work in the customer service department at *National Geographic* magazine. In due time, I wound up with a career, indeed, owning and running a firm that publishes research reports for architects and real estate developers.

Apparently, schools have changed their approach. Today's students are told they know everything in order to succeed in a career. Career talk often begins in seventh grade or earlier, and the career is offered as the reward one receives upon graduation. No one is satisfied with this system. Businesses complain that they get new graduates who are unhappy with anything less than high-level, decision-making jobs as their first assignments. And parents are shocked that the child without a job can graduate traumatized by the fear of rejection.

As I see it, parents are a principal cause of the problem. Who among us hasn't thought, "What's wrong with that kid?" when we hear that a recent college graduate is a checker at a grocery store because "he can't find a job." At the same time, how many of us can put the screws on a recruiter's reject and convince him that he must abandon his idea of a career and take up the idea of finding work?

This is a distasteful task, especially when we have shipped our children off to expensive colleges, believing that simply by footing the tuition bill we are making them economically secure. The kids believe this, too, but the reality is that when they graduate, they are no more prepared for careers than we were.

Entry-level positions: It is not a disgrace to go out and pound the pavement. I used just this expression the other day with a friend of my son who, though he had graduated in December with a degree in philosophy, has not yet found a job. He had never heard the saying before. He is bright, personable and would do well in almost any kind of business. But he complains that he can't find work in the want ads—he has not visited any personnel agencies—and so he talks about going to law school instead. He was crushed by not having been recruited before graduation.

Which brings me back to my daughter. After some yelling and screaming by her parents, she did make the rounds of *headhunters* and found one who specialized in entry-level positions. This gentleman was wonderful; he helped her assess her skills and prepared her for interviews. She also read the newspapers and answered different types of ads. Not surprisingly, she got many responses. After a few weeks she had the exhilarating experience of having three job offers at once. Two were the products of answering newspaper ads and one came through the headhunter's efforts. She landed an excellent position as an insurance underwriter—a job she didn't even know existed when she graduated.

Happy in her job, Maureen also fell in love; and when she began to look for employment in Chicago where she and her husband will live, she needed no help from her parents. She was confident and aggressive. She used headhunters, the want ads, her friends and ours. She had a new resource—business contacts. Yet as she was typing letters one day, I offered some sympathy about how hard it is to hunt for a job.

"It's OK, Mom," she said. "This isn't like the first time. Now I know how to look for a job!"

And she found one as a senior underwriter. She'll make more money and more decisions.

It's beginning to look like a career.

Vocabulary

As you think about this essay, these definitions may be helpful to you:

1. **recruiter** a representative of a company or organization who is seeking to secure the services of or hire individuals to work for that organization
2. **demeaning** degrading
3. **delusion** something that is falsely believed
4. **evolutionary** characterized by a process of change in a certain direction
5. **headhunters** paid recruiters of personnel

Discussion Questions

1. Why do some students feel like failures if they do not have a job at graduation, according to Sherry?
2. How did Sherry's daughter approach the job-search process?
3. What is the difference between a job and a career?
4. What advice does Sherry give for finding entry-level jobs? Do you agree?
5. How did Sherry's daughter finally find her first job? Subsequent jobs?

Suggestions for Your Journal

Do you know any college graduates who are still searching for a job? If so, what have you learned from their experiences?

What type of entry-level job are you preparing for when you graduate? What kinds of experiences (such as internships, volunteer work, co-op or work experiences) would enhance your chances of getting the job you desire? What resources exist on your campus to help you obtain these experiences? What other steps can you take to make yourself more marketable when you graduate?

Outlooks and Insights: Succeeding on the Job and in Life
Carol Carter

Carol Carter received her education from the University of Arizona. She is assistant vice president and director of college marketing for Prentice-Hall publishers. This essay appears in her book *Majoring in the Rest of Your Life* and discusses what might happen after you obtain your first job. Her latest book *Keys to Effective Learning* focuses on effective learning techniques that can serve for a lifetime.

No matter what your first job after college happens to be, it is a first step. But it is also a point of departure. If you started with the company and the position your dreams, great. Your job might also be less than terrific. But you have to start somewhere, building your skills, meeting people and developing work habits. That's a positive, exciting challenge.

You'll go from there to a string of promotions, to a better job with another company, to a smaller company, back to graduate school or to begin your own company. Your first job is like a blank page. You fill it in as you go. And your options are limitless as long as you pursue them.

Games People Play

In the real world, people measure themselves by all kinds of things—how much money they make, what their job is, how many people they know, how many dates they have, what kind of clothes they wear or what kind of car they drive.

Many of these things have to do with *appearances*, not reality. They reflect what people want others to think, not necessarily what they really are. Know the difference between the two and be true to yourself and your values. The best job in the world isn't worth much if you are not happy. Similarly, no amount of money or possessions you can buy will satisfy you if you aren't content with who you are.

[You need to define] those things that are important to *you*, and you alone. So resist comparing yourself with those around you. That's a game you'll never win. There will always be people who are better and worse off than you. In college and in life, it's important to do what you believe and what you feel is right.

People may not always agree with you, especially if they feel threatened by your abilities. That's okay. Preserve your *integrity* and don't let someone get the better of you. Your satisfaction will come from knowing that you took the high road.

President John F. Kennedy said it best in his inaugural address: "For of those to whom much is given, much is required. And when at some future date the high court of history sits in judgment on each of us, recording whether in our brief span of service we fulfilled our responsibilities to the state, our success or failure, in whatever office we hold, will be measured by four questions: First, were we truly men of courage? . . . Second, were we truly men of judgment? . . . Third, were we truly men of integrity? . . . Finally, were we truly men of dedication?"

Is It Ethical?

Ask yourself these questions: Would others approve of my behavior if they knew about it? Would I want someone else to behave similarly? Is what I'm doing right for the company? Is what the company doing right? If not, how do I handle it? What are my own personal standards and how do I define them?

In journalism, the accepted rule for quotes is that if someone says something to you and then says, "Don't print that," only *after* he made the statement, you are allowed to print it. But several journalists I've talked to said they would not print the quote if it was made by a "civilian," a nonpolitician or anyone not familiar with the rules of the press. The reason? Plain fairness.

On Being Happy

Once you've landed your job, take pride in what you do. Concentrate not just on job success but on overall happiness. If there is any one point that this book makes, it's the importance of balancing several goals—personal and professional. Your job is only one aspect of your life.

It takes a strong commitment and hard work to maintain a healthy balance on the job and off. Being happy won't just happen. Like anything else, you have to work at it.

In a graduation speech to students at his alma mater, MIT, Kenneth Olsen, CEO of Digital Equipment Corporation, reflected on his thirty years of work since graduating from college: "Running a business is not the important thing. Making a commitment to do a good job, to improve things, to influence the world is where it's at. I would also suggest that one of the most satisfying things is to help others to be creative and take responsibility. These are the important things."

"Your most precious *commodity* is not material," says Charles S. Sanford, Jr., CEO of Bankers Trust New York Corporation. "It is and always will be your time." If you keep work in balance with other things in your life, Sanford says, you can accomplish even more on the job. "Read a little poetry, enjoy friends, and most of all, don't take yourself too seriously. In the final analysis, whatever you have accomplished won't be worth much unless you've had fun."

Okay, so the *cynic* in you cries: How much time did these CEOs spend working in their twenties and thirties? Good point. They probably spent a lot of time, but you have to ask yourself: Do you want to be a CEO? Most people would say, "No, thanks." You have to carefully weigh the trade-offs of your long-term goals against what you are doing—and enjoying—in the short term. The majority of the population thrive quite happily between entry-level positions and the top of the heap. They enjoy their work and still have the time to be with their friends and raise a family.

Maybe you won't have all the money in the world, but you will have had time to enjoy those things that count the most when you're ninety—a job you liked, a lifestyle you enjoyed and the opportunity to contribute to your own growth and that of others.

Thoughts for the Journey

I'd like to tell you a personal anecdote. It has to do with becoming discouraged.

About three months before I finished this manuscript, I was exhausted. My job was quite *tedious*—not because the work itself had changed, but because my approach to it had. I made little time to see my friends, and at night I just wanted to go to sleep early. Boring. In short, I was doing all those things I have said never to do. Realizing that I wasn't being myself, and knowing for a fact that I wasn't having a good time, I decided to take a break to get back the *perspective* I knew was missing.

Egypt was the place for perspective. Why Egypt? It was exotic, distant and vastly different from life as I knew it. Moreover, one of my interests is travel, and after my junior year in Spain, I made a personal promise to visit as many countries as I could. So off I went for the first time on a vacation by myself, leaving my "normal" life and my work behind me.

When I saw the pyramids at dusk, a renewed energy and inspiration filled me. The 4,500-year-old pyramids symbolize balance, perfection, human achievement and teamwork. (Fortunately, today we can work in teams in business and organizations; the Egyptians dictated to slaves in the most oppressive style.) Witnessing the achievements of an ancient culture that survived 4,500 years left me with a feeling of great awe and real humility. I wondered how many American monuments would survive 450 years, let alone into the year 6500.

Clearly, the Egyptians saw no limits to what they could accomplish. They saw things not in terms of what they were in the moment, but in terms of what they could become in time. They made dreams into realities.

Well, bully for Tut, you say, but what has this got to do with college and careers and human potential? The pyramids helped me to recover my "edge," my own potential. The tensions loosened inside of me and confidence took over.

My perspective restored, I was free to concentrate on challenges, including work, the book and my personal life, with confidence and energy.

Throughout your life, the inspirations that motivate you will ebb and flow. You won't always feel inspired and you won't always perform at peak. The important thing to remember when you reach an impasse is not to panic. Remove yourself from the ordinary—through reading *Don Quixote* or going to a concert or exhibit or taking a day trip by yourself. Maybe your most relaxing time is spent watching a football game or a weekly sitcom. That's fine. Just allow yourself time to unwind and replenish your own central energy source.

The Blue Sky Ahead

You have a lot to be proud of. If you are reading this book for the first time as a freshman, you get credit for getting this far and for committing yourself to making college and your career pursuit everything they can be. Good for you.

When you graduate and you are wondering how four or more years could come and go so fast, take time to pat yourself on the back. Look down from where you are now, realize how far you've come and be proud of your accomplishments. The next peak you scale, your first job, is very similar to what you've learned in the last few years. Accept the challenges that are before you. And in addition to doing a good or a great job, give to the world something of what it has given to you through your family, your friends, your activities and your actions. Don't be typical. You are unique. Show the world the special gifts and contributions that only you have to offer.

And so here's to your unique success story. Here's to the ability that you have to dream the dream and make it real. Go change the world.

Vocabulary

As you think about this essay, these definitions may be helpful to you:

1. **integrity**   firm adherence to a code of moral or artistic values
2. **commodity**   something useful or valuable
3. **cynic**   a fault-finding critic who believes that human conduct is motivated wholly by self-interest
4. **tedious**   tiresome because of length or dullness
5. **perspective**   point of view

Discussion Questions

1. How is your first job like a blank page, according to Carter?
2. Do you agree that many measurements of success that people use only have to do with "appearances"? Explain.
3. What are some "games people play"?
4. Why is ethical behavior so important in the workplace?
5. Why is it important to balance your personal and professional life?

How Can These Ideas Apply to You?

1. How will you measure success in the "real world"?
2. List three work values that are important to you. Why are they important?
3. How do you define your personal standards as they relate to ethical behavior?
4. How do you "unwind and replenish your central energy source"?
5. What can you do now while still in school to facilitate a better personal transition into the workplace?

Credits

▬

This page constitutes an extension of the copyright page. We have made every effort to trace the ownership of all copyrighted material and to secure permission from copyright holders. In the event of any question arising as to the use of any material, we will be pleased to make the necessary corrections in future printings. Thanks are due to the following authors, publishers, and agents for permission to use the material indicated.

Atwell, "What Does Society Need from Higher Education?"
    Reprinted by permission of the Johnson Foundation, Racine, WI. Excerpt from "What Does Society Need from Higher Education?" in A Wingspread Group on Higher Education. An American Imperative: Higher Expectations in Higher Education (Racine, WI: The Johnson Foundation, 1993), pp. 51-53. Reprinted by permission of the Johnson Foundation, Racine, WI.
"Patrick Awuah on Educating Leaders", copyright TED.com
Ballard, "Job Search: Chance or Plan?"
    Mark Ballard, "Job Search: Chance or Plan?" reprinted by permission of the author.
Bok, "Purposes"
    Derek Bok, UNDERACHIEVING COLLEGES © 2006 by Princeton University Press. Reprinted by permission of Princeton University Press.
Bowen, "The Baccalaureate Degree: What Does It Mean? What Should It Mean?," Howard R.
    "The Baccalaureate Degree: What Does It Mean?," excerpt from AMERICAN ASSOCIATION FOR HIGHER EDUCATION BULLETIN, Vol. 34, No. 3, November 1981, pp. 11-15. Reprinted with permission.
Boyoumi, "How Does it Feel to Be a Problem"
    "How Does it Feel to Be a Problem" by Moustafa Boyoumi From Amerasia Journal 27:3 (2001)/28:1 (2002): 69-77. Reprinted by permission.
Brown, "Why I Don't Let Students Cut My Classes"
    William R. Brown, "Why I Don't Let Students Cut My Classes," reprinted by permission of the author.
Burtchaell, "Major Decisions"
    James T. Burtchaell, "Major Decisions" in Notre Dame Magazine. Winter, 1986-87. Copyrights (c). by Notre Dame Magazine. All rights reserved. Reproduced by permission.
Carter, "Outlooks and Insights,"
    "Outlooks and Insights," from MAJORING IN THE REST OF YOUR LIFE: Career Secrets for College Freshman, fourth editon, by Carol Carter at LifeBound (www. lifebound.com). Copyright (c) 2005 LifeBound, LLC. Reprinted by permission of the author and publisher.

Cicarelli, "A New Debate Is Joined Over an Old Question: Is College an Investment or an End in Itself?"
James Cicarelli, "A New Debate is Joined over an Old Questions: Is College an Investment or and End in Itself?" (c) 1987 James Cicarelli. Reprinted by permission of the author.

Delgado-Romero, "The Face of Racism"
From Edward A. Delgado-Romero, The Face of Racism, from the Journal of Counseling and Development, vol. 77. Copyright © 1999 by The American Counseling Association. No further reproduction authorized without written permission of the American Counseling Association.

Erickson, "Fitting In"
From Betty LaSere Erickson and Diane Weltner Strommer, TEACHING COLLEGE FRESHMEN. Copyright (c) 1991 John Wiley & Sons, Inc. This material is used by permission of John Wiley & Sons, Inc.

Finster, "Freshman Can Be Taught to Think Creatively, Not Just Amass Information,"
David C. Finster, "Freshman Can Be Taught to Think Creatively, Not Just Amass Information," July 13, 1988. Reprinted by permission of the author.

Fox-Hines, "Standing Up for Yourself - Without Stepping on Others".
Ruthann Fox-Hines, "Standing Up for Yourself - Without Stepping on Others". Used by permission. Sears, Susan J.& Virginia N. Gordon, BUILDING YOUR CAREER: A GUIDE TO YOUR FUTURE, 3rd Edition, © 2002, 101-105, 108-109, 111, 114-115. Reprinted by permission of Pearson Education, Inc., Upper Saddle River, NJ.

Gardner, "Decoding Your Professors"
John N. Gardner, "Decoding Your Professors," from COLLEGE IS ONLY THE BEGINNING. Copyright © 1989 Thomson Wadsworth. Used by permission.

Gordon, "The Developing College Student"
Virginia Gordon, "The Developing College Student" from Foundations: A Reader for New College Students, pp. 175-179. Copyright © 2005 Thomson Wadsworth. Used by permission.

Halverson, "American Higher Education: A Brief History"
"American Higher Education: A Brief History," by William Halverson. Reprinted by permission of the author.

Halverson, "On Academic Freedom"
James Carter and William Halverson, "On Academic Freedom," reprinted by permission of the authors.

The Harvard Guide to Happiness

James, "Understanding Who Is Smart"
Adult Publishing Group from THINKING IN THE FUTURE TENSE: A Workout for the mind by Jennifer James. Copyright (c) 1996 by Jennifer James, Inc. All rights reserved.

Jobs, "Connecting the Dots"
Commencement address by Steve Jobs, June 12, 2005. Stanford Report, June 14, 2005

Jones, "The Educated Person"
Excerpt from "The Educated Person" in THE EDUCATED PERSON: A COLLECTION OF CONTEMPORARY AMERICAN ESSAYS edited by Thomas B. Jones (St. Paul, MN: Metropolitan State University). Revised edition, 1989 pp. 101-105. Reprinted with permission from Thomas B. Jones, Professor, Metropolitan State University.

Lacey, "Job Outlook for College Graduates"
Jill Lacey and Olivia Crosby, "Job Outlook for College Graduates" from Master Student Reader, © 2007 Cengage Learning

Leondar-Wright, "Are There Class Cultures"
"Are There Class Cultures", Reprinted courtesy of Betsy Leondar-Wright, www.classmatters.org, from her book CLASS MATTERS: CROSS-CLASS ALLIANCE BUILDING FOR MIDDLE-CLASS ACTIVISTS. New Society Publishers. Copyright© 2005

Leonhardt, "The College Dropout Boom"
David Leonhardt, "The College Dropout Boom," from New York Times, May 24, 2005. Reprinted by permission of the author.

Malcolm X, "Saved"
"Saved", Autobiography of Malcolm X, as told to Alex Haley. From THE NEXT FIFTY YEARS, edited by John Brockman, copyright (c) 2002 by John Brockman. Used by permission of Vintage Books, a division of Random House, Inc.

McGuire, "Growing Up With Two Moms"
"Growing Up With Two Moms" by Megan McGuire, from 'Newsweek' (Nov. 4, 1996). Copyright © 1996 by Newsweek, Inc.

McIntosh, "White Privilege: Unpacking the Invisible Knapsack"
White Privilege: Unpacking the Invisible Knapsack, by Peggy McIntosh, from White Privilege and Male Privilege. Reprinted with permission. May not be reprinted without the permission of the author.

Meiland, "The Difference Between High School and College"
From Jack Meiland, "The Difference Between High School and College," from COLLEGE THINKING. Mentor Book/The New American Library, New York, 1981. © 1981 by Jack W. Meiland. Reprinted by permission of the author's estate.

Minnick, "Ideas as Property"
Thomas L. Minnick, "Ideas as Property" from Foundations: A Reader for New College Students, pp. 175-179. Copyright © 2005 Thomson Wadsworth. Used by permission.

Minnick, "Fourteen Ways of Looking at Electives"
Thomas L. Minnick, "Fourteen Ways of Looking at Electives" from Foundations With Infotrac: A Reader For New College Students. Wadsworth Publishing, 2004. Used by permission.

Morrill, "Developing a Personal System of Values"
Richard L. Morrill, "Developing a Personal System of Values". Reprinted with permission.

Newman, "Loneliness"
Barbara M. Newman and Philip R. Newman, "Loneliness," pp. 87-90 from WHEN KIDS GO TO COLLEGE. Copyright (c) 1992 by Ohio State University Press. Reprinted by permission of the publisher.

Pellegrino, "Having a Degree and Being Educated"
Edmund D. Pellegrino, "Having a Degree and Being Educated" from UNIVERSITY SURVEY: A GUIDEBOOK AND READINGS FOR NEW STUDENTS. Guidebook edited by Thomas L. Minnick and Patrick Royster; Readings selected and edited by Virginia N. Gordon, Patrick Royster and Thomas L. Minnick, pp. 155-156. Ohio State University Press, 2000. Copyright (c) 2000 by Edmund D. Pellegrino. Reprinted by permission. All rights reserved.

Pierce, "What Does Society Need From Higher Education?"
Excerpt from "What Does Society Need from Higher Education?" in A Wingspread Group on Higher Education. An American Imperative: Higher Expectations in Higher Education (Racine, WI: The Johnson Foundation, 1993), pp. 122-124.

Raspberry, "College Major Doesn't Mean All That Much"
William Raspberry, "College Major Doesn't Mean All That Much," Copyright © 1990, The Washington Post Writers Group. Reprinted with permission.

Roosevelt, "Student Expectations Seen as Causing Grade Disputes"
Max Roosevelt, "Student Expectations Seen as Causing Grade Disputes," from New York Times, February 18, 2009. Reprinted by permission of the author.

Seligman, "Work and Personal Satisfaction"
Martin E. P. Seligman, "Work and Personal Satisfaction," from AUTHENTIC HAPPINESS, (Free Press, 2002), pp 165-177. Reprinted by permission of the author.

Sherry, "Postgraduate Paralysis,"
Mary Sherry, "Postgraduate Paralysis," from NEWSWEEK, July 11, 1988. Reprinted by permission of the author.

Staley, "Technology Skills: Wireless, Windowed, Webbed, and Wikied"
"Technology Skills: Wireless, Windowed, Webbed, and Wikied," from Focus on College Success Learning About Learning. Stanley, Constance. © Copyright 2011 Cengage Learning.

Staley, "How Do You Perceive and Process Information"
"How Do You Perceive and Process Information?" from Success Learning about Learning. Stanley, Constance. © Copyright 2011 Cengage Learning. Reprinted with the permission of Simon & Schuster

Stepp, "School's Out: One Young Man Puzzles Over His Future Without College"
Laura Sessions Stepp, "School's Out: One Young Man Puzzles Over His Future Without College," Copyright © 1990, The Washington Post Writers Group. Reprinted with permission.

Sue, "A Racial/Cultural Identity Development Model"
"A Racial/Cultural Identity Development Model" by Sue & Sue. Counseling The Culturally Diverse: Theory and Practice, pp 214-226. © 2003 by John Wiley & Sons Inc. All rights reserved.

Takaki. "We Will All Be Minorities"
Ronald Takaki. "We Will All Be Minorities" from A Different Mirror: A History of Multicultural America ©2003 Back Bay Books

Twining, "Active Learning"
From James E. Twining, STRATEGIES FOR ACTIVE LEARNING. Published by Allyn and Bacon, Boston, MA. Copyright © 1991 by Pearson Education. Reprinted by permission of the publisher.

Uchida, "What Students Must Know to Succeed in the 21st Century"
Donna Uchida, "What Students Must Know to Succeed in the 21st Century," pp. 6-11 from PREPARING STUDENTS FOR THE 21st CENTURY. Reprinted by permission of the AASA.

Wagner, "Rigor Redefined"
Tony Wagner, "Rigor Redefined," from Expecting Excellence, October 2008. Reprinted by permission of the author.

SACRAMENTO STATE DIRECTORY
All phone numbers listed are area code 916
When dialing from on campus, dial 8 and then the last 4-digits

ACADEMIC DEPARTMENTS

Department	Location	Phone
Anthropology	Mendocino 4010	278-6452
Art	Kadema 185	278-6166
Biological Sciences	Sequoia 202	278-6535
Business Administration	Tahoe 1030	278-6771
Chemistry	Sequoia 506	278-6684
Child Development	Brighton 137	278-7192
Civil Engineering	Riverside 4024	278-6982
Communication Studies	Mendocino 5014	278-6688
Computer Engineering	Riverside 3018	278-6844
Computer Science	Riverside 3018	278-6834
Construction Management	Riverside 4024	278-6616
Criminal Justice	Alpine 137	278-6487
Design (Graphic Des, Interior Des, Photogr)	Mariposa 5001	278-3962
Economics	Tahoe 3028	278-6223
Education—Bilingual/Multicultural Education	Eureka 401	278-5942
Education—Counselor Education	Eureka 414	278-5399
Education—Spec Ed, Rehab, Sch Psy, Deaf Std	Eureka 316	278-6622
Education—Teacher Education	Eureka 201	278-6155
Electrical Engineering	Riverside 3018	278-6873
English	Calaveras 103	278-6586
Environmental Studies	Amador 554A	278-6620
Ethnic Studies	Amador 463	278-6646
Family & Consumer Sciences	Mariposa 3000	278-6393
Film	Mendocino 5027	278-6285
Foreign Languages	Mariposa 2051	278-6333
Geography	Amador 550	278-6109
Geology	Placer 2003	278-6337
Gerontology	El Dorado 1030	278-7163
Government	Tahoe 3104	278-6202
History	Tahoe 3080	278-6206
Humanities & Religious Studies	Mendocino 2011	278-6444
Journalism	Mendocino 5014	278-6688
Kinesiology & Health Science	Solano 3002	278-6441
Learning Skills	Lassen 2200	278-6725
Liberal Studies	Lassen 2008	278-6342

Math/Statistics	Brighton 141	278-6534
Mechanical Engineering	Riverside 4024	278-6624
Music	Capistrano 103	278-5155
Nursing	El Dorado 1016	278-6525
Philosophy	Mendocino 3000	278-6424
Physical Therapy	Solano 4000	278-6426
Physics & Astronomy/Physical Science	Sequoia 230	278-6518
Psychology	Amador 350	278-6254
Recreation, Parks & Tourism Admin.	Solano 4000	278-6752
ROTC- Air Force	Publ Serv Bldng 214	278-7449
ROTC- Army	Publ Serv Bldng 202	278-7682
Social Science	Lassen 2008	278-6207
Social Work	Mariposa 4010	278-6943
Sociology	Amador 450	278-6522
Speech Pathology & Audiology	Shasta 172	278-6601
Theatre & Dance	Shasta 104	278-6368
Women's Studies	Amador 561B	278-6817

CAMPUS RESOURCES

Academic Advising	Lassen 1013	278-6351
Admissions & Outreach	Lassen 1102	278-7766
Alcohol & Drug Prevention Education	The Well	278-5422
Aquatic Center	Lake Natoma	278-2842
Associated Students, Inc. (ASI)	Univ Union, 3rd Floor	278-6784
Bike Shop	Univ Union, Peak Adventures	278-6662
Bookstore	Bookstore	278-6446
Career Center	Lassen 1013	278-6231
Central Ticket Office	Univ Union, 1st Floor	278-4323
Children's Center	Child Development Center	278-6216
Commencement	Sacramento 104	278-4724
Community Engagement Center	Library 4028	278-4610
Copy Graphics Center	River Front Center	278-6960
Educational Opportunity Prog. (EOP)	Lassen 2205	278-6183
Financial Aid & Scholarships	Lassen 1006	278-6554
Global Education	Lassen 2304	278-6686
Graduate Studies	River Front Center 206	278-6470
Housing & Res Life	Sierra Hall	278-6655
Information Resources & Technology	AIRC 3010	278-6606
Intercollegiate Athletics	Yosemite 134	278-6481

Library-Circulation Desk	Library 1023	278-3463
Lost & Found	Publ Serv Bldng	278-3463
Math Lab	Brighton 118	278-6796
MESA Engineering and Computer Sci.	Santa Clara 1213	278-6699
Multicultural Center	Library 1010	278-6101
One Card Center	Brighton Annex	278-7878
Orientation	Lassen 1010	278-7841
Peak Adventures	Univ Union, 1st Floor	278-6321
Police Department	Publ Serv Bldng 1	278-6851
Pride Center	Lassen 3011	278-8720
Psychological Counseling Services	Student Health Center 203	278-6416
Recreational Sports	Univ Union, 1st Floor	278-4111
Registrar's Office / Records	Lassen 1011	278-3625
Registration Help Line		278-8088
Sac Link Help Desk	AIRC 2005	278-7337
Services to Students w/ Disabilities	Lassen 1008	278-6955
State Hornet Newspaper	Univ Union, 2nd Floor	278-6583
Student Affairs	Lassen 3008	278-6060
Student Athlete Resource Center	Lassen 3002/3004	278-7796
Student Financial Services	Lassen 1001	278-6736
Student Health Center	Student Health Center	278-6461
Student Organizations & Leadership	University Union, 3rd Floor	278-6595
Student Services Counter	Lassen 1011	278-3625
Teaching Cred Advising	Eureka 216	278-6403
Testing Center	Lassen 2302	278-6296
Transportation & Parking	7667 Folsom Blvd	278-7275
UNIQUE Programs	Univ Union, 3rd Floor	278-3928
Veteran's Affairs	Lassen 3000	278-6733
Women's Resource Center	Lassen 3005	278-7388
Writing Center	Calaveras 128	278-6356

EMERGENCY

Alcoholics Anonymous: 916-454-1100	UC Davis Med Center: 916-734-2011
Mercy Hospital: 916-453-4545	University Police: 916-278-6851
Sacramento Co. Mental Health: 916-875-1055	WEAVE: 916-920-2952
Suicide Prevention: 916-368-3111	24 Hour Crisis Line: 916-732-3637
Sutter Memorial Hospital: 916-454-3333	EMERGENCY: 911

SACRAMENTO STATE UNDERGRADUATE PROGRAMS
Majors by College
*For list of minors please refer to the 2008-2010 Catalog, pages 22-23

College of Arts and Letters
www.al.csus.edu
- Art
- Communication Studies
- Design (Graphic Design, Interior Design, Photography)
- English
- Film Studies
- Foreign Languages
- History
- Humanities and Religious Studies
- Journalism
- Learning Skills Center
- Liberal Arts
- Music
- Philosophy
- Theatre and Dance

College of Business Administration
www.cba.csus.edu
- Accountancy
- Accounting Information Systems
- Entrepreneurship
- Finance
- General Management
- Management of Human Resources/ Organizational Behavior
- International Business
- Management Information Systems
- Marketing
- Operations Management
- Real Estate and Land Use Affairs
- Risk Management and Insurance

College of Education
www.coe.csus.edu
- American Sign Language/Deaf Studies
- Child Development
- Vocational Education

College of Engineering and Computer Science
www.ecs.csus.edu
- Civil Engineering
- Computer Engineering
- Computer Science
- Construction Management

- Electrical and Electronic Engineering
- Mechanical Engineering

College of Health and Human Services
www.hhs.csus.edu
- Criminal Justice
- Kinesiology and Health Science
- Nursing
- Physical Therapy
- Recreation, Parks and Tourism Administration
- Social Work
- Speech Pathology and Audiology

College of Natural Sciences and Mathematics
www.csus.edu/nsm
- Biological Sciences
- Chemistry
- Earth Science
- Geography
- Geology
- Mathematics and Statistics
- Physics and Astronomy

College of Social Sciences and Interdisciplinary Studies
www.csus.edu/ssis
- Anthropology
- Asian Studies
- Economics
- Environmental Studies
- Ethnic Studies
- Family and Consumer Sciences
- Gerontology
- Government
- Liberal Studies
- Psychology
- Social Science
- Sociology
- Women's Studies

354 Sacramento State Map

SACRAMENTO STATE
6000 J Street, Sacramento, CA 95819

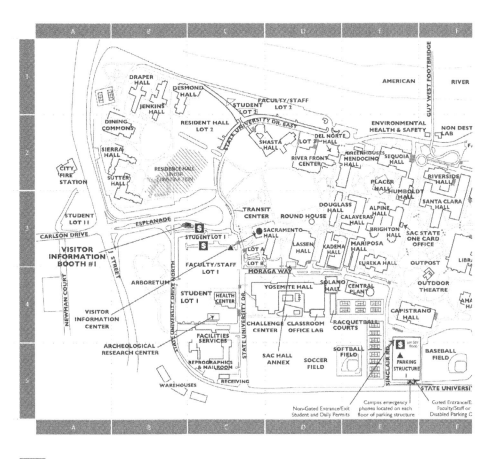

S **Daily Permit Machines**
▲ **Carpool Parking**
••• **Bollards**
▬ **Access Gates**
▬ **Loading Zones**

Vehicles must display a valid Sac State parking permit while parked in a campus parking area. California State laws and Sac State parking regulations are enforced 24 hours a day, 365 days per year. With a Sac State OneCard, parking permits may be purchased at the Student Financial Services Center in Lassen Hall and the UTAPS office.

See reverse side of

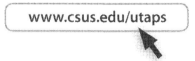

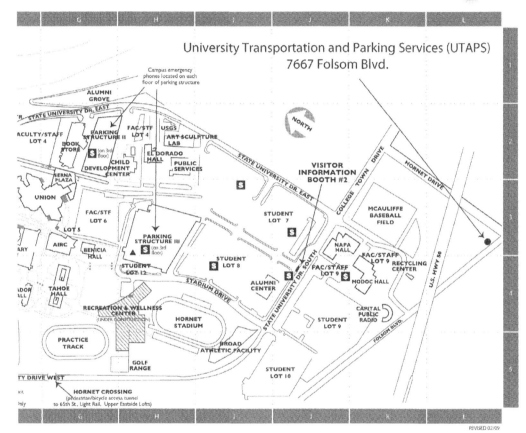

REVISED 02/09

Daily parking permits may be purchased from any daily permit machine (indicated by $). Parking lot signs designate which permits are valid in each parking lot section, unless otherwise indicated at specific spaces. Daily parking permits are valid in student lots.

For additional parking information, call University Transportation and Parking Services (UTAPS) at 278-7275 (278-PARK), come to the office at 7667 Folsom Blvd., or visit our web site at www.csus.edu/utaps.

map for building locations.

Parking Facility	Location
Parking Structure I	E5
Parking Structure II	G2
Parking Structure III	H3
Lot 1	C3
Lot 2	C2
Lot 3	D2
Lot 4	G2
Lot 5	G3
Lot 6	G3
Lot 7	J3
Lot 8	I3
Lot 9	J4
Lot 10	J5
Lot 11	J5
Lot 12	H4

Physical Address:
California State University, Sacramento
University Transportation and Parking Services
7667 Folsom Blvd., Sacramento, CA

Mailing Address:
California State University, Sacramento
6000 J Street, Sacramento, CA 95819-6076

SACRAMENTO
STATE
Leadership begins here.

www.csus.edu/utaps